# The
# FIVE THOUSAND
# YEAR LEAP

## *28 Great Ideas*
## *that Changed the World*

### BY

### W. CLEON SKOUSEN

### 30 Year Anniversary Edition

Library of Congress Cataloging-in-Publication Data is available from the Library of Congress
Catalogue # TX0006840354
ISBN 0-9815596-6-2
American Documents Publishing, L.L.C.
2020 Fieldstone Pkwy Ste. 900
Franklin, TN. 37069
Visit us at www.usconstitutioncoach.com

Cover Design: Evan Frederickson

Printed in the United States of America
10 9 8 7 6 5 4 3 2 1

# Dedication

**THIS WORK IS DEDICATED TO** that generation of resolute Americans whom we call the Founding Fathers. They created the first free people to survive as a nation in modern times. They wrote a new kind of Constitution which is now the oldest in existence. They built a new kind of commonwealth designed as a model for the whole human race. They believed it was thoroughly possible to create a new kind of civilization, giving freedom, equality, and justice to all.

Their first design for a free-people nation was to encompass all of North America, accommodating, as John Adams said, two to three hundred million freemen. They created a new cultural climate that gave wings to the human spirit. They encouraged exploration to reveal the scientific secrets of the universe. They built a free-enterprise culture to encourage industry and prosperity. They gave humanity the needed ingredients for a gigantic 5,000-year leap!

– W. Cleon Skousen

# Table of Contents

Author Preface & Acknowledgements..................................................................iii

Why It Is Important to Study the Founders' Success Formula Today...............vi

Foreword by Glenn Beck..................................................................................1
    A Hard Beginning....................................................................................1
    Why Jamestown Was Different ...............................................................3
    Two Hundred Years Later.......................................................................3
    Can We Lose It? .....................................................................................4
    The 28 Great Ideas That Are Changing the World .................................5
    Time to Get Back to Basics ....................................................................5
    I Want Your Solemn Promise .................................................................6


Part I: The Founders' Monumental Task
    The Founder's Political Spectrum ........................................................11
    What Is Left? What Is Right?...............................................................11
    The Founding Fathers Used a More Accurate Yardstick.......................12
    Rulers Law ...........................................................................................12
    The Founders' Attraction to People's Law ...........................................13
    Characteristics of Anglo-Saxon Common Law......................................14
    Similarities between Anglo-Saxons's and Ancient Israel.......................15
    Memorializing The Two Examples of People's Law ..............................18
    The Founders' Struggle to Establish People's Law ..............................18
    First Constitution Too Close to Anarchy...............................................19
    The Genius of the Constitutional Convention in 1787...........................20
    A Special Device to Encourage Open Discussion..................................21
    Birth of Bill of Rights...........................................................................21
    The Balanced Center ...........................................................................22
    America's Three-Headed Eagle.............................................................23
    The Two Wings of the Eagle ................................................................24
    Thomas Jefferson Describes the Need for Balance................................25
    The Problem of Political Extremists .....................................................25
    Jefferson's Conversation with Washington ...........................................25
    Jefferson's Concern About Radicals.....................................................26
    The Founders Warn Against the Collectivist Left .................................27
    The Need for an "Enlightened Electorate".............................................28
    The Founders' Common Denominator of Basic Beliefs .........................28
    Fundamental Principles ........................................................................29

Part II: The Founders' Basic Principles
    1st Principle: The Genius of Natural Law ................................................33
    2nd Principle: A virtuous and Moral People ........................................41
    3rd Principle: Virtuous and Moral Leaders...........................................47
    4th Principle: The Role of Religion.......................................................59
    5th Principle: The Role of the Creator...................................................73
    6th Principle: All Men Are Created Equal.............................................79
    7th Principle: Equal Rights, Not Equal Things ....................................87
    8th Principle: Man's Unalienable Rights...............................................93
    9th Principle: The Role of Revealed Law..............................................99
    10th Principle: Sovereignty of the People ...........................................105
    11th Principle: Who Can Alter the Government?.................................109
    12th Principle: Advantages of a Republic............................................113
    13th Principle: Protection Against Human Frailty................................119
    14th Principle: Property Rights Essential to Liberty ...........................123
    15th Principle: Free-market Economics ...............................................131
    16th Principle: The Separation of Powers ...........................................141
    17th Principle: Checks and Balances....................................................149
    18th Principle: Importance of a Written Constitution...........................157
    19th Principle: Limiting and Defining the Powers of Government..........161
    20th Principle: Majority Rule, Minority Rights ...................................165
    21st Principle: Strong Local Self-government .....................................169
    22nd Principle: Government by Law, Not by Men ...............................173
    23rd Principle: Importance of an Educated Electorate .........................177
    24th Principle: Peace Through Strength ...............................................183
    25th Principle: Avoid Entangling Alliances.........................................189
    26th Principle: Protecting the Role of the Family ...............................199
    27th Principle: Avoiding the Burden of Debt ......................................203
    28th Principle: The Founders' Sense of Manifest Destiny ...................215

Bibliography ...............................................................................................221
Appendix A: The Mystery of the Anglo-Saxons, by W. Cleon Skousen........225
Appendix B: The Secret To America's Strength, by W. Cleon Skousen ........233
About the Author ........................................................................................253
Index .........................................................................................................255


**Bonus Material**
The United States Constitution..................................................................271
The Declaration of Independence...............................................................287


Common Sense by Thomas Paine ..............................................................291
    Of the Origin and Design of Government in General ...........................292
    Of Monarchy and Hereditary Succession............................................297
    Thoughts on the Present State of American Affairs .............................303
    Of the Present Ability of America .......................................................316
    Appendix ...........................................................................................325


101 Constitutional Questions To Ask Candidates .......................................337

"The happy union of these states is a wonder; their Constitution is a miracle; their example of the hope and liberty throughout the world. Woe to the ambition that would meditate the destruction of either!"
James Madison

---

"The adversaries of the Constitution seem to have lost sight of the People altogether in their reasonings on this subject… These gentlemen must here be reminded of their error. They must be told that the ultimate authority, wherever the derivative may be found, reside in the People alone." — Federalist Papers No. 46, page 294.

# Preface

**By W. Cleon Skousen**

The publication of this book is the fulfillment of a dream gestated over forty years ago at the George Washington University Law School in the nation's capital.

As I studied Constitutional law, there was always a nagging curiosity as to why someone had not taken the time and trouble to catalogue the ingredients of the Founding Fathers' phenomenal success formula so it would be less complex and easier to digest. It seemed incredible that these gems of political sagacity had to be dug out of obscurity by each individual doing it piecemeal and never really knowing for certain that the whole puzzle had been completely assembled.

All of this introspective cogitation was taking place during the Great Depression, while this writer was working full time at the FBI and going to law school at night.

A short time before, a brand new majority in Congress had been swept into power, and our professor of Constitutional law was constantly emphasizing the mistakes these newly elected "representatives of the people" were making. He would demonstrate how they were continually seeking answers to the nation's ills through remedies which were not authorized by the Constitution, and in most cases by methods which had been strictly forbidden by historical experience and the teachings of the Founders.

As I talked to some of these enthusiastic new Congressmen, it soon became apparent that their zeal was sincere and that any mistakes they might be making were the results of ignorance, not malicious intent. In fact, all of us belonged to a generation that had never been taught the clear-cut, decisive principles of sound politics and economics enunciated by the Founders. Somebody had apparently decided these were not very important anymore.

To this extent it could be said that, ideologically speaking, we were a generation of un-Americans. Even those of us who had come up through political science had never been required to read the Federalist Papers, John Locke, Algernon Sidney, Montesquieu, Adam Smith, Cicero, or the original writings of the men who put it all together in the first place. One of my undergraduate professors had even said that the Constitution was obsolete. He said it wasn't designed for a modern industrial society.

Nevertheless, one of my friends in Congress said he would like to study the Founders' ideas. What he wanted was a simple, easy-to-understand book. So did the rest of us. My text on Constitutional law was three inches thick and was so cluttered up with complex, legalistic rhetoric that it would only confuse a farmer, businessman, or real estate broker who had just been elected to Congress. It was even confusing to those of us who were trying to get a handle on "the system" so we could pass the bar examination. The fact that some of us did pass the bar "the very first time around" was always counted within our secret circle as a providential miracle!

As the years went by, I continued to look for a book which laid out the great ideas of the Founders so that even a new Congressman could "read as he ran" and get a fairly good comprehension of the Founders' ingenious success formula. I did find a number of writers who seemed to come within striking distance of the target, only to back away and never complete the task. Often their tomes were long, tedious conglomerates of abstract complexity. Of course, there were lots of books on Constitutional "nuts and bolts," or the mechanics of government, which were similar to my texts in political science. However, none of these ever portrayed a philosophical comprehension of why it was all supposed to be so great.

Eventually, circumstances were such that this writer overcame a prevailing sense of apprehension and undertook the task of trying to do something along these lines just as a matter of personal insight. Now, a hundred digested volumes later, and after a most gratifying visit with many of the Founders through their letters, biographies, and speeches, this book has been assembled.

It may appear to some to be a very modest contribution, but it has been a monumental satisfaction to the author. Never before have I fully appreciated the intellectual muscle and the quantum of solid character required to produce the first modern republic. I have gained a warm affection for the Founders. I have learned to see them as men imbued with all of our common weaknesses called "human nature," and yet capable of becoming victorious at a task which would have decimated weaker men. I have learned to glory in their successes and have felt an overtone of personal sorrow when they seemed to attain less than they had hoped. It has been a marvelous adventure in research to perceive the ramifications of the Founders' formula for a model commonwealth of freedom and prosperity which became the United States of America.

When it comes to acknowledgments, I find myself, like other writers, overwhelmed with obligations.

How can one thank a thousand researchers and writers on at least three continents who have spent much of their lives digging up and recording the detailed treasures concerning the lives and thoughts of those distinguished nation-builders whom we are pleased to call our Founding Fathers?

At closer range, the task of expressing appreciation is not so difficult, provided that this author can be forgiven for not including all who deserve meritorious thanks.

First and foremost, I must do what so many writers seem to be admitting lately, and that is expressing a frank confession that their books would never have been written without the patient and enduring support of a loving wife. This is particularly true in my case.

Her task of assisting an author-husband has been intermingled with raising eight children, trying to run a household with more than 5,000 books scattered about, answering dozens of telephone calls each day, and trying to locate her husband in time to eat dinner or meet a group of visiting dignitaries. All this and much more has been the continuous routine of my beautiful and patient helpmeet who was appropriately named by her parents, "Jewel."

Also involved in a most significant way with the completion of this book has been the working staff of the National Center for Constitutional Studies (NCCS). Going the eleventh mile, I appreciate Glenn J. Kimber, vice president in charge of our nationwide operations, Andrew M. Allison, editor of monthly publications, and my son, Harold Skousen, in charge of layout and graphics. To these and the many others not specifically mentioned, I am eternally grateful.

And to the student who has a longing to appreciate the pioneers who built the American commonwealth, this book is offered. It is hoped that it will be helpful and understandable, and will to some degree provide the stimulating inspiration which the research and writing of it brought to the author.

W. Cleon Skousen

# Why It Is Important to Study the Founders' Success Formula Today

"The American people are now two centuries away from the nation's original launching. Our ship of state is far out to sea and is being tossed about in stormy waters, which the Founders felt could have been avoided if we had stayed within sight of our initial moorings.

"They also felt that each ingredient set forth in their great success formula was of the highest value. They would no doubt be alarmed to see how many of those ingredients have been abandoned, or have been allowed to become seriously eroded."

*The Making of America: The Meaning and Substance of the Constitution*
by W. Cleon Skousen

# Foreword

## By Glenn Beck

This is a story you won't believe.

It starts with a hundred famished, starving people so desperate for food they had to eat their milk cows, slaughter their plough horses, and kill their dogs. When that ran out they hunted birds and squirrels, and then trapped rats and mice, and finally boiled the leather of their shoes to chew. When that was gone, they turned to each other, waiting on the dying for their next meal.

It's an ugly tale of starvation and desperation that didn't happen at some far away place, it happened right here in our own backyard—Jamestown, Virginia.

### A Hard Beginning

By Christmas day of 1607, more than two thirds of those first colonists in Jamestown were dead. The next year, more settlers arrived but most of them died that winter. The year after that came additional arrivals and more deaths—from starvation. It was an experiment in failure that repeated its deadly tally for seven terrible years.

The plan was simple, really: plant the first English settlement in America—more of a business venture than a colonization—and gather up all that gold. You know, all that gold that lies around everywhere?

When word of the colony spread around England, hundreds more crossed the ocean to Virginia, each anxious to out-perform the dead who preceded them and prove that a fresh load of strong backs and keen minds could stand the rigors of the wilds—after all, English settlers had been colonizing faraway places for ages, all over the world, why should the Americas be any different?

But the "starving times" kept killing them off. Of the estimated 9,000 who sailed to Virginia, only 1,000 survived.

There were two main reasons why Jamestown wasn't working, and this is my point.

The first was the problem of habit—everybody had been doing things the same old way for more than 5,000 years.

Okay, we made *some* improvements since the pyramids, but not many. The Jamestown settlers traveled in boats not much better than those that sailed the Nile. Their farm tools consisted of a shovel, a stick plow and a scythe—about the same as you could pick up at your local *Baghdad Hardware and Feed* back in 3000 B.C. And even though there was an early form of China, there was still no Walmart, so their clothing had to be handspun and hand-woven. Transportation was by cart and oxen, and their medicine was more superstition than substance—and worst of all, most of them died young.

The second reason the colony wasn't working was that the leadership didn't bother updating the way they ran the place. They started off with communalism—every man could take from the general storehouse what he needed and was supposed to give back what he could. In theory, everybody would give back enough so they all could survive. After all, shouldn't the welfare of the colony be more important than individual welfare? While people would like to believe otherwise, the real answer is a resounding *no*.

The Jamestown experiment backfired. Worse than that, it was a pure disaster—uglier than Plato had promised.

It was in fact pure socialism in action.

The men were divided into threes—a third to start the farm, a third to build the fort, and a third to head off into the woods and find gold. Naturally everybody slipped away to go hunt for gold and they neglected the fort and the farm. Oh yes, some of them bothered the local Indians and were shot with arrows—back in those days the welcome wagon was nowhere in sight.

The big fix didn't come until 1614. That's when the colony leadership realized it wasn't a lack of food that kept killing off the settlers—it was a famine of knowledge of correct principles.

Sir Thomas Dale spotted it immediately that year when he first stepped off the boat and into a stagnated mass of unmotivated colonists. It seemed obvious what the problem was—the men were lazy because they had no investment in the land—they had no private property.

Without asking permission from the colony's shareholders, Dale went ahead and gave three acres of land to the old timers, less to the newly arrived, and asked only that in return they provide two barrels of corn for the store house at harvest time.

It's amazing what a little freedom can do for the downtrodden!

The colonists were thrilled. They dropped what they were doing and hurried about clearing *their* land, plowing *their* ground, planting, dunging, watering—whatever they could to have *their own* food for the winter. By that fall, the storehouse was full thanks to the two-barrel tax, and the people were alive. Tobacco came later, and suddenly the colony took root and started on the road to prosperity.

## Why Jamestown Was Different

Jamestown was different from other colonies because it finally shed its failing ways and started practicing free enterprise principles—the freedom to own and control property, and enjoy its fruits. Years later these ideas worked their way into Adam Smith and his famous book, *The Wealth of Nations*.

The blood of these pioneers started the groundswell that brought us the first popular assembly of legislative representatives in the western hemisphere. Their descendants included many of the foremost intellects who built the framework for our future United States of America: Thomas Jefferson, author of the Declaration of Independence; James Madison, "Father of the Constitution;" George Washington, hero-general of the War for Independence; George Mason, author of the first American Bill of Rights in Virginia. Four of the first five presidents of the United States sprung from this fire-tested colony.

## Two Hundred Years Later

What's two hundred years in the history of the world? Nothing really—maybe an average Chinese dynasty—it's a blink. Two hundred years after the Constitution was signed, the great "noble experiment" of America's Declaration of Independence and free-enterprise economics had produced phenomenal results.

The United States started accumulating a fantastic list of achievements in technology, politics and economics never before witnessed in the history of humankind. The spirit of freedom infected people all around the globe, and free-market economics unleashed creativity and brilliance in nations everywhere. A literal explosion of progress crackled wherever freedom could reach. Electricity, the internal combustion engine, nuclear energy, aircraft, electronics, communications, travel to the moon or the bottom of the sea—suddenly, nearly anything seemed possible.

People started living longer—double the average lifespan of a few centuries before. Our homes, quality of food and clothing, the luxuries of central air and heat, running water and flushing toilets, common-day travel around the globe, tens of millions of books, increased capacity to invent and understand, educational advances for the average student, cures, entertainment, and non-stop movies on TV or your iPod—all came about not just in America but to benefit the entire world.

In just 200 years, the human race made a 5,000-year leap!

### Can we lose it?

Every generation feels it must re-invent the sociological wheel. If we were still taught these basics in school, maybe we could skip a few years of stupidity, but it's too late for our generation. We have to pay our stupid tax.

For a hundred years, social and political experiments outside of the Constitution and prosperity principles have played havoc with our culture, and now we're making the same dumb mistakes prior failed cultures have made.

So, we've got to ask: Are we really better off under the decay of freedom that we have today, than we were back when that nasty old Constitution dictated everything?

Dr. Skousen points out when it comes to the physical sciences, knowledge and discovery is added to the main body of knowledge as time passes—it builds on the lessons of the past.

But the same doesn't happen with the social sciences.

Dr. Skousen warns us that when we don't teach the rising generation those cultural and moral lessons that keep society healthy and safe, the people end up making all the same mistakes—and not just once, but half a dozen times or more. We're doing it right now, he says, and muddle our lives with "drugs, riots, revolutions, and terrorism; predatory wars; unnatural sexual practices; merry-go-round marriages; organized crime; neglected and sometimes brutalized children; plateau intoxication; debt-ridden prosperity; and all the other ingredients of insanity which have shattered twenty mighty civilizations in the past." And he made that list 30 years ago!

To that list I would add these other mistakes that are leading us down a dead-end road: the bailout "un-stimulus program," nationalization of our banks and auto industry, the loss of secret balloting for union activities, taxation without representation, morally bankrupt standard bearers, tax cheats running government programs, pork-barrel spending, locking up natural resources, punishing the productive, rewarding the lazy, squelching opposing viewpoints, redistributing the wealth, creating an entitlement mentality, granting more rights to illegals than our own citizens, a fear of our fellow citizens and loss of pride in the greatness of this nation—and generally the ignoring of our Constitutional rights, privileges and opportunities.

## The 28 Great Ideas That Helped Change the World

There is no reason why our American way of life should be drowning in the same mistakes of those failed empires of the past, except for perhaps this one—as a culture we've stopped teaching and practicing the true principles of prosperity.

There are 28 great ideas that helped change our world, and the funny thing is, the American Founding Fathers hardly invented a single one of them. But they did find them, and brought them all together in a single document that has blessed this great nation and the entire world.

These ideas didn't all come together at once. After Jamestown, it took 180 years to pull these great concepts together so that true and lasting freedom was born.

It worked so well so fast that after just two years as a nation, George Washington was able to write, "The United States enjoy a scene of prosperity and tranquility under the new government that could hardly have been hoped for." And the very next day in another letter he said, "Tranquility reigns among the people with that disposition towards the general government which is likely to preserve it....Our public credit stands on that [high] ground which three years ago it would have been considered as a species of madness to have foretold." (*The Writings of George Washington,* Vol. 31: 316-317, 318-319)

## It's Time to Get Back to Basics

In some ways, during parts of 2007 and 2008 I experienced one of the most difficult periods of my life. There had been other times where I experienced financial and family troubles, but this was bigger. I had begun to lose hope. I began to see the massive problems that we – as a nation and as a people – were facing. It seemed like no matter how hard I tried, I couldn't come up with a way it could resolve itself. The more I looked, the more I wished I hadn't looked. How can I hand this country to my children and grand children in better shape than it was given to me?

Without any answers, I spiraled into a sort of despair. How do you fix these problems? How do you fix the economic nightmare that is on its way caused by overspending, massive debt, and giant social programs? How do you protect your kids and country from a force that doesn't have a uniform? What's the right balance between security and liberty? How do you cure American's lack of faith in their government when the political parties are intentionally dividing us?

Then one day in the spring, I was walking down the Avenue of the Americas in Manhattan and the answer came to me. It was so dramatic that it made me stop in the middle of the sidewalk and laugh out loud. The answer was obvious and best of all, the thinking and worrying had already been done for me. The questions that we face were foreseen by the greatest group of Americans to ever live; our Founding Fathers. They knew we would be grappling with issues like the ones we face today at some point, so they designed a ship that could withstand even the mightiest storm. They also knew that we would eventually lose our way and that we would need a beacon to lead our way back.

I often times have wondered why the constitution appears as it does. Why those three words "We the people," are so large. After all, it's not like James Madison wrote those three words then realized, "Oh shoot, I can't use this sized font or we'll run out of space!" They did it for a reason. The answer is not the government, it's not a politician, it's not a policy; it's always, "We the people."

Unfortunately, many of us have been so misinformed or suffer from such a high degree of apathy, that we have no idea who our founders really were. We don't understand how they lived, what rights they were actually trying to protect, and what our responsibilities are to ensure that protection.

Within a couple of weeks after that revelation on the sidewalk a friend—without solicitation—sent me a copy of this book. He said, "Glenn, I don't know if you've ever read this, but it's the simplest, easiest way for Americans of all ages to understand the simple yet brilliant principles our founders based this country on."

After reading it, I realized a couple of things. One, its author—was years ahead of his time. And secondly, our founders were thousands of years ahead of their time. My hope is that all Americans young and old will spend the time with this book to understand why we are who we are. The words of our Founding Fathers have a way of reaching across any political divide. They are words of wisdom that I can only describe as divinely inspired. They are here for us to help solve the unsolvable—and they are the reason why we have for so long been the greatest nation on earth. But most importantly, in these pages, you will find hope.

I know that I have.

### I Want Your Solemn Promise

Right now, right this very moment, I want you to make me a promise.

Promise me you will read this book cover to cover in the next 30 days—sooner if you can. Promise me you will pass this book along to somebody else when you're done. Commit them to read it in 30 days.

Promise me you will write down the 28 ideas and teach them to your children, your neighbors, your friends—*Now* is the time to get out of our comfort zone.

You, me, all of us were born for this day, to stand responsible before God and future generations to keep this torch of freedom lit, and bear it away from ruin. Twenty failed empires of the past give ample proof that no generation having tasted freedom and then lost it *has ever tasted it again*.

Do you remember our resolve on September 12, our promise to each other to link arms and face the coming storms together? Those storms are now boiling overhead—our Republic is at stake. You don't have to be like Washington's troops and track bloody footprints through the snow at Valley Forge, let's pray to God we never have to go there again. To fight this battle you need to read, to *understand*. Learn these 28 ideas, make them your own, put them on the fridge, the bathroom mirror, on your forehead, I don't care—just know them by heart, that's all I ask. And yes—there will be a quiz, there's *always* a quiz.

Remember those minutemen in the days of our Revolutionary War? Do you remember their job, to be ready to defend the encroachment of the Redcoats with a minute's notice? If you were called upon to preserve our freedom, to save our Constitution, could you be ready—could you answer in a minute?

I want you to think of this—

One of my favorite Bible stories is Joshua and the battle of Jericho. Remember how they marched around the city and all at once blew their horns and the walls went tumbling down? That's us all over the place. We are the troops. The truth is our trumpet. And the walls are those same old tired ideas forced on us today—ideas that didn't work at Jamestown, and certainly won't work now.

The power is ours to blast our horns and shake those rotted scales off our freedoms, shake them to rubble and get our country back.

Read this book and discover we're a lot like Joshua—*They* don't surround us, we surround *Them*!

But you've got to have your horn ready—*now* is the time.

Promise me.

—Glenn Beck, March 2009

# PART I

# The Founders' Monumental Task

The Constitutional Convention of 1787

# Structuring a Government with All Power in the People

### The Founders' Political Spectrum

Part of the genius of the Founding Fathers was their political spectrum or political frame of reference. It was a yardstick for the measuring of the political power in any particular system of government. They had a much better political yardstick than the one which is generally used today. If the Founders had used the modern yardstick of "Communism on the left" and "Fascism on the right," they never would have found the balanced center which they were seeking.

### What Is Left? What Is Right?

It is extremely unfortunate that the writers on political philosophy today have undertaken to measure various issues in terms of political parties instead of political power. No doubt the American Founding Fathers would have considered this modern measuring stick most objectionable, even meaningless.

Today, as we mentioned, it is popular in the classroom as well as the press to refer to "Communism on the left," and "Fascism on the right." People and parties are often called "Leftist," or "Rightist." The public do not really understand what they are talking about.

These terms actually refer to the manner in which the various parties are seated in the parliaments of Europe. The radical revolutionaries (usually the Communists) occupy the far left and the military dictatorships (such as the Fascists) are on the far right. Other parties are located in between.

Measuring people and issues in terms of political parties has turned out to be philosophically fallacious if not totally misleading. This is because the platforms or positions of political parties are often superficial and structured on shifting sand. The platform of a political party of one generation can hardly be recognized by the next. Furthermore, Communism and Fascism turned out to be different names for approximately the same thing -- the police state. They are not opposite extremes but, for all practical purposes, are virtually identical.

### The American Founding Fathers Used a More Accurate Yardstick

Government is defined in the dictionary as "a system of ruling or controlling," and therefore the American Founders measured political systems in terms of the amount of coercive power or systematic control which a particular system of government exercises over its people. In other words, the yardstick is not political parties, but political power.

Using this type of yardstick, the American Founders considered the two extremes to be *anarchy* on the one hand, and *tyranny* on the other. At the one extreme of anarchy there is no government, no law, no systematic control and no governmental power, while at the other extreme there is too much control, too much political oppression, too much government. Or, as the Founders called it, "tyranny."

The object of the Founders was to discover the "balanced center" between these two extremes. They recognized that under the chaotic confusion of anarchy there is "no law," whereas at the other extreme the law is totally dominated by the ruling power and is therefore "Ruler's Law." What they wanted to establish was a system of "People's Law," where the government is kept under the control of the people and political power is maintained at the balanced center with enough government to maintain security, justice, and good order, but not enough government to abuse the people.

The Founders' political spectrum might be graphically illustrated as follows:

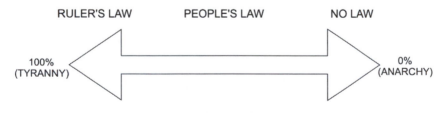

RULER'S LAW          PEOPLE'S LAW          NO LAW

100%                                         0%
(TYRANNY)                               (ANARCHY)

### Ruler's Law

The Founder's seemed anxious that modern man recognize the subversive characteristics of oppressive Ruler's Law which they identified primarily with a tyrannical monarchy. Here are its basic characteristics:

1. Authority under Ruler's Law is nearly always established by force, violence and conquest.
2. Therefore, all sovereign power is considered to be in the con-

queror or his descendants.

3. The people are not equal, but are divided into classes, and are all looked upon as subjects of the king.
4. The entire country is considered to be the property of the ruler, who speaks of it as his "realm."
5. The thrust of government power is from the top down, not from the people upward.
6. The people have no unalienable rights. The King giveth and the King taketh away.
7. Government is by the whims of men, not by the fixed rule of law which the people need in order to govern the affairs with confidence.
8. The Ruler issues edicts which are called "The Law," who then interprets the law and enforces it, thus maintaining tyrannical control over the people.
9. Problems are always solved by issuing more edicts or laws, setting up more bureaus, harassing the people with more regulators, and charging the people for these "services" by continually adding to their burden of taxes.
10. Freedom is never looked upon as a viable solution to anything.
11. The long history of Ruler's Law is one of blood and terror, both anciently and in modern times. Under it, the people are stratified into an aristocracy of the Ruler's retinue while the law to the common people is one of perpetual poverty, excessive taxation, stringent regulations and a continuous existence of misery.

### The Founders' Attraction to People's Law

In direct contrast to the harsh oppression of Ruler's Law, the Founders, particularly Jefferson, admired the institutes of freedom under People's Law as originally practiced among the Anglo-Saxons. As one authority on Jefferson points out:

> "Jefferson's great ambition at that time [1776] was to promote a renaissance of Anglo-Saxon primitive institutions on the new continent. Thus presented, the American Revolution was nothing but the reclamation of the Anglo-Saxon birthright of which the colonists had been deprived by a 'long trend of abuses.' Nor does it appear that there was anything in this theory which surprised or shocked his contemporaries; Adams apparently did not disapprove of it, and it would be easy to bring in many similar expressions of the same idea in documents of the time." (Gilbert Chinard, *Thomas Jefferson: The Apostle of American-*

*ism*, 2nd edition, revised, The University of Michigan Press, Ann
Arbor, Michigan, 1975, pp. 86-87.)

### Characteristics of Anglo-Saxon Common Law or People's Law

Here are the principle points of People's Law as practiced by the
Anglo-Saxons (for a more extensive examination of the Anglo-Saxons,
see Appendix A, "The Mystery of the Anglo-Saxons"):

1. The Anglo-Saxons considered themselves a commonwealth of
   freemen.
2. All decisions and the selection of leaders had to be with the consent of the people, preferably by full consensus, not just a majority.
3. The laws by which they were governed were considered natural
   laws given by divine dispensation, and were so well known by the
   people they did not have to be written down.
4. Power was dispersed among the people and never allowed to concentrate in any one person or group. Even in time of war, the authority granted to the leaders was temporary and the power of the
   people to remove them was direct and simple.
5. Primary responsibility for resolving problems rested first of all
   with the individual, then the family, then the tribe or community,
   then the region, and finally, the nation.
6. They were organized into small, manageable groups where every
   adult had a voice and a vote. They divided the people into units
   of ten families who elected a leader; then fifty families who
   elected a leader; then a hundred families who elected a leader;
   and then a thousand families who elected a leader.
7. They believed the rights of the individual were considered unalienable and could not be violated without risking the wrath of
   divine justice as well as civil retribution by the people's judges.
8. The system of justice was structured on the basis of severe punishment unless there was complete reparation to the person who
   had been wronged. There were only four "crimes" or offenses
   against the whole people. These were treason, by betraying their
   own people; cowardice, by refusing to fight or failing to fight
   courageously; desertion; and homosexuality. These were considered capital offenses. All other offenses required reparation to the
   person who had been wronged.
9. They always attempted to solve problems on the level where the
   problem originated. If this was impossible they went no higher

than was absolutely necessary to get a remedy. Usually only the most complex problems involving the welfare of the whole people, or a large segment of the people, ever went to the leaders for solution.

The contrast between Ruler's Law (all power in the ruler) and People's Law (all power in the people) is graphically illustrated below. Note where the power base is located under each of these systems. Also compare the relationship between the individual and the rest of society under these two systems.

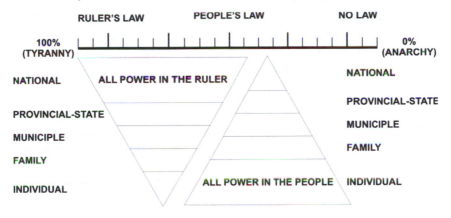

## The Founders Note the Similarities between Anglo-Saxon Common Law and People's Law

As the Founders studied the record of the ancient Israelites they were intrigued by the fact that they also operated under a system of laws remarkably similar to those of the Anglo-Saxons. The two systems were similar both in precept and operational structure. In fact, the Reverend Thomas Hooker wrote the "Fundamental Orders of Connecticut" based on the principles recorded by Moses in the first chapter of Deuteronomy. These "Fundamental Orders" were adopted in 1639 and constituted the first written constitution in modern times. This constitutional charter operated so successfully that it was adopted by Rhode Island. When the English colonies were converted over to independent states, these were the only two states which had constitutional documents which readily adapted themselves to the new order of self-government. All of the other states had to write new constitutions.

Here are the principal characteristics of the People's Law in ancient Israel which were almost identical with those of the Anglo-Saxons:

1.  First of all, they were set up as a commonwealth of freemen. A basic tenant was: "Proclaim liberty throughout all the land unto all the inhabitants thereof." (Leviticus 25:10.) These same words are inscribed on the American Liberty Bell.

    Whenever the Israelites fell into the temptation to have slaves or bond-servants, they were reprimanded. Around 600 B.C., a divine reprimand was given through Jeremiah: "Ye have not hearkened unto me, in proclaiming liberty every one to his brother, and every man to his neighbor: behold, I proclaim a liberty for you, saith the Lord." (Jeremiah 34:17)

2.  All the people were organized into small manageable units where the representative of each family had a voice and a vote. This organizing process was launched after Jethro, the father-in-law of Moses, saw him trying to govern the people under Ruler's Law. (See Exodus 18:13-26.)

    When the structure was completed the Israelites were organized as follows:

    Moses
    V.P. (Aaron) and V.P. (Joshua)
    A Senate or Council of 70
    A Congress of Elected Representatives
    1000 Families
    100 Families
    50 Families
    10 Families
    Single family

3.  There was specific emphasis on strong, local self-government. Problems were solved to the greatest possible extent on the level where they originated.

    The record says: "The hard causes they brought unto Moses, but every small matter they judged themselves." (Exodus 18:26)

4.  The entire code of justice was based primarily on reparation to the victim rather than fines and punishment by the commonwealth. (Reference to this procedure will be found in Exodus, chapters 21 and 22.) The one crime for which no "satisfaction" could be given was first-degree murder. The penalty was death. (See Numbers 35:31.)

5.  Leaders were elected and new laws were approved by the common consent of the people. (See 2 Samuel 2:4; 1 Chronicles 29:22; for the rejection of a leader, see 2 Chronicles 10:16; for the

approval of new laws, see Exodus 19:8.)

6. Accused persons were presumed to be innocent until proven guilty. Evidence had to be strong enough to remove any question of doubt as to guilt. Borderline cases were decided in favor of the accused and he was released. It was felt that if he were actually guilty, his punishment could be left to the judgment of God in the future life.

When the structure was completed the Israelites were organized as follows:

MOSES

Vice President over Internal Affairs   AARON - JOSHUA   Vice President over the Military

COUNCIL OF 70
(A Senate)

ELECTED REPRESENTATIVES
(A Congress)

600 GROUPS OF        1,000 FAMILIES
6,000 GROUPS OF         100 FAMILIES
12,000 GROUPS OF          50 FAMILIES
60,000 GROUPS OF          10 FAMILIES
(78,600 assistants to help govern the people)

MORE THAN 600 THOUSAND FAMILIES

MORE THAN 3 MILLION PEOPLE WITH POWER TO GOVERN THEMSELVES

*Note: These numbers are approximations based on the census recorded in the first chapter of the book of Numbers of the Old Testament.*

Howard B. Rand, an American lawyer, reviewed these principles and wrote:

"When the time came for the United States of America to adopt a constitution, our forefathers modeled it after the perfect Israelite system of administration." (Howard B. Rand, *Digest of the Divine Law*, Merrimac, Massachusetts: Destiny Publishers, 1943, pp. 130-31.)

These solid principles became the tow ropes down the stream of history for over a thousand years. Today Americans must take hold of those tow ropes if our nation is to survive. We must:

1.  Acknowledge the inspiration of the Founders' Success Formula.

2.  Reinstate Constitutional principles in our government.

3.  Revive our love for God, family, and country.

4.  Rejuvenate morality in our lives, in our businesses, and in our country.

### Memorializing These Two Examples of People's Law on the U.S. Seal

It was the original intent of the Founders to have both the ancient Israelites and the Anglo-Saxons represented on the official seal of the United States. The members of the committee were Thomas Jefferson, John Adams, and Benjamin Franklin.

They recommended that one side of the seal show the profiles of two Anglo-Saxons representing Hengist and Horsa. These brothers were the first Anglo-Saxons to bring their people to England around A.D. 450 and introduce the institutes of People's Law into the British Isles. On the other side of the seal this committee recommended that there be a portrayal of ancient Israel going through the wilderness led by God's pillar of fire. In this way the Founders hoped to memorialize the two ancient peoples who had practiced People's Law and from whom the Founders had acquired many of their basic ideas for their new commonwealth of freedom. (See Gilbert Chinard, *Thomas Jefferson: The Apostle of Americanism*, p. 86.)

As it turned out, all of this was a little complicated for a small seal, and therefore a more simple design was utilized. However, here is a modern artist's rendition of the original seal as proposed by Jefferson, Adams, and Franklin. Obviously, this is a segment of America's rich heritage of the past which has disappeared from most history books.

### The Founders' Struggle to Establish People's Law in the Balanced Center

In the Federalist Papers, No. 9, Hamilton refers to the "sensations of horror and disgust " which arise when a person studies the histories of those nations that are always "in a state of perpetual vibration between the extremes of tyranny and anarchy." (*The Federalist Papers*, Mentor Books, New York, 1961, No. 9, p. 71)

Washington also refers to the human struggle wherein "there is a natural and necessary progression, from the extreme of anarchy to the extreme of tyranny." (Fitzpatrick, *Writings of George Washington*, 26:489)

Franklin noted that "there is a natural inclination in mankind to kingly government." He said it gives people the illusion that somehow a king will establish "equality among citizens; and that they like." Franklin's great fear was that the states would succumb to this gravitational pull toward a strong central government symbolized by a royal establishment. He said: "I am apprehensive, therefore – perhaps too apprehensive – that the Government of these States may in future times end in a monarchy. But this catastrophe, I think, may be long delayed, if in our proposed system we do not sow the seeds of contention, faction, and tumult, by making our posts of honor places of profit." (Albert Henry Smyth, ed., *The Writings of Benjamin Franklin*, 10 vols., The Macmillan Company, New York, 1905-1907, 9:593; modern spelling.)

The Founders' task was to somehow solve the enigma of the human tendency to rush headlong from anarchy to tyranny -- the very thing which later happened in the French Revolution. How could the American people be constitutionally structured so that they would take a fixed position at the balanced center of the political spectrum and forever maintain a government "of the people, by the people, and for the people," which would not perish from the earth?

It took the Founding Fathers 180 years (1607 to 1787) to come up with their American formula. In fact, just eleven years before the famous Constitutional Convention at Philadelphia, the Founders wrote a constitution which almost caused them to lose the Revolutionary War. Their first attempt at constitutional writing was called "The Articles of Confederation."

## The Founders' First Constitution Ends Up Too Close to Anarchy

The American Revolutionary War did not commence as a war for independence but was originally designed merely to protect the rights of the people from the arrogant oppression of a tyrannical king. Nevertheless, by the spring of 1776 it was becoming apparent that a complete separation was the only solution.

It is interesting that even before the Declaration of Independence, the Continental Congress appointed a committee on June 11, 1776, to write a constitution. John Dickinson served as chairman of the committee and wrote a draft based on a proposal made by Benjamin Franklin in 1775.

However, the states felt that Dickinson's so-called "Articles of Confederation" gave too much power to the central government. They therefore hacked away at the draft until November 15, 1777, when they proclaimed that the new central government would have no powers whatsoever except those "expressly" authorized by the states. And the states did not expressly authorize much of anything.

Under the Articles of Confederation as finally adopted, there was no executive, no judiciary, no taxing power, and no enforcement power. The national government ended up being little more than a general "Committee of the States." It made recommendations to the states and then prayed they would respond favorably. Very often they did not.

On the Founders' political spectrum the Articles of Confederation would appear as follows:

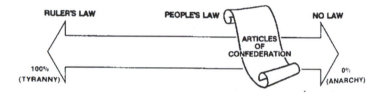

The suffering and death at Valley Forge and Morristown were an unforgettable demonstration of the abject weakness of the central government and its inability to provide food, clothes, equipment, and manpower for the war. At Valley Forge the common fare for six weeks was flour, water, and salt, mixed together and baked in a skillet -- fire cakes, they were called. Out of approximately 8,000 soldiers, around 3,000 abandoned General Washington and went home. Approximately 200 officers resigned their commissions. Over 2,000 soldiers died of starvation and disease. Washington attributed this near-disaster at Valley Forge to the constitutional weakness of the central government under the Articles of Confederation.

### The Genius of the Constitutional Convention in 1787

Not one of the Founding Fathers could have come up with the much-needed Constitutional formula by himself, and the delegates who attended the Convention knew it. At that very moment the states were bitterly divided. The Continental dollar was inflated almost out of existence. The economy was deeply depressed, and rioting had broken out. New England had threatened to secede, and both England and Spain were standing close by, ready to snatch up the dis-United States at the first propitious opportunity.

Writing a Constitution under these circumstances was a frightening experience. None of the delegates had expected the Convention to require four tedious months. In fact, within a few weeks many of the delegates, including James Madison, were living on borrowed funds.

From the opening day of the Convention it was known that the brain-storming discussions would require frequent shifting of positions and changing of minds. For this reason the Convention debates were held in secret to avoid public embarrassment as the delegates made concessions, reversed earlier positions, and moved gradually toward some kind of agreement.

### A Special Device Employed to Encourage Open Discussion

To encourage the delegates to freely express themselves without the usual formalities of a convention, the majority of the discussions were conducted in what they called "the Committee of the Whole." This committee consisted of all the members of the Convention, but, as a committee, decisions were always tentative and never binding in the same way they would have been if voted upon by the Convention. Only after a thorough ventilating of the issues would the Committee of the Whole turn themselves back into a sitting of the Convention and formally approve what they had just discussed in the Committee.

The object of the Founders was to seek a consensus or general agreement on what the Constitution should provide. After four months of debate they were able to reach general agreement on just about everything except the issues of slavery, proportionate representation, and the regulation of commerce. All three of these issues had to be settled by compromise.

It is a mistake however, to describe the rest of the Constitution as a "conglomerate of compromises," because extreme patience was used to bring the minds of the delegates into agreement rather than simply force the issue to finality with a compromise. This is demonstrated in the fact that over 60 ballots were taken before they resolved the issue of how to elect the President. They could have let the matter lie after the first ballot, but they did not. They were anxious to talk it out until the vast majority felt good about the arrangement. That is why it took 60 ballots to resolve the matter.

### Birth of Bill of Rights

When the Founders had finished their work on September 17, 1787, President Washington attached a letter to the signed draft and sent it to the Congress. The Congress ratified the Constitution without any changes and sent it to the states. When several of the larger states threatened to reject the Constitution, they were invited to ratify the main body of the Constitution but attach suggested amendments. They submitted 189! At the first session of Congress, these suggested amendments were reduced to 12 by James Madison, and 10 of them were finally approved and ratified by the states. Thus was born America's famous Bill of Rights.

### The Balanced Center

This was the polemic process by which the Founders struggled to get the American eagle firmly planted in the balanced center of the political spectrum. James Madison later described the division of labor between the states and the federal government as follows:

> "The powers delegated by the proposed Constitution to the federal government are few and defined. Those which are to remain in the State governments are numerous and indefinite.... The powers reserved to the several States will extend to all the objects which, in the ordinary course of affairs, concern the lives, liberties, and properties of the people, and the internal order, improvement, and prosperity of the State." (*The Federalist Papers*, No. 45, pp. 292-293.)

The fixing of the American eagle in the center of the spectrum was designed to maintain this political equilibrium between the people in the states and the federal government. The idea was to keep the power base close to the people. The emphasis was on strong local self-government. The states would be responsible for internal affairs and the federal government would confine itself to those areas which could not be fairly or effectively handled by the individual states. This made the Founders' political spectrum look approximately like this:

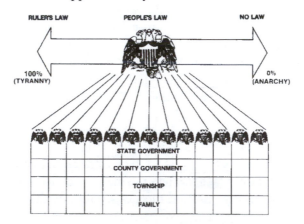

### America's Three-Headed Eagle

Although Polybius, John Locke, and Baron Charles de Montesquieu had all advocated the separation of the governmental functions into three departments – legislative, executive, and judicial – the American Founders were the first to carefully structure what might be described as a three-headed eagle.

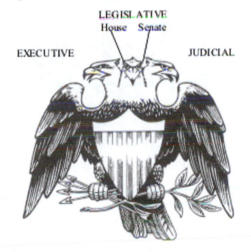

The central head was the law-making or legislative function with two eyes – the House and the Senate – and these must both see eye-to-eye on any piece of legislation before it can become law. A second head is the administrative or Executive Department with all authority centered in a single, strong President, operating within a clearly defined framework of limited power. The third head is the judiciary, which was assigned the task of acting as guardian of the Constitution and the interpretation of its principles as originally designed by the Founders.

The genius of this three-headed eagle was not only the separation of powers but the fact that all three heads operated through a single neck. By this means the Founders carefully integrated these three departments so that each one was coordinated with the others and could not perform independently of them. It was an ingeniously structured pattern of political power which might be described as "coordination without consolidation."

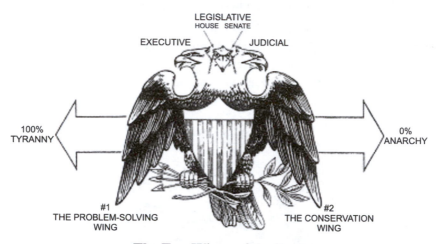

LEGISLATIVE
HOUSE  SENATE

EXECUTIVE　　　　　　JUDICIAL

100%
TYRANNY

0%
ANARCHY

#1
THE PROBLEM-SOLVING
WING

#2
THE CONSERVATION
WING

### The Two Wings of the Eagle

The Founder's view of their new form of government can be further demonstrated by using the symbol of the eagle and referring to its two wings:

Wing #1 of the eagle might be referred to as the problem-solving wing or the wing of compassion. Those who function through this dimension of the system are sensitive to the unfulfilled needs of the people. They dream of elaborate plans to solve these problems.

Wing #2 has the responsibility of conserving the nation's resources and the people's freedom. Its function is to analyze the programs of wing #1 with two questions. First, can we afford it? Secondly, what will it do to the rights and individual freedom of the people?

Now, if both of these wings fulfill their assigned function, the American eagle will fly straighter and higher than any civilization in the history of the world. But if either of these wings goes to sleep on the job, the American eagle will drift toward anarchy or tyranny. For example, if wing #1 becomes infatuated with the idea of solving all the problems of the nation regardless of the cost, and wing #2 fails to bring its power into play to sober the problem-solvers with a more realistic approach, the eagle will spin off toward the left, which is tyranny.

On the other hand, if wing #1 fails to see the problems which need solving and wing #2 becomes inflexible in its course of not solving problems simply to save money, or not disturb the status quo, then the machinery of government loses its credibility and the eagle drifts over toward the right where the people decide to take matters into their own hands. This can eventually disintegrate into anarchy.

### Thomas Jefferson Describes the Need for Balance

When Thomas Jefferson became President, he used his first inaugural address to describe the need to make room for the problem-solving wing, to which his own Democratic-Republican party belonged, and also make room for the conservation wing, to which the Federalist party of John Adams belonged. He tried to stress the fact that all Americans should have some elements of both of these party dimensions in their thinking. In his inaugural address he said: "We have called by different names brethren of the same principle. We are all republicans – we are all federalists." (Albert Ellery Bergh, editor, *The Writings of Thomas Jefferson*, 20 volumes, The Thomas Jefferson Memorial Association, Washington, D.C., 1907, 3:319)

### The Problem of Political Extremists

Nevertheless, Jefferson saw fringe elements in both of these parties which were political extremists. In the Federalist party were those who would pull the eagle away from its balanced center toward the tyrannical left and form a central government so strong that it would border on a monarchy. Concerning the monarchist fringe of the Federalist Party, he wrote:

> "I have spoken of the Federalists as if they were a homogeneous body, but this is not the truth. Under that name lurks the heretical sect of monarchists. Afraid to wear their own name, they creep under the mantle of Federalism, and the Federalists, like sheep permit the fox to take shelter among them, when pursued by dogs. These men have no right to office. If a monarchist be in office, anywhere, and it be known to the President, the oath he has taken to support the Constitution imperiously requires the instantaneous dismissing of such officer; and I hold the President criminal if he permitted such to remain. To appoint a monarchist to conduct the affairs of a Republic is like appointing an atheist to the priesthood. As to the real federalists, I take them to my bosom as brothers. I view them as honest men, friends to the present Constitution." (From a newspaper letter, June 1803; Paul Leicester Ford, editor, *The Writings of Thomas Jefferson*, 10 volumes, G.P. Putnam's Sons, New York, 1892-1899, 8:237.)

### Jefferson's Conversation with Washington

Jefferson reports a conversation with President Washington in August 1793 in which Jefferson expressed deep concern that some elements of the President's administration were pushing toward oppressive monarchial-type powers. The President immediately responded that republican principles must be maintained and that, "the Constitution we have is an excellent one, if we can keep it where it is." With reference to the possibility of a monarchial party arising, President Washington stated that, "there was not a man in the United States who would set his face more decidedly against it than himself." Jefferson nevertheless pointed out to the President that:

> "There does not pass a week, in which we cannot prove declarations dropping from the monarchical party [the branch of the administration pushing for a central government with massive powers and saying] that our government is good for nothing, is a milk and water thing which cannot support itself, we must knock it down, and set up something of more energy."

President Washington replied that if anyone were guilty of such nonsense, it would be "a proof of their insanity." (Bergh, *Writings of Thomas Jefferson*, 1:257.)

### Jefferson's Concern About the Radical Fringe Element in His Own Party

In May 1805, while serving as President, Jefferson wrote to Dr. George Logan. He was concerned with elements of extremism pushing toward the extreme right which, to the Founders, meant "anarchy." He wrote:

> "I see with infinite pain the bloody schism which has taken place among our friends in Pennsylvania and New York, and will probably take place in other States. The main body of both sections mean well, but their good intensions will produce great public evil." (Bergh, *Writings of Thomas Jefferson*, 10:440.)

Like President Washington, Jefferson saw the need for maintaining the government in the balanced center where the Constitution had placed it. He wrote to Governor George Clinton in 1803, "Our business is to march straight forward ... without either turning to the right or left." (*Ibid.*)

With both of the eagle's wings flying – one solving problems, the other preserving resources and freedom – the American future could not help but ascend to unprecedented heights of wealth and influence.

### The Founders Warn Against the Drift Toward the Collectivist Left Welfare State

Since the genius of the American system is maintaining the eagle in the balanced center of the spectrum, the Founders warned against a number of temptations which might lure subsequent generations to abandon their freedoms and their rights by subjecting themselves to a strong federal administration operating on the collectivist Left.

They warned against the "welfare state" where the government endeavors to take care of everyone from the cradle to the grave. Jefferson wrote:

"If we can prevent the government from wasting the labors of the people, under the pretense of taking care of them, they must become happy." (*Ibid.*, p. 342)

They warned against confiscatory taxation and deficit spending. Jefferson said it was immoral for one generation to pass on the results of its extravagance in the form of debts to the next generation. He wrote: "... we shall all consider ourselves unauthorized to saddle posterity with our debts, and morally bound to pay them ourselves; and consequently within what may be deemed the period of a generation, or the life [expectancy] of the majority." (*Ibid.*, p. 358)

Every generation of Americans struggled to pay off the national debt up to the present one.

The Founders also warned that the only way for the nation to prosper was to have equal protection of "rights," and not allow the government to get involved in trying to provide equal distribution of "things." They also warned against the pooling of property as advocated by the proponents of communism. Samuel Adams said they had done everything possible to make the ideas of socialism and communism unconstitutional. Said he:

"The Utopian schemes of leveling [re-distribution of the wealth] and a community of goods [central ownership of the means of production and distribution], are as visionary and impractical as those which vest all property in the Crown. [These ideas] are arbitrary, despotic, and, in our government, unconstitutional." (William V. Wells, *The Life and Public Services of Samuel Adams*, 3 volumes, Little, Brown and Company, Boston, 1865, 1:154.)

## The Need for an "Enlightened Electorate"

To prevent the American eagle from tipping toward anarchy on the right, or tyranny on the left, and to see that the American system remained in a firm, fixed position in the balanced center of the political spectrum, the Founders campaigned for a strong program of widespread education. Channels were needed through which the Founders and other leaders could develop and maintain an intelligent, informed electorate.

Jefferson hammered home the necessity for an educated electorate on numerous occasions. Here are some samples: "If a nation expects to be ignorant and free, in a state of civilization, it expects what never was and never will be." (Ford, *Writings of Thomas Jefferson*, 10:4.)

> "No other sure foundation can be devised for the preservation of freedom and happiness.... Preach ... a crusade against ignorance; establish and improve the law for educating the common people. Let our countrymen know that the people alone can protect us against these evils [of misgovernment]." (Bergh, *Writings of Thomas Jefferson*, 5:396-397.)

What the Founders really wanted was a system of educational communication through which they could transfer their great body of fundamental beliefs based on self evident truths. They knew they had made a great discovery, and they wanted their posterity to maintain it. As Madison said, it is something which "it is incumbent on their successors to improve and perpetuate." (*The Federalist Papers*, No. 14, p. 105.)

## The Founders' Common Denominator of Basic Beliefs

One of the most amazing aspects of the American story is that while the nation's founders came from widely divergent backgrounds, their fundamental beliefs were virtually identical. They quarreled bitterly over the most practical plan of implementing those beliefs, but rarely, if ever, disputed about their final objectives or basic convictions.

These men came from several different churches, and some from no churches at all. They ranged in occupation from farmers to presidents of universities. Their social background included everything from wilderness pioneering to the aristocracy of landed estates. Their dialects included everything from the loquacious drawl of South Carolina to the clipped staccato of Yankee New England. Their economic origins included everything from frontier poverty to opulent wealth.

Then how do we explain their remarkable unanimity in fundamental beliefs?

Perhaps the explanation will be found in the fact that they were all remarkably well-read, and mostly from the same books. Although the level of their formal training varied from spasmodic doses of home tutoring to the rigorous regimen of Harvard's classical studies, the debates in the Constitutional Convention, and the writings of the Founders reflect a far broader knowledge of religious, political, historical, economic, and philosophical studies than would be found in any cross-section of American leaders today.

The thinking of Polybius, Cicero, Thomas Hooker, Coke, Montesquieu, Blackstone, John Locke, and Adam Smith salt-and-peppered their writings and their conversations. They were also careful students of the Bible, especially the Old Testament, and even though some did not belong to any Christian denomination, the teachings of Jesus were held in universal respect and admiration.

Their historical readings included a broad perspective of Greek, Roman, Anglo-Saxon, European, and English history. To this writer, nothing is more remarkable about the early American leaders than their breadth of reading and depth of knowledge concerning the essential elements of sound nation building.

## Fundamental Principles

The relative uniformity of fundamental thought shared by these men included strong and unusually well-defined convictions concerning religious principles, political precepts, economic fundamentals, and long-range social goals. On particulars, of course, they quarreled, but when discussing fundamental precepts and ultimate objectives they seemed practically unanimous.

They even had strong criticism of one another as individual personalities, yet admired each other as laborers in the common cause. John Adams, for example, felt a strong personality conflict between himself and Benjamin Franklin and even Thomas Jefferson. Yet Adams' writings are steeped in accolades for both of them, and their writings carried the same for him. One of George Washington's most vehement critics was Dr. Benjamin Rush, and yet that Pennsylvania physician boldly supported everything for which Washington worked and fought.

We will now proceed to carefully examine the 28 major principles on which the American Founders established the first free people in modern times. These are the great ideas which provided the intellectual, political, and economic climate for the 5,000-year leap.

# Part II

# The Founders' Basic Principles

# 1st
## Principle

**The only reliable basis for sound government and just human relations is Natural Law.**

Marcus Tullius Cicero
The Founders' Favorite Expositor of Natural Law

**M**ost modern Americans have never studied Natural Law. They are therefore mystified by the constant reference to Natural Law by the Founding Fathers. Blackstone confirmed the wisdom of the Founders by stating that it is the only reliable basis for a stable society and a system of justice. Then what is Natural Law? A good place to seek out the answer is in the writings of one of the American Founders' favorite authors, Marcus Tullius Cicero.

### The Life and Writings of Cicero

It was Cicero who cut sharply through the political astigmatism and philosophical errors of both Plato and Aristotle to discover the touchstone for good laws, sound government, and the long-range formula for happy human relations. In the Founders' roster of great political thinkers, Cicero was high on the list.

Dr. William Ebenstein of Princeton says:

"The only Roman political writer who has exercised enduring influence throughout the ages is Cicero (106-43 B.C.)... Cicero studied law in Rome, and philosophy in Athens... He became the leading lawyer of his time and also rose to the highest office of state [Roman Consul].

"...Yet his life was not free of sadness; only five years after he had held the highest office in Rome, the consulate, he found himself in exile for a year.... Cicero nevertheless showed considerable personal courage in opposing the drift toward dictatorship based on popular support. Caesar was assassinated in 44 B.C., and a year later, in 43 B.C., Cicero was murdered by the henchmen of Antony, a member of the triumvirate set up after Caesar's death." (William Ebenstein, *Great Political Thinkers*, Holt, Rinehart and Winston, New York, 1963, pp. 122-123.)

So out of Cicero's maelstrom of turbulent experience with power politics, plus his intense study of all forms of political systems, he wrote his landmark books on the Republic and the Laws. In these writings Cicero projected the grandeur and promise of some future society based on Natural Law.

The American Founding Fathers obviously shared a profound appreciation of Cicero's dream because they envisioned just such a commonwealth of prosperity and justice for themselves and their posterity. They saw in Cicero's writings the necessary ingredients for their model society which they eventually hoped to build.

## Cicero's Fundamental Principles

To Cicero, the building of a society on principles of Natural Law was nothing more nor less than recognizing and identifying the rules of "right conduct" with the laws of the Supreme Creator of the universe. History demonstrates that even in those nations sometimes described as "pagan" there were sharp, penetrating minds like Cicero's who reasoned their way through the labyrinths of natural phenomena to see behind the cosmic universe, as well as the unfolding of their own lives, the brilliant intelligence of a supreme Designer with an ongoing interest in both human and cosmic affairs.

Cicero's compelling honesty led him to conclude that once the reality of the Creator is clearly identified in the mind, the only intelligent approach to government, justice, and human relations is in terms of the laws which the Supreme Creator has already established. The Creator's order of things is called Natural Law.

A fundamental presupposition of Natural Law is that man's reasoning power is a special dispensation of the Creator and is closely akin to the rational or reasoning power of the Creator himself. In other words, man shares with his Creator this quality of utilizing a rational approach to solving problems, and the reasoning of the mind will generally lead to common-sense conclusions based on what Jefferson called "the laws of Nature and of Nature's God." (The Declaration of Independence)

Let us now examine the major precepts of Natural Law which so profoundly impressed the Founding Fathers.

## Natural Law Is Eternal and Universal

First of all, Cicero defines Natural Law as "true law." Then he says:

"True law is right reason in agreement with nature; it is of universal application, unchanging and everlasting; it summons to duty by its commands, and averts from wrongdoing by its prohibitions.... It is a sin to try to alter this law, nor is it allowable to repeal any part of it, and it is impossible to abolish it entirely. We cannot be freed from its obligations by senate or people, and we need not look outside ourselves for an expounder or interpreter of it. And there will not be different laws at Rome and Athens, or different laws now and in the future, but one eternal and unchangeable law will be valid for all nations and all times, and there will be one master and ruler, that is God, over us all, for he is the author of this law, its promulgator, and its enforcing judge. Whoever is disobedient is fleeing from himself and denying his human nature, and by reason of this very fact he will suffer the worst punishment." (Quoted in Ebenstein, *Great Political Thinkers*, p. 133.)

In these few lines the student encounters concepts which were repeated by the American Founders a thousand times. The Law of Nature or Nature's God is eternal in its basic goodness; it is universal in its application. It is a code of "right reason" from the Creator himself. It cannot be altered. It cannot be repealed. It cannot be abandoned by legislators or the people themselves, even though they may pretend to do so. In Natural Law we are dealing with factors of absolute reality. It is basic in its principles, comprehensible to the human mind, and totally correct and morally right in its general operation. To the Founding Fathers as well as to Blackstone, John Locke, Montesquieu, and Cicero, this was a monumental discovery.

## The Divine Gift of Reason

To Cicero it was an obvious and remarkable thing that man had been endowed with a rich quality of mind that does not exist among other forms of life except in the most minuscule proportions. Between man and other creatures there is a gigantic gap insofar as mental processes are concerned. Cicero as well as the Founders viewed this as a special, divine endowment from the Creator. Cicero wrote:

> "The animal which we call man, endowed with foresight and quick intelligence, complex, keen, possessing memory, full of reason and prudence, has been given a certain distinguished status by the Supreme God who created him; for he is the only one among so many different kinds and varieties of living beings who has a share in reason and thought, while all the rest are deprived of it. But what is more divine, I will not say in man only, but in all heaven and earth, than reason? And reason, when it is full grown and perfected, is rightly called wisdom. Therefore, since there is nothing better than reason, and since it exists both in man and God, the first common possession of man and God is reason.

> "But those who have reason in common must also have right reason in common. And since right reason is law we must believe that men have Law also in common with the gods. Further, those who share Law must also share Justice; and those who share these are to be regarded as members of the same commonwealth. If indeed they obey the same authorities and powers, this is true in a far greater degree; but as a matter of fact they do obey this celestial system, the divine mind, and the God of transcendent power. Hence we must now conceive of this whole universe as one commonwealth of which both gods and men are members." (Quoted in Ebenstein, *Great Political Thinkers*, p. 133.)

No prophet of the Old Testament or the Gospel teachers of the New Testament ever said it any better.

### The First Great Commandment

Cicero had comprehended the magnificence of the first great commandment to love, respect, and obey the all-wise Creator. He put this precept in proper perspective by saying that God's law is "right reason." When perfectly understood it is called "wisdom." When applied by government in regulating human relations it is called "justice." When people unite together in a covenant or compact under this law, they become a true "commonwealth" and since they intend to administer their affairs under God's law, they belong to his commonwealth. Thus Cicero came to what Jews and Christians call the first great commandment.

It will be recalled that a lawyer tried to discredit Jesus by asking him, *"Master, which is the great commandment in the Law?"* Of course, there were hundreds of commandments, and the question was designed as a clever stratagem to embarrass Jesus. However, Jesus was not embarrassed. He simply replied: *"Thou shalt love the Lord thy God with all thy heart, and with all thy soul, and with all thy mind. This is the first and great commandment."*

The lawyer was amazed by this astute and ready response from the Galilean carpenter. But Jesus was not through. He added: *"And the second is like unto it. Thou shalt love thy neighbor as thyself. On these two commandments hang all the law and the prophets."* (Matthew 22:36-40.)

The astonished lawyer simply replied: *"Well, Master, thou hast said the truth!"*

Jesus had picked out what he considered to be the foremost commandment from Deuteronomy 6:4-5, and then selected what he considered to be the second most important commandment clear over in Leviticus 19:18.

## The Second Great Commandment

It is interesting that Cicero, without being either a Christian or a Jew, was able to discover the power and fundamental significance of obedience, not only to the first great commandment, but to the second one as well. His great mind instinctively led him to comprehend the beauty and felicity of what Jesus had identified as the second great commandment: *"Thou shalt love thy neighbor as thyself."*

Dr. William Ebenstein comments on this rather fascinating insight among Cicero's writings by saying:

> "There is another note, too, in Cicero that points forward, toward Christianity, rather than backward, to Plato and Aristotle: Cicero's consciousness of love as a mighty social bond." (Ebenstein, *Great Political Thinkers*, p. 124.)

Cicero raises this point in connection with his discussion of Justice. He points out that Justice is impossible except under the principles of God's just law:

> "... For these virtues originate in our natural inclination to love our fellow-men, and this is the foundation of justice." (*Ibid.*, p. 134)

So to Cicero, the glue which holds a body of human beings together in the commonwealth of a just society is love – love of God; love of God's great law of Justice; and love of one's fellow-men which provides the desire to promote true justice among mankind.

### All Mankind Can Be Taught God's Law or Virtue

Cicero projected throughout his writings a particularly optimistic view of the potential improvement of human beings by teaching them the elements of virtue through education. He wrote:

> "Out of all the material of the philosophers' discussion, surely there comes nothing more valuable than the full realization that we are born for justice, and the right is based, not upon men's opinions, but upon Nature. This fact will immediately be plain if you once get a clear conception of man's fellowship and union with his fellow-men.... However we may define man, a single definition will apply to all. This is a sufficient proof that there is no difference in kind between man and man.... in fact, there is no human being of any race who, if he finds a guide, cannot attain to virtue." *(Ibid.)*

### Legislation in Violation of God's Natural Law is a Scourge to Humanity

We cannot complete our review of Cicero's discourse on Natural Law without including his warning against legislators who undertake to pass laws which violate the "laws of Nature and of Nature's God." Cicero wrote:

> "But the most foolish notion of all is the belief that everything is just which is found in the customs or laws of nations.... What of the many deadly, the many pestilential statutes which nations put in force? These no more deserve to be called laws than the rules a band of robbers might pass in their assembly. For if ignorant and unskillful men have prescribed deadly poisons instead of healing drugs, these cannot possibly be called physicians' prescriptions; neither in a nation can a statute of any sort be called a law, even though the nation, in spite of being a ruinous regulation has accepted it." *(Ibid.)*

### All Law Should Be Measured Against God's Law

Cicero then set forth the means by which people may judge between good and evil laws. All laws must be measured by God's Law, which is described by Cicero as follows:

"Therefore Law [of the Creator] is the distinction between things just and unjust, made in agreement with that primal and most ancient of all things, Nature; and in conformity to Nature's standard are framed those human laws which inflict punishment upon the wicked and protect the good." (*Ibid.*, p. 135)

Cicero also emphasizes that the essence of an evil law cannot be mended through ratification by the legislature or by popular acclaim. Justice can never be expected from laws arbitrarily passed in violation of standards set up under the laws of Nature or the laws of the Creator. Here is his argument:

"But if the principles of Justice were founded on the decrees of peoples, the edicts of princes, or the decisions of judges, then Justice would sanction robbery and adultery and forgery of wills, in case these acts were approved by the votes or decrees of the populace. But if so great a power belongs to the decisions and decrees of fools that the laws of Nature can be changed by their votes, then why do they not ordain that what is bad and baneful shall be considered good and salutary? Or, if a law can make Justice injustice can it not also make good out of bad?" *(Ibid.)*

### Cicero's Conclusion

It was clear to Cicero as he came toward the close of his life that men must eliminate the depravity that had lodged itself in society. He felt they must return to the high road of Natural Law. They must pledge obedience to the mandates of a loving and concerned Creator. What promise of unprecedented grandeur awaited that future society which would undertake it! He wrote:

"As one and the same Nature holds together and supports the universe, all of whose parts are in harmony with one another, so men are united in Nature; but by reason of their depravity they quarrel, not realizing that they are of one blood and subject to one and the same protecting power. If this fact were understood, surely man would live the life of the Gods!" *(Ibid.)*

The American Founders believed this. They embraced the obvious necessity of building a highly moral and virtuous society. The Founders wanted to lift mankind from the common depravity and chicanery of past civilizations, and to lay the foundation for a new kind of civilization built on freedom for the individual and prosperity for the whole common-wealth. This is why they built their system on Natural Law.

Let us consider a few examples.

### Examples of Natural Law

It may be surprising, even to Americans, to discover how much of their Constitution and their life-style is based on principles of Natural Law. For example:

The concept of *unalienable rights* is based on Natural Law. Twenty-two of these unalienable rights are listed in this book.

The concept of *unalienable duties* is based on Natural Law. Twenty of these unalienable duties are listed in this book.

The concept of *habeas corpus* is based on Natural Law.

The concept of *limited government* is based on Natural Law.

The concept of *separation of powers* is based on Natural Law.

The concept of *checks and balances* to correct abuses by peaceful means is based on Natural Law.

The right of *self-preservation* is based on Natural Law.

The right to *contract* is based on Natural Law.

Laws protecting the *family* and the institution of *marriage* are all based on Natural Law.

The concept of *justice by reparation* or paying for damages is based on Natural Law.

The right to *bear arms* is based on Natural Law.

The principle of no *taxation without representation* is based on Natural Law.

These few examples will illustrate how extensively the entire American constitutional system is grounded in Natural Law. In fact, Natural Law is the foundation and encompassing framework for everything we have come to call "People's Law."

This is precisely what Thomas Jefferson was talking about when he wrote in the Declaration of Independence:

> "We hold these truths to be self-evident, that all men are created equal, that they are endowed by their Creator with certain inalienable rights, that among these are Life, Liberty and the Pursuit of Happiness."

These well-remembered phrases from America's initial charter of liberty are all primary pre-suppositions under the principles of Natural law. Now, having covered the highlights of the Founders' first fundamental precept, let us proceed to the second.

# 2nd

## Principle

**A free people cannot survive under a republican constitution unless they remain virtuous and morally strong.**

Modern Americans have long since forgotten the heated and sometimes violent debates which took place in the thirteen colonies between 1775 and 1776 over the issue of morality. For many thousands of Americans the big question of independence hung precariously on the single, slender thread of whether or not the people were sufficiently "virtuous and moral" to govern themselves. Self-government was generally referred to as "republicanism," and it was universally acknowledged that a corrupt and selfish people could never make the principles of republicanism operate successfully. As Franklin wrote:

> "Only a virtuous people are capable of freedom. As nations become corrupt and vicious, they have more need of masters." (Smyth, *Writings of Benjamin Franklin*, 9:569.)

George Washington later praised the American Constitution as the "palladium of human rights," but pointed that it could survive only "so long as there shall remain any virtue in the body of the people." (Saul K. Padover, ed., *The Washington Papers*, Harper & Brothers, NY, 1955, p. 244.)

## What Is "Public Virtue"?

Morality is identified with the Ten Commandments and obedience to the Creator's mandate for "right conduct," but the early Americans identified "public virtue" as a very special quality of human maturity in character and service closely akin to the Golden Rule. As a modern historian epitomized it:

> "In a Republic, however, each man must somehow be persuaded to submerge his personal wants into the greater good of the whole. This willingness of the individual to sacrifice his private interest for the good of the community -- such patriotism or love of country -- the eighteenth century termed public virtue.... The eighteenth century mind was thoroughly convinced that a popularly based government 'cannot be supported without virtue'." (Gordon S. Wood, *The Creation of the American Republic*, 1776-1787, The University of North Carolina Press, Chapel Hill, 1969, p. 68.)

### Self-Doubts

The people had an instinctive thirst for independence, but there remained a haunting fear that they might not be "good enough" to make it work.

These self-doubts were actually the eye of the hurricane during those final pre-revolutionary years when Americans were trying to decide whether they had the moral capacity for self-government. Great names of later years were among the doubters in those pre-revolutionary days. John Jay, Robert Morris, Robert Livingston, and even John Dickinson were among them. Their doubts gradually diminished as their patriotic indignation was aroused by the harsh and sometimes brutal policies of the British crown. They were also moved by the powerful expressions of faith and confidence pouring forth from men of "admired virtue" such as John Adams, George Washington, Richard Henry Lee, and Josiah Quincy.

Spirits continued to rise so that by the spring of 1776, thousands of confident voices were heard throughout the colonies affirming that there was sufficient "public virtue" in the people to make republican principles work successfully.

### Thomas Paine

One of the most strident voices in the debate was Thomas Paine, whose Common Sense had been a best-seller. He followed up this initial success with other writings assuring Americans they were ripe for independence. He pointed out that most of the people were "industrious, frugal, and honest."

He added that few Americans had been corrupted with riches the way people had been debilitated in Europe, where all they wanted was "luxury, indolence, amusement, and pleasure." Furthermore, there was a spirit of equality and public virtue unheard of in other nations because "the people of America are a people of property, almost every man is a freeholder." (Quoted in Wood, *The Creation of the American Republic*, p. 100.)

Nevertheless, there were many newspapers in New York, Boston, Philadelphia, and Charleston which printed numerous letters pointing out dramatically and gruesomely the deficiencies of American society in many serious respects.

This self-examination over a period of several years resulted in a remarkable reform movement which spread up and down the entire Atlantic seaboard.

### The Tide of Reform

Many Americans became extremely self-conscious about their lack of "public virtue" because of non-involvement in the affairs of government. They began to acknowledge their obsession with self-interest, the neglect of public affairs, and their disdain for the needs of the community as a whole. Gradually, a spirit of "sacrifice and reform" became manifest in all thirteen colonies.

Looking back on that period, one historian wrote:

In the eyes of the Whigs, the two or three years before the Declaration of Independence always appears to be the great period of the Revolution, the time of greatest denial and cohesion, when men ceased to extort and abuse one another, when families and communities seemed peculiarly united, when the courts were wonderfully free of that constant bickering over land and credit that had dominated their colonial life. (*Ibid.*, p. 102)

### How the Moral Reform Accelerated the Revolution

Many Americans became so impressed with the improvement in the quality of life as a result of the reform movement that they were afraid they might lose it if they did not hurriedly separate from the corrupting influence of British manners. They attributed this corruption to the monarchial aristocracy of England. Even Americans such as John Jay, Robert Morris, and Robert Livingston were beginning to see that the people were exhibiting a potential capacity for virtue and morality which would guarantee the success of a free, self-governing society. Therefore, it became popular to express the sentiment that the sooner they became independent the better.

The non-importation resolution of the Continental Congress, which required great sacrifice and devastating losses to many business houses, was carried out extensively even though it operated on a voluntary basis. It was so successful that John Page wrote to Jefferson that it appeared to him "a spirit of public virtue may transcend every private consideration." *(Ibid.)*

Young James Madison gloried in the atmosphere of national purpose, saying that "a spirit of liberty and patriotism animates all degrees and denominations of men." *(Ibid.)*

It was in this climate of reform and commitment that Americans saw themselves sublimating and improving their social consciousness to the point where the continuing presence of British manners did indeed seem to be a threat to the new reform. As Gordon Wood relates it:

> "By 1776 it had become increasingly evident that if they were to remain the kind of people they wanted to be they must become free of Britain. The calls for independence thus took on a tone of imperativeness.... Only separating from the British monarch and instituting republicanism, it seemed, could realize the social image the Enlightenment had drawn of them." *(Ibid., p. 108)*

British influence was already taking its toll. One alarmed American wrote, "Elegance, luxury and effeminacy begin to be established." David Ramsay declared that if Americans had not revolted "our frugality, industry, and simplicity of manners, would have been lost in an imitation of British extravagance, idleness, and false refinements." *(Ibid. p. 110)*

### The Lessons of History

It is only in this historical context that the modern American can appreciate the profound degree of anxiety which the Founders expressed concerning the quality of virtue and morality in their descendants. They knew that without these qualities, the Constitution they had written and the republican system of government which it provided could not be maintained. As James Madison said:

> "Is there no virtue among us? If there be not, we are in a wretched situation. No theoretical checks, no form of government, can render us secure. To suppose that any form of government will secure liberty or happiness without any virtue in the people, is a chimerical [imaginary] idea. If there be sufficient virtue and intelligence in the community, it will be exercised in

the selection of these men; so that we do not depend upon their virtue, or put confidence in our rulers, but in the people who are to choose them." (Quoted in Jonathan Elliot, ed., *The Debates in the Several State Conventions on the Adoption of the Federal Constitution,* 5 vols., J. B. Lippincott Company,)

Of course, as Jefferson said, "Virtue is not hereditary." (Ford, *Writings of Thomas Jefferson*, p. 227.)

Virtue has to be earned and it has to be learned. Neither is virtue a permanent quality in human nature. It has to be cultivated continually and exercised from hour to hour and from day to day. The Founders looked to the home, the school, and the churches to fuel the fires of virtue from generation to generation.

In his Farewell Address, George Washington declared:

"Of all the dispositions and habits which lead to political prosperity, religion and morality are indispensable supports. In vain would that man claim the tribute of patriotism, who should labor to subvert these great pillars of human happiness, these firmest props of the duties of men and citizens... Let it simply be asked, where is the security for property, for reputation, for life, if the sense of religious obligation desert the oaths which are the instruments of investigation in courts of justice? And let us with caution indulge the supposition that morality can be maintained without religion. Whatever may be conceded to the influence of refined education ... reason and experience both forbid us to expect that national morality can prevail in exclusion of religious principle." (Padover, *The Washington Papers*, pp. 318-319.)

Benjamin Franklin stressed the same point and added how precious good teachers are:

"I think with you, that nothing is of more importance for the public weal, than to form and train up youth in wisdom and virtue. Wise and good men are in my opinion, the strength of the state; more so than riches or arms...

"I think also, that general virtue is more probably to be expected and obtained from the education of youth, than from the exhortations of adult persons; bad habits and vices of the mind being, like diseases of the body, more easily prevented [in youth] than cured [in adults.] I think, moreover, that talents for the education of youth are the gift of God; and that he on whom they are bestowed, whenever a way is opened for the use of them, is as strongly called as if he heard a voice from heaven...." (Quoted in Adrienne Koch, ed., *The American Enlightenment*, George Braziller, New York, 1965, p. 77.)

## A Warning from the Founders

At the conclusion of the Revolutionary War, Samuel Adams, who is sometimes called the "father of the revolution," wrote to Richard Henry Lee:

> "I thank God that I have lived to see my country independent and free. She may long enjoy her independence and freedom if she will. It depends on her virtue." (Wells, *Life of Samuel Adams*, 3:175.)

John Adams pointed out why the future of the United States depended upon the level of virtue and morality maintained among the people. He said:

> "Our Constitution was made only for a moral and religious people. It is wholly inadequate to the government of any other." (Quoted in John R. Howe, Jr., *The Changing Political Thought of John Adams*, Princeton University Press, Princeton, N.J., 1966, p. 189.)

Samuel Adams knew the price of American survival under a Constitutional form of government when he wrote:

> "The sum of all is, if we would most truly enjoy the gift of Heaven, let us become a virtuous people; then shall we both deserve and enjoy it. while, on the other hand, if we are universally vicious and debauched in our manners, though the form of our Constitution carries the face of the most exalted freedom, we shall in reality be the most abject slaves." (Wells, *Life of Samuel Adams*, 1:22-23.)

## What is the Key to Preserving a Virtuous Nation?

Since the quality of virtue and morality in the character of a nation is the secret to its survival, one cannot help but wonder if there is some special ingredient which is fundamentally necessary to provide the greatest assurance that these qualities of our national life will be preserved. The Founders had an answer to this question, which brings us to our next basic precept.

# 3rd

## Principle

**The most promising method of securing a virtuous and
morally stable people is to elect virtuous leaders.**

"...thou shalt provide out of all the people able men, such as
fear God, men of truth, hating covetousness [unjust gain]; and
place such over them, to be rulers..." - Exodus 18:21

Samuel Adams pointed out a sobering fact concerning our political survival as a free people when he said:

> "But neither the wisest constitution nor the wisest laws will
> secure the liberty and happiness of a people whose manners are
> universally corrupt. He therefore is the truest friend to the liberty
> of his country who tries most to promote its virtue, and who, so
> far as his power and influence extend, will not suffer a man to be
> chosen into any office of power and trust who is not a wise and
> virtuous man." (Wells, *Life of Samuel Adams*, 1:22.)

He then went on to say that public officials should not be chosen if
they are lacking in experience, training, proven virtue, and demonstrated
wisdom. He said the task of the electorate is to choose those whose "fidelity has been tried in the nicest and tenderest manner, and has been ever
firm and unshaken." (*Ibid.*)

A favorite scripture of the day was *Proverbs* 29:2, which says: "When
the righteous are in authority, the people rejoice; but when the wicked
beareth rule, the people mourn."

### In the Absence of Angels

The Founders recognized human nature for what it is – a mixture of
good and evil. They reasoned that if people are to govern themselves and

have the best possible government, then a political process should be developed through which the wisest, the most experienced, and the most virtuous can be precipitated to the surface and elected to public office. Actually, mankind has no sensible option. As Madison said:

> "If men were angels, no government would be necessary. If angels were to govern men, neither external nor internal controls on government would be necessary." (*The Federalist Papers*, No. 51, p. 322.)

Unfortunately, that utopian dream will never be possible in view of the obvious limitations of human nature. The next best thing is to take the most promising element in society and draft them into public service. What the Founders hoped to do was develop a spirit of public virtue by having leaders of strong private virtue. It would be a new kind of "freemen aristocracy" or "natural aristocracy" which would be open to all, but inheritable by none. Every leader would have to rise to his high office on personal merit, not the wealth and reputation of his ancestors.

### Jefferson's "Natural Aristocracy"

Thomas Jefferson typified the Founders' philosophy of social responsibility. They strongly believed that the best citizens should accept major roles in public life. They believed people with talent and demonstrated qualities of leadership should have the same sense of duty as that which Washington exhibited when he allowed himself to be called out of retirement three separate times to serve the country. Jefferson referred to such people as the nation's "natural aristocracy." He said it was an aristocracy of virtue, talent, and patriotism without which the nation could not survive.

In contrast to the natural aristocracy, he said there was an "artificial" aristocracy which dominated the elite ruling class of Europe. These were those who obtained their high offices because of wealth, their station in life, or some special influence which had been brought to bear in their behalf. He wanted no artificial aristocracy in America. Jefferson wrote in 1813:

> "There is a natural aristocracy among men. The grounds of this are virtue and talents.... There is, also, an artificial aristocracy, founded on wealth and birth, without either virtue or talents; for with these it would belong to the first class. The natural aristocracy I consider as the most precious gift of nature for the instruction, the trusts, and government of society. And indeed, it would have been inconsistent in creation to have formed man for

the social state, and not to have provided virtue and wisdom enough to manage the concerns of the society. May we not even say, that that form of government is the best, which provides the most effectually for a pure selection of these natural aristoi into the offices of government?" (Ford, *Writings of Thomas Jefferson*, 9:425.)

Jefferson felt it should be the goal of the whole nation to use education and every other means to stimulate and encourage those citizens who clearly exhibited a special talent for public service. He felt one of the greatest threats to the new government would be the day when the best qualified people refused to undertake the tedious, arduous, and sometimes unpleasant task of filling important public offices. In 1779 he said:

"For promoting the public happiness, those persons whom nature has endowed with genius and virtue, should be rendered by liberal education worthy to receive, and able to guard the sacred deposit of the rights and liberties of their fellow citizens; and they should be called to that charge without regard to ... birth, or other accidental condition or circumstance." (Ford, *Writings of Thomas Jefferson*, 2:221.)

### Capturing the Founders' Perspective on "Politics"

The natural tendency of nearly all people is to encourage others to run for office, but not get involved themselves. The Founders knew we could never enjoy strong self-government unless this general perspective were changed. They wanted it to be counted an honor to be drafted into "politics." A popular quotation from Cicero emphasized this theme. He had said:

"For there is really no other occupation in which human virtue approaches more closely the august function of the gods than that of founding new States or preserving those already in existence." (Quoted in Ebenstein, *Great Political Thinkers*, p. 128.)

### John Adams on the "Divine Science of Politics"

American history will show that both Samuel Adams and his younger cousin, John Adams, sacrificed their fortunes to serve in politics. They both considered politics to be a "divine science."

John Adams had this to say about the high calling of a servant of the people in politics:

"Politics are the divine science, after all. How is it possible that any man should ever think of making it subservient to his own little passions and mean private interests? Ye baseborn sons of fallen Adam, is the end of politics a fortune, a family, a gilded coach, a train of horses, and a troop of livery servants, balls at Court, splendid dinners and suppers? Yet the divine science of politics is at length in Europe reduced to a mechanical system composed of these materials." (Quoted in Koch, *The American Enlightenment*, p. 189.)

Some might feel inclined to smile at such a puritanical ideology in a practical politician such as John Adams, but he had a ready answer for the skeptic. Said he:

"What is to become of an independent statesman, one who will bow the knee to no idol, who will worship nothing as a divinity but truth, virtue, and his country? I will tell you; he will be regarded more by posterity than those who worship hounds and horses; and although he will not make his own fortune, he will make the fortune of his country." (*Ibid.*)

### Preparation for Service in Politics

John Adams, like so many of the Founders, laid great stress on the importance of broad, in-depth preparation for a career in public service. Early in his professional life, John Adams wrote to his wife explaining what he felt he must do to prepare himself for leadership in the "divine science" of politics. He wrote:

"The science of government is my duty to study, more than all other sciences; the arts of legislation and administration and negotiation ought to take place of, indeed to exclude, in a manner, all other arts. I must study politics and war, that my sons may have liberty to study mathematics and philosophy. My sons ought to study mathematics and philosophy, geography, natural history and naval architecture, navigation, commerce, and agriculture, in order to give their children a right to study painting, poetry, music, architecture, statuary, tapestry, and porcelain." (*Ibid.*, p. 188)

John Adams was never very popular as an individual, but the people knew he could be trusted. He was elected over and over again, finally becoming President of the United States. Years later, he wrote:

"I do not curse the day when I engaged in public affairs.... I cannot repent of any thing I ever did conscientiously and from a sense of duty. I never engaged in public affairs for my own interest, pleasure, envy, jealousy, avarice, or ambition, or even the desire of fame. If any of these had been my motive, my conduct would have been very different. In every considerable transaction of my public life, I have invariably acted according to my best judgment, and I can look up to God for the sincerity of my intentions." (*Ibid.*, p. 208-209))

If one is astonished by the level of idealism which Founders such as Adams and Jefferson attached to the role of political public service, it cannot be more surprising than the supreme desire they expressed to prevent those offices from becoming monetary attractions. Benjamin Franklin remonstrated both in Europe and America against extravagant compensation for positions of public service.

## Making Public Office an Honor Rather Than a Position of Profit

As Benjamin Franklin traveled in Europe, he noted that there was a violent struggle for appointments to public offices because they paid so well. He felt this was a serious mistake.

In the early history of the United States, community offices were looked upon as stations of honor granted to the recipients by an admiring community, state, or nation. These offices were therefore often filled by those who performed their services with little or no compensation. Even when an annual salary of $25,000 was provided in the Constitution for President Washington, he determined to somehow manage without it. Some might think that this was no sacrifice because he had a large plantation. However, the Mount Vernon plantation had been virtually ruined during the Revolutionary War, and he had not yet built it back into efficient production when he was called to be President. Washington declined his salary on principle. He did the same thing while serving as Commander-in-Chief of the armed forces during the Revolutionary War. Not all could afford to do this, but it was considered the proper procedure when circumstances permitted it.

While in Europe in 1777, Franklin explained to a friend the widespread support for the American attitude concerning public service:

"In America, salaries, where indispensable, are extremely low; but much of public business is done gratis. The honor of serving the public ably and faithfully is deemed sufficient. Public spirit really exists there, and has great effects. In England it is universally deemed a nonentity, and whoever pretends to it is laughed at as a fool, or suspected as a knave." (Smyth, *Writings of Benjamin Franklin*, 7:4.)

### Franklin's Address to the Constitutional Convention

Franklin fervently hoped this policy could be perpetuated in America from generation to generation. At the Constitutional Convention in 1787, he gave a discourse on the need to fix the course of American public service so that it would always attract men of public virtue and repel scoundrels scrambling for a soft job. He said:

> "Sir, there are two passions which have a powerful influence in the affairs of men. These are ambitions and avarice; the love of power and the love of money. Separately, each of these has great force in prompting men to action; but when united in view of the same object, they have in many minds the most violent effects. Place before the eyes of such men a post of honor, that shall at the same time be a place of profit, and they will move heaven and earth to obtain it. The vast number of such places it is that renders the British government so tempestuous. The struggles for them are the true source of all those factions which are perpetually dividing the nation, distracting its councils, hurrying it sometimes into fruitless and mischievous wars, and often compelling a submission to dishonorable terms of peace." (Smyth, *Writings of Benjamin Franklin*, 9:591.)

### Haggling for High-Salaried Public Offices Was Repugnant to the Founders

Franklin had seen enough of the world to make a general observation to the Constitutional Convention which the members could not help but hear with deep respect. The men at the Convention were there at great personal sacrifice; some, like Madison, on borrowed money. Franklin warned that high salaries for government offices are the best way to attract scoundrels and drive from the halls of public office those men who possess true merit and virtue. He asked:

> "And of what kind are the men that will strive for this profitable preeminence, through all the bustle of cabal, the heat of contention, the infinite mutual abuse of parties, tearing to pieces the best of characters? It will not be the wise and moderate, the lovers of peace and good order, the men fittest for the trust. It

will be the bold and the violent, the men of strong passions and indefatigable activity in their selfish pursuits. These will thrust themselves into your government, and be your rulers. And these, too, will be mistaken in the expected happiness of their situation; for their vanquished competitors, of the same spirit, and from the same motives, will perpetually be endeavoring to distress their administration, thwart their measures, and render them odious to the people." (Smyth, *Writings of Benjamin Franklin*, 9:591-592.)

### Benjamin Franklin's Prophecy

Peering down through the corridor of time, Franklin proclaimed his prophetic judgment as to what could be expected if future generations of Americans permitted the lure of high salaries to be associated with public offices. Here are the remarkably profound insights from the "Sage of Philadelphia" to the members of the Constitutional Convention:

"Sir, though we may set out in the beginning with moderate salaries, we shall find that such will not be of long continuance. Reasons will never be wanting for proposed augmentations; and there will always be a party for giving more to the rulers, that the rulers may be able in return to give more to them. Hence, as all history informs us, there has been in every state and kingdom a constant kind of warfare between the governing and the governed, the one striving to obtain more for its support, and the other to pay less. And this has alone occasioned great convulsions, actual civil wars, ending either in dethroning of the princes or enslaving of the people. Generally, indeed, the ruling power carries its point, and we see the revenues of princes constantly increasing, and we see that they are never satisfied, but always in want of more. The more the people are discontented with the oppression of taxes, the greater need the prince has of money to distribute among his partisans, and pay the troops that are to suppress all resistance, and enable him to plunder at pleasure." (Smyth, *Writings of Benjamin Franklin*, 9:592.)

### Prelude to Monarchy

Franklin foresaw the possibility of profit in public office becoming the means by which an American monarchy could eventually arise; not called a monarchy, of course, but an executive with monarchial powers. He continued his speech as follows:

"There is scarce a king in a hundred who would not, if he could, follow the example of Pharaoh – get first all the people's money, then all their lands, and then make them and their children servants forever. It will be said that we do not propose to establish kings. I know it. But there is a natural inclination in mankind to kingly government. It sometimes relieves them from aristocratic domination. They had rather have one tyrant than 500. It gives more of the appearance of equality among citizens; and that they like. I am apprehensive – therefore – perhaps too apprehensive – that the government of these states may in future times end in a monarchy. But this catastrophe, I think, may be long delayed, if in our proposed system we do not sow the seeds of contention, faction, and tumult, by making our posts of honor places of profit. If we do, I fear that, though we employ at first a number and not a single person, the number will in time be set aside; it will only nourish the fetus of a king (as the honorable gentleman from Virginia very aptly expressed it), and a king will the sooner be set over us." (Smyth, *Writings of Benjamin Franklin*, 9:592-593.)

### Franklin Cites an Exceptional but Admirable Example in England

"It may be imagined by some that this is a utopian idea, and that we can never find men to serve us in the executive department without paying them well for their services. I conceive this to be a mistake. Some existing facts present themselves to me, which incline me to a contrary opinion. The high sheriff of a county in England is an honorable office, but it is not a profitable one. It is rather expensive, and therefore not sought for. But yet it is executed, and well executed, and usually by some of the principal gentlemen of the county... I only bring the instance to show that the pleasure of doing good and serving their country, and the respect such conduct entitles them to, are sufficient motives with some minds to give up a great portion of their time to the public, without the mean inducement of pecuniary satisfaction." (Smyth, *Writings of Benjamin Franklin*, 9:593-594.)

### Franklin Points to the Example of George Washington

The most notable example of such altruistic service in the United States was George Washington. At that moment he was presiding over the Convention which Franklin was addressing. Had Washington been elsewhere, Franklin undoubtedly would have gone into a comprehensive history of the notable example which Washington represented in practicing the principles that Franklin was trying to have institutionalized as a part of the American philosophy of government. To avoid embarrassing Washington, however, he simply said:

> "To bring the matter nearer home, have we not seen the greatest and most important of our offices, that of general of our armies, executed for eight years together, without the smallest salary, by a patriot whom I will not now offend by any other praise; and this, through fatigues and distresses, in common with the other brave men, his military friends and companions, and the constant anxieties peculiar to his station? And shall we doubt finding three or four men in all the United States, with public spirit enough to bear sitting in peaceful council, for perhaps an equal term, merely to preside over our civil concerns, and see that our laws are duly executed? Sir, I have a better opinion of our country.

> "I think we shall never be without a sufficient number of wise and good men to undertake, and execute well and faithfully, the office in question." (Smyth, *Writings of Benjamin Franklin*, 9:594-595.)

Franklin then concluded his remarks by emphasizing that his plea for giving modest salaries to those filling public office was not motivated by a parsimonious passion for saving taxes, but simply to avoid the evils that go with high salaries. He said:

> "Sir, the saving of the salaries, that may at first be proposed, is not an object with me. The subsequent mischiefs of proposing them are what I apprehend. And therefore it is that I move the amendment. If it is not seconded or accepted, I must be contented with the satisfaction of having delivered my opinion frankly, and done my duty." (Smyth, *Writings of Benjamin Franklin*, 9:595.)

### Putting Principles into Practice

For nearly a half century, Franklin and most of the Founders had practiced these principles in their own lives. No better example can be found than Franklin himself. Take the summer of 1775, for instance, when Franklin was serving as a businessman, a member of Congress, and chairman of the Pennsylvania Committee of Safety. This committee had to provide weapons, munitions, gunboats, and stockades in preparation for the coming conflict. He describes a typical day to a friend in England as follows:

> "My time was never more fully employed. In the morning at six, I am at the Committee of Safety, appointed by the [Pennsylvania] Assembly to put the province in a state of defense; which committee holds till near nine, when I am in Congress, and that sits till after four in the afternoon. Both of these bodies proceed with the greatest unanimity, and their meetings are well attended. It will scarce be credited in Britain, that men can be as diligent with us from zeal for the public good, as with you for thousands per annum. Such is the difference between uncorrupted new states, and corrupted old ones." (Smyth, *Writings of Benjamin Franklin*, 6:409.)

Long before the Constitutional Convention, where Franklin had made his plea for modest salaries, Pennsylvanians had put the following provision in their State Constitution:

> "As every freeman, to preserve his independence, (if he has not a sufficient estate) ought to have some profession, calling, trade, or farm, whereby he may honestly subsist, there can be no necessity for, nor use in, establishing offices of profit; the usual effects of which are dependence and servility, unbecoming freemen, in the possessors and expectants; faction, contention, corruption, and disorder among the people. Wherefore, whenever an office, through increase of fees or otherwise, becomes so profitable, as to occasion many to apply for it, the profits ought to be lessened by the legislature." (*Ibid.*)

## The Formula for Producing Leaders of Character and Virtue

A modern American cannot read the writings of men such as Jefferson, Adams, Franklin, or Washington without feeling a certain sense of pride that the United States produced and had available leaders of this supreme quality to launch the first "noble experiment" for freedom in modern times.

However, one important question remains: "How are such qualities of superior character and virtue developed in human beings?"

The answer will be found in the writings of the Founders themselves. As we shall see in the numerous quotations appearing in the following pages, the beliefs of the Founders were based on careful study. They had also been carefully taught. In their respective churches, families, schools, or elsewhere, they had been allowed to acquire a comprehensive system of strong, basic beliefs. Throughout their writings and speeches, the Founders project themselves as positive believers in a broad spectrum of fundamental precepts which they called "self-evident truths."

These beliefs are remarkable in and of themselves, but the fact that they all seem to have shared them in common is even more remarkable.

## Beliefs Which the Founders Rejected

It is interesting that their acceptance of these beliefs necessarily required that they categorically reject some of the more popular intellectual fads which were widespread in Europe during their day. It further required that they reject some of the less tenable positions of certain popular denominations; even denominations to which some of them belonged.

What we are seeing in the Founders, therefore, is a group of very independent, tough-minded men whose beliefs were based on empirical evidence and the light of careful reasoning. Even their acceptance of things which are not seen – the existence of the Creator, for example – were based on observable phenomena and precise reasoning.

The well-known psychologist Abraham Maslow, in his book entitled The Third Force, concludes after extensive testing that a mind-set based on a spectrum of well-established beliefs, such as the Founders possessed, definitely produces a higher quality of human behavior and a more positive adjustment to the stresses of life.

No doubt Cicero would respond to such a conclusion with the observation that these results should have been expected. Beliefs based on reason and self-evident truth bring a human being into harmony with natural law and the eternal realities of the cosmic universe.

Now we will examine what the Founders had to say about some of their better-known basic beliefs.

# 4th

## Principle

**Without religion the government of a
free people cannot be maintained.**

Americans of the twentieth century often fail to realize the supreme importance which the Founding Fathers originally attached to the role of religion in the structure of the unique civilization which they hoped would emerge as the first free people in modern times. Many Americans also fail to realize that the Founders felt the role of religion would be as important in our own day as it was in theirs.

In 1787, the very year the Constitution was written and approved by Congress, that same Congress passed the famous Northwest Ordinance. In it they emphasized the essential need to teach religion and morality in the schools. Here is the way they said it:

> "Article 3: Religion, morality, and knowledge being necessary to good government and the happiness of mankind, schools and the means of education shall forever be encouraged." (George B. de Huszar, Henry W. Littlefield, and Arthur W, Littlefield, editors, *Basic American Documents,* Littlefield, Adams & Co., Ames, Iowa, 1953, p, 66.)

Notice that formal education was to include among its responsibilities the teaching of three important subjects:

1. **Religion**, which might be defined as a "fundamental system of beliefs concerning man's origin and relationship to the cosmic universe as well as his relationship with his fellowmen."
2. **Morality**, which may be described as "a standard of behavior distinguishing right from wrong."
3. **Knowledge**, which is "an intellectual awareness and understanding of established facts relating to any field of human experience or inquiry (i.e., history, geography, science, etc.)"

### Washington Describes the Founders' Position

The position set forth in the Northwest Ordinance was re-emphasized by President George Washington in his Farewell Address:

"Of all the dispositions and habits which lead to political prosperity, religion and morality are indispensable supports.... And let us with caution indulge the supposition that morality can be maintained without religion ... Reason and experience both forbid us to expect that national morality can prevail to the exclusion of religious principle.

"It is substantially true that virtue or morality is a necessary spring of popular government. (*Basic American Documents*, pp. 108-109.)

### The Teaching of Religion in Schools Restricted to Universal Fundamentals

Having established that "religion" is the foundation of morality and that both are essential to "good government and the happiness of mankind," the Founders then set about to exclude the creeds and biases or dissensions of individual denominations so as to make the teaching of religion a unifying cultural adhesive rather than a divisive apparatus. Jefferson wrote a Bill for Establishing Elementary Schools in Virginia and made this point clear by stating:

"No religious reading, instruction, or exercise shall be prescribed or practiced inconsistent with the tenets of any religious sect or denomination." (J. Randolph, ed., *Early History of the University of Virginia*, 1856, pp. 96-97.)

Obviously, under such restrictions the only religious tenets to be taught in public schools would have to be those which were universally accepted by all faiths and completely fundamental in their premises.

## Franklin Describes the Five Fundamentals
## of "All Sound Religion"

Several of the Founders have left us with descriptions of their basic religious beliefs, and Benjamin Franklin summarized those which he felt were the "fundamental points in all sound religion." This is the way he said it in a letter to Ezra Stiles, president of Yale University:

> "Here is my creed: I believe in one God, the Creator of the universe. That he governs it by his providence. That he ought to be worshipped. That the most acceptable service we render to him is in doing good to his other children. That the soul of man is immortal, and will be treated with justice in another life respecting its conduct in this. These I take to be the fundamental points in all sound religion." (Smyth, *Writings of Benjamin Franklin*, 10:84.)

### The "Fundamental Points" to Be Taught in the Schools

The five points of fundamental religious belief expressed or implied in Franklin's statement are these:

1. There exists a Creator who made all things and mankind should recognize and worship him.
2. The Creator has revealed a moral code of behavior for happy living which distinguishes right from wrong.
3. The Creator holds mankind responsible for the way they treat each other.
4. All mankind live beyond this life.
5. In the next life mankind are judged for their conduct in this one.

All five of these tenets run through practically all of the Founders' writings. These are the beliefs which the Founders sometimes referred to as the "religion of America" and they felt these Fundamentals were so important in providing "good government and the happiness of mankind" that they wanted them taught in the public schools along with morality and knowledge.

### Statements of the Founders Concerning These Principles

Samuel Adams said that this group of basic beliefs which constitute "the religion of America is the religion of all mankind." (Wells, Life of Samuel Adams, 3:23.) In other words, these fundamental beliefs belong to all world faiths and could therefore be taught without being offensive to any "sect or denomination" as indicated in the Virginia bill for establishing elementary schools.

John Adams called these tenets the "general principles" on which the American civilization had been founded. (Letter to Jefferson cited in Bergh, *Writings of Thomas Jefferson*, 13:293.)

Thomas Jefferson called these basic beliefs the principles "in which God has united us all." (*Ibid.*, 14:198.)

From these statements it is obvious how significantly the Founders looked upon the fundamental precepts of religion and morality as the cornerstones of free government. This gives additional importance to the previously quoted warning of Washington when he said: "Of all the dispositions and habits which lead to political prosperity, religion and morality are indispensable supports... Who that is a sincere friend to it can look with indifference upon attempts to shake the foundation of the fabric?" (*Basic American Documents*, pp. 108-109.)

Washington issued this solemn warning because in France, shortly before he wrote his Farewell Address (1796), the promoters of atheism and amorality had seized control and turned the French Revolution into a shocking blood bath of wild excesses and violence. Washington obviously never wanted anything like that to happen in the United States. Therefore he had said: "In vain would that man claim the tribute of patriotism who should labor to subvert these great pillars of human happiness [religion and morality]." (*Ibid.*)

### Alexis de Tocqueville Discovers the
### Importance of Religion in America

When the French jurist, Alexis de Tocqueville, visited the United States in 1831, he became so impressed with what he saw that he went home and wrote one of the best definitive studies on the American culture and Constitutional system that had been published up to that time. His book was called *Democracy in America*. Concerning religion in America, de Tocqueville said:

"On my arrival in the United States the religious aspect of the country was the first thing that struck my attention; and the longer I stayed there, the more I perceived the great political consequences resulting from this new state of things." (Alexis de Tocqueville, *Democracy in America*, 2 vols., 1840, Vintage Books, New York, 1945, 1:319.)

He described the situation as follows:

"Religion in America takes no direct part in the government of society, but it must be regarded as the first of their political institutions.... I do not know whether all Americans have a sincere faith in their religion -- for who can search the human heart? -- but I am certain that they hold it to be indispensable to the maintenance of republican institutions. This opinion is not peculiar to a class of citizens or to a party, but it belongs to the whole nation and to every rank of society." (*Ibid.*, p. 316)

## European Philosophers Turned Out to Be Wrong

In Europe, it had been popular to teach that religion and liberty were enemies of each other. De Tocqueville saw the very opposite happening in America. He wrote:

"The philosophers of the eighteenth century explained in a very simple manner the gradual decay of religious faith. Religious zeal, said they, must necessarily fail the more generally liberty is established and knowledge diffused. Unfortunately, the facts by no means accord with their theory. There are certain populations in Europe whose unbelief is only equaled by their ignorance and debasement; while in America, one of the freest and most enlightened nations in the world, the people fulfill with fervor all the outward duties of religion." (*Ibid.*, p. 319)

## A New Kind of Religious Vitality Emerges in America

De Tocqueville pointed out that "in France I had almost always seen the spirit of religion and the spirit of freedom marching in opposite directions. But in America I found they were intimately united." (*Ibid.*) He then pointed out that the early American colonists "brought with them into the New World a form of Christianity which I cannot better describe than by styling it a democratic and republican religion. This contributed powerfully to the establishment of a republic and a democracy in public affairs; and from the beginning, politics and religion contracted an alliance which has never been dissolved." (*Ibid.*, p. 311)

However, he emphasized the fact that this religious under-girding of the political structure was a common denominator of moral teachings in different denominations and not the political pressure of some national church hierarchy. Said he:

"The sects [different denominations] that exist in the United States are innumerable. They all differ in respect to the worship which is due to the Creator; but they all agree in respect to the duties which are due from man to man. Each sect adores the Deity in its own peculiar manner, but all sects preach the same moral law in the name of God.... All the sects of the United States are comprised within the great unity of Christianity, and Christian morality is everywhere the same... There is no country in the world where the Christian religion retains a greater influence over the souls of men than in America." (*Ibid.*, p. 314)

It was astonishing to de Tocqueville that liberty and religion could be combined in such a balanced structure of harmony and good order. He wrote:

"The revolutionists of America are obliged to profess an ostensible respect for Christian morality and equity, which does not permit them to violate wantonly the laws that oppose their designs.... Thus, while the law permits the Americans to do what they please, religion prevents them from conceiving, and forbids them to commit, what is rash and unjust." (*Ibid.*, p. 316)

### De Tocqueville Describes the Role of Religion in the Schools

De Tocqueville found that the schools, especially in New England, incorporated the basic tenets of religion right along with history and political science in order to prepare the student for adult life. He wrote:

"In New England every citizen receives the elementary notions of human knowledge; he is taught, moreover, the doctrines and the evidences of his religion, the history of his country, and the leading features of its Constitution. In the states of Connecticut and Massachusetts, it is extremely rare to find a man imperfectly acquainted with all these things, and a person wholly ignorant of them is a sort of phenomenon." (*Ibid.*, p. 327)

### De Tocqueville Describes the Role of the American Clergy

Alexis de Tocqueville saw a unique quality of cohesive strength emanating from the clergy of the various churches in America. After noting that all the clergy seemed anxious to maintain "separation of church and state," he nevertheless observed that collectively they had a great influence on the morals and customs of public life. This indirectly reflected itself in the formulating of laws and ultimately in fixing the moral and political climate of the American commonwealth. As a result, he wrote:

"This led me to examine more attentively than I had hitherto done the station which the American clergy occupy in political society. I learned with surprise that they filled no public appointments; I did not see one of them in the administration, and they are not even represented in the legislative assemblies." (*Ibid.*, p. 320)

How different this was from Europe, where the clergy nearly always belonged to a national church and occupied seats of power. He wrote:

"The unbelievers in Europe attack the Christians as their political opponents rather than as their religious adversaries; they hate the Christian religion as the opinion of a [political] party much more than as an error of belief; and they reject the clergy less because they are the representatives of the Deity than because they are the allies of government." (*Ibid.*, p. 325)

In America, he noted, the clergy remained politically separated from the government but nevertheless provided a moral stability among the people which permitted the government to prosper. In other words, there was separation of church and state but not separation of state and religion.

### The Clergy Fueled the Flame of Freedom, Stressed Morality, and Alerted the Citizenry To Dangerous Trends

The role of the churches to perpetuate the social and political culture of the United States provoked the following comment from de Tocqueville:

"The Americans combine the notions of Christianity and of liberty so intimately in their minds that it is impossible to make them conceive the one without the other.... I have known of societies formed by Americans to send out ministers of the Gospel into the new Western states, to found schools and churches there, lest religion should be allowed to die away in those remote settlements, and the rising states be less fitted to enjoy free institutions than the people from whom they came." (*Ibid.*, p. 317)

De Tocqueville discovered that while the clergy felt it would be demeaning to their profession to become involved in partisan politics, they nevertheless believed implicitly in their duty to keep a message of religious principles and moral values flowing out to the people as the best safeguard for America's freedom and political security. In one of de Tocqueville's most frequently quoted passages, he stated:

> "I sought for the greatness and genius of America in her commodious harbors and her ample rivers, and it was not there; in her fertile fields and boundless prairies, and it was not there; in her rich mines and her vast world commerce, and it was not there. Not until I went to the churches of America and heard her pulpits aflame with righteousness did I understand the secret of her genius and power. America is great because she is good, and if America ever ceases to be good, America will cease to be great." (Quoted in Ezra Taft Benson, *God, Family, Country: Our Three Great Loyalties*, Deseret Book Company, Salt Lake City, 1975, p. 360.)

### The Founders' Campaign for Equality of All Religions

One of the most remarkable undertakings of the American Founders was to do something no other nation had ever successfully achieved – the task of providing legal equality for all religions, both Christian and non-Christian.

Jefferson and Madison were undoubtedly the foremost among the Founders in pushing through the first of these statutes in Virginia. Jefferson sought to disestablish the official church of Virginia in 1776, but this effort was not completely successful until ten years later.

Meanwhile, in 1784, Patrick Henry was so enthusiastic about strengthening the whole spectrum of Christian churches that he introduced a bill "Establishing a Provision for Teachers of the Christian Religion." (This document is reproduced in the supplementary appendix of *Everson v. Board of Education*, 330 U.S. 1, p. 72.)

It was the intention of this bill to provide that each taxpayer would designate "to what society of Christians" his money should go. The funds collected by this means were to make "provision for a minister or teacher of the Gospel ... or the providing places of divine worship [for that denomination], and to none other use whatever...." (*Ibid.*, p. 94.)

Madison immediately reacted with his famous "Memorial and Remonstrance" against religious assessments, in which he proclaimed with the greatest possible energy the principle that the state government should not prefer one religion over another. Equality of religions was the desired goal. He wrote:

> "Who does not see that the same authority which can establish Christianity, in exclusion of all other religions, may estab-

lish with the same ease any particular sect of Christians, in exclusion of all other sects? ... The bill violates that equality which ought to be the basis of every law." (William C. Rives and Philip R. Fendall, eds., *Letters and Other Writings of James Madison*, 4 vols., J. B. Lippincott, Philadelphia, 1865, 1:163-164.)

## Why the Founders Wanted the Federal Government Excluded from All Problems Relating to Religion and Churches

The Supreme Court has stated on numerous occasions that to most people freedom of religion is the most precious of all the unalienable rights next to life itself. When the United States was founded, there were many Americans who were not enjoying freedom of religion to the fullest possible extent. At least seven of the States had officially established religions or denominations at the time the Constitution was adopted. These included: (Kruse, The Historical Meaning and Judicial Construction *of the Establishment of Religion Clause* of the First Amendment, 1962, 2:65 and 2:94-107.)

Connecticut (Congregational church)
Delaware (Christian faith)
Maryland (Christian faith)
Massachusetts (Congregational church)
New Hampshire (Protestant faith)
New Jersey (Protestant faith)
South Carolina (Protestant faith)

Under these circumstances the Founders felt it would have been catastrophic and might have precipitated civil strife if the federal government had tried to establish a national policy on religion or disestablish the denominations which the states had adopted. Nevertheless, the Founders who were examining this problem were anxious to eventually see complete freedom of all faiths and an equality of all religions, both Christian and non-Christian. How could this be accomplished without stirring up civil strife?

## Justice Story Describes the Founders' Solution

In his famous Commentaries on the Constitution, Justice Joseph Story of the Supreme Court pointed out why the Founders as well as the states themselves felt the federal government should be absolutely excluded from any authority in the field of settling questions on religion. He stated:

"In some of the states, Episcopalians constituted the predominant sect; in others, Presbyterians; in others, Congregationalists; in others, Quakers; and in others again, there was a close numerical rivalry among contending sects. It was impossible that there should not arise perpetual strife and perpetual jealousy on the subject of ecclesiastical ascendancy, if the national government were left free to create a religious establishment. The only security was in extirpating the power. But this alone would have been an imperfect security, if it had not been followed up by a declaration of the right of the free exercise of religion, and a prohibition (as we have seen) of all religious tests. Thus, the whole power over the subject of religion is left exclusively to the state governments, to be acted upon according to their own sense of justice, and the state constitutions." (Joseph Story, *Commentaries on the Constitution of the United States*, 3rd ed,, 2 vols. Little, Brown and Company, Boston, 1858, 2:666-667, art. 1879; emphasis added.)

This is why the First Amendment of the Constitution provides that "Congress shall make NO law respecting an establishment of religion, or prohibiting the free exercise thereof."

### Jefferson and Madison Emphasize the Intent of the Founders

It is clear from the writings of the Founders as well as the Commentaries of Justice Story that the First Amendment was designed to eliminate forever the interference of the federal government in any religious matters within the various states. As Madison stated during the Virginia ratifying convention: "There is not a shadow of right in the general government to intermeddle with religion. Its least interference with it should be a most flagrant usurpation." (Elliot, *Debates in the State Conventions*, 3:330.)

Jefferson took an identical position when he wrote the Kentucky Resolutions of 1798: "It is true, as a general principle, ... that no power over the freedom of religion, freedom of speech, or freedom of the press being delegated to the United States by the Constitution ... all lawful powers respecting the same did of right remain and were reserved to the states, or to the people." (Mortimer J. Adler et al., eds., *The Annals of America*, 18 vols., Encyclopedia Britannica, Inc., Chicago, 1968, 4:63.)

### The Supreme Court as Well as Congress Excluded from Jurisdiction over Religion

In the Kentucky Resolutions, Thomas Jefferson also made it clear that the federal judicial system was likewise prohibited from intermeddling with religious matters within the states. He wrote:

"Special provision has been made by one of the amendments to the Constitution, which expressly declares that 'Congress shall make no law respecting an establishment of religion, or prohibiting the free exercise thereof ...', thereby guarding in the same sentence, and under the same words, the freedom of religion, of speech, and of the press, insomuch that whatever violates either throws down the sanctuary which covers the others; and that libels, falsehood, and defamation, equally with heresy and false religions, are withheld from the cognizance of federal tribunals." (*Ibid.*)

## The Federal "Wall" Between Church and State

When Thomas Jefferson was serving in the Virginia legislature he helped initiate a bill to have a day of fasting and prayer, but when he became President, Jefferson said there was no authority in the federal government to proclaim religious holidays. In a letter to the Danbury Baptist Association dated January 1, 1802, he explained his position and said the Constitution had created "a wall of separation between Church and State." (Bergh, *Writings of Thomas Jefferson*, 16:282.)

In recent years the Supreme Court has undertaken to use this metaphor as an excuse for meddling in the religious issues arising within the various states. It has not only presumed to take jurisdiction in these disputes, but has actually forced the states to take the same hands-off position toward religious matters even though this restriction originally applied only to the federal government. This obvious distortion of the original intent of Jefferson (when he used the metaphor of a "wall" separating church and state) becomes entirely apparent when the statements and actions of Jefferson are examined in their historical context.

It will be recalled that Jefferson and Madison were anxious that the states intervene in religious matters so as to provide for equality among all religions, and that all churches or religions assigned preferential treatment should be disestablished from such preferment. They further joined with the other Founders in expressing an anxiety that ALL religions be encouraged in order to promote the moral fiber and religious tone of the people. This, of course, would be impossible if there were an impenetrable "wall" between church and state on the state level. Jefferson's "wall" was obviously intended only for the federal government, and the Supreme Court application of this metaphor to the states has come under severe criticism. (Dallin Oaks, ed., *The Wall Between Church and State*, University of Chicago Press, Chicago, 1963, pp. 2-3.)

### Religious Problems Must Be Solved Within the Various States

In Thomas Jefferson's second inaugural address, he virtually signaled the states to press forward in settling their religious issues since it was within their jurisdiction and not that of the federal government:

> "In matters of religion, I have considered that its free exercise is placed by the Constitution independent of the powers of the general government. I have therefore undertaken on no occasion to prescribe the religious exercises suited to it; but have left them, as the Constitution found them, under the direction and discipline of state or church authorities acknowledged by the several religious societies." (Bergh, *Writings of Thomas Jefferson*, 3:378.)

Jefferson, along with the other Founders, believed that it was within the power of the various states to eliminate those inequalities which existed between the various faiths, and then pursue a policy of encouraging religious institutions of all kinds because it was in the public interest to use their influence to provide the moral stability needed for "good government and the happiness of mankind." (*Northwest Ordinance of 1787*, Article 3.)

Jefferson's resolution for disestablishing the Church of England in Virginia was not to set up a wall between the state and the church but simply, as he explained it, for the purpose of "taking away the privilege and preeminence of one religious sect over another, and thereby [establishing] ... equal rights among all." (Julian P. Boyd, ed., *The Papers of Thomas Jefferson*, 19 vols. by 1974, Princeton University, Princeton, N.J., 1950, 1:531, note 1; emphasis added.)

### Affirmative Programs to Encourage All Religions on the State Level

In view of the extremely inflexible and rigid position which the U.S. Supreme Court has taken in recent years concerning the raising up of a "wall" between state government and religion, it is remarkable how radically different the Founders' views were upon such matters.

Take, for example, their approval of religious meetings in tax-supported public buildings. With the Founders there was no objection as to the propriety of using public buildings for religious purposes, for that was to be encouraged. The only question was whether or not the facilities could be made available equally to all denominations desiring them. Notice how Jefferson reflects his deep satisfaction in the way the churches were using the local courthouse in Charlottesville, near Jefferson's home:

"In our village of Charlottesville, there is a good degree of religion, with a small spice only of fanaticism. We have four sects, but without either church or meeting-house. The court-house is the common temple, one Sunday in the month to each. Here, Episcopalian and Presbyterian, Methodist and Baptist, meet together, join in hymning their Maker, listen with attention and devotion to each others' preachers, and all mix in society with perfect harmony." (Bergh, *Writings of Thomas Jefferson*, 15:404.)

One cannot help asking the modern Supreme Court: "Where is the wall of separation between church and state when the courthouse is approved for the common temple of all the religious sects of a village?"

Of course, Jefferson would be the first to require some other arrangement if all of the churches could not be accommodated equally, but so long as they were operating equally and harmoniously together, it was looked upon as a commendable situation. The fact that they were utilizing a tax-supported public building was not even made an issue.

## Religious Principles Undergird Good Government

What doctrines were Americans so anxious to teach one another in order that they might remain united and well governed? These religious precepts turned out to be the heart and soul of the entire American political philosophy. They were taken from the books of John Locke, Sir William Blackstone, and other great thinkers of the day, who took them directly from the Bible. Thus, religion and the American institutions of freedom were combined. In fact, the Founders had taken the five truths we have already identified as "religion" and had built the whole Constitutional framework on top of them.

The sanctity of civil rights and property rights, as well as the obligation of citizens to support the Constitution in protecting their unalienable rights, were all based on these religious precepts. Therefore, having established the general principle that "without religion the government of a free people cannot be maintained," we now turn to the specific principles on which this general concept was based.

# 5th

## Principle

**All things were created by God, therefore upon Him all mankind are equally dependant and to Him they are equally responsible.**

### The Reality of a Divine Creator

The Founders vigorously affirm throughout their writings that the foundation of all reality is the existence of a Creator, who is the designer of all things in nature and the promulgator of all the laws which govern nature.

The Founders were in harmony with the thinking of John Locke as expressed in his famous Essay Concerning Human Understanding. In it Locke pointed out that it defies the most elementary aspects of reason and experience to presuppose that everything in existence developed as a result of fortuitous circumstance. The mind, for example, will not accept the proposition that the forces of nature, churning about among themselves, would ever produce a watch, or even a lead pencil, let alone the marvelous intricacies of the human eye, the ear, or even the simplest of the organisms found in nature. All these are the product of intelligent design and high-precision engineering.

Locke felt that a person who calls himself an "atheist" is merely confessing that he has never dealt with the issue of the Creator's existence. Therefore, to Locke an atheist would be to that extent "irrational," and out of touch with reality; in fact, out of touch with the most important and fundamental reality.

## How Can One Know There Is a God?

In his Essay Concerning Human Understanding, John Locke insisted that everyone can know there is a divine Creator. It is simply a case of thinking about it. (*Concerning Human Understanding*, Great Books of the Western World, vol. 35, Encyclopedia Britannica, Inc., Chicago, 1952, pp. 349-352.)

To begin with, each person knows that he exists. With Descartes each person can say, "Cogito ergo sum." With God, each person can say, "I Am!"

Furthermore, each person knows that he is something. He also knows that a something could not be produced by a nothing. Therefore, whatever brought man and everything else into existence also had to be something.

It follows that this something which did all of this organizing and arranging would have to be all-knowing to the full extent required for such an organization and arrangement.

This something would therefore have to be superior to everything which had resulted from this effort. This element of superiority makes this something the ultimate "good" for all that has been organized and arranged. In the Anglo-Saxon language, the word for supreme or ultimate good is "God."

## Getting to Know God

Man is capable of knowing many things about God, Locke said. The Creator must of necessity be a cogitative (reasoning or thinking) being, for man is a cogitative (reasoning) being. Certainly a non-cogitative being like a rock could never have produced a cogitative being like a man. We may also know that the divine Creator has a sense of compassion and love, for he gave mankind these sublime qualities.

The Creator would also reflect a fine sense of right and wrong, and also a sense of indignation or even anger with those who violate the laws of "right" action. In other words, God has a strong sense of "justice." Remorse for wrong also arouses a sense of compassion in the Creator, just as it does in human beings whom he designed.

There are other attributes of man which human beings must necessarily share with their Creator if man is "made in the image of God." One would be a sense of humor. The Creator must also be a great artist on the visual plane. Everything the Creator organizes is in terms of beauty through color, form, and contrasts. Obviously, man can enjoy only to a finite degree the capacity of his Creator to appreciate the vast panorama of sensory satisfaction which we call "beauty."

So, as John Locke says, there are many things man can know about God. And because any thoughtful person can gain an appreciation and conviction of these many attributes of the Creator, Locke felt that an atheist has failed to apply his divine capacity for reason and observation.

The American Founding Fathers agreed with Locke. They considered the existence of the Creator as the most fundamental premise underlying all self-evident truth. It will be noted as we proceed through this study that every single self-evident truth enunciated by the Founders is rooted in the presupposition of a divine Creator.

## Concerning God's Revealed Law Distinguishing Right from Wrong

The Founders considered the whole foundation of a just society to be structured on the basis of God's revealed law. These laws constituted a moral code clearly distinguishing right from wrong. This concept was not new with the Founders. This was the entire foundation of all religious cultures world-wide. It was particularly emphasized in the Judeo-Christian structure of the English law. No authority on the subject was more widely read than William Blackstone (1723-1780). He established the classes for the first law school at Oxford in 1753. His lectures on the English law were published in 1765 and were as widely read in America as they were in England.

In his Commentaries on the Laws of England, Blackstone propounded the generally accepted idea that "when the Creator formed the universe" he organized it and then "impressed certain principles upon that matter, from which it can never depart and without which it would cease to be." (Blackstone, *Commentaries on the Laws of England*, ed. William Carey Jones, 2 vols., Bancroft-Whitney Co., San Francisco, 1916, 1:52.)

He then went on to say that the will of God which is expressed in the orderly arrangement of the universe is called "the law of nature," and that there are laws for "human" nature just as surely as they exist for the rest of the universe. (*Ibid.*, pp. 56-58) He said the laws for human nature had been revealed by God, whereas the laws of the universe (natural law) must be learned through scientific investigation. (*Ibid.*, p. 64) Blackstone stated that "upon these two foundations, the law of nature and the law of revelation, depend all human laws...." (*Ibid.*, p. 65)

As we shall see later, the attitude of the Founders toward God's law (both natural and revealed) gave early Americans a very high regard for the "law" as a social institution. They respected the sanctity of the law in the same way that it was honored among the Anglo-Saxons and by ancient Israel.

## The Nearness of God

It is also important to note that the Founders did not look upon God as some mysterious teleological force operating automatically and indifferently in nature (as modern Deists claim), but they believed in a Creator who is both intelligent and benevolent and therefore anxious and able to respond to people's petitions when they are deserving of needed blessings and engaged in a good cause. Days of fasting and prayer were commonplace in America. Most of the Founders continually petitioned God in fervent prayers, both public and private, and looked upon his divine intervention in their daily lives as a singular blessing. They were continually expressing gratitude to God as the nation survived one major crisis after another.

## George Washington

George Washington was typical of the Founders in this respect: Charles Bracelen Flood discovered in his research that during the Revolutionary War there were at least sixty-seven desperate moments when Washington acknowledged that he would have suffered disaster had not the hand of God intervened in behalf of the struggle for independence. (Charles Bracelen Flood, *Rise and Fight Again*, Dodo, Mead & Co., New York, 1976, p. 377.)

After being elected President, Washington stressed these sentiments in his first inaugural address when he said:

> "No people can be bound to acknowledge and adore the invisible hand which conducts the affairs of men more than the people of the United States. Every step, by which they have advanced to the character of an independent nation, seems to have been distinguished by some token of providential agency." (Fitzpatrick, *Writings of George Washington*, 30:292.)

## James Madison

Madison was equally emphatic on this point when he contemplated the work of the Constitutional Convention and saw the guiding influence of God just as Washington had seen it on the battlefield. Said he:

> "The real wonder is that so many difficulties should have been surmounted ... with a unanimity almost as unprecedented as it must have been unexpected. It is impossible for any man of candor to reflect on this circumstance without partaking of the astonishment. It is impossible for the man of pious reflection not to perceive in it a finger of that Almighty hand which has been so

frequently and signally extended to our relief in the critical stages of the revolution." (*The Federalist Papers*, No. 37, pp. 230-231.)

### "In God We Trust"

From all of this it will be seen that the Founders were not indulging in any idle gesture when they adopted the motto, "In God we trust." Neither was it a matter of superfluous formality when they required that all witnesses who testify in the courts or before Congressional hearings must take an oath and swear or affirm before God that they will tell the truth. As Washington pointed out in his Farewell Address: "Where is the security for property, for reputation, for life, if the sense of religious obligation desert the oaths which are the instruments of investigation in courts of justice?" (Fitzpatrick, *Writings of George Washington*, 35:229.) In fact, it was not at all uncommon, as Alexis de Tocqueville discovered, to look with the greatest precaution upon an individual who had no religious convictions. He wrote:

> "While I was in America, a witness who happened to be called at the Sessions of the county of Chester (state of New York) declared that he did not believe in the existence of God or in the immortality of the soul. The judge refused to admit the evidence, on the ground that the witness had destroyed beforehand all the confidence of the court in what he was about to say." (Alexis de Tocqueville, *Democracy in America*, 1:317.)

In a note de Tocqueville added:

> "The New York Spectator of August 23, 1831, related the fact in the following terms: "...The presiding judge remarked that he had not before been aware that there was a man living who did not believe in the existence of God; that this belief constituted the sanction [in law, that which gives binding force] of all testimony in a court of justice; and that he knew of no case in a Christian country where a witness had been permitted to testify without such belief." (*Ibid.*)

This now brings us to the next important principle enunciated by the Founders.

# 6th

## Principle

**All men are created equal.**

The Founders wrote in the Declaration of Independence that some truths are self-evident, and one of these is the fact that all men are created equal.

Yet everyone knows that no two human beings are exactly alike in any respect. They are different when they are born. They plainly exhibit different natural skills. They acquire different tastes. They develop along different lines. They vary in physical strength, mental capacity, emotional stability, inherited social status, in their opportunities for self-fulfillment, and in scores of other ways. Then how can they be equal?

The answer is, they can't, except in three ways. They can only be treated as equals in the sight of God, in the sight of the law, and in the protection of their rights. In these three ways all men are created equal. It is the task of society, as it is with God, to accept people in all their vast array of individual differences, but treat them as equals when it comes to their role as human beings. As members of society, all persons should have their equality guaranteed in two areas. Constitutional writer Clarence Carson describes them:

> "First, there is equality before the law. This means that every man's case is tried by the same law governing any particular case. Practically, it means that there are no different laws for different classes and orders of men [as there were in ancient times]. The definition of premeditated murder is the same for the millionaire as for the tramp. A corollary of this is that no classes are created or recognized by law.

"Second, the Declaration refers to an equality of rights... Each man is equally entitled to his life with every other man; each man has an equal title to God-given liberties along with every other." (Clarence Carson, *The American Tradition, Foundation for Economic Education*, Irvington-on-Hudson, New York, 1970, pp. 112-113.)

## Rousseau's Error

John Adams was in France when Jean Jacques Rousseau was teaching that all men were designed to be equal in every way. Adams wrote:

"That all men are born to equal rights is true. Every being has a right to his own, as clear, as moral, as sacred, as any other being has.... But to teach that all men are born with equal powers and faculties, to equal influence in society, to equal property and advantages through life, is as gross a fraud, as glaring an imposition on the credulity of the people, as ever was practiced by monks, by Druids, by Brahmins, by priests of the immortal Lama, or by the self-styled philosophers of the French Revolution." (Quoted in Koch, *The American Enlightenment*, p. 222.)

## What It Means to Have Equal "Rights"

The goal of society is to provide "equal justice," which means protecting the rights of the people equally.

- At the bar of justice, to secure their rights.
- At the ballot box, to vote for the candidate of their choice.
- At the public school, to obtain their education.
- At the employment office, to compete for a job.
- At the real estate agency, to purchase or rent a home.
- At the pulpit, to enjoy freedom of religion.
- At the podium, to enjoy freedom of speech.
- At the microphone or before the TV camera, to present views on issues of the day.
- At the meeting hall, to peaceably assemble.
- At the print shop, to enjoy freedom of the press.
- At the store, to buy the essentials or desirable things of life.
- At the bank, to save and prosper.
- At the tax collector's office, to pay no more than their fair share.

♦ At the probate court, to pass on to their heirs the fruits of life's labors.

## The Problem of Minorities

Admittedly, equal rights have not been completely established in all of these areas, but the Founders struck a course which has thus far provided a better balance in administering the equality of rights than has occurred at any time in history. The breakdown occurs in connection with the treatment of minorities.

Minorities in any country consider themselves "outsiders" who want to become "insiders." As long as they are treated as outsiders they do not feel equal. The interesting part of it is that every ethnic group in the American society was once a minority. We are a nation of minorities!

There is no spot on the planet earth where so many different ethnic groups have been poured into the same milieu as in the United States. It was appropriate that America should be called the melting pot of the world.

Two things are especially notable about this. First of all, it is remarkable that the Founders were able to establish a society of freedom and opportunity which would attract so many millions of immigrants. Secondly, it is even more remarkable that within two or three generations nearly all of these millions of immigrants became first-class citizens.

As we noted above, newcomers to any nation are not considered first-class citizens immediately. Human nature does not allow it. In some countries "outsiders" are still treated with hostility after they have resided in those countries for three or four hundred years. In the United States, immigrants or outsiders can become insiders much more rapidly. Nevertheless, the transition is painful.

## Crossing the Culture Gap

Being a minority, even in the United States, is painful because acceptance depends on "crossing the culture gap." This means learning the English language – with an American dialect more or less; attaining the general norm of education – which in America is fairly high; becoming economically independent – which often means getting out of the ghetto; and becoming recognized as a social asset to the community – which always takes time. Usually it requires far more time than the minority group can patiently endure.

But the impatience of a minority can be an advantage. It expedites their assimilation by motivating greater effort to gain acceptance. In the United States, as a result, many members of a minority group are assimilated in a single generation. Others must wait until the second generation, and a few are still struggling in the third. But these are the exceptions. They can't quite get across the culture gap. It is a fact of life in America, as everywhere else, that no ethnic group is going to be entirely comfortable or treated completely as equals in an adopted society until they have crossed the culture gap.

### A Nation of Minorities

As mentioned above, there is not a single ethnic group in the United States but what has been treated at one time or another as a minority, or less than first-class citizens.

The story of minorities in the United States is a fascinating tale. Beginning with the French in the 1500s and the English in the 1600s (and the Dutch, Germans, Swedes, Scots, and Irish in between,) it was one grand conglomerate of tension, discrimination, malice, and sometimes outright persecution. But the miracle of it all is the fact that they fought side by side for freedom in the Revolutionary War, and all of them could boast of descendants in the White House or the Congress as the years passed by. So all of this became America – a nation of minorities.

### The Japanese and Chinese

One of the best examples of minority adjustment under adverse circumstances is the American saga of the Japanese and Chinese.

The treatment they received is an embarrassment to modern Americans. They were not only shabbily treated, but sometimes they were treated brutally. (In certain situations this happened to other minorities as well.) But practically none of the Japanese and Chinese went home. They became domestics, field workers, and truck farmers; they ran laundries, worked for a pittance on railroads, ate their simple fare, and slept on bare boards. Meanwhile, they sent their

children to school and endured their mistreatment with patience. By 1940 the Chinese were virtually assimilated and the Japanese had almost made it. Then came the attack on Pearl Harbor.

Within weeks the vast Japanese population in California had been hauled off to concentration camps in the Rocky Mountains. J. Edgar Hoover knew there were practically no espionage agents among them. The few security risks had already been identified and incarcerated. He vigorously protested the Japanese evacuation and so did many others, but all to no avail.

The Japanese could have been very bitter, but to the ultimate embarrassment and chagrin of those who had engineered this fiasco, they loyally mobilized their sons and sent them into the American armed services as volunteers! Japanese-American regiments were among the most decorated in World War II. They went into the military ranks under suspicion and resentment, but they came out in hero roles. A few years later the entire State of California was represented in the Senate by a Japanese-American.

## The Black Minority

But of all the minorities in America, the blacks have undertaken assimilation as first-class citizens under the greatest number of handicaps. Many early political leaders of the United States, including Abraham Lincoln, were fearful the blacks might never achieve complete adjustment because of the slavery culture in which the first few generations were raised.

Nevertheless, freedom and education brought a whole new horizon of hope to the blacks within three generations. Tens of thousands of them hurdled the culture gap, and soon the blacks in other countries saw their ethnic cousins in the United States enjoying a higher standard of living than blacks in any part of the world. In fact, by 1970 a black high school student in Alabama or Mississippi had a better opportunity to get a college education than a white student in England.

Providing equality for the blacks has never been approached with any degree of consensus. Some felt that with education and job opportunities the blacks could leap the culture gap just as other minorities had done. Others felt they should be made the beneficiaries of substantial government gratuities. Experience soon demonstrated, however, that government gratuities are as corrupting and debilitating to blacks as they are to the Indians or any other minorities. The blacks themselves asked for equal opportunity at the hiring hall. Thus, the trend began to shift in the direction which no doubt the Founders such as Washington, Jefferson, and Franklin would have strongly approved.

## Violence Proves Counter-Productive

In the mid-sixties there were groups of Marxist agitators who moved in among the blacks to promote direct action by violence. One of these was Eldridge Cleaver, who had been trained in Marxist philosophy and tactics while serving a fifteen-year sentence in a California state penitentiary. In 1967 he became the Minister of Information for the Black Panthers. In his books, Eldridge Cleaver describes the rationale behind their philosophy of violence. It was to destroy the whole economic and social structure of the United States so that blacks could enjoy equal rights under an American Communist regime. The crescendo of violence increased year after year. During the summer of 1968 over a hundred American cities were burning. But the burning was always in black ghettos. The idea was to put the blacks in direct confrontation with the police and state militia in order to solidify their apparent need to become a racial bloc for the coming revolution.

But the burning and fire-bombing backfired. The black population began to realize it was only the homes of the blacks that were being burned. Other than police, it was primarily blacks that were being hurt in the melee of the riots. In the shoot-outs with the police, nineteen of the Black Panther leaders were killed. Eldridge Cleaver was wounded. He and his wife later fled to Cuba and then to other Communist countries.

The whole scenario of violence had proved tragically counter-productive. It temporarily jolted out of joint a broad spectrum of reforms which the blacks were really seeking and the rest of the nation was trying to provide.

### A Dissident Returns

After nearly eight years as an exile in Communist and Socialist countries, Eldridge Cleaver asked to be allowed to return to the United States and pay whatever penalty was due on charges pending against him. He and his wife were no longer atheists. They were no longer Communists. Those bitter years behind the iron and bamboo curtains had dispelled all the propaganda concerning "equality" and "justice" under Communism. Cleaver told the press: "I would rather be in jail in America than free anywhere else." He then went on to say:

> "I was wrong and the Black Panthers were wrong.... We [black Americans] are inside the system and I feel that the number one objective for Black America is to recognize that they have the same equal rights under the Constitution as Ford or Rockefeller, even if we have no blue-chip stocks. But our membership in the United States is the supreme blue-chip stock and the one we have to exercise." (Laile Bartlett, "The Education of Eldridge Cleaver," *Reader's Digest*, September 1976, pp. 65-72.)

By 1981 Eldridge Cleaver had paid his final debt to society. No further charges were pending against him. Although he had been involved in a police shoot-out in Oakland, California, he had not been accused of causing any deaths. In fact, it was in the Oakland shoot-out that he was wounded. As he was released on parole, the judge required that he finish his obligation to society by putting in several hundred hours of public service at a California college.

Soon after that he began accepting speaking engagements before schools, churches, community gatherings, and even prison groups to describe his new and yet profound appreciation for America. He described the despondency which came over him when he found what a betrayal of human rights and human dignity Communism turned out to be. He described the long and strenuous intellectual struggle with his Marxist atheism before he recognized its fraudulent fallacies. He frankly and patiently dialogued with university students still struggling with similar philosophical problems. He assured them, as Locke had done, that a persistent pursuit of the truth would bring them to the threshold of reality, where the Creator could be recognized and thereafter have a place in their lives.

The Eldridge Cleaver story is simply the account of a prodigal American who found himself and returned home.

### Constitutional Amendments to Insure Equal Rights

After the Constitution was adopted in 1789, Americans added four amendments to make certain that everyone, including racial minorities, could enjoy equal rights. These amendments are as follows:

The Thirteenth Amendment to provide universal freedom.

The Fourteenth Amendment to provide universal rights of citizenship.

The Fifteenth and the Nineteenth Amendments to provide universal voting rights regardless of race, color, or sex.

The Founders distinguished between equal rights and other areas where equality is impossible. They recognized that society should seek to provide equal opportunity but not expect equal results; provide equal freedom but not expect equal capacity; provide equal rights but not equal possessions; provide equal protection but not equal status; provide equal educational opportunities but not equal grades.

They knew that even if governmental compulsion were used to force its citizens to appear equal in material circumstances, they would immediately become unequal the instant their freedom was restored to them. As Alexander Hamilton said:

> "Inequality would exist as long as liberty existed.... It would unavoidably result from that very liberty itself." (Harold C. Syrett et al., eds., *The Papers of Alexander Hamilton*, 19 vols. by 1973, Columbia University Press, New York, 1961, 4:218.)

Nevertheless, there are some who insist that people do not have equal rights unless they have "equal things." The Founding Fathers were well acquainted with this proposition and set forth their belief concerning it in the next principle.

# 7th

## Principle

**The proper role of government is to protect
equal rights, not provide equal things.**

Federal Government Transfer Payments

In Europe, during the days of the Founders, it was very popular to proclaim that the role of government was to take from the "haves" and give to the "have nots" so that all might be truly "equal." However, the American Founders perceived that this proposition contained a huge fallacy.

### What Powers Can Be Assigned to Government

The Founders recognized that the people cannot delegate to their government the power to do anything except that which they have the lawful right to do themselves.

For example, every person is entitled to protection of his life and property. Therefore it is perfectly legitimate to delegate to the government the task of setting up a police force to protect the lives and property of all the people.

But suppose a kind-hearted man saw that one of his neighbors had two cars while another neighbor had none. What would happen if, in a spirit of benevolence, the kind man went over and took one of the cars from his prosperous neighbor and generously gave it to the neighbor in need? Obviously, he would be arrested for car theft. No matter how kind his intentions, he is guilty of flagrantly violating the natural rights of his prosperous neighbor, who is entitled to be protected in his property.

Of course, the two-car neighbor could donate a car to his poor neighbor, if he liked, but that is his decision and not the prerogative of the kind-hearted neighbor who wants to play Robin Hood.

### How Governments Sometimes Commit "Legal" Crimes

But suppose the kind-hearted man decided to ask the mayor and city council to force the man with two cars to give one to his pedestrian neighbor. Does that make it any more legitimate? Obviously, this makes it even worse because if the mayor and city council do it in the name of the law, the man who has lost his car has not only lost the rights to his property, but (since it is the "law") he has lost all right to appeal for help in protecting his property.

The American Founders recognized that the moment the government is authorized to start leveling the material possessions of the rich in order to have an "equal distribution of goods," the government thereafter has the power to deprive any of the people of their "equal" rights to enjoy their lives, liberties, and property.

### A Popular Fallacy

Those on the receiving end of the program may think this is very "just" to take from the "haves" and give to the "have nots." They may say, "This is the way the government provides equal justice for all." But what happens when the government comes around and starts taking from those who count themselves "poor"? They immediately declare with indignation that they have "rights" in the property the government gave them. The government replies, "WE decide who has rights in things."

The power given to the government to take from the rich automatically cancelled out the principle of "guaranteed equal rights." It opened the floodgate for the government to meddle with everybody's rights, particularly property rights.

### A Lesson from Communism

When the Communists seized power in Hungary, the peasants were delighted with the "justice" of having the large farms confiscated from their owners and given to the peasants. Later the Communist leaders seized three-fourths of the peasant land and took it back to set up government communal farms. Immediately the peasants howled in protest about their property "rights."

Those who protested too loudly or too long soon found that they not only lost their land, but also their liberty. If they continued to protest, they lost their lives.

## Equal Rights Doctrine Protects the Freedom to Prosper

The American Founders took a different approach. Their policy was to guarantee the equal protection of all the people's rights and thus insure that all would have the freedom to protest. There was to be no special penalty for getting rich. The French philosophers cried out in protest, "But then some of the people will become very rich!" "Indeed they will," the Founders might have responded -- "the more the better."

In fact, it was soon discovered that the new industrial age required large quantities of private funds in order to build factories, purchase complicated machinery and tools, and provide millions of jobs which had never before existed.

The Founders felt that America would become a nation dominated by a prosperous middle class with a few people becoming rich. As for the poor, the important thing to insure was the freedom to prosper so that no one would be locked into the poverty level the way people have been in all other parts of the world.

## Making A Whole Nation Prosperous

It was realized, of course, that some would prosper more than others. That is inevitable as long as there is liberty. Some would prosper because of talent, some because of good fortune, some because of an inheritance, but most would prosper because of hard work.

The entire American concept of "freedom to prosper" was based on the belief that man's instinctive will to succeed in a climate of liberty would result in the whole people prospering together. It was thought that even the poor could lift themselves through education and individual effort to become independent and self-sufficient.

The idea was to maximize prosperity, minimize poverty, and make the whole nation rich. Where people suffered the loss of their crops or became unemployed, the more fortunate were there to help. And those who were enjoying "good times" were encouraged to save up in store for the misfortunes which seem to come to everybody someday. Hard work, frugality, thrift, and compassion became the key words in the American ethic.

## Why the Founders Made European Theories Unconstitutional

What happened in America under these principles was remarkable in every way. Within a short time the Americans, as a people, were on the way to becoming the most prosperous and best-educated nation in the world (which was amazing to de Tocqueville when he arrived in 1831). They were also the freest people in the world. Eventually, the world found that they were also the most generous people on earth. And all this was not because they were Americans. The Founders believed these same principles would work for any nation. The key was using the government to protect equal rights, not to provide equal things. As previously mentioned, Samuel Adams said the ideas of a welfare state were made unconstitutional:

> "The utopian schemes of leveling [redistribution of the wealth], and a community of goods [central ownership of all the means of production and distribution], are as visionary and impracticable as those which vest all property in the Crown. [These ideas] are arbitrary, despotic, and, in our government, unconstitutional." (Wells, *Life of Samuel Adams*, 1:154.)

## Nevertheless, the Founders Had a Deep Concern for the Poor and Needy

As mentioned earlier, disciples of the collectivist Left in the Founders' day as well as our own have insisted that compassion for the poor requires that the Federal government become involved in taking from the "haves" and giving to the "have nots." Benjamin Franklin had been one of the "have nots," and after living several years in England where he saw government welfare programs in operation, he had considerable to say about these public charities of counterproductive compassion.

Franklin wrote a whole essay on the subject and told one of his friends, "I have long been of your opinion, that your legal provision for the poor [in England] is a very great evil, operating as it does to the encouragement of idleness. We have followed your example, and begin now to see our error, and, I hope, shall reform it." (Smyth, Writings of Benjamin Franklin, 10:64.)

A survey of Franklin's views on counter-productive compassion might be summarized as follows:

1. Compassion which gives a drunk the means to increase his drunkenness is counter-productive. (Ibid., 5:538)
2. Compassion which breeds debilitating dependency and weakness is counter-productive. (Ibid., 5:123)
3. Compassion which blunts the desire or necessity to work for a living is counter-productive. (Ibid., 3:135-136)
4. Compassion which smothers the instinct to strive and excel is counter-productive. (Ibid., 3:136-137)

Nevertheless, the Founders recognized that it is a mandate of God to help the poor and underprivileged. It is interesting how they said this should be done.

## The Founders' Formula for "Calculated" Compassion

Franklin wrote:

"To relieve the misfortunes of our fellow creatures is con-curring with the Deity; it is godlike; but, if we provide encour-agement for laziness, and supports for folly, may we not be found fighting against the order of God and Nature, which perhaps has appointed want and misery as the proper punishments for, and cautions against, as well as necessary consequences of, idleness and extravagance? Whenever we attempt to amend the scheme of Providence, and to interfere with the government of the world, we had need be very circumspect, lest we do more harm than good." (*Ibid.*, 3:135)

Nearly all of the Founders seem to have acquired deep convictions that assisting those in need had to be done through means which might be called "calculated" compassion. Highlights from their writings suggest the following:

1. Do not help the needy completely. Merely help them to help themselves.
2. Give the poor the satisfaction of "earned achievement" instead of rewarding them without achievement.
3. Allow the poor to climb the "appreciation ladder" -- from tents to cabins, cabins to cottages, cottages to comfortable houses.
4. Where emergency help is provided, do not prolong it to the point where it becomes habitual.
5. Strictly enforce the scale of "fixed responsibility." The first and foremost level of responsibility is with the individual himself; the second level is the family; then the church; next the commu-nity; finally the county, and, in a disaster or emergency, the state. Under no circumstances is the federal government to become in-volved in public welfare. The Founders felt it would corrupt the government and also the poor. No Constitutional authority exists for the federal government to participate in charity or welfare.

## Motives of the Founders

By excluding the national government from intervening in the local affairs of the people, the Founders felt they were protecting the unalien-able rights of the people from abuse by an over-aggressive government. But just what are "unalienable" rights? This brings us to our next princi-ple.

# 8th

## Principle

**Men are endowed by their Creator
with certain unalienable rights.**

The Founders did not believe that the basic rights of mankind originated from any social compact, king, emperor, or governmental authority. Those rights, they believed, came directly and exclusively from
God. Therefore, they were to be maintained sacred and inviolate. John
Locke said it this way:

> "The state of Nature has a law of Nature to govern it, which
> ... teaches all mankind who will but consult it, that being all equal
> and independent, no one ought to harm another in his life, health,
> liberty or possessions; for men being all the workmanship of one
> omnipotent and infinitely wise maker; all the servants of one sov-
> ereign master, sent into the world by His order and about His
> business; they are His property....

> "And, being furnished with like faculties, sharing all in one
> community of Nature, there cannot be supposed any such subor-
> dination among us that may authorize us to destroy one another."
> (John Locke, *Second Essay Concerning Civil Government,* Great
> Books of the Western World, vol. 35, Encyclopedia Britannica,
> Inc., Chicago, 1952, p. 26, par. 6.)

## When Is a Right Unalienable?

The substantive nature of those rights which are inherent in all mankind was described by William Blackstone in his Commentaries on the Laws of England:

> "Those rights, then, which God and nature have established, and are therefore called natural rights, such as are life and liberty, need not the aid of human laws to be more effectually invested in every man than they are; neither do they receive any additional strength when declared by the municipal laws to be inviolable. On the contrary, no human legislature has power to abridge or destroy them, unless the owner shall himself commit some act that amounts to a forfeiture." (William Blackstone, *Commentaries on the Laws of England*, 1:93.)

In other words, we may do something ourselves to forfeit the unalienable rights endowed by the Creator, but no one else can take those rights from us without being subject to God's justice. This is what makes certain rights unalienable. They are inherent rights given to us by the Creator. That is why they are called natural rights.

We also have certain other rights called *vested* rights which are created by the community, state, or nation for our protection and well-being. However, these can be changed any time the lawmakers feel like it.

Examples of vested rights would be the right to go hunting during certain seasons, or the right to travel on the public highway. Notice that the government can change both of these "rights" or prohibit them altogether. The region could be declared off-limits for hunting. The highway could be closed.

But the government could not pass a law to destroy all babies under the age of two, or lock up everybody with blonde hair. In the one case it would be destroying the unalienable right to life, and in the other case it would be destroying the unalienable right to liberty. A person can lose his liberty through his own misbehavior, but not because he has blonde hair!

## The Founders Did Not List All of the Unalienable Rights

When the Founders adopted the Declaration of Independence, they emphasized in phrases very similar to those of Blackstone that God has endowed all mankind "with certain unalienable rights, that *among* these are life, liberty, and the pursuit of happiness."

Let us identify some of the unalienable or natural rights which the Founders knew existed but did not enumerate in the Declaration of Independence:

The right of self-government.

The right to bear arms for self-defense.

The right to own, develop, and dispose of property.

The right to make personal choices.

The right of free conscience.

The right to choose a profession.

The right to choose a mate.

The right to beget one's kind.

The right to assemble.

The right to petition.

The right to free speech.

The right to a free press.

The right to enjoy the fruits of one's labors.

The right to improve one's position through barter and sale.

The right to contrive and invent.

The right to explore the natural resources of the earth.

The right to privacy.

The right to provide personal security.

The right to provide nature's necessities -- air, food, water, clothing, and shelter.

The right to a fair trial.

The right of free association.

The right to contract.

### Many Founders Used Similar Language
### Emphasizing "Unalienable Rights"

It was very common among the Founders to express their sentiments concerning man's unalienable rights in almost the same language as Jefferson. Here are the words of the Virginia Declaration of Rights adopted by the Virginia assembly June 12, 1776 (before the Declaration of Independence!):

> "All men are by nature equally free and independent and have certain inherent rights, of which, when they enter into a state of society, they cannot, by any compact, deprive or divest their posterity; namely, the enjoyment of life and liberty, with the means of acquiring and possessing property, and pursuing and obtaining happiness and safety." (*Annals of America*, 2:432.)

Notice that the words of the Declaration of Independence are very similar when it says, "We hold these truths to be self-evident, that all men are created equal, that they are endowed by their Creator with certain unalienable rights, that among these are life, liberty, and the pursuit of happiness."

### Property Rights Essential to the Pursuit of Happiness

Some scholars have wondered just what Jefferson mean by "the pursuit of happiness," but the meaning of this phrase was well understood when it was written. Perhaps John Adams said it even more clearly:

"All men are born free and independent, and have certain natural, essential, and unalienable rights, among which may be reckoned the right of enjoying and defending their lives and liberties; that of acquiring, possessing, and protecting property; in fine, that of seeking and obtaining their safety and happiness." (George A. Peek, Jr., ed., *The Political Writings of John Adams,* Liberal Arts Press, New York, 1954, p. 96.)

### Three Great Natural Rights

Of course, the concept of unalienable rights was by no means exclusive to the American Founders. It was well understood by English defenders of the common law. Eleven years before the Declaration of Independence, Sir William Blackstone had written this concerning the natural rights of man:

"And these [great natural rights] may be reduced to three principal or primary articles: the right of *personal security*, the right of *personal liberty,* and the right of *private property*; because as there is no other known method of compulsion, or of abridging man's natural free will, but by an infringement or diminution of one or other of these important rights, the preservation of these, inviolate, may justly be said to include the preservation of our civil immunities in their largest and most extensive sense." (Blackstone, *Commentaries on the Laws of England,* 1:219-220; emphasis added.)

### State Constitutions

The protection of these rights was later carried over into the constitutions of the various states. Here is how the Constitution of Pennsylvania stated it:

"Article I, Section 1. All men are born equally free and independent, and have certain inherent and indefeasible rights, among which are those of enjoying and defending life and lib-

erty, of acquiring, possessing, and protecting property and reputation, and of pursuing their own happiness." (Quoted in Judson
A. Crane, *Natural Law in the United States*, University of Pittsburgh, Pittsburgh, 6:144.)

## All Rights Founded in the Protection of Life

Over a century ago, Frederic Bastiat, who was trying to preserve freedom in France, wrote that man's unalienable rights are actually those
which relate to life itself and that the preservation of those rights is primarily a matter of self-preservation. He wrote:

"We hold from God the gift which includes all others. This
gift is life--physical, intellectual, and moral life. But life cannot
maintain itself alone. The Creator of life has entrusted us with
the responsibility of preserving, developing, and perfecting it. In
order that we may accomplish this, He has provided us with a
collection of marvelous faculties. And He has put us in the midst
of a variety of natural resources. By the application of our faculties to these natural resources we convert them into products, and
use them. The process is necessary in order that life may run its
appointed course.

"Life, faculties, production -- in other words, individuality,
liberty, property -- this is man. And in spite of the cunning of artful political leaders, these three gifts from God precede all human
legislation, and are superior to it.

"Life, liberty, and property do not exist because men have
made laws. On the contrary, it was the fact that life, liberty, and
property existed beforehand that caused men to make laws [for
the protection of them] in the first place." (Frederic Bastiat, *The
Law, The Foundation for Economic Education, Inc.,* Irvington-
on-Hudson, New York, 1974], pp. 5-6.)

But on what basis are the unalienable rights of mankind to be protected? This brings us to the principle which is a corollary to the one we
have just discussed.

# 9th

## Principle

**To protect man's rights, God has revealed
certain principles of divine law.**

Rights, though endowed by God as unalienable prerogatives, could not remain unalienable unless they were protected as enforceable rights under a code of divinely proclaimed law. William Blackstone pointed out that the Creator is not only omnipotent (all-powerful):

> "... but as He is also a Being of infinite wisdom. He has laid down only such laws as were founded in those relations of justice, that existed in the nature of things ... These are the eternal, immutable laws of good and evil, to which the Creator Himself in all His dispensations conforms; and which He has enabled human reason to discover, so far as they are necessary for the conduct of human actions. Such, among others, are these principles: that we should live honestly, should hurt nobody, and should render to everyone his due." (Blackstone, *Commentaries on the Laws of England*, 1:59-60.)

### Sound Principles of Law All Based on God's Law

Blackstone also said it was necessary for God to disclose these laws to man by direct revelation:

"The doctrines thus delivered we call the revealed or divine law, and they are to be found only in the Holy Scriptures. These precepts, when revealed, are found upon comparison to be really a part of the original law of nature, as they tend in all their consequences to man's felicity." (*Ibid.*, 1:64.)

An analysis of the essential elements of God's code of divine law reveals that it is designed to promote, preserve, and protect man's unalienable rights. This divine pattern of law for human happiness requires a recognition of God's supremacy over all things; that man is specifically forbidden to attribute God's power to false gods; that the name of God is to be held in reverence, and every oath taken in the name of God is to be carried out with the utmost fidelity, otherwise the name of God would be taken in vain; that there is also a requirement that one day each week be set aside for the study of God's law; that it is also to be a day of worship and the personal renewing of one's commitment to obey God's law for happy living; that there are also requirements to strengthen family ties by children honoring parents and parents maintaining the sanctity of their marriage and not committing adultery after marriage; that human life is also to be kept sacred; that he who willfully and wantonly takes the life of another must forfeit his own; that a person shall not lie; that a person shall not steal; that every person must be willing to work for the things he desires from life and not covet and scheme to get the things which belong to his neighbor.

These principles will be immediately recognized as the famous Ten Commandments. There are many additional laws set forth in the Bible which clarify and define these principles. (For a complete codification of these laws, see W. Cleon Skousen, *The Third Thousand Years*, Bookcraft, Inc., Salt Lake City, 1964, pp. 651-682.)

### Divine Law Endows Mankind with Unalienable Duties as Well as Unalienable Rights

In recent years the universal emphasis on "rights" has seriously obscured the unalienable duties which are imposed upon mankind by divine law. As Thomas Jefferson said, man "has no natural right in opposition to his social duties." (Bergh, *Writings of Thomas Jefferson*, 16:282.)

There are two kinds of duties – public and private. Public duties relate to public morality and are usually supported by local or state ordinances which can be enforced by the police power of the state. Private duties are those which exist between the individual and his Creator. These are called principles of private morality. The only enforcement agency is the self-discipline of the individual himself. William Blackstone was referring to public and private morality when he said:

> "Let a man therefore be ever so abandoned in his principles, or vicious in his practice, provided he keeps his wickedness to himself, and does not offend against the rules of public decency, he is out of the reach of human laws. But if he makes his vices public, though they be such as seem principally to affect himself (as drunkenness, or the like), they then become by the bad example they set, of pernicious effects to society; and therefore it is then the business of human laws to correct them.... Public sobriety is a relative duty [relative to other people], and therefore enjoined by our laws; private sobriety is an absolute duty, which, whether it be performed or not, human tribunals can never know; and therefore they can never enforce it by any civil sanction." (Blackstone, *Commentaries on the Laws of England*, 1:208.)

In a sense we could say that our unalienable duties, both public and private, are an inherent part of Natural Law. They constitute a responsibility imposed on each individual to respect the absolute rights or unalienable rights of others.

### Examples of Public and Private Duties

Here are some of the more important responsibilities which the Creator has imposed on every human being of normal mental capacity:

1. The duty to honor the supremacy of the Creator and his laws. As Blackstone states, the Creator's law is the supreme law of the world: "This law of nature, being coeval with mankind and dictated by God himself, is of course superior in obligation to any other. It is binding over all the globe in all countries, and at all times; no human laws are of any validity, if contrary to this...." (Ibid., sec. 2, par. 39.)
2. The duty not to take the life of another except in self-defense.
3. The duty not to steal or destroy the property of others.
4. The duty to be honest in all transactions with others.
5. The duty of children to honor and obey their parents and elders.
6. The duty of parents and elders to protect, teach, feed, clothe, and provide shelter for children.
7. The duty to support law and order and keep the peace.
8. The duty not to contrive through a covetous heart to despoil another.
9. The duty to provide insofar as possible for the needs of the help-

less -- the sick, the crippled, the injured, the poverty-stricken.

10. The duty to honorably perform contracts and covenants both with God and man.
11. The duty to be temperate.
12. The duty to become economically self-sufficient.
13. The duty not to trespass on the property or privacy of another.
14. The duty to maintain the integrity of the family structure.
15. The duty to perpetuate the race.
16. The duty not to promote or participate in the vices which destroy personal and community life.
17. The duty to perform civic responsibilities -- vote, assist public officials, serve in official capacities when called upon, stay informed on public issues, volunteer where needed.
18. The duty not to aid or abet those involved in criminal or anti-social activities.
19. The duty to support personal and public standards of common decency.
20. The duty to follow rules of moral rectitude.

### The Creator's Superior Law of Criminal Justice

The Creator revealed a divine law of criminal justice which is far superior to any kind being generally followed in the world today. This is a most important element of God's revealed law, and let us therefore emphasize it again even though we discussed it earlier.

It will be recalled that God's revealed law provided true "justice" by requiring the criminal to completely restore the property he had stolen or to otherwise pay the damages for losses he had caused. It was the law of "reparation" -- repairing the damage. In addition, the criminal had to pay his victim punitive damages for all the trouble he had caused. This was also to remind him not to do it again.

This system of justice through reparation was practiced by the ancient Israelites and also the Anglo-Saxons. In recent years a number of states have begun to adopt the "reparation" system. This requires the judge to call in the victim and consult with him or her before passing sentence. This discussion includes the possibility of the criminal's working to pay back the damages he caused his victim.

If the criminal is too irresponsible to be trusted to get a job and repay his victim, then he is given a heavy prison term with the provision that he cannot be considered for parole until he will guarantee full cooperation in repayment to his victim.

The State of Utah adopted such a law. Judges are required to have offenders indemnify their victims for damages wherever possible. A copy of this law may be obtained from the Secretary of State, Utah Capitol Building, Salt Lake City, Utah 84104.

### Should Taxpayers Compensate Victims of Crimes?

In some states, the victims of criminal activities may apply to the state for damages. This most unfortunate policy is a counter-productive procedure which encourages crime rather than deters it. It encourages a bandit to say to his victim, "Don't worry, mister. You'll get it all back from the state."

Now we must respond to one final question concerning God's revealed laws of "true justice": What if a law is passed by Congress or some legislature which is contrary to God's law? What then?

### God's Law the Supreme Law of the Land

Among the Anglo-Saxons and the ancient Israelites, the law enunciated by God was looked upon as sacred and not subject to change by human legislative bodies. In an authoritative text entitled English Constitutional and Legal History, Dr. Colin Rhys Lovell of the University of Southern California writes this concerning the Anglo-Saxons:

> "To most Anglo-Saxons the law was either divinely inspired or the work of their ancestors, [being] of such antiquity that it was unthinkable that it should be changed. Alfred the Great ... was one of the few rulers of the period who issued new laws, but he too regarded the body of traditional Anglo-Saxon law as sacred and God-given." (Colin Rhys Lovell, English *Constitutional and Legal History*, Oxford University Press, New York, 1962, p. 36.)

Dr. Lovell explains the attitude of the Anglo-Saxon race toward their divine code of law. He says they considered it:

> "... immutable [emphasis in the original]. Even the all-powerful tribal assembly had no legislative power, and this theory of legislative impotence endured for a long time in the development of the English constitution and disappeared only very gradually; even many centuries later the fiction that specific legislation was not making new law but reinforcing ancient customs was preserved. Most of the great steps forward in the development of the

English constitution have been taken with loud assertions that nothing new was being contemplated, only the old was being restored." (*Ibid.*, p. 7)

## Natural Law Constitutes Eternal Principles

Even when it was finally acknowledged that Parliament was writing new statutes and dealing with problems not mentioned in the law of ancient times, it was still required that none of the new laws contradict the provisions of divine law. John Locke set forth the principle which carried over into the thinking of the American Founders when he wrote:

> "The law of Nature stands as an eternal rule to all men, legislators as well as others. The rules that they make for man's actions must ... be conformable to the law of Nature -- i.e., to the will of God." (John Locke, *Second Essay Concerning Civil Government*, p. 56, par. 135.)

Sir William Blackstone, contemporary of the Founders, wrote:

> "Man, considered as a creature, must necessarily be subject to the laws of his Creator.... This will of his Maker is called the Law of Nature....This law of nature, being coeval with mankind, and dictated by God, Himself, is of course superior in obligation to any other. It is binding over all the globe in all countries, and at all times: no human laws are of any validity, if contrary to this." (William Blackstone, *Commentaries on the Laws of England*, 1:54, 56, 63.)

But who will decide? When it comes to lawmaking, the nations of most of the world throughout history have been subject to the whims and arbitral despotism of kings, emperors, rulers, and magistrates. How can the people be protected from the autocratic authority of their rulers? Where does the source of sovereign authority lie?

The Founders had strong convictions on this point.

# 10th

## Principle

**The God-given right to govern is vested in the
sovereign authority of the whole people.**

During the 1600s, the royal families of England did everything in their
power to establish the doctrine that they governed the people by "divine right of kings." In other words, it was declared a "God-given right."

### Algernon Sidney Is Beheaded

King Charles II beheaded Algernon Sidney in 1683 for saying that
there is no divine right of kings to rule over the people. Sidney insisted
that the right to rule is actually in the people and therefore no person can
rightfully rule the people without their consent.

In responding to the question, "Whether the supreme power be ... in
the people," he replied:

> "I say, that they [including himself] who place the power [to
> govern] in a multitude, understand a multitude composed of
> freemen, who think it for their convenience to join together, and
> to establish such laws and rules as they oblige themselves to observe." (Algernon Sidney, *Discourses on Government*, 3 vols.,
> Printed for Richard Lee by Deare and Andres, New York, 1805,
> 2:18.)

### John Locke on the Source of Political Power

The very year Algernon Sidney was beheaded, John Locke fled from
England to Holland where he could say the same thing Sidney did, but
from a safer distance. After the "Glorious Revolution" which he helped
in plotting, Locke returned from Holland on the same boat as the new

Queen (Mary). In 1890 he published his two famous essays on The Original Extent and End of Civil Government. In the second essay he wrote:

"In all lawful governments, the designation of the persons who are to bear rule being as natural and necessary a part as the form of the government itself, and that which had its establishment *originally from the people* ... all commonwealths, therefore, with the form of government established, have rules also of appointing and conveying the right to those who are to have any share in the public authority; and whoever gets into the exercise of any part of the power by other ways than what the laws of the community have prescribed hath no right to be obeyed, though the form of the commonwealth be still preserved, since he is not the person the laws have appointed, and, consequently, not the person the people have consented to. Nor can such an usurper, or any deriving from him, ever have a title till *the people are both at liberty to consent, and have actually consented,* to allow and confirm in him the power he hath till then usurped." (John Locke, *Second Essay Concerning Civil Government*, pp. 70-71, par. 198; emphasis added.)

### View of the American Founders

There was no place for the idea of a divine right of kings in the thinking of the American Founders. They subscribed to the concept that rulers are servants of the people and all sovereign authority to appoint or remove a ruler rests with the people. They pointed out how this had been so with the Anglo-Saxons from the beginning.

Dr. Lovell describes how the tribal council, consisting of the entire body of freemen, would meet each month to discuss their problems and seek a solution through consensus. The chief or king (taken from the Anglo-Saxon word *cyning*--chief of the kinsmen) was only one among equals:

"The chief owed his office to the tribal assembly, which selected and could also depose him. His authority was limited at every turn, and though he no doubt commanded respect, his opinion carried no more weight in the debates of the assembly than that of any freeman" (Lovell, *English Constitutional and Legal History*, p. 5.)

## Alexander Hamilton

In this same spirit, Alexander Hamilton declared:

"The fabric of American empire ought to rest on the solid basis of the consent of the people. The streams of national power ought to flow immediately from that pure, original fountain of all legitimate authority." (*The Federalist Papers*, No. 22, p. 152.)

The divine right of the people to govern themselves and exercise exclusive power of sovereignty in their official affairs was expressed by the Commonwealth of Massachusetts in its Proclamation of January 23, 1776:

"It is a maxim that in every government, there must exist, somewhere, a supreme, sovereign, absolute, and uncontrollable power; but this power resides always in *the body of the people*; and it never was, or can be, delegated to any man, or a few; the great Creator has never given to men a right to vest others with authority over them, unlimited either in duration or degree." (Quoted by Hamilton Albert Long, *Your American Yardstick*, Your Heritage Books, Inc., Philadelphia, 1963, p. 167; emphasis added.)

## James Madison

James Madison discovered many people frightened by the Constitution when it was presented for ratification because they felt a federal government was being given autocratic authority. Madison declared:

"The adversaries of the Constitution seem to have lost sight of the *people* altogether in their reasonings on this subject; and to have viewed these different establishments not only as mutual rivals and enemies, but as uncontrolled by any common superior in their efforts to usurp the authorities of each other. These gentlemen must be here reminded of their error. They must be told that the *ultimate authority*, wherever the derivative may be found, *resides in the people alone.*" (*The Federalist Papers*, No. 46, p. 294; emphasis added.)

But even if it is acknowledged that the *people* are divinely endowed with the sovereign power to govern, what happens if elected or appointed officials usurp the authority of the people to impose a dictatorship or some form of abusive government on them?

This brings us to the fundamental principle on which the Founders based their famous Declaration of Independence.

# 11th

## Principle

**The majority of the people may alter or abolish a government which has become tyrannical.**

Philadelphia, 1776

The Founders were well acquainted with the vexations resulting from an abusive, autocratic government which had imposed injuries on the American colonists for thirteen years in violation of the English constitution. Thomas Jefferson's words in the Declaration of Independence therefore emphasized the feelings of the American people when he wrote:

"Prudence, indeed, will dictate that governments long established should not be changed for light and transient causes; and, accordingly, all experience has shown, that mankind are more disposed to suffer, while evils are sufferable, than to right themselves by abolishing the forms to which they are accustomed.

"But, when a long train of abuses and usurpations, pursuing invariably the same object, evinces a design to reduce them under absolute despotism, it is their right, it is their duty, to throw off such government, and to provide new guards for their future security." (*Annals of America*, 2:447-48.)

Once again, we find John Locke setting forth this same doctrine in his classical Second Essay Concerning Civil Government:

"The reason why men enter into society is the preservation of their property.... [Therefore,] whenever the legislators endeavor to take away and destroy the property of the people, or to reduce them to slavery under arbitrary power, they [the officials of government] put themselves into a state of war with the people, who are thereupon absolved from any further obedience, and are left to the common refuge which God hath provided for all men against force and violence. Whensoever, therefore, the legislative shall transgress this fundamental rule of society, and either by ambition, fear, folly, or corruption, endeavor to grasp themselves, or put into the hands of any other, an absolute power over the lives, liberties, and estates of the people, by this breach of trust they [the government officials] forfeit the power the people had put into their hands ... and it devolves to the people, who have a right to resume their original liberty, and ... provide for their own safety and security." ( John Locke, *Second Essay Concerning Civil Government*, pp. 75-76, par. 222; emphasis added.)

### Power Rests in the Majority

However, it is important to recognize that the "government" was established by the majority of the people, and only a majority of the people can authorize an appeal to alter or abolish a particular establishment of government. As Locke pointed out:

"When any number of men have, by the consent of every individual, made a community, they have thereby made that community one body, with a power to act as one body, which is only by the will and determination of the majority... And thus every man, by consenting with others to make one body politic under one government, puts himself under an obligation to every one of that society to submit to the determination of the majority, and to be concluded by it." (*Ibid.*, p. 47, par. 96- 97.)

### No Right of Revolt in a Minority

This being true, Locke pointed out that there is no right of revolt in an individual, a group, or a minority. Only in the majority. As he stated elsewhere:

"For if it [the unlawful act of government] reach no farther than some private men's cases, though they have a right to defend themselves ... yet the right to do so will not easily engage them in a contest ... it being as impossible for one or a few oppressed men to disturb the government where the body of the people do not think themselves concerned in it... But if either these illegal acts have extended to the *majority* of the people, or if the mischief and oppression has light [struck] only on some few, but in such cases as the precedent and consequences seem to *threaten all,* and they are persuaded in their consciences that their laws, and with them, their estates, liberties, and lives are in danger, and perhaps their religion too, *how they will be hindered from resisting illegal force used against them I cannot tell.*" (*Ibid.*, p. 73, par. 208-9; emphasis added.)

## Virginia Declaration of Rights

In other words, the majority are then likely to revolt just as the American Founders did when their plight had finally become intolerable. Certainly there was no significant confusion in the minds of the Founders as to their rights and proper recourse when they approached their moment of critical decision in 1776. The Virginia assembly passed the Virginia Declaration of Rights on June 12, 1776, which provided in Section 3 as follows:

"That government is, or ought to be, instituted for the common benefit, protection, and security of the people... And that, when any government shall be found inadequate or contrary to these purposes, a *majority* of the community hath an indubitable, inalienable, and indefeasible right to reform, alter, or abolish it, in such manner as shall be judged most conducive to the public weal." (*Annals of America*, 2:432; emphasis added.)

So, granted that the people are sovereign and the majority of them can take over whenever necessary to restructure the political machinery and restore liberty, what is likely to be the best form of government which will preserve liberty? The answer to this question was a favorite theme of the American nation-builders.

# 12th

## Principle

**The United States of America shall be a Republic.**

This principle is highlighted in the pledge of allegiance when it says:

> I pledge allegiance to the flag
> Of the United States of America
> And to the Republic
> For which it [the flag] stands...

There are many reasons why the Founders wanted a republican form of government rather than a democracy. Theoretically, a democracy requires the full participation of the masses of the people in the legislative or decision making processes of government. This has never worked because the people become so occupied with their daily tasks that they will not properly study the issues, nor will they take the time to participate in extensive hearings before the vote is taken. The Greeks tried to use democratic mass participation in the government of their city-states, and each time it ended in tyranny.

### A Democracy and a Republic Compared

A democracy becomes increasingly unwieldy and inefficient as the population grows. A republic, on the other hand, governs through elected representatives and can be expanded indefinitely. James Madison contrasted these two systems when he wrote:

"Democracies have ever been spectacles of turbulence and contention; have ever been found incompatible with personal security or the rights of property; and have in general been as short in their lives as they have been violent in their deaths....

"A republic, by which I mean a government in which the scheme of representation takes place, opens a different prospect and promises the cure for which we are seeking." (*The Federalist Papers*, No. 10, p. 81.)

Madison later went on to point out how an expanding country like the United States could not possibly confine itself to the limitations of a democracy, but must rely upon a representative or republican form of government to protect the ever-expanding interests of its people. He said:

"In a democracy the people meet and exercise the government in person; in a republic they assemble and administer it by their representatives and agents. A democracy, consequently, must be confined to a small spot. A republic may be extended over a large region." (*Ibid.*, No. 14, p. 100.)

### A Republic Defined

To make his position completely clear, Madison offered a concise definition of a republic as follows:

"We may define a republic to be ... a government which derives all its powers directly or indirectly from the great body of the people, and is administered by persons holding their offices during pleasure for a limited period, or during good behavior. It is essential to such a government that it be derived from the great body of the society, not from an inconsiderable proportion or a favored class of it; otherwise a handful of tyrannical nobles, exercising their oppressions by a delegation of their powers, might aspire to the rank of republicans and claim for their government the honorable title of republic." (*Ibid.*, No. 39, p. 241.)

### Modern Emphasis on "Democracy"

During the early 1900s an ideological war erupted, and the word "democracy" became one of the casualties. Today, the average American uses the term "democracy" to describe America's traditional Constitutional republic. But technically speaking, it is not. The Founders had hoped that their descendants would maintain a clear distinction between a democracy and a republic.

The creation of the current confusion developed as a result of a new movement in the United States. Approximately 100 people met in New York in 1905 and organized what they called the Intercollegiate Socialist Society (ISS). Chapters were established on more than sixty college and university campuses coast-to-coast. In time the co-directors of the movement became Harry W. Laidler and Norman Thomas. Laidler explained that the ISS was set up to "throw light on the world-wide movement of industrial democracy known as socialism." (*The New York Times*, January 28, 1919.)

What was this new movement attempting to accomplish? Socialism is defined as "government ownership or control of all the means of production (farms, factories, mines, and natural resources) and all the means of distribution (transportation, communications, and the instruments of commerce)." Obviously, this is not a "democracy" in the classical sense. And it is the very antithesis of a free-market economy in a republic.

The ISS adopted a snappy slogan for the times: "Production for use, not for profit." This seemed to catch on. Hundreds of men and women who later became big names in government, press, radio, television, and motion pictures were among the early recruits.

### The League for Industrial Democracy

However, by 1921 the violence associated with the Union of Soviet Socialist Republics (USSR) had given the term "socialism" a strongly repugnant meaning to many people. The ISS therefore decided to change its name to "The League for Industrial Democracy." The word "democracy" was supposed to carry the message that through the nationalization (government expropriation) of all the means of production and distribution, the nation's fabulous resources would become the property of "all the people" -- hence a democracy. Then America could enjoy "production for use, not for profit." This meant that the word "democracy" was deceptive. Various devices were used to alert the public to the true meaning of the word. For example, the U.S. Army's Training Manual No. 2000-25, published in 1928, contained a whole section explaining the difference between a democracy and a republic in their original, historical sense.

### Government Manual Defines a "Democracy"

The manual had the following to say concerning the characteristics of a democracy:

1. A government of the masses.
2. Authority derived through mass meetings or any other form of "direct" expression.

3. Results in mobocracy.
4. Attitude toward property is communistic -- negating property rights.
5. Attitude toward law is that the will of the majority shall regulate, whether it is based upon deliberation or government by passion, prejudice, and impulse, without restraint or regard to consequences.
6. Results in demagogism, license, agitation, discontent, anarchy.

It will be recalled that James Madison was almost as strong in his own historical evaluation of past democracies. His words, as indicated above, were:

"Democracies have ever been spectacles of turbulence and contention; have ever been found incompatible with personal security or the rights of property; and have in general been as short in their lives as they have been violent in their deaths." (*The Federalist Papers*, No. 10, p. 81.)

## Government Manual Defines a Republic

The government manual then proceeded to outline the characteristics of a republic, which all of the Founders had vigorously recommended over a pure democracy or any other form of government.

1. Authority is derived through the election by the people of public officials best fitted to represent them.
2. Attitude toward property is respect for laws and individual rights, and a sensible economic procedure.
3. Attitude toward law is the administration of justice in accord with fixed principles and established evidence, with a strict regard for consequences.
4. A greater number of citizens and extent of territory may be brought within its compass.
5. Avoids the dangerous extreme of either tyranny or mobocracy.
6. Results in statesmanship, liberty, reason, justice, contentment, and progress.

James Madison, as we mentioned earlier, had defined a republic along the same lines:

"We may define a republic to be ... a government which derives all its powers directly or indirectly from the great body of the people, and is administered by persons holding their offices during [the people's] pleasure for a limited period, or during good behavior." (*Ibid.*, No. 39, p. 241.)

## Identifying the United States as a "Democracy"

In spite of these efforts to clarify the difference between a democracy and a republic, the United States began to be consistently identified in both the press and the school books as a "democracy." President Wilson helped contribute to the confusion when he identified World War I as the effort of the allied forces to "make the world safe for democracy." President Wilson had surrounded himself with many of the early recruits of the ISS movement, and these may have encouraged the adoption of this slogan just as they later changed the name of their ISS organization to the League for Industrial Democracy.

A review of the roster of early ISS members will also reveal that by the 1930s the more brilliant young leaders of the movement from World War I days had risen to some of the most prestigious positions in politics, press, publishing houses, radio, academic circles, teacher-training colleges, the National Council of Churches, and just about every other major center of opinion-molding influence.

However, the intellectual development of the ISS members had not followed the same line of maturation. Some wanted the new "United States democracy" to become a socialist's state with the people's consent (democratic socialism). Others wanted a "mixed system" of part socialism, part free-enterprise. Some were becoming disillusioned and had started swinging back to the Founders' traditional formula. A few had become enamored with the seizure of power by force and violence and had become leaders in the Communist party movement. Nevertheless, all of them continued to refer to the United States as a democracy.

## "Democracy" Loses Its Identification with Socialism

Following World War II, an interesting semantic transition began to take place in the American mind with reference to the use of the word "democracy."

To begin with, the Communists, the National Socialists of Germany, and the Democratic Socialists throughout the rest of Europe had all misused the word "democracy" to the point where it had become virtually meaningless as a descriptive term. As a euphemism for socialism, the word had become totally innocuous.

Furthermore, socialism, whether spelled with a capital or small "s," had lost its luster. All over the world, socialist nations – both democratic and communistic – were drifting into deep trouble. All of them were verging on economic collapse in spite of tens of billions of dollars provided by the United States to prop them up. Some had acquired a notorious and abhorrent reputation because of the violence, torture, starvation, and concentration-camp tactics they had all used against their own civilian population. All over the world, socialism had begun to emerge as an abject failure formula. To the extent it was tried in America (without ever being called "socialism,") it had created colossal problems which the Founding Fathers' formula would have avoided.

All of this created a subtle change in the American mind set. People continued referring to the United States as a "democracy," but mentally they had begun to equate "democracy" with the traditional Constitutional republic. It became popular to refer to American democracy as though it were quite different from everybody else's kind of democracy. That is the status of the word "democracy" in the United States today. The majority of the people are instinctively leaning more and more toward the fundamental thinking of the Founders. They will probably end up calling the United States a "democratic republic," which is the term used by the followers of Thomas Jefferson!

### The Attack on the Constitution

With the preceding historical picture in mind, it will be readily appreciated that the introduction of the word "democracy" (to describe the United States) was actually designed as an attack on the Constitutional structure of government and the basic rights it was designed to protect. As Samual Adams pointed out, the Founders had tried to make socialism "unconstitutional." Therefore, to adopt socialism, respect and support for traditional constitutionalism had to be eroded and then emasculated. In view of this fact, it should not surprise the student of history to discover that those who wanted to have "democracy" identified with the American system were also anxious to have Americans believe their traditional Constitution was outdated, perhaps totally obsolete.

In this author's college days, it was popular in political science and economics classes to point out that the Constitution was written some two centuries ago by a people who were about 95 percent farmers. Now, they would say, we live in an industrial society, and the needs of the people can no longer be accommodated under the archaic system provided under the U.S. Constitution. Not only certain teachers expressed this opinion, but U.S. Senators proclaimed it. Occasionally, even a President would say it! In this writer's file there is an interesting collection of such statements.

But this does raise an important question. No doubt our economic and social circumstances have changed tremendously since the days of the Founders. Has this made the Constitution obsolete? In the next chapter we will address this.

# 13th

## Principle

**A constitution should be structured to permanently protect the people from the human frailties of their rulers.**

"Let no more be said of confidence in man, but bind him down from mischief by the chains of the Constitution." -- Thomas Jefferson

At the Constitutional Convention, the Founding Fathers were concerned with the one tantalizing question which no political scientist in any age had yet been able to answer with complete satisfaction. The question was, "How can you have an efficient government but still protect the freedom and unalienable rights of the people?"

### Distrust of Power Not Necessarily Disrespect for Leaders

The Founders had more confidence in the people than they did in the leaders of the people, especially trusted leaders, even themselves. They felt the greatest danger arises when a leader is so completely trusted that the people feel no anxiety to watch him. Alexander Hamilton wrote:

"For it is a truth, which the experience of all ages has attested, that the people are commonly most in danger when the means of injuring their rights are in the possession of those [toward] whom they entertain the least suspicion." (*The Federalist Papers*, No. 25, p. 164.)

Two hundred years of American history have demonstrated the wisdom of the Founders in proclaiming a warning against the frailties of human nature in the people's elected or appointed leaders. Every unconstitutional action has usually been justified because it was for a "good cause." Every illegal transfer of power from one department to another has been excused as "necessary." The whole explosion of bureaucratic power in Washington has been the result of "trusting" benign political leaders, most of whom really did have good intentions. Thomas Jefferson struck out with all the force that tongue and pen could muster against trusting in human nature. Said he:

> "It would be a dangerous delusion were a confidence in the men of our choice to silence our fears for the safety of our rights; that confidence is everywhere the parent of despotism; free government is founded in jealousy, and not in confidence; it is jealousy, and not confidence, which prescribes limited constitutions to bind down those whom we are obliged to trust with power; that our Constitution has accordingly fixed the limits to which, and no farther, our confidence may go... In questions of power, then, let no more be said of confidence in man, *but bind him down from mischief by the chains of the Constitution.*" ("The Kentucky Resolutions of 1798," *Annals of America*, 4:65-66; emphasis added.)

## Government Is Coercive Force

George Washington made it very clear why all of this was necessary. The Founders looked upon "government" as a volatile instrument of explosive power which must necessarily be harnessed within the confines of a strictly interpreted Constitution, or it would destroy the very freedom it was designed to preserve. Said he:

> "Government is not reason, it is not eloquence – it is force! Like fire, it is a dangerous servant and a fearful master." (Quoted in Jacob M. Braude, *Lifetime Speaker's Encyclopedia*, 2 vols., Prentice-Hall, Inc., Englewood Cliffs, N.J., 1962, 1:326.)

## Leaders Are Not Angels but Fragile Human Beings

James Madison saw the problem of placing power in the hands of fallible human beings who, by nature, contain a complexity of elements reflecting both good and evil. The purpose of a constitution is to define the area in which a public official can serve to his utmost ability, but at the same time provide strict limitations to chain him down from mischief. In every human being there is a natural tendency to practice Parkinson's law of perpetual expansion and to exercise personal proclivities toward ego-mania and self-aggrandizement. As we indicated earlier, Madison was very concerned about human frailties in the leaders of the people. He said:

> "It may be a reflection on human nature that such devices [as Constitutional chains] should be necessary to control the abuses of government. But what is government itself but the greatest of all reflections on human nature? ... If angels were to govern men, neither external nor internal controls on government would be necessary. [But lacking these,] in framing a government which is to be administered by men over men, the great difficulty lies in this: *you must first enable the government to control the governed; and in the next place oblige it to control itself.*" (*The Federalist Papers*, No. 51, p. 322; emphasis added.)

### Why the Original Constitution Will Never Be Obsolete

And that is what the Constitution is all about -- providing freedom from abuse by those in authority. Anyone who says the American Constitution is obsolete just because social and economic conditions have changed does not understand the real genius of the Constitution. It was designed to control something which *has not changed and will not change -- namely, human nature.*

### Danger of Losing Constitutional Rights

Furthermore, the Founders knew from experience that the loss of freedom through the gradual erosion of Constitutional principles is not always so obvious that the people can readily detect it. Madison stated:

> "I believe there are more instances of the abridgement of the freedom of the people by gradual and silent encroachments of those in power, than by violent and sudden usurpations.... This danger ought to be wisely guarded against." (Elliot, *Debates in the State Conventions*, 3:87.)

### When Erosion Occurs, Act Quickly

In 1785, Madison had occasion to issue a vigorous warning to his home state of Virginia:

> "It is proper to take alarm *at the first experiment on our liberties*. We hold this prudent jealousy to be the first duty of citi-

zens and one of the noblest characteristics of the late Revolution. *The freemen of America* did not wait till usurped power had strengthened itself by exercise and entangled the question in precedents. They saw all the consequences [of governmental abuses] in the principle, and they avoided the consequences by denying the principle [on which the abuses were based]. We revere this lesson too much ... to forget it." ("Memorial and Remonstrance," in Rives and Fendall, *Letters and Other Writings of James Madison*, 1:163; emphasis added.)

But where are the encroachments of abusive rulers most likely to attack? Is there some basic right which self-aggrandizing politicians seek to destroy first? The Founders said there was. Mankind has so many rights that it is sometimes difficult to keep a watchful eye on all of them. Therefore, the Founders said we should especially concentrate on the preservation of one particular right because all other rights are related to it. This special object of concern is identified in the next principle.

# 14th

## Principle

**Life and liberty are secure only so long as the right to property is secure.**

Under English common law, a most unique significance was attached to the unalienable right of possessing, developing, and disposing of property. Land and the products of the earth were considered a gift of God which were to be cultivated, beautified, and brought under dominion. As the Psalmist had written:

> "... even the heavens are the Lord's: but the earth hath he given to the children of men." (*Psalm* 115:16.)

### Mankind Given the Earth "In Common"

John Locke pointed out that the human family originally received the planet earth as a common gift and that mankind was given the capacity and responsibility to improve it. Said he:

> "God, who hath given the world to men in common, hath also given them reason to make use of it to the best advantage of life and convenience." (John Locke, *Second Essay Concerning Civil Government*, p. 30, par. 25.)

## Development of the Earth Mostly by Private Endeavor

Then Locke pointed out that man received the commandment from his Creator to "subdue" the earth and "have dominion" over it. (*Genesis* 1:28.) But because dominion means control, and control requires exclusiveness, private rights in property became an inescapable necessity or an inherent aspect of subduing the earth and bringing it under dominion.

It is obvious that if there were no such thing as "ownership" in property, which means legally protected exclusiveness there would be no subduing or extensive development of the resources of the earth. Without private "rights" in developed or improved property, it would be perfectly lawful for a lazy, covetous neighbor to move in as soon as the improvements were completed and take possession of the fruits of his industrious neighbor. And even the covetous neighbor would not be secure, because someone stronger than he could take it away from him.

## Without Property Rights, Four Things Would Occur

Note that if property rights did not exist, four things would occur which would completely frustrate the Creator's command to multiply and replenish the earth and subdue it and bring it under dominion:

1.  One experience like the above would tend to completely destroy the incentive of an industrious person to develop and improve any more property.
2.  The industrious individual would also be deprived of the fruits of his labor.
3.  Marauding bands would even be tempted to go about the country confiscating by force and violence the good things which others had frugally and painstakingly provided.
4.  Mankind would be impelled to remain on a bare subsistence level of hand-to-mouth survival because the accumulation of anything would invite attack.

## A Person's Property is a Projection of Life Itself

Another interesting point made by Locke is the fact that all property is an extension of a person's life, energy, and ingenuity. Therefore, to destroy or confiscate such property is, in reality, an attack on the essence of life itself.

The person who has worked to cultivate a farm, obtained food by hunting, carved a beautiful statue, or secured a wage by his labor, has projected his very being – the very essence of his life – into that labor. This is why Locke maintained that a threat to that property is a threat to the essence of life itself. Here is his reasoning:

"Though the earth and all inferior creatures be common [as the gift from God] to all men, yet every man has a "property" in his own "person." This, nobody has any right to but himself. The "labor" of his body and the "work" of his hands, we may say, are properly his. Whatsoever, then, he removes out of the state that Nature hath provided and left it in, he hath mixed his labor with it, and joined to it something that is his own, and thereby makes it his property....

"He that is nourished by the acorns he picked up under an oak, or the apples he gathered from the trees in the wood, has certainly appropriated them to himself. Nobody can deny but the nourishment is his. I ask, then, when did they begin to be his? When he digested? or when he ate? or when he boiled? or when he brought them home? or when he picked them up? And it is plain, if the first gathering made them not his, nothing else could." (John Locke, *Second Essay Concerning Civil Government*, pp. 30-31, par. 26-27.)

### How Is Ownership Acquired?

Locke then deals with a very important question: If all things were originally enjoyed in common with the rest of humanity, would a person not have to get the consent of every other person on earth before he could call certain things his own? Locke answers by saying:

"That labor ... added something to them [the acorns or apples] more than Nature, the common mother of all, had done, and so they became his private right. And will any one say he had no right to those acorns or apples he thus appropriated because he had not the consent of all mankind to make them his?... If such a consent as that was necessary, [the] man [would have] starved, notwithstanding the plenty God had given him...

"It is the taking any part of what is common, and removing it out of the state Nature leaves it in, which begins the property, without which the common [gift from God] is of no use.... Thus the law of reason makes the deer that [property of the Indian] who hath killed it; it is allowed to be his goods who hath bestowed his labor upon it, though, before, it was the common right of every one." (*Ibid.*, p. 31, par. 27-29.)

### Property Rights Sacred?

It is important to recognize that the common law does not make property sacred, but only the right which someone has acquired in that property. Justice George Sutherland of the U.S. Supreme Court once told the New York State Bar Association:

> "It is not the right of property which is protected, but the right to property. Property, per se, has no rights; but the individual -- the man -- has three great rights, equally sacred from arbitrary interference: the right to his life, the right to his liberty, the right to his property... The three rights are so bound together as to be essentially one right. To give a man his life but deny him his liberty, is to take from him all that makes his life worth living. To give him his liberty but take from him the property which is the fruit and badge of his liberty, is to still leave him a slave." (George Sutherland, "Principle or Expedient?", Annual Address to the New York State Bar Association, 21 January 1921, p. 18.)

In this same spirit Abraham Lincoln once said:

> "Property is the fruit of labor. Property is desirable, is a positive good in the world. That some should be rich shows that others may become rich and hence is just encouragement to industry and enterprise. Let not him who is houseless pull down the house of another, but let him work diligently to build one for himself, thus by example assuring that his own shall be safe from violence... I take it that it is best for all to leave each man free to acquire property as fast as he can. Some will get wealthy. I don't believe in a law to prevent a man from getting rich; it would do more harm than good." (Quoted in *The Freeman: Ideas on Liberty*, May 1955, p. 7.)

### Primary Purpose of Government Is to Protect Property

The early American colonists had much to say about property and property rights because it was a critical issue leading to the Revolutionary War. The effort of the Crown to take their property through various kinds of taxation without their consent (either individually or through their representatives) was denounced as a violation of the English constitution and English common law. They often quoted John Locke, who had said:

"The supreme power cannot take from any man any part of his property without his own consent. For the preservation of property being the end of government, and that for which men enter into society, it necessarily supposes and requires that the people should have property, without which they must be supposed to lose that [property] by entering into society, which was the end for which they entered into it." (John Locke, *Second Essay Concerning Civil Government*, p. 57, par. 138.)

## Property Rights Essential to Liberty

John Adams saw private property as the most important single foundation stone undergirding human liberty and human happiness. He said:

"The moment the idea is admitted into society that property is not as sacred as the laws of God, and that there is not a force of law and public justice to protect it, anarchy and tyranny commence. *Property must be secured or liberty cannot exist.*" (Charles Francis Adams, ed., *The Works of John Adams*, 10 vols., Little, Brown and Company, Boston, 1850-1856, 6:9, 280; emphasis added.)

## Should Government Take from the "Haves" and Give to the "Have Nots"?

As we have pointed out earlier, one of the worst sins of government, according to the Founders, was the exercise of its coercive taxing powers to take property from one group and give it to another. In our own day, when the government has imposed a multi-hundred-billion- dollar budget on the American people with about one half being "transfer payments" from the tax-paying public to the wards of the government, the following words of James Madison may sound strange:

"Government is instituted to protect property of every sort.... This being the end of government, that alone is not a just government, ... nor is property secure under it, where the property which a man has in his personal safety and personal liberty is violated by arbitrary seizures of one class of citizens for the service of the rest." (Saul K. Padover, ed., *The Complete Madison*, Harper & Bros., New York, 1953, p. 267.)

## Redistribution of the Wealth Unconstitutional

In earlier years the American courts held that the expropriating of property to transfer to other citizens was unlawful, being completely outside the constitutional power delegated to the government. It was not until after 1936 (the Butler case) that the Supreme Court began arbitrarily distorting the meaning of the "general welfare" clause to permit the distribution of federal bounties as a demonstration of "concern" for the poor and the needy. Before that time, this practice was prohibited. The Supreme Court had declared:

> "No man would become a member of a community in which he could not enjoy the fruits of his honest labor and industry. The preservation of property, then, is a primary object of the social compact.... The legislature, therefore, had no authority to make an act divesting one citizen of his freehold, and vesting it in another, without a just compensation. It is inconsistent with the principles of reason, justice and moral rectitude; it is incompatible with the comfort, peace and happiness of mankind; it is contrary to the principles of social alliance in every free government; and lastly, it *is contrary to the letter and spirit of the Constitution.*" (2 Dall 304, 310 [Pa. 1795]; emphasis added.)

## Property Rights the Foundation of All Civilizations

One of the world's foremost economists, Dr. Ludwig von Mises, pointed out that the preservation of private property has tremendous social implications as well as legal ramifications. He wrote:

> "If history could prove and teach us anything, it would be the private ownership of the means of production as a necessary requisite of civilization and material well-being. All civilizations have up to now been based on private property. Only nations committed to the principle of private property have risen above penury and produced science, art, and literature. There is no experience to show that any other social system could provide mankind with any of the achievements of civilization." (Ludwig von Mises, *Socialism*, Yale University Press, New Haven, Connecticut, 1951, p. 583.)

## Caring for the Poor Without Violating Property Rights

But, of course, the nagging question still remains. If it corrupts a society for the government to take care of the poor by violating the principle of property rights, who will take care of the poor? The answer of those who built America seems to be: "Anybody but the federal government."

Americans have never tolerated the suffering and starvation which have plagued the rest of the world, but until the present generation help was given almost exclusively by the private sector or on the community or state level. President Grover Cleveland vetoed legislation in his day designed to spend federal taxes for private welfare problems. He wrote:

> "I can find no warrant for such an appropriation in the Constitution, and I do not believe that the power and duty of the General Government ought to be extended to the relief of individual suffering which is in no manner properly related to the public service or benefit. A prevalent tendency to disregard the limited mission of this power and duty should, I think, be steadfastly resisted, to the end that the lesson should be constantly enforced that though the people support the Government the Government should not support the people.

> *"The friendliness and charity of our countrymen can always be relied upon to relieve their fellow-citizens in misfortune.* This has been repeatedly and quite lately demonstrated. Federal aid in such cases encourages the expectation of paternal care on the part of the Government and weakens the sturdiness of our national character, while it prevents the indulgence among our people of that kindly sentiment and conduct which strengthens the bonds of a common brotherhood." ("Why the President Said No," in *Essays on Liberty*, 12 vols., The Foundation for Economic Education, Inc., Irvington-on-Hudson, New York, 1952-65, 3:255; emphasis added.)

# 15th

## Principle

**The highest level of prosperity occurs when there is a free-market economy and a minimum of government regulations.**

Freedom to TRY     Freedom to BUY     Freedom to SELL     Freedom to FAIL

The Founders were fascinated with the possibility of setting up a political and social structure based on natural law, but what about economics? Were there natural laws for the marketplace?

A tome of five books on the subject was published just in the nick of time which gave them the answer. It came out in 1776 and was called The Wealth of Nations. It was written by a college professor in Scotland named Adam Smith.

This brilliant work is not easy reading, but it became the watershed between mercantilism and the doctrines of free market economics. It fitted into the thinking and experiences of the Founders like a hand in a glove. Thomas Jefferson wrote: "In political economy, I think Smith's Wealth of Nations the best book extant." (Bergh, *Writings of Thomas Jefferson*, 8:31.)

### Adam Smith's Free-enterprise Economics Tried First in America

Other writers in Europe, such as the Physiocrats in France, were advocating a free-market economy, but nowhere on earth were these principles being practiced by any nation of size or consequence. Therefore, the United States was the first people to undertake the structuring of a whole national economy on the basis of natural law and the free-market concept described by Adam Smith. Among other things, this formula called for the following:

1. Specialized production -- let each person or corporation of persons do what they do best.
2. Exchange of goods takes place in a free-market environment without governmental interference in production, prices, or wages.
3. The free market provides the needs of the people on the basis of supply and demand, with no government imposed monopolies.
4. Prices are regulated by competition on the basis of supply and demand.
5. Profits are looked upon as the means by which production of goods and services is made worthwhile.
6. Competition is looked upon as the means by which quality is improved, quantity is increased, and prices are reduced.

## The Four Laws of Economic Freedom

Prosperity also depends on a climate of wholesome stimulation protected by law. Reduced to its simplest formula, there are four laws of economic freedom which a nation must maintain if its people are to prosper at the maximum level. These are:

1. The Freedom to try.
2. The Freedom to buy.
3. The Freedom to sell.
4. The Freedom to fail.

By 1905 the United States had become the richest industrial nation in the world. With only five percent of the earth's continental land area and merely six percent of the world's population, the American people were producing over half of almost everything -- clothes, food, houses, transportation, communications, even luxuries. It was a great tribute to Adam Smith.

## The Role of Government in Economics

The Founding Fathers agreed with Adam Smith that the greatest threat to economic prosperity is the arbitrary intervention of the government into the economic affairs of private business and the buying public. Historically, this has usually involved fixing prices, fixing wages, controlling production, controlling distribution, granting monopolies, or subsidizing certain products.

Nevertheless, there are four areas of legitimate responsibility which properly belong to government. These involve the policing responsibilities of government to prevent:

1.  Illegal force in the market place to compel purchase or sale of products.
2.  Fraud in misrepresenting the quality, location, or ownership of the item being sold or bought.
3.  Monopoly which eliminates competition and results in restraint of trade.
4.  Debauchery of the cultural standards and moral fiber of society by commercial exploitation of vice -- pornography, obscenity, drugs, liquor, prostitution, or commercial gambling.

The perspective of the Founders in the economic role of government may be gathered from sentiments such as these by Washington:

> "Let vigorous measures be adopted; not to limit the prices of articles, for this I believe is inconsistent with the very nature of things, and impracticable in itself, but to punish speculators, forestallers, and extortioners, and above all to sink the money by heavy taxes. To promote public and private economy; encourage manufacturers, etc." (Fitzpatrick, *Writings of George Washington*, 14:313.)

### After 1900 Adam Smith Got Lost in the Shuffle

In spite of the fact that the fruits of the free-market economy were making the United States the biggest and richest industrial nation in the world, the beginning of the twentieth century saw many prominent and influential leaders losing confidence in the system. These included wealthy industrialists, heads of multi-national banking institutions, leaders in the academic world, and some of the more innovative minds in the media. The same feverish restlessness was taking hold in similar circles in Europe.

It was true, as it is with all systems, that the free market economy was in need of some adjustments and fine tuning, but these leaders were getting ready to throw the entire system overboard. The problems of the day included a number of large-scale strikes, the rise of powerful trusts, the mysterious recurrence of boom-and-bust cycles, and the rise of a new Populist movement in which certain agriculture and labor groups were demanding that the government get involved in the redistribution of the wealth.

Many of these problems were either caused or aggravated by the very people who were demanding "a new system." The new system would involve extensive government regulation if not outright expropriation of major industries and natural resources. In Europe, certain confederations of wealthy families had gained control of their respective governments and were making a financial killing. Some of the wealthy families in America coveted the rich government monopolies of their trans-Atlantic cousins.

It was in this climate that Adam Smith and the free market economy fell out of favor. We have already discussed the rise of the Intercollegiate Socialist Society, which was billed on major university campuses as the vanguard of the new era. Collectivism, socialism, government ownership of industry, subsidy of the farmers, and a whole spectrum of similar ideas were permeating the country when World War I broke out. This greatly accelerated the idea of strong centralized government with regulatory power over every aspect of the marketplace.

### John Chamberlain Describes What Happened to Adam Smith

By the 1920s, the debunking of the Founding Fathers was in full swing. The obsolescence of the Constitution was discussed openly. The ideas of Adam Smith were considered archaic. John Chamberlain, one of the foremost writers of our own day, was just coming up through college. He describes the academic climate of that era:

> "When I was taking a minor in economics as a congruent part of a history major back in the 1920s, Robert Hutchins had not yet started his campaign to restore a reading of the "great books" to college courses. So we never read Adam Smith's The Wealth of Nations. We heard plenty about it, however. The professors treated it condescendingly; we were told it was the fundamentalist Bible of the old dog-eat-dog type of businessman.

> "The businessmen, in that Menckenian time, were considered the natural enemies of disinterested learning. We, as students, regarded them as hypocrites. They talked competition, and invoked the name of Adam Smith to bless it. Then they voted for the high-tariff Republican Party. Somehow Adam Smith, as the man who had justified a business civilization, got the blame for everything. We weren't very logical in those days, and we were quite oblivious to our own hypocrisy in making use of our businessmen fathers to pay our college tuition fees and to stake us to trips to Europe." (Introduction to *The Wealth of Nations*, "Heirloom Edition," 2 vols., Arlington House, New Rochelle, New York, no date, page v.)

## Adam Smith Out, Karl Marx In

John Chamberlain eventually came to realize what the intellectual leaders of the day were doing. They were deprecating the Founders and the free-market economy to create a vacuum which would then be filled with a completely new formula. Their new economic nostrum was the very toxin the Founders had warned against. Chamberlain describes what happened:

> "The depression that began in 1929 is generally considered the watershed that separates the new (collectivist) age from the old, or rugged individualist, age. Before Franklin Roosevelt, we had had the republic (checks and balances, limited government, inalienable rights to liberty and property, and all that). After 1933 we began to get the centralized state and interventionist controls of industry. Actually, however, the inner spirit of the old America had been hollowed out in the Twenties. The colleges had ceased to teach anything important about our heritage. You had to be a graduate student to catch up with The Federalist Papers, or with John Calhoun's Disquisition on Government, or with anything by Herbert Spencer, or with The Wealth of Nations. We were the ignorant generation.

> "The depression began our education. But the first "great book" in economics that we read was Marx's *Capital*. We had nothing to put against it. Talk of "planning" filled the air. We read George Soule and Stuart Chase on the need for national blueprints and national investment boards and "government investment." Keynes was still in the future, but his system was already being laid brick by brick. And Adam Smith was still a word of derision." (*Ibid.*, pp. v-vi.)

## The Rediscovery of Adam Smith

My own education was similar to that of John Chamberlain. I was less than a decade behind him. We were all part of a generation of lost Americans who had to rediscover our heritage the hard way. For nearly a quarter of a century the Founders had been relegated to the pre-industrial past. Certain professors spoke disparagingly of what they called the "myths the Founders believed." The Founding Fathers were all very old-fashioned.

Gradually, however, the intellectual light of day dawned on many thousands of that lost generation. Ivor Thomas wrote his book, *The Socialist Tragedy* (New York: The Macmillan Company, 1951), explaining what socialism had done to Europe. Max Eastman wrote his Reflections on the *Failure of Socialism* (New York: The Devin-Adair Company, 1962), explaining what socialism had done to America and the world.

For some, there was a genuine awakening. The traditional values of the Founders began to emerge with a new message of promise so long neglected. John Chamberlain describes his rediscovery of Adam Smith:

> "We had to rediscover the real Adam Smith the hard way, by living our mistakes, and by being led to the whole body of the literature of freedom that had created the American federal system. Only then were we able to appreciate Smith. Ironically, our education paralleled that of Adam Smith himself, which took place over a period of a dozen years between the close of the Seven Years War and the outbreak of the American Revolution. We would have been saved so much trouble if we had only been compelled to read -- and digest -- The Wealth of Nations in the first college course in economics, with James Madison's political theory as a side dressing.

> "Smith's book is, indeed, the beginnings of everything that is important to economic theory, the lack of clarity on value theory notwithstanding. It should be the natural starting point for students of economics for the simple and compelling reason that it anticipated Ludwig von Mises by a full century and a half in considering economics as part of a wider science of human choices. Smith backed into his study by way of a general preoccupation with human destiny in a way that should be utterly convincing to our own pragmatic day." (*Introduction to The Wealth of Nations*, page vi.)

As this book goes to press, America is strenuously struggling to restore a few of the lost jewels from the Founders' treasury. An appreciation for Adam Smith is looming larger. If it continues, there is hope for a brighter future for the next generation than for the one just passing.

A genuine return to the Founders, however, will also involve the completion of something which has never been done, neither in the Founders' day nor in ours. It is the need for a genuine monetary reform along the lines the Founders envisioned but were never able to launch.

### One Responsibility of Government Never Completely Fulfilled

At the Constitutional Convention, the Founders determined that they would make the American dollar completely independent of any power or combination of powers outside of the American people. They therefore gave the exclusive power to issue and control money to the people's representatives—the Congress—and forbade anybody, even the states, to meddle with it. Not only was Congress to be held responsible for the issuing of money, but it was to see that its purchasing power remained fixed. In other words, the "value" of the money was to remain steady and reliable not only in the United States, but also in relation to foreign money. They therefore stated in the Constitution that Congress would have the power "To coin money, regulate the value thereof, and of foreign coin...." (Article I, Section 8, clause 5.)

All money was to be "coined" in precious metal. Paper "notes" were to be "promises to pay" in gold or silver, not legal tender as such. States were strictly forbidden to allow debts to be paid except in terms of gold or silver (Article I, Section 10).

Washington stated:

> "We should avoid ... the depreciation of our currency; but I conceive this end would be answered, as far as might be necessary, by stipulating that all money payments should be made in gold and silver, being the common medium of commerce among nations." (Fitzpatrick, *Writings of George Washington*, 11:217.)

### What Went Wrong?

Here is one area where a great idea of the Founders was never adequately implemented. The Founders were just coming out of a devastating depression when the Constitution was adopted, and under pressure from both European and American financial interests, a whole series of policy errors were committed which have continued to this day. For example:

The issuing of money was turned over to a private consortium of bankers who set up a privately owned bank called the Bank of the United States. (A similar arrangement exists today under the Federal Reserve System.)

The indignant protest of Thomas Jefferson can be heard across the vista of two whole centuries:

> "If the American people ever allow the banks to control the issuance of their currency, first by inflation and then by deflation, the banks and corporations that will grow up around them will deprive the people of all property until their children will wake up homeless on the continent their fathers occupied. The issuing power of money should be taken from the banks and re-

stored to Congress and the people to whom it belongs." (Quoted in Olive Cushing Dwinell, *The Story of Our Money*, 2nd ed., Forum Publishing Company, Boston, 1946], p. 84.

### Fractional Banking

The bank was allowed to issue three or four times more paper notes or loans than it had in assets. This is called "fractional banking" because the bank has only a fraction of the assets needed to back up the paper money or credit which it has issued.

Once again Jefferson protested: "The banks themselves were doing business on capitals [assets], three-fourths of which were fictitious...." (Ford, *Writings of Thomas Jefferson*, 10:133.)

Jefferson saw that the banks would inflate the economy by loaning out fictitious paper money (with no assets behind it). This would "boom" the economy. Then, when the financiers had lured borrowers into a precarious position, they would call for a "bust" and foreclose on the property for which the bank had virtually furnished nothing.

At the first signs of a pending "bust," Jefferson lamented:

> "This fictitious capital ... is now to be lost, and to fall on somebody; it [the bank] must take on those who have property to meet it, and probably on the less cautious part, who, not aware of the impending catastrophe, have suffered themselves to contract, or to be in debt and must now sacrifice their property of a value many times the amount of the debt. We have been truly sowing the wind, and are now reaping the whirlwind." (*Ibid.*, 10:133.)

Amazingly, this disastrous pattern of "boom and bust" has been repeated off and on for over 200 years without the cause of it being corrected. A sound monetary reform program is still begging for a hearing.

### An Economy of Debt Instead of Wealth

The financiers who gained control of American finance built the economy on debt instead of wealth. Jefferson's protest came out as follows:

> "At the time we were funding our national debt, we heard much about 'a public debt being a public blessing,' that the stock representing it was a creation of active capital for the aliment of commerce, manufactures and agriculture. This paradox was well adapted to the minds of believers in dreams..." (Bergh, *Writings of Thomas Jefferson*, 13:420.)

Jefferson, Jackson, and Lincoln all tried to get the monetary program turned around so that Congress would issue its own money and banks would be required to loan on existing assets rather than use fictitious money based on merely a fraction of their assets. In other words, they wanted to get rid of the "boom and bust" cycle. At one point when the idea seemed to be catching on, the London Times came out with a frantic editorial stating:

> "If that mischievous financial policy, which had its origin in the North American Republic during the late war in that country (the Civil War), should become indurated down to a fixture, then that Government will furnish its own money without cost. It will pay off its debts and be without debt. It will have all the money necessary to carry on its commerce. It will become prosperous beyond precedent in the history of the civilized governments of the world. The brains and the wealth of all countries will go to North America. That government must be destroyed or it will destroy every monarchy on the globe." (Quoted in Gertrude Margaret Coogan, *Money Creators*, Omni Publications, Hawthorne, California, 1974, p. 217.)

## A Pressing Opportunity

All of this should demonstrate that somewhere up the trail, the leadership of the United States has an opportunity to add one more burst of momentum to the upward thrust of the 5,000 year leap. It will be a monumental monetary reform based on the principles which the Founders understood but were never able to implement. As Jefferson said toward the latter days of his life:

> "We are overdone with banking institutions, which have banished the precious metals, and substituted a more fluctuating and unsafe medium... These have withdrawn capital from useful improvements and employments to nourish idleness... [These] are evils more easily to be deplored than remedied." (Bergh, *Writings of Thomas Jefferson*, 12:379-80.)

On another occasion, Jefferson lamented:

> "We are completely saddled and bridled, and... the bank is so firmly mounted on us that we must go where [it] will guide." (*Ibid.*, 9:337-338.)

# 16th

## Principle

**The government should be separated into three branches:
Legislative, Executive, and Judicial.**

### America's Three-Headed Eagle

A popular pastime among political writers in ancient times was attempting to decide what form of government was best. Some argued for a monarchy, with a single, powerful ruler. Others preferred an aristocracy where the "best families" of the nation were allowed to rule. Yet a third favored a pure democracy where decisions were to be made by the whole people. Unfortunately none of these systems furnished the security and justice which were expected of them.

Then came Polybius. Polybius was a Greek who lived 204 to 122 B.C. Next to Herodotus and Thucydides, Polybius is recognized as the greatest of all Greek historians. When Greece was conquered by Rome, Polybius was deported to the Roman capital. Previously, Polybius had rendered illustrious public service to the Achaean League, a confederation of city states. However, he quickly recognized the advantages of the Roman republic which had been set up to govern millions. Polybius became a friend and ally of Rome, traveling widely on military and diplomatic missions to Europe, Asia, and Africa. His rich practical and scholarly experience finally culminated in his writing forty books of history!

## The Political Insights of Polybius

Polybius felt there was an element of genius in each of the three types of government being discussed by philosophers. A monarchy had the executive strength needed to direct the administration of the government, particularly in time of war. An aristocracy, on the other hand, represented the vested interests of wealth and the developed resources of the nation. A democracy, meanwhile, represented the interests of the masses of the population without which neither a monarchy nor an aristocracy could exist.

Unfortunately, none of these systems, when allowed to govern, provided equality, prosperity, justice, or domestic tranquility for the whole society. Polybius felt he understood why this was so:

> "Even more keenly than Aristotle, he [Polybius] was aware that each form carried within itself the seed of its own degeneration, if it were allowed to operate without checks and balances provided by opposing principles. Monarchy could easily become tyranny, aristocracy sink into oligarchy [oppressive government by a few rich families], and democracy turn into mob rule of force and violence." (William Ebenstein, *Great Political Thinkers*, p. 110.)

## Polybius Proposes a "Mixed" Constitution

But since all three systems represented unique and essential elements for the governing of a people, why not combine them into a single system? Polybius saw the synthesizing process of all three ingredients beginning to develop in the Roman system, but shortly after Polybius died, the Romans abandoned their principles of a republic and eventually set up an emperor. Thus came to an end what Polybius had hoped would be the first three department constitution in history. He visualized the strength of a monarchy being assigned the executive duties of government; the interests of wealth and the "established order" would be represented in the Senate; the interests of the general populace would be represented in the popular Assembly. Polybius felt that if these three departments were set up as coordinated equals they could perform their necessary functions, but at the same time counter-balance one another as a restraining mechanism so that no one of them would acquire sufficient power to abuse the people.

This new approach to government was called a "mixed" constitution. It was a great idea, but it virtually died with Polybius. Not until the middle 1700s did the genius of Baron Charles de Montesquieu undertake to resurrect the inspired potentialities of a "mixed" constitution and submit it for the consideration of modern man.

### Baron Charles de Montesquieu

Montesquieu became one of the best-educated scholars in France. Although his mother died when he was seven, and his father died when he was twenty-four, a wealthy uncle left him a title, a judicial office, and his whole fortune. Montesquieu traveled extensively throughout England and continental Europe. Then he spent approximately twenty years of research before he wrote his philosophical history called *The Spirit of Laws*. This has been described as "one of the most important books ever written," and certainly ranks as "the greatest book of the French 18th century." (George Saintsbury, "Montesquieu," *Encyclopedia Britannica*, 11th ed., 29 vols., University Press, Cambridge, England, 1910-1911, 18:776.)

The final writing required two solid years of uninterrupted labor and was completed in his huge study hall, sixty by forty feet, at his palatial residence in France. However, the book was so full of praise for the English system that it was never popular in France and was scarcely read. Nevertheless, it became famous elsewhere and was greatly admired by the Founders. It documented the practical possibility of a government based on "separation of powers" or a "mixed" constitution.

In Book XI, Montesquieu actually set forth the ingredients for a model constitution. The Founders admired it sufficiently to use many portions of it as a guide in their own work. However, the Founders' joint effort in constitution writing greatly excelled even that of Montesquieu. Nevertheless, to him must go the well-deserved credit for illuminating the minds of the Founders with the exciting possibilities of a government based on "separated" but "coordinated" powers.

### The Foundation for What Became America's Three-headed Eagle

Montesquieu saw the separation of powers developing under the English system somewhat differently than Polybius had seen it in Rome.

Instead of the three departments of government being the executive, the senate, and the people's assembly, Montesquieu saw the powers of government developing along the lines of an executive, a legislature (of both an upper and a lower house), and an independent judiciary. In England the developing process was still in progress, but Montesquieu felt it was moving in the right direction.

The Parliament was gradually exercising increasing independence, which Montesquieu pronounced essential to liberty. However, he recognized that a legislature could be tyrannical if the executive did not retain some of its power to check it. Said he:

> "When the legislative and executive powers are united in the same person, or in the same body of magistrates, there can be no liberty, because apprehensions may arise, lest the same monarch *OR* senate [legislature] should enact tyrannical laws, to execute them in a tyrannical manner." (The Spirit of Laws, Great Books of the Western World, vol. 38, Encyclopedia Britannica, Inc., Chicago, 1952, p. 70; emphasis added.)

Montesquieu saw the legislature enacting the laws and the executive administering them. But he felt it was just as important to have an independent judiciary to interpret and enforce the laws:

> "Again, there is no liberty, if the judiciary power be not separated from the legislative and executive. Were it joined with the legislative, the life and liberty of the subject would be exposed to arbitrary control, for the judge would then be the legislator. Were it joined to the executive power, the judge might behave with violence and oppression." ("The Spirit of Laws," *Great Books of the Western World*, vol. 38, Encyclopedia Britannica, Inc., Chicago, 1952, p. 70.)

## A Single Executive

Montesquieu recognized the weakness of the Roman system in setting up two or more consuls to preside over the people. On one occasion there were thirty executives in Greece. Montesquieu said this responsibility should be concentrated in a single person who can make decisions quickly and decisively and cannot escape either credit or blame for the consequences.

It is interesting that in the American Constitutional Convention, there was a heated debate over the number of Presidents. The New Jersey Plan called for several. Governor Randolph of Virginia wanted at least three. James Wilson argued along the lines of Montesquieu that there should be only one.

## Development of "Separation of Powers" in America

It may come as a surprise to modern Americans to learn how slowly the doctrine of "separation of powers" was accepted in America. The states were perfectly willing to set up a single executive, a separate legislature (usually with an upper and a lower house), and also an independent judiciary, but they were certainly not agreeable to setting up a three department government on the federal level.

It will be recalled that when the Articles of Confederation were written, neither an executive nor a judiciary was provided for. Provision was made for a Congress of representatives from the various states, but even the Congress had no taxing power or enforcement power. It was simply a "committee of the states."

### John Adams Pushes Separation-of-Powers Doctrine

In 1776, when it first became apparent that the American people would have to set up their own government, John Adams practically stood alone in advocating a government built on a separation of powers. Even before the Declaration of Independence he was advocating a new national government with three separate departments but found himself severely criticized for such a revolutionary idea. Many years later John Adams wrote a letter to one of the other Founders, Dr. Benjamin Rush, dated April 12, 1809, in which he described his initial effort to get this principle adopted:

> "I call you to witness that I was the first member of Congress who ventured to come out in public, as I did in January 1776, in my 'Thoughts on Government,' ... in favor of a government with three branches, and an independent judiciary. This pamphlet, you know, was very unpopular. No man appeared in public to support it but yourself. You attempted in the public papers to give it some countenance, but without much success. Franklin leaned against it. Dr. Young, Mr. Timothy Matlack and Mr. James Cannon, and I suppose Mr. George Bryan were alarmed and displeased at it. Mr. Thomas Paine was so highly offended with it that he came to visit me at my chamber at Mrs. Yard's to remonstrate and even scold at me for it, which he did in very ungenteel terms. In return, I only laughed heartily at him... Paine's wrath was excited because my plan of government was essentially different from the silly projects that he had published in his 'Common Sense.' By this means I became suspected and unpopular with the leading demagogues and the whole constitutional party in Pennsylvania." (Koch, *The American Enlightenment*, p. 163.)

### John Adams Studies the "Divine Science" of Good Government

It is interesting that John Adams should have been the first among the Founding Fathers to capture the vision of Montesquieu in setting up a self-repairing national government under the separation-of-powers doctrine. As we pointed out earlier, he looked upon politics as a "divine science," and determined to devote his life to its study. It will be recalled that during the Revolutionary War he wrote to his wife:

> "The science of government is my duty to study, more than all other sciences; the arts of legislation and administration and negotiation ought to take [the] place of, indeed to exclude, in a manner, all other arts. I must study politics and war, that my sons may have liberty to study mathematics and philosophy. My sons ought to study mathematics and philosophy, geography, natural history and naval architecture, navigation, commerce, and agriculture, in order to give their children a right to study painting, poetry, music, architecture, statuary, tapestry, and porcelain." (*Ibid.*, p. 188.)

## Basic Principles of Sound Constitutionalism Unpopular at First

As indicated earlier, he had discovered that the selling of the principles of his "divine science" was not designed for the career of a man who wanted to become a popular politician. Here's the way he described his experiences:

> "Upon my return from France in 1779, I found myself elected by my native town of Braintree a member of the Convention for forming a Constitution for the State of Massachusetts. I attended that Convention of near four hundred members. Here I found such a chaos of absurd sentiments concerning government that I was obliged daily, before that assembly, and afterwards in a Grand Committee, to propose plans and advocate doctrines, which were extremely unpopular with the greater number. Lieutenant-Governor Cushing was avowedly for a single assembly, like Pennsylvania. Samuel Adams was of the same mind. Mr. Hancock kept aloof, in order to be governor. In short, I had at first no support but from the Essex junta, who had adopted my ideas in the letter to Mr. Wythe.... They made me, however, draw up the Constitution, and it was finally adopted, with some amendments very much for the worse." (*Ibid.*, pp. 163-64.)

## John Adams Writes Separation of Powers into a State Constitution

It is interesting that in spite of all the opposition John Adams encountered, he did succeed, almost single-handedly, in getting his state to adopt a constitution based on separation of powers. For the first time in the world a constitution read:

> "In the government of the Commonwealth of Massachusetts the legislative, executive and judicial powers shall be placed in separate departments, to the end that it might be a government of laws and not of men...." (*Ibid.*, p. 252.)

### The Modern Apostle of the Divine Science of Good Government Unappreciated for a Century

In later years, Adams was successful in getting his ideas incorporated in the U.S. Constitution, but he was never able to gain a genuine acceptance of himself. Even though he was elected the first Vice President of the United States and the second President, he very shortly disappeared into history with scarcely a ripple. A hundred years after the founding of the country, neither Washington nor Massachusetts had erected any kind of monument to John Adams. (*Ibid.*, p. 154) It was only as scholars began digging into the origins of American constitutionalism that John Adams suddenly loomed up into proper perspective. Even he suspected there would be very few who would remember what he had attempted to accomplish. He wrote to a friend:

> "Mausoleums, statues, monuments will never be erected to me. Panegyrical romances will never be written, nor flattering orations spoken to transmit me to posterity in brilliant colors." (*Ibid.*)

### A Constitution for 300 Million Freemen

Nevertheless his political precepts of the "divine science" of government caught on. Even Pennsylvania revised its constitution to include the separation of powers principle, and Benjamin Franklin, one of the last to be converted, finally acknowledged that the Constitution of the United States with its separation of powers was as perfect as man could be expected to produce. He urged all of the members of the Convention to sign it so that it would have unanimous support.

John Adams said it was his aspiration, "...to see rising in America an empire of liberty, and the prospect of two or three hundred millions of freemen, without one noble or one king among them." (*Ibid.*, p. 191)

# 17th
## Principle

**A system of checks and balances should be adopted to prevent the abuse of power.**

"The necessity of reciprocal checks in the exercise
of political power ..." – George Washington

It must have been astonishing to John Adams to discover that after he had sold the people on the separation of powers doctrine, some of them wanted the separation to be so complete that it would have made the system unworkable.

These people who took this puritanical view opposed the adoption of the Constitution on the grounds that it did not make the separation of power between the three departments complete and absolute.

They missed a most important factor in Montesquieu's presentation. He said each of the departments was to be separate in its functions, but subject to the checks of the other two departments in case it became abusive in performing those functions.

### James Madison Explains "Checks and Balances"

It is interesting that James Madison had to spend five Federalist Papers (numbers 47 to 51) explaining that the separation of powers between the executive, legislative, and judicial departments should not be absolute, but should make allowances for a built-in system of checks and balances. He said the trick was to separate the powers and then delicately lace them back together again as a balanced unit.

Madison conceded, however, that keeping the three departments of government separated was fundamental to the preservation of liberty. He wrote:

> "The accumulation of all powers, legislative, executive, and judiciary, in the same hands, whether of one, a few, or many, and whether hereditary, self appointed, or elective, may justly be pronounced the very definition of tyranny." (*The Federalist Papers*, No. 47, p. 301.)

Madison then proceeded to explain how Montesquieu recommended that the powers be separated as to function but coordinated for the prevention of usurpation or abuse. Note his opening tribute to Montesquieu:

> "The oracle who is always consulted and cited on this subject is the celebrated Montesquieu. If he be not the author of this invaluable precept in the science of politics, he has the merit at least of displaying and recommending it most effectually to the attention of mankind." (*Ibid.*, No. 47, p. 301.)

In the Federalist Papers, No. 47, Madison indicated that even those states which demanded an absolute separation of powers in the federal constitution employed a blending of power in their own state constitutions. He pointed out that just as those safeguards were necessary for the states, they were equally important to include in the federal constitution. In fact, he said:

> "I shall undertake ... to show that unless these departments be so far connected and blended as to give each a constitutional control over the others, the degree of separation which the maxim [of Montesquieu] requires, as essential to a free government, can never in practice be duly maintained." (*Ibid.*, No. 48, p. 308.)

### Blending Does Not Mean Usurping

Notice that the purpose of "checks and balances" is a constitutional control in the hands of each department of government to prevent any usurpation of power by another department or abusive administration of the power granted to it. This "blending" does not, therefore, intrude into the legitimate functions of each of the departments. As Madison explained it:

> "It is agreed on all sides that the powers properly belonging to one of the departments ought not to be directly and completely

administered by either of the other departments. It is equally evident that none of them ought to possess, directly or indirectly, an overruling influence over the others in the administration of their respective powers. It will not be denied that power is of an encroaching nature and that it ought to be effectually restrained from passing the limits assigned to it.... The next and most difficult task is to provide some practical security for each, against the invasion of the others." (*Ibid.*, No. 48, p. 308.)

Just how difficult this task turned out to be is demonstrated in a number of problems which have arisen in our own day. The failure to use the checks and balances effectively has allowed the judiciary to create new laws (called judicial legislation) by pretending to be merely interpreting old ones. Failure to use the checks and balances has also allowed the President to make thousands of new laws, instead of Congress, by issuing executive orders. It has allowed the federal government to invade the reserved rights of the states on a massive scale. It has allowed the legislature to impose taxes on the people never contemplated by the Founders or the Constitution.

The whole spectrum of checks and balances needs to be more thoroughly studied and more vigorously enforced. Madison appropriately anticipated that "parchment barriers" in the Constitution would not prevent usurpation. Each department of government has the responsibility to rise up and protect its prerogatives by exercising the checks and balances which have been provided. At the same time, the people have the responsibility to keep a closer watch on their representatives and elect only those who will function within Constitutional boundaries.

### Checks Were Designed to Protect the "Will of the People"

All of these aberrations in the administration of government have done violence to the intent and desires of the people. The Founders felt that if the checks and balances as originally provided were to prove inadequate, the remedy should be a device by which the people might more directly influence the power centers of government so that decisions would be more in harmony with their wishes. James Madison said it this way:

"As the people are the only legitimate fountain of power and it is from them that the constitutional charter under which the [power of the] several branches of government ... is derived, it seems strictly consonant to the republican theory to recur to the same original authority ... whenever any one of the departments may commit encroachments on the chartered authorities of the others." (*Ibid.*, No. 49, pp. 313-314.)

But how do the people protect themselves? There must be adequate legal machinery provided so that the representatives of the people have more direct input to project the will of the people when the officials of government are ignoring it. Madison discussed the various overseer devices which had been considered in the past to keep the departments of government within their Constitutional channels. None had proven particularly successful.

Pennsylvania tried out a Council of Censors to enforce its constitution. The council was effective in determining what violations had occurred, but was powerless to remedy the evil.

Others suggested that the people be allowed to vote on critical constitutional issues at specified times. However, the tremendous emotional anguish displayed during the ratification of the U.S. Constitution demonstrated that this was not something to be undertaken very often. Said Madison:

> "The danger of disturbing the public tranquility by interesting too strongly the public passions is a still more serious objection against a frequent reference of constitutional questions to the decision of the whole society. Notwithstanding the success which has attended the revisions of our established forms of government [the ratification conventions] and which does so much honor to the virtue and intelligence of the people of America, it must be confessed that the experiments are of too ticklish a nature to be unnecessarily multiplied." (*Ibid.*, No. 49, p. 315.)

In the end, Madison contended, there is no better device to curb the departments of government than the internal machinery of checks and balances provided in the Constitution as written. Said he:

> "The only answer that can be given is that as all these exterior provisions are found to be inadequate, the defect must be supplied by so contriving the interior structure of the government as that its several constituent parts may, by their mutual relations, be the means of keeping each other in their proper places." (*Ibid.*, No. 51, p. 320.)

What the Founders finally devised is recognized as an ingenious device when properly implemented. The fact that it has sometimes fallen into neglect in recent times does not detract from the fact that it is still the most effective way to maintain the American eagle in the balanced center of the political spectrum. The Constitution made the departments separate as to their assigned function, but made them dependant upon one another to be fully operative. As we depicted in an earlier section of this book, the symbolic American eagle has three heads, but they operate from one neck. As a former Under-Secretary of State, J. Reuben Clark, Jr., explained it:

> "The Framers ... separated the three functions of government, and set each of them up as a separate branch -- the legislative, the executive, and the judicial. Each was wholly independent of the other. No one of them might encroach upon the other. No one of them might delegate its power to another.

> "Yet by the Constitution, the different branches were bound together, unified into an efficient, operating whole. These branches stood together, supported one another. While severally independent, they were at the same time, mutually dependent. It is this union of independence and dependence of these branches -- legislative, executive, and judicial -- and of the governmental functions possessed by each of them, that constitutes the marvelous genius of this unrivalled document. The Framers had no direct guide in this work, no historical governmental precedent upon which to rely. As I see it, it was here that the divine inspiration came. It was truly a miracle." (J. Reuben Clark, *Stand Fast by Our Constitution*, Deseret Book Company, Salt Lake City, 1973, pp. 147-148.)

### The Original Intent of the Founders

As it turned out, the American Founding Fathers achieved a system of checks and balances far more complex than those envisioned by Montesquieu. These included the following provisions:

1. The House of Representatives serves as a check on the Senate since no statute can become law without the approval of the House.
2. At the same time the Senate (representing the legislatures of the states before the 17th Amendment) serves as a check on the House of Representatives since no statute can become law without its approval.

3.  A President can restrain both the House and the Senate by using his veto to send back any bill not meeting with his approval.

4.  The Congress has, on the other hand, a check on the President by being able to pass a bill over the President's veto with a two-thirds majority of each house.

5.  The legislature also has a further check on the President through its power of discrimination in appropriating funds for the operation of the executive branch.

6.  The President must have the approval of the Senate in filling important offices of the executive branch.

7.  The President must also have the approval of the Senate before any treaties with foreign nations can go into effect.

8.  The Congress has the authority to conduct investigations of the executive branch to determine whether or not funds are being properly expended and the laws enforced.

9.  The President has a certain amount of political influence on the legislature by letting it be known that he will not support the re-election of those who oppose his program.

10. The executive branch also has a further check on the Congress by using its discretionary powers in establishing military bases, building dams, improving navigable rivers, and building interstate highways so as to favor those areas from which the President feels he is getting support by their representatives.

11. The judiciary has a check on the legislature through its authority to review all laws and determine their constitutionality.

12. The Congress, on the other hand, has a restraining power over the judiciary by having the constitutional authority to restrict the extent of its jurisdiction.

13. The Congress also has the power to impeach any of the judges who are guilty of treason, high crimes, or misdemeanors.

14. The President also has a check on the judiciary by having the power to nominate new judges subject to the approval of the Senate.

15. The Congress has further restraining power over the judiciary by having the control of appropriations for the operation of the federal court system.

16. The Congress is able to initiate amendments to the Constitution which, if approved by three-fourths of the states, could seriously affect the operation of both the executive and judicial branches.

17. The Congress, by joint resolution, can terminate certain powers granted to the President (such as war powers) without his consent.
18. The people have a check on their Congressmen every two years; on their President every four years; and on their Senators every six years.

### The Importance of Preserving the Founders' System

President Washington felt that the separation of powers with its accompanying checks and balances was the genius of the American system of government. The task was to maintain it. In his Farewell Address he stated:

> "It is important, likewise, that the habits of thinking in a free country should inspire caution in those entrusted with its administration to confine themselves within their respective constitutional spheres, avoiding in the exercise of the powers of one department to encroach upon another.

> "The spirit of encroachment tends to consolidate the powers of all the departments in one and thus to create, whatever the form of government, a real despotism. A just estimate of that love of power and proneness to abuse it which predominates in the human heart is sufficient to satisfy us of the truth of this position.

> "The necessity of reciprocal checks in the exercise of political power, by dividing and distributing it into different depositories and constituting each the guardian of the public weal against invasions by the others, has been evinced by experiments ancient and modern, some of them in our country and under our own eyes. To preserve them must be as necessary as to institute them. If, in the opinion of the people, the distribution or modification of the constitutional powers be in any particular wrong, let it be corrected by an amendment in the way which the Constitution designates. But let there be no change by usurpation; for though this, in one instance, may be the instrument of good, it is the customary weapon by which free governments are destroyed." (Fitzpatrick, *Writings of George Washington*, 35:228.)

### The Founders' Device for "Peaceful" Self-Repair

During nearly two centuries that the Constitution has been in operation, it has carried the nation through a series of traumatic crises. Not the least of these have been those occasions when some branch of government became arrogantly officious in the administration of its assigned task or flagrantly violated the restrictions which the Constitution placed upon it. As President Washington indicated, there is a tendency for some of this to occur continually, as is the case in our own day, but when it reaches a point of genuine crisis there is built-in Constitutional machinery to take care of it.

By way of contrast, we have scores of nations which claim to have copied the United States Constitution, but which failed to incorporate adequate checks and balances. In those countries, the only remedy, when elected presidents have suspended the constitution and used the army to stay in power, has been to resort to machine guns and bombs to oust the usurper. This occurs time after time. What the Founders wished to achieve in the Constitution of 1787 was machinery for the peaceful means of self-repair when the system went out of balance.

## Watergate

One of the most dramatic illustrations of the peaceful transfer of power in a time of crisis was in connection with the Watergate scandal. A President was found to have used his high office for purposes which were beyond the scope of his authority and outside the ramifications of legal conduct. Under threat of impeachment, he resigned. At the time, he was Commander-in-Chief of the Armed Services of the United States. He made no attempt to use these military forces to keep himself in power. In fact, under the American Constitution, it would have been useless for him to have attempted it. The transfer of power was made quietly and peacefully once the issue came to a point of decision.

## The Blessing of Domestic Tranquility

Some of us have had to travel or live in nations during a time of turmoil and revolution. Even one such experience will usually convince the most skeptical activist that there is nothing to be gained and a great deal to be lost by resorting to violence to bring about political change. Once a constitution has been established and the machinery developed for remedy or repair by peaceful means, this is the most intelligent and satisfactory route to pursue. It requires more patience, but given time, the results are more certain.

To solve problems by peaceful means was the primary purpose of the United States Constitution.

# 18th
## Principle

**The unalienable rights of the people are most likely to be preserved if the principles of government are set forth in a written constitution.**

The one weakness of the Anglo-Saxon common law was that it was unwritten. Since its principles were known among the whole people, they seemed indifferent to the necessity of writing them down. As Dr. Colin Rhys Lovell of the University of Southern California states:

> "The law applied by any of these Anglo-Saxon assemblies was customary. Until the Anglo-Saxon conversion to Christianity it was unwritten and like all customary law was considered immutable." (*English Constitutional and Legal History*, p. 7.)

### England's Need for a Written Bill of Rights

However, the Norman Conquest taught the Anglo-Saxons in England a bitter lesson. Many of their most treasured rights disappeared in a flood of blood and vindictive oppression. In fact, these rights were regained very slowly over a period of centuries and gradually they were written down. In 1215 A.D., during a national crisis, the sword was virtually put to the throat of King John in order to compel him to sign the Magna Charta, setting forth the traditional rights of freemen as well as the feudal barons who had been serving under King John.

During that same century the "Model Parliament" came into being, which compelled the King to acknowledge the principle of no taxation without representation. Charles I was later pressured into signing the people's Petition of Rights in 1628, and the English Bill of Rights was signed by William and Mary in 1689.

Through the centuries, the British have tried to manage their political affairs with no written constitution and have merely relied upon these fragmentary statutes as a constitutional reference source. These proved helpful to the American Founders, but they felt that the structure of government should be codified in a more permanent, comprehensive form. It will be appreciated, therefore, that the tradition of written constitutions in modern times is not of English origin but is entirely American, both in principle and practice.

### Beginnings of a Written Constitution in America

The first written charter in America was in 1620, when the Mayflower Compact came into being. Later the charter concept evolved into a more comprehensive type of constitution when Thomas Hooker and his associates adopted the Fundamental Orders of Connecticut in 1639. It is interesting that the Connecticut charter makes no reference to the Crown or the British Government as the source of its authority. It is a compact of "We, the people." As historian John Fiske writes:

> "On the 14th of January, 1639, all the freemen of the three towns assembled at Hartford and adopted a written constitution in which the hand of the great preacher [the Reverend Thomas Hooker] is clearly discernible. It is worthy of note that this document contains none of the conventional references to a "dread sovereign" or a "gracious King," nor the slightest allusion to the British or any other government outside of Connecticut itself, nor does it prescribe any condition of church-membership for the right of suffrage. It was the first written constitution known to [modern] history, that created a government, and it marked the beginnings of American democracy, of which Thomas Hooker deserves more than any other man to be called the father.

> "The government of the United States today is in lineal descent more nearly related to that of Connecticut than to that of any of the other thirteen colonies.... This little federal republic ... silently grew till it became the strongest political structure on the continent, as was illustrated in the remarkable military energy and the unshaken financial credit of Connecticut during the Rev-

olutionary War." (John Fiske, *The Beginnings of New England,* The Historical Writings of John Fiske, vol. 6, Houghton Mifflin Company, Boston, 1902, pp. 155-156.)

## American Constitution Represents Wisdom of Many

Montesquieu pointed out that when it comes to legislating (which includes the setting up of constitutions), the writing of the statute or charter is "oftentimes better regulated by many than by a single person." (*The Spirit of Laws*, p. 72.) In harmony with this same sentiment, the American Founding Fathers considered it wise to "legislate" their constitution by filtering it through the wisdom and experiences of many delegates assembled in a convention rather than leaving it to the genius of some individual. James Madison commented on this:

> "It is not a little remarkable that in every case reported by ancient history in which government has been established with deliberation and consent, the task of framing it has not been committed to an assembly of men, but has been performed by some individual citizen of preeminent wisdom and approved integrity.

> "Minos, we learn, was the primitive founder of the government of Crete, as Zaleucus was of that of the Locrians. Theseus first, and after him Draco and Solon, instituted the government of Athens. Lycurgus was the lawgiver of Sparta. The foundation of the original government of Rome was laid by Romulus, and the work completed by two of his elective successors, Numa and Tullius Hostilius. On the abolition of royalty the consular administration was substituted by Brutus, who stepped forward with a project for such reform, which, he alleged, had been prepared by Servius Tullius, and to which his address obtained the assent and ratification of the senate and people. This remark is applicable to confederate governments also. Amphictyon, we are told, was the author of that which bore his name. The Achaean league received its first birth from Achaeus, and its second from Aratus." (*The Federalist Papers*, No. 38, pp. 231-232.)

It is always difficult to operate through a committee, a group, or a convention as the Founding Fathers did. Nevertheless, the history of the convention demonstrates that the final product was far stronger than any individual could have written it. Time has also proven the tremendous advantage of having a completely written document for reference purposes rather than relying upon tradition and a few scattered statutes as the fundamental law of the land.

# 19th

## Principle

**Only limited and carefully defined powers should be delegated to government, all others being retained in the people.**

No principle was emphasized more vigorously during the Constitutional Convention than the necessity of limiting the authority of the federal government. Not only was this to be done by carefully defining the powers delegated to the government, but the Founders were determined to bind down its administrators with legal chains codified in the Constitution.

It will be recalled that one of the reasons many of the states would not adopt the original draft of the Constitution was that they feared the encroachments of the federal government on the rights of the states and the people The first ten amendments were therefore added to include the ancient, unalienable rights of Anglo-Saxon freemen so there could be no question as to the strictly limited authority the people were conferring on their central government. Notice how carefully the Ninth and Tenth Amendments are worded:

### The Ninth Amendment

The enumeration in the Constitution, of certain rights, shall not be construed to deny or disparage others retained by the people.

### The Tenth Amendment

The powers not delegated to the United States by the Constitution, nor prohibited by it to the States, are reserved to the States respectively, or to the people.

The people felt that the hedging up of federal authority was absolutely essential because of their experience with corrupt and abusive governments in the past. Alexander Hamilton commented on this by saying:

"There is, in the nature of sovereign power, an impatience of control that disposes those who are invested with the exercise of it to look with an evil eye upon all external attempts to restrain or direct its operations.... This tendency is not difficult to be accounted for. It has its origin in the love of power. Power controlled or abridged is almost always the rival and enemy of that power by which it is controlled or abridged. This simple proposition will teach us how little reason there is to expect that the persons entrusted with the administration of the affairs of the particular members of a confederacy [the federal government] will at all times be ready with perfect good humor and an unbiased regard to the public weal to execute the resolutions or decrees of the general authority. The reverse of this [expectation] results from the constitution of man." (*The Federalist Papers*, No. 15, p. 111.)

### Original Balance Between Federal Government and States

The separation of powers between the states and the federal government was designed to reinforce the principle of limited government. The federal government was supreme in all matters relating to its responsibility, but it was specifically restricted from invading the independence and sovereign authority reserved to the States. The Founders felt that unless this principle of dual sovereignty was carefully perpetuated, the healthy independence of each would deteriorate and eventually one or the other would become totally dominant. If the federal government became dominant, it would mean the end of local self-government and the security of the individual. On the other hand, if the states became dominant, the federal government would become so weak that the structure of the nation would begin to fractionalize and disintegrate into smaller parts. Alexander Hamilton emphasized these views of the Founders when he wrote:

"This balance between the national and state governments ought to be dwelt on with peculiar attention, as it is of the utmost importance. It forms a double security to the people. If one encroaches on their rights, they will find a powerful protection in the other. Indeed, they will both be prevented from over-passing their constitutional limits, by certain rivalship which will ever subsist between them." (Quoted in Lord Acton, *Essays on Freedom and Power*, The Free Press, Glencoe, Illinois, 1949, p. 218.)

## Where Power Rivals Power

The Founders felt that by having a wholesome balance between the federal and state governments, the people would have recourse to one or the other in case of usurpation or abuse by either. Commenting further on this, Hamilton said:

> "Power being almost always the rival of power, the general government will at all times stand ready to check the usurpations of the state governments, and these will have the same disposition towards the general government. The people, by throwing themselves into either scale, will infallibly make it preponderate. If their rights are invaded by either, they can make use of the other as the instrument of redress." (*The Federalist Papers*, No. 28, p. 181.)

## Why the Founders Would Have Frowned on the 17th Amendment

But would the states be able to protect themselves from the might of the federal government if the Congress began legislating against states' rights? Originally, the states could protect themselves because U.S. Senators were appointed by the state legislatures, and the Senate could veto any legislation by the House of Representatives which they considered a threat to the rights of the individual states. Unfortunately, the protection of states' rights by this means was completely wiped out by the passage of the Seventeenth Amendment in 1913.

That amendment provided that Senators would thenceforth be elected by popular ballot rather than appointed by the state legislatures. This meant the states as sovereign commonwealths had lost their representation on the federal level, and their Senators would be subject to the same popular pressures during an election campaign as those which confront the members of the House of Representatives.

Since that time, there has been no veto power which the states could exercise against the Congress in those cases where a federal statute was deemed in violation of states' rights. The Senators who used to be beholden to their state legislatures for their conduct in Washington are now beholden to the popular electorate. Federal funds appropriated for a state are generally a source of popular acclaim, and Senators, like Congressmen, usually hasten to get them approved. Too often it has been of little consequence that those funds might be expended in violation of basic powers reserved to the state.

Sometime in the not-too-distant future, the people may want to take another look at the present trend and consider the advantages of returning to the Founders' policy of having state legislatures in the United States Senate. It might give us another generation of Senators like Daniel Webster, John Calhoun, and Henry Clay.

# 20th
## Principle

**Efficiency and dispatch require government to operate according to the will of the majority, but constitutional provisions must be made to protect the rights of the minority.**

*"Give me your tired, your poor,*
*your huddled masses yearning to breathe free ..."*
— Inscription on the Statue of Liberty,
from a poem written by Emma Lazarus

One of the most serious mistakes in the structure of the Articles of Confederation was the requirement that no changes could be made without the approval of every one of the states. During the Revolutionary War several vital changes were suggested, but in each instance a single state was able to prevent the needed change from being adopted.

### Basis for the "Majority" Rule

Delaying action until it had the unanimous approval of all concerned can be disastrous in a time of emergency. It even inhibits healthy progress in normal times. Unanimity is the ideal, but majority rule becomes a necessity. The theory of majority rule was explained by John Locke as follows:

> "When any number of men have ... consented to make one community or government, they are thereby presently incorporated, and make one body politic, wherein the majority have a

right to act and conclude [bind] the rest.... It being one body ... it is necessary the body should move that way whither the greater force carries it, which is the consent of majority, or else it is impossible it should act or continue one body.... And thus every man, by consenting with others to make one body politic under one government, puts himself under an obligation to every one of that society to submit to the determination of the majority, and to be concluded [bound] by it." (John Locke, *Second Essay Concerning Civil Government*, pp. 46-47, par. 95-97.)

## Problem of Securing "Unanimous Consent"

John Locke then dealt with the problem of having to wait on unanimous decision before any action can be taken. He stated:

"For if the consent of the majority shall not in reason be received as the act of the whole ... nothing but the consent of every individual can make anything to be the act of the whole, which, considering the infirmities of health and avocations of business which ... will necessarily keep many away from the public assembly; and the variety of opinions and contrariety of interests which unavoidably happen in all collections of men, it is next [to] impossible ever to be had." (*Ibid.*, p. 98)

## Majority Rule a Necessity

It has sometimes been argued that a bare majority of one person scarcely justifies the making of a final decision for the whole body. It has been argued that it would be better to have a substantial majority of perhaps two-thirds or three-fourths. In the Constitution a provision of this type was incorporated in the text for the purpose of initiating amendments. A two-thirds majority is also required for the purpose of overriding a Presidential veto. Nevertheless, this requirement was considered dangerous when applied to the routine business of the Congress. Alexander Hamilton explained it as follows:

"To give a minority a negative upon the majority (which is always the case where more than a majority is requisite to a decision) is, in its tendency, to subject the sense of the greater number to that of the lesser number.... The necessity of unanimity in public bodies, or something approaching towards it, has been founded upon a supposition that it would contribute to security. But its real operation is to embarrass the administration, to destroy the energy of the government, and to substitute the pleasure, caprice, or artifices of an insignificant, turbulent, or corrupt junta to the regular deliberations and decisions of a respectable majority....

"The public business must in some way or other go forward. If a pertinacious minority can control the opinion of a majority, respecting the best mode of conducting it, the majority in order that something may be done must conform to the views of the minority; and thus the sense of the smaller number will overrule that of the greater and give a tone to the national proceedings. Hence, tedious delays; continual negotiation and intrigue; contemptible compromises of the public good." (*The Federalist Papers*, No. 22, pp. 147-48.)

### Minorities Have Equal Rights

Nevertheless, the American Founders had suffered enough from the tyrannical conduct of Parliament to feel highly sensitive to the rights of minorities. Thomas Jefferson referred to this in his first inaugural address on March 4, 1801, when he said:

"All, too, will bear in mind this sacred principle, that though the will of the majority is in all cases to prevail, that will to be rightful must be reasonable; that the minority possess their equal rights, which equal laws must protect, and to violate would be oppression." (Bergh, *Writings of Thomas Jefferson*, 3:318.)

We have already treated the problems faced by minorities. It is important for us to remember that every ethnic group in the United States was once a minority. We are literally a nation of minorities. However, it is the newcomers who feel they are not yet first-class citizens.

It is the responsibility of the minorities themselves to learn the language, seek needed education, become self-sustaining, and make themselves recognized as a genuine asset to the community. Meanwhile, those who are already well established can help. The United States has built a reputation of being more generous and helpful to newcomers than any other nation. It is a reputation worth preserving. Once upon a time, we were all minorities.

# 21st

## Principle

### Strong local self-government is the
### keystone to preserving human freedom.

Political power automatically gravitates toward the center, and the purpose of the Constitution is to prevent that from happening. The centralization of political power always destroys liberty by removing the decision-making function from the people on the local level and transferring it to the officers of the central government. This process gradually benumbs the spirit of "voluntarism" among the people, and they lose the will to solve their own problems. They also cease to be involved in community affairs. They seek the anonymity of oblivion in the seething crowds of the city and often degenerate into faceless automatons who have neither a voice nor a vote.

### The Golden Key to Preserving Freedom

How different from the New England town spirit, where every person had a voice and a vote. How different from the Anglo-Saxon tribal meetings, where the people were considered sovereign and every man took pride in participating. And how different from ancient Israel, where the families of the people were governed in multiples of tens, fifties, hundreds, and thousands, and where problems were solved on the level where those problems originated. All of those societies had strong local self-government. This is what the Founding Fathers considered the golden key to preserving freedom.

### Jefferson Compares New England with Virginia

Thomas Jefferson saw the advantages of the close-knit New England town over the aristocratic rural life of Virginia. Said he:

"These wards, called townships in New England, are the vital principle of their governments, and have proved themselves the wisest invention ever devised by the wit of man for the perfect exercise of self government, and for its preservation." (Bergh, *Writings of Thomas Jefferson*, 15:38.)

Jefferson was anxious to have all the English colonists in America revive the customs of their Anglo-Saxon ancestors, including strong local self-government. As historian Richard Frothingham points out:

"In ancient England, local self-government is found in connection with the political and territorial divisions of *tythings*, *hundreds*, *burghs*, *counties*, and *shires*, in which the body of inhabitants had a voice in managing their own affairs. Hence it was the germinal idea of the Anglo-Saxon polity.

"In the course of events, the Crown deprived the body of the people of this power of local rule, and vested it in a small number of persons in each locality, who were called municipal councils, were clothed with the power of filling vacancies in their number, and were thus self-perpetuating bodies. In this way, the ancient freedom of the municipalities was undermined, and the power of the ruling classes was installed in its place. Such was the nature of the local self-government in England, not merely during the period of the planting of her American colonies (1607 to 1732), but for a century later.... It was a noble form robbed of its life-giving spirit." (Richard Frothingham, *The Rise of the Republic of the United States*, Little, Brown and Company, Boston, 1873, pp. 14-15.)

### The Instinct for Self-Government Survives

Nevertheless, Frothingham points out that these ancient institutions were not entirely forgotten by the people. He quotes the French historian and statesman Francois Guizot as saying:

"When there scarcely remained traces of popular assemblies, the remembrance of them, of the right of freemen to deliberate and transact their business together, resided in the minds of men as a primitive tradition, and a thing which might come about again." (*Ibid.*, p. 15.)

Frothingham says this is exactly what happened as Englishmen pulled away from the mother country and migrated to America. He says that in the colonies, "These assemblies reappeared, and old rights were again en-joyed, when the emigrants to the soil now the United States began to frame the laws under which they were to live." (*Ibid.*)

### Jefferson Emphasizes the Role of Strong Local Self-Government

As the Founders wrote their laws, they were determined to protect the freedom of the individual and provide a vigorous climate of healthy, local self-government. Only those things which related to the interest of the entire commonwealth were to be delegated to the central government. Thomas Jefferson probably said it better than anyone when he wrote:

> "The way to have good and safe government is not to trust it all to one, but to divide it among the many, distributing to every one exactly the functions he is competent to [perform best]. Let the national government be entrusted with the defense of the na-tion, and its foreign and federal relations; the State governments with the civil rights, laws, police, and administration of what con-cerns the State generally; the counties with the local concerns of the counties, and each ward [township] direct the interests within itself. It is by dividing and subdividing these republics, from the great national one down through all its subordinations, until it ends in the administration of every man's farm by himself; by placing under every one what his own eye may superintend, that all will be done for the best. What has destroyed liberty and the rights of man in every government which has ever existed under the sun? The generalizing and concentrating all cares and powers into one body, no matter whether of the autocrats of Russia or France, or of the aristocrats of a Venetian senate." (Bergh, *Writings of Thomas Jefferson*, 14:421.)

### Deployment of Power Between the Federal Government and the States

James Madison, who is sometimes described as "the father of the Constitution," emphasized the necessity to reserve all possible authority in the states and the people. The Constitution delegates to the federal gov-ernment only that which involves the whole people as a nation. He wrote:

> "The powers delegated by the proposed Constitution to the federal government are few and defined. Those which are to re-main in the State governments are numerous and indefinite. The former [federal powers] will be exercised principally on external objects, as war, peace, negotiation, and foreign commerce.... The powers reserved to the several States will extend to all the ob-

jects which, in the ordinary course of affairs, concern the lives, liberties, and properties of the people, and the internal order, improvement, and prosperity of the State." (*The Federalist Papers*, No. 45, pp. 292-293.)

## Federal Government to Remain Relatively Small

Thomas Jefferson emphasized that if the oncoming generations perpetuated the Constitutional pattern, the federal government would be small and cohesive and would serve as an inexpensive operation because of the limited problems which would be assigned to it. He wrote:

> "The true theory of our Constitution is surely the wisest and best, that the states are independent as to everything within, themselves, and united as to everything respecting foreign nations. Let the general government be reduced to foreign concerns only, and let our affairs be disentangled from those of all other nations, except as to commerce, which the merchants will manage the better, the more they are left free to manage for themselves, and our general government may be reduced to a very simple organization, and a very inexpensive one; a few plain duties to be performed by a few servants." (Bergh, *Writings of Thomas Jefferson*, 10:168.)

## A Prophecy

One of the greatest American historians of the last generation was John Fiske. He caught the spirit of the Founders and studied their writings. He knew the secret to the 5,000 year leap which was then well on its way. He also saw some dangerous trends away from the Founders' basic formula of sound government. He therefore wrote a prophecy which Americans of our own day might ponder with profit:

> "If the day should ever arrive (which God forbid!) when the people of the different parts of our country shall allow their local affairs to be administered by prefects sent from Washington, and when the self government of the states shall have been so far lost as that of the departments of France, or even so closely limited as that of the counties of England -- on that day the political career of the American people will have been robbed of its most interesting and valuable features, and the usefulness of this nation will be lamentably impaired." (John Fiske, *The Critical Period of American History,* 1783-1789, The Historical Writings of John Fiske, vol. 12, Houghton Mifflin Company, Boston, 1916,)

# 22nd
## Principle

**A free people should be governed by
law and not by the whims of men.**

To be governed by the whims of men is to be subject to the ever-changing capriciousness of those in power. This is ruler's law at its worst. In such a society nothing is dependable. No rights are secure. Things established in the present are in a constant state of flux. Nothing becomes fixed and predictable for the future.

### Law as a "Rule of Action"

The American Founders and their Anglo-Saxon forebears had an entirely different point of view. They defined law as a "rule of action" which was intended to be as binding on the ruler as it was upon the people. It was designed to give society a stable frame of reference so the people could feel secure in making plans for the future. As John Locke said:

> "Freedom of men under government is to have a standing rule to live by, common to everyone of that society, and made by the legislative power erected in it." (*Second Essay Concerning Civil Government*, p. 29, par. 21.)

Under established law every person's rights and duties are defined. Anglo-Saxon common law provided a framework of relative security and a sense of well-being for people and things, both present and future. This is the security which is designed to provide a high degree of freedom from fear and therefore freedom to act. Such a society gives its people a sense of liberty -- liberty under law. The American Founders believed that without the protection of law there can be no liberty.

### Responsibility of Society to Establish Fixed Laws

John Locke pointed out that unless a society can provide a person with a code of fixed and enforceable laws, he might as well have stayed in the jungle:

> "To this end it is that men give up all their natural power to the society they enter into, and the community put the legislative power into such hands as they think fit, with this trust, that they shall be governed by declared laws, or else their peace, quiet, and property will still be at the same uncertainty as it was in the state of Nature." (*Ibid.*, p. 56, par. 136.)

### John Adams

John Adams expressed the same tenor of thought when he said:

> "No man will contend that a nation can be free that is not governed by fixed laws. All other government than that of permanent known laws is the government of mere will and pleasure." (*A Defense of the Constitutions of Government of the United States*, 3 vols., Bud and Bartram, Philadelphia, 1797, 1:124.)

### Aristotle

Human experience has taught mankind this same principle down through the ages. Here are the words of Aristotle in his Politics:

> "Even the best of men in authority are liable to be corrupted by passion. We may conclude then that the law is reason without passion, and it is therefore preferable to any individual." (Quoted by Edwin S. Corwin in "The Higher Law — Background of American Constitutional Law," *Harvard Law Review*, 1928, 42:155.)

### Plato Was Wrong

We deduct from this that Aristotle had concluded that the teachings of his mentor, Plato, were wrong. Plato believed that in the ideal society the people should be governed "by the few" who would rule according to "scientific principles" and make on-the-spot decisions to force the people to do what is good for them. (Benjamin Jowett, trans., *The Dialogues of Plato*, Great Books of the Western World, vol. 7, Encyclopedia Britannica, Inc., Chicago, 1952, p. 599.) Plato argued that these men must not be restricted by written laws but should govern the people in whatever manner they felt was for the best. He said:

> "The best thing of all is not that the law should rule, but that a man should rule, supposing him to have wisdom and royal power." (*Ibid.*)

Plato acknowledged that in the absence of rulers with the "scientific" wisdom to govern, a code of laws would be needed, but he insisted that this would be the "second best thing."

### Law Is a Positive Good in Preserving Liberty

As we have seen, the American Founding Fathers would have agreed with Aristotle rather than Plato. Part of this was due to the fact that the Founders looked upon law differently than Plato. Instead of treating law as merely a code of negative restraints and prohibitions, they considered law to be a system of positive rules by which they could be assured of enjoying their rights and the protection of themselves, their families, and their property. In other words, law was a positive good rather than a necessary evil. This was precisely the view of John Locke when he wrote:

> "The end of law is not to abolish or restrain but to preserve and enlarge freedom. For in all the states of created beings, capable of laws, where there is no law there is no freedom. For liberty is to be free from restraint and violence from others, which cannot be where there is no law." (*Second Essay Concerning Civil Government*, p. 37, par. 57.)

### Law Should Be Understandable and Stable

The Founders were sensitive to the fact that the people have confidence in the law only to the extent that they can understand it and feel that it is a rule of relative permanence which will not be continually changed. James Madison emphasized both of these points when he wrote:

> "It will be of little avail to the people that the laws are made by men of their own choice if the laws be so voluminous that they cannot be read, or so incoherent that they cannot be understood; if they be repealed or revised before they are promulgated, or undergo such incessant changes that no man, who knows what the

law is today, can guess what it will be tomorrow. Law is defined to be a rule of action; but how can that be a rule, which is little known and less fixed?" (*The Federalist Papers*, No. 62, p. 381.)

It will be recalled that Thomas Jefferson resigned from Congress in 1776 to hasten back to Virginia and volunteer for the task of rewriting the state laws so that, when independence had been won, the people would have a model system of legal principles which they could understand and warmly support. The complex codes of laws and regulations in our own day could be greatly improved through a similar housecleaning.

# 23rd
## Principle

**A free society cannot survive as a republic
without a broad program of general education.**

The English colonists in America undertook something which no nation had ever attempted before -- the educating of the whole people. The colonists had a sense of "manifest destiny" which led them to believe that they must prepare themselves for a most unique and important role in the unfolding of modern world history. Universal education was therefore considered an indispensable ingredient in this preparation.

### John Adams Describes Beginning of Public Education

The movement for universal education began in New England. Clear back in 1647 the legislature of Massachusetts passed a law requiring every community of fifty families or householders to set up a free public grammar school to teach the fundamentals of reading, writing, ciphering, history, geography, and Bible study. In addition, every township containing 100 families or more was required to set up a secondary school in advanced studies to prepare boys for attendance at Harvard. John Adams stated that this whole program was designed to have "knowledge diffused generally through the whole body of the people." He said:

> "They made an early provision by law that every town consisting of so many families should be always furnished with a grammar school. They made it a crime for such a town to be des-

titute of a grammar schoolmaster for a few months, and subjected it to heavy penalty. So that the education of all ranks of people was made the care and expense of the public, in a manner that I believe has been unknown to any other people, ancient or modern.

"The consequences of these establishments we see and feel every day [written in 1765]. A native of America who cannot read and write is as rare ... as a comet or an earthquake. It has been observed that we are all of us lawyers, divines, politicians, and philosophers. And I have good authorities to say that all candid foreigners who have passed through this country and conversed freely with all sorts of people here will allow that they have never seen so much knowledge and civility among the common people in any part of the world.... liberty cannot be preserved without a general knowledge among the people.... They have a right, an indisputable, unalienable, indefeasible, divine right to that most dreaded and envied kind of knowledge -- I mean, of the characters and conduct of their rulers." (Koch, *The American Enlightenment*, p. 239.)

## Importance of Good Local School Boards

The success of this educational effort was due largely to the careful selection of highly conscientious people to serve on the school committees in each community and supervise the public schools. Historian John Fiske says these school committees were bodies of "great importance." Then he adds:

"The term of service of the members is three years, one third being chosen annually. The number of members must therefore be some multiple of three. The slow change in the membership of the board insures that a large proportion of the members shall always be familiar with the duties of the place. The school committee must visit all the public schools at least once a month, and make a report to the town every year. It is for them to decide what textbooks are to be used. They examine candidates for the position of teacher and issue certificates to those whom they select." (Fiske, *Civil Government in the United States*, Houghton, Mifflin and Company, Boston, 1890], pp. 22-23.)

## European and American Literacy Compared

The unique and remarkable qualities of this program are better appreciated when it is realized that this was an age when illiteracy was the common lot of most people in Europe. John Adams, who spent many years in France, commented on the fact that of the 24 million inhabitants of France, only 500,000 could read and write. (Koch, *The American Enlightenment*, pp. 213, 217.)

In the American colonies the intention was to have all children taught the fundamentals of reading, writing, and arithmetic so that they could go on to become well informed citizens through their own diligent self-study. No doubt this explains why all of the American Founders were so well read, and usually from the same books, even though a number of them had received a very limited formal education. The fundamentals were sufficient to get them started, and thereafter they became remarkably well informed in a variety of areas through self-learning. This was the pattern followed by both Franklin and Washington.

## De Tocqueville Comments on American Education in 1831

Gradually, the zeal for universal education spread from New England to all of the other colonies. By 1831, when Alexis de Tocqueville of France visited the United States, he was amazed by the fruits of this effort. He wrote:

> "The observer who is desirous of forming an opinion on the state of instruction among the Anglo Americans must consider the same object from two different points of view. If he singles out only the learned, he will be astonished to find how few they are; but if he counts the ignorant, the American people will appear to be the most enlightened in the world....

> "In New England every citizen receives the elementary notions of human knowledge; he is taught, moreover, the doctrines and the evidences of his religion, the history of his country, and the leading features of its Constitution. In the states of Connecticut and Massachusetts, it is extremely rare to find a man imperfectly acquainted with all these things, and a person wholly ignorant of them is a sort of phenomenon." (Alexis de Tocqueville, *Democracy in America*, 1:326-327.)

## Excursions in the Wilderness

De Tocqueville pointed out that as the visitor advanced toward the West or the South, "the instruction of the people diminishes." Nevertheless, he said, "there is not a single district in the United States sunk in complete ignorance...." (*Ibid.*, 1:327.) De Tocqueville made extensive excursions along the frontier and commented on his observations as follows:

> "At the extreme borders of the confederated states, upon the confines of society and wilderness, a population of bold adventurers have taken up their abode, who pierce the solitudes of the American woods.... As soon as the pioneer reaches the place which is to serve him for a retreat, he fells a few trees and builds a log house. Nothing can offer a more miserable aspect than these isolated dwellings.... Yet no sort of comparison can be drawn between the pioneer and the dwelling that shelters him. Everything about him is primitive and wild, but he is himself the result of the labor and experience of eighteen centuries. He wears the dress and speaks the language of cities; he is acquainted with the past, curious about the future, and ready for argument about the present; he is, in short, a highly civilized being, who consents for a time to inhabit the backwoods, and who penetrates into the wilds of the New World with the Bible, an axe, and some newspaper. It is difficult to imagine the incredible rapidity with which thought circulates in the midst of these deserts [wilderness]. I do not think that so much intellectual activity exists in the most enlightened and populous districts of France." (*Ibid*, 1:328-29.)

## Education Includes Morality and Politics

He then went on to comment concerning the close relationship between the program of universal education and the preservation of freedom:

> "It cannot be doubted that in the United States the instruction of the people powerfully contributes to the support of the democratic republic; and such must always be the case, I believe, where the instruction which enlightens the understanding is not separated from the moral education.... An American should never be led to speak of Europe, for he will then probably display much presumption and very foolish pride.... But if you question him respecting his own country, the cloud that dimmed his intelli-

gence will immediately disperse; his language will become as clear and precise as his thoughts. He will inform you what his rights are and by what means he exercises them; he will be able to point out the customs which obtain in the political world. You will find that he is well acquainted with the rules of the administration, and that he is familiar with the mechanism of the laws.... The American learns to know the laws by participating in the act of legislation; and he takes a lesson in the forms of government from governing. The great work of society is ever going on before his eyes and, as it were, under his hands.

"In the United States, politics are the end and aim of education...." (*Ibid.*, 1:329-330.)

### Even Young Children Trained in the Constitution

To appreciate the literal reality of the emphasis on politics in early American education, one need only examine the popular textbook on political instruction for children. It was called a "Catechism on the Constitution," and it contained both questions and answers concerning the principles of the American political system. It was written by Arthur J. Stansbury and published in 1828.

Early Americans knew they were in possession of a unique and valuable invention of political science, and they were determined to promote it on all levels of education.

### Early Americans Educated to Speak with Eloquence

In 1843, Daniel Webster made a statement which might surprise Americans of our own day:

"And whatever may be said to the contrary, a correct use of the English language is, at this day [1843], more general throughout the United States than it is throughout England herself." (*The Works of Daniel Webster*, 6 vols., Little, Brown and Company, Boston, 1851, 1:102.)

It was commonplace for the many people on the frontier, as well as on the Atlantic seaboard, to speak with a genuine flavor of eloquence. Sermons and orations by men of limited formal education reflected a flourish and style of expression which few Americans could duplicate today. Many of these attributed their abilities to extensive reading of the Bible. Such was the case with Abraham Lincoln. Certainly the classical beauty of the Gettysburg Address and his many other famous expressions cannot be attributed to college training, for he had none.

## Cultural Influence of Extensive Bible Reading

Not only did the Bible contribute to the linguistic habits of the people, but it provided root strength to their moral standards and behavioral patterns. As Daniel Webster stated, wherever Americans went, "the Bible came with them." Then he added:

> "It is not to be doubted, that to the free and universal reading of the Bible, in that age, men were much indebted for right views of civil liberty. The Bible is a book of faith, and a book of doctrine, and a book of morals, and a book of religion, of especial revelations from God; but it is also a book which teaches man his own individual responsibility, his own dignity, and his equality with his fellow-man." (*Ibid.*)

In our own day the public schools have been secularized to the point where no Bible reading is permitted. The Founding Fathers would have counted this a serious mistake.

# 24th

## Principle

**A free people will not survive unless they stay strong.**

Afree people in a civilized society always tend toward prosperity. In the case of the United States, the trend has been toward a super-abundant prosperity. Only as the federal government has usurped authority and intermeddled with the free-market economy has this surge of prosperity and high production of goods and services been inhibited.

But prosperity in the midst of thriving industry, fruitful farms, beautiful cities, and flourishing commerce always attracts the greedy aspirations of predatory nations. Singly, these covetous predators may not pose a threat, but federated together they may present a spectre of total desolation to a free, prosperous people. Before the nation's inhabitants are aware, their apocalypse of destruction is upon them.

It was the philosophy of the Founders that the kind hand of Providence had been everywhere present in allowing the United States to come forth as the first free people in modern times. They further felt that they would forever be blessed with freedom and prosperity if they remained a virtuous and adequately armed nation.

### Franklin's Philosophy of Defense

Clear back in 1747, Benjamin Franklin vividly comprehended the task ahead. Said he:

"Were this Union formed, were we once united, thoroughly armed and disciplined, were everything in our power done for our security, as far as human means and foresight could provide, we might then, with more propriety, humbly ask the assistance of heaven and a blessing on our lawful endeavors." (Smyth, *Writings of Benjamin Franklin*, 2:352.)

Peace was the goal, but strength was the means. Franklin envisioned the day when a prudent policy of national defense would provide the American people with the protection which their rise to greatness would require. He wrote:

"The very fame of our strength and readiness would be a means of discouraging our enemies; for 'tis a wise and true saying, that 'One sword often keeps another in the scabbard.' The way to secure peace is to be prepared for war. They that are on their guard, and appear ready to receive their adversaries, are in much less danger of being attacked than the supine, secure and negligent." (*Ibid.*)

Franklin further saw that those in authority have the inherent responsibility to initiate the means by which adequate defenses can be provided. He declared:

"Protection is as truly due from the government to the people, as obedience from the people [is due] to the government." (*Ibid.*, p. 347)

In later life he held to the same solid philosophy of peace through strength as an assurance of survival in the future:

"Our security lies, I think, in our growing strength, both in numbers and wealth, that creates an increasing ability of assisting this nation in its wars, which will make us more respectable, our friendship more valued, and our enmity feared; thence it will soon be thought proper to treat us not with justice only, but with kindness, and thence we may expect in a few years a total change of measures with regard to us; unless, by a neglect of military discipline, we should lose all martial spirit, and our western people become as tame as those in the eastern dominions of Britain [India], when we may expect the same oppressions; for there is much truth in the Italian saying, 'Make yourselves sheep, and the wolves will eat you.' (*Ibid.*, 6:3-4.)

### Franklin Disgusted with Popular Apathy

Franklin had a low opinion of people who waved the flag of liberty but would do little or nothing to provide the means for defending it. His mind-set called for action to back up the words. Writing from England, he declared:

> "Our people certainly ought to do more for themselves. It is absurd, the pretending to be lovers of liberty while they grudge paying for the defense of it. It is said here, that an impost of five percent on all goods imported, though a most reasonable proposition, had not been agreed to by all the States, and was therefore frustrated; and that your newspapers acquaint the world with this, with the non-payment of taxes by the people, and with the non-payment of interest to the creditors of the public. The knowledge of these things will hurt our credit." (*Ibid.*, 8:645.)

### The Thoughts of George Washington

George Washington is often described as "First in peace, first in war, first in the hearts of his countrymen."

No American occupied a more substantive position, either then or now, to proclaim what he considered to be a necessary posture for the preservation of the nation. He had literally risked "his life, his fortune, and his sacred honor" for the cause of freedom and performed that task under circumstances which would have smothered the endurance of men with lesser stamina and courage. He fought the Revolutionary War with no navy of any consequence, no trained professional army of either size or stability, and no outpouring of genuine support from the very states he was striving to save. He could have retired in bitterness after Valley Forge and Morristown, but that was not his character. He did not relish the anguish of it all, but he endured it. To George Washington, it was all part of "structuring a new nation."

Washington's position on national defense was in terms of grim realities experienced on the field of battle. No man wanted peace more than he. And no man was willing to risk more in life and property to achieve it. In nearly the same words as Franklin he declared:

> "To be prepared for war is one of the most effectual means of preserving peace." (Fitzpatrick, *Writings of George Washington*, 30:491.)

Washington also saw the fallacy of waiting until an attack had occurred before marshalling available resources. He wrote:

"A free people ought not only to be armed, but disciplined to which end a uniform and well-digested plan is requisite." (*Ibid.*)

Washington also saw the fallacy of a policy of indepenence with other nations which made the United States vulnerable in time of war. In his first annual address to Congress, he spoke of the people's general welfare, then stated:

"And their safety and interest require that they should promote such manufactories as tend to render them independent of others for essentials, particularly military supplies." (*Ibid.*)

Washington felt that neither politics nor world circumstances should lure the American people into a posture of complacency. He felt that vigilance was indeed the price of freedom, and unless it was promoted with firmness and consistency the future of the United States would be in jeopardy. In another speech he said:

"The safety of the United States, under divine protection, ought to rest on the basis of systematic and solid arrangements, exposed as little as possible to the hazards of fortuitous circumstances." (*Ibid.*, 31:403.)

### Washington's Fifth Annual Address to Congress

As President, Washington perceived the tendency of Congress to avoid its responsibility to provide adequate defenses. Because the President was personally responsible for the nation's foreign relations, he was well aware that the new born United States had a long way to go to insure decent respect and deference from the arrogant European powers. In his fifth annual address to Congress, he said:

"I cannot recommend to your notice measures for the fulfillment of our duties to the rest of the world, without again pressing upon you the necessity of placing ourselves in a condition of complete defense, and of exacting from them the fulfillment of their duties toward us." (*Ibid.*, 33:165.)

Washington could already see the predatory monarchs of Europe planning to slice up the United States and divide it among them unless the people alerted themselves to the exigencies of the day. The British still had their troops stationed along the northern border of U.S. territory. The Spanish had definite aspirations to make a thrust into the Mississippi heartland. From Washington's point of view, all was not well in America's happy valley. Therefore he told the Congress:

"There is a rank due to the United States among nations, which will be withheld, if not absolutely lost, by the reputation of weakness. If we desire to avoid insult, we must be able to repel it; if we desire to secure peace, one of the most powerful instruments of our rising prosperity, it must be known that we are at all times ready for war." (*Ibid.*, 33:165.)

## A Duty to the Creator to Preserve Freedom and Unalienable Rights

Samuel Adams emphasized the moral responsibility of Americans to preserve the heritage of freedom and unalienable rights with which the Creator had endowed them. Once these blessings have been vouchsafed to a human being, Sam Adams felt it was a wicked and unnatural thing to allow those great fruits of liberty to languish by neglect or apathy. When individuals combine into a society, they bring all of their natural rights with them. Under no circumstances must these be allowed to dwindle away. Said he:

"It is the greatest absurdity to suppose it [would be] in the power of one, or any number of men, at the entering into society, to renounce their essential natural rights, or the means of preserving those rights; when the grand end of civil government, from the very nature of its institution, is for the support, protection, and defense of those very rights; the principal of which ... are life, liberty, and property. If men, through fear, fraud, or mistake, should in terms renounce or give up any essential natural right, the eternal law of reason and the grand end of society would absolutely vacate such renunciation. The right to freedom being the gift of God Almighty, it is not in the power of man to alienate this gift and voluntarily become a slave." (Quoted in Wells, *Life of Samuel Adams*, 1:504.)

## The American Inheritance

Thus the Founders passed on to their posterity a policy of peace through strength. They were peace-loving, but not pacifists. They called for a rugged kind of strength bolted to a broad base. They saw the foundation for their security in a bustling, prosperous economy with a high standard of public morality; and they saw the necessity for a level of preparedness which discouraged attack from potential enemies by creating a rate of risk so high that the waging of war against this nation would be an obviously unprofitable undertaking.

As Samuel Adams wrote to a sympathetic friend in England:

"It is the business of America to take care of herself; her situation, as you justly observe, depends upon her own virtue." (*Ibid.*, 1:376.)

# 25th

## Principle

**"Peace, commerce, and honest friendship with
all nations -- entangling alliances with none."**

"Friendship with all ... alliances with none." -- Thomas Jefferson

These are the words of Thomas Jefferson, given in his first inaugural address. (Bergh, *Writings of Thomas Jefferson*, 3:321.)

As the United States emerged on the world scene in the eighteenth century, American leaders took a united and fixed position against entangling alliances with any foreign powers unless an attack against the United States made such alliances temporarily necessary.

This was the Founders' doctrine of "separatism." This was far different from the modern term of "isolationism." The latter term implies a complete seclusion from other nations, as though the United States were to be detached and somehow incubated in isolation from other nations.

In point of fact, the policy of the Founders was just the opposite. They desired to cultivate a wholesome relationship with all nations, but they wished to remain aloof from sectional quarrels and international disputes. They wanted to avoid alliances of friendship with one nation which would make them enemies of another nation in a time of crisis. They wanted to keep American markets open to all countries unless certain countries engaged in hostilities toward the United States.

### Switzerland Followed the Founders' Policy

The Founders' original policy was similar in many ways to that of modern Switzerland, which has successfully remained neutral and aloof from entangling alliances during two world wars and numerous European quarrels. During these periods of intense military action, Switzerland did not follow a policy of "isolationism," but one of universal diplomatic relations with all who might wish to come to Switzerland to buy, sell, borrow, or bank. She took a hostile posture toward none unless threatened. In general terms, this is analogous to the doctrine of "separatism" practiced by the early American leaders.

## Washington Describes the Founders' Plans

The universality of foreign relations which Washington hoped to engender is reflected in the following statement from his famous Farewell Address:

"Observe good faith and justice toward all nations. Cultivate peace and harmony with all. Religion and morality enjoin this conduct; and can it be that good policy does not equally enjoin it? It will be worthy of a free, enlightened, and, at no distant period, a great nation to give to mankind the magnanimous and too novel example of a people always guided by an exalted justice and benevolence." (Fitzpatrick, *Writings of George Washington*, 35:231.)

From experience Washington was well aware of the natural tendency to classify nations as "friends" or "enemies." He felt that in the absence of political, military, or commercial hostility toward the United States, every effort should be made to cultivate friendship with all. He wrote:

"In the execution of such a plan nothing is more essential than that permanent, inveterate antipathies against particular nations and passionate attachments for others should be excluded, and that in place of them just and amicable feelings toward all should be cultivated. The nation which indulges toward another an habitual hatred or an habitual fondness is in some degree a slave. It is a slave to its animosity or to its affection, either of which is sufficient to lead it astray from its duty and its interest." (*Ibid.*)

Washington pointed out that "antagonism by one nation against another disposes each more readily to offer insult and injury, to lay hold of slight causes of umbrage, and to be haughty and intractable when accidental or trifling occasions of dispute occur." (*Ibid.*)

## The Problem with "Playing Favorites"

By the same token, the United States could become overly attached to some nations because the people feel a special kinship or affection toward them. Washington warned:

> "So, likewise, a passionate attachment of one nation for another produces a variety of evils. Sympathy for the favorite nation, facilitating the illusion of an imaginary common interest in cases where no real common interest exists, and infusing into one the enmities of the other, betrays the former into a participation in the quarrels and wars of the latter without adequate inducement or justification. It leads also to concessions to the favorite nation of privileges denied to others, which is apt doubly to injure the nation making the concessions, by unnecessarily parting with what ought to have been retained, and by exciting jealousy, ill will, and disposition to retaliate in the parties from whom equal privileges are withheld." (*Ibid.*, p. 232)

## Concerning Most-favored Nations

Washington also warned that giving a more favored status to particular nations could open up the United States to strong foreign influences which could subvert the security or best interests of the United States. In fact, American officials seeking to accommodate friendly allies could inadvertently compromise American interests to a very dangerous extent. Washington said:

> "Against the insidious wiles of foreign influence, I conjure you to believe me, fellow citizens, the jealousy of a free people ought to be constantly awake, since history and experience prove that foreign influence is one of the most baneful foes of republican government. But that jealousy, to be useful, must be impartial, else it becomes the instrument of the very influence to be avoided instead of a defense against it. Excessive partiality for one foreign nation and excessive dislike of another cause those whom they actuate to see danger only on one side and serve to veil and even second the arts of influence on the others. Real patriots, who may resist the intrigues of the favorite, are liable to become suspected and odious, while its tools and dupes usurp the applause and confidence of the people to surrender their interests." (*Ibid.*, p. 233)

### What American Foreign Policy Should Be

Washington then made his famous declaration of the Founders' policy of foreign relations:

> "The great rule of conduct for us, in regard to foreign nations, is in extending our commercial relations to have with them as little political connection as possible. So far as we have already formed engagements, let them be fulfilled with perfect good faith. Here let us stop." (*Ibid.*)

Even within the previous few years, Washington had seen the tendency to get the United States embroiled in European disputes, and he saw them operating to the distinct disadvantage of the United States. Therefore, he warned:

> "Europe has a set of primary interests which to us have none, or a very remote relation. Hence she must be engaged in frequent controversies, the causes of which are essentially foreign to our concerns. Hence, therefore, it must be unwise in us to implicate ourselves, by artificial ties, in the ordinary combinations and collisions of her friendships or enmities.... Why, by interweaving our destiny with that of any part of Europe, entangle our peace and prosperity in the toils of European ambition, rivalship, interests, humor, or caprice?" (*Ibid.*, p. 234)

### A World Policy

And what he had said concerning Europe he would say to the rest of the world:

> "It is our true policy to steer clear of permanent alliances with any portion of the foreign world. So far, I mean, as we are now at liberty to do it, for let me not be understood as capable of patronizing infidelity to existing engagements (I hold the maxim no less applicable to public than to private affairs that honesty is always the best policy). I repeat it, therefore: let those engagements be observed in their genuine sense. But, in my opinion, it is unnecessary and would be unwise to extend them." (*Ibid.*)

He said that "temporary alliances" may be justified for "extraordinary emergencies," but other than that, "harmony, liberal intercourse with all nations are recommended by policy, humanity, and interest." (*Ibid.*, p. 235)

## Commercial Relations with Other Nations

Washington felt the same policy should apply to America's commercial relations with foreign countries:

> "But even our commercial policy should hold an equal and impartial hand, neither seeking nor granting exclusive favors or preferences; consulting the natural course of things; diffusing and diversifying by gentle means the streams of commerce but forcing nothing; establishing with powers so disposed, in order to give to trade a stable course, to define the rights of our merchants, and to enable the government to support them, conventional rules of intercourse, the best that present circumstances and mutual opinion will permit, but temporary and liable to be from time to time abandoned or varied, as experience and circumstances shall dictate." (*Ibid.*)

Washington was not in favor of the United States government begging for special privileges, monopolies, or advantages from other nations in commercial treaties. He said:

> "It is folly in one nation to look for disinterested favors from another; that it must pay with a portion of its independence for whatever it may accept under that character; that, by such acceptance, it may place itself in the condition of having given equivalents for nominal favors and yet of being reproached with ingratitude for not giving more. There can be no greater error than to expect, or calculate, upon real favors from nation to nation. It is an illusion which experience must cure, which a just pride ought to discard." (*Ibid.*)

Long after Washington was dead, Jefferson reiterated these same basic principles in a letter to James Monroe dated October 24, 1823:

> "Our first and fundamental maxim should be, never to entangle ourselves in the broils of Europe. Our second, never to suffer Europe to intermeddle with cis-Atlantic [western hemisphere] affairs. America, north and south, has a set of interests distinct from those of Europe, and peculiarly her own. She should therefore have a system of her own, separate and apart from that of Europe. While the last [Europe] is laboring to become the domicile of despotism, our endeavors should surely be to make our hemisphere that of freedom." (Bergh, *Writings of Thomas Jefferson*, 15:477.)

## The Founders' Effort to Reconcile
## "Separatism" with Manifest Destiny

American separatism did have one aspect which was clearly distinct from Swiss neutrality: the Founders accepted the doctrine of "Manifest Destiny." This placed upon the American people the responsibility of serving as the vanguard nation for the moral and political emancipation of all mankind. Freedom, education, and progress for all men were a common denominator in the thinking of early American leaders. As John Adams wrote:

> "I always consider the settlement of America with reverence and wonder, as the opening of a grand scene and design in Providence for the illumination of the ignorant, and the emancipation of the slavish part of mankind all over the earth." (Quoted in Ernest Lee Tuveson, *Redeemer Nation*, University of Chicago Press, Chicago, 1974, p. 25.)

> In the same spirit, James Madison wrote: "Happily for America, happily we trust for the whole human race, they [the Founders] pursued a new and more noble course." (*The Federalist Papers*, No. 14, p. 104.)

The Monroe Doctrine was specifically designed to insulate the western hemisphere from further contamination by quarreling European monarchs. The Founders hoped Mexico and each of the Latin American countries would gradually follow the example of the United States in becoming free, self-governing people. Once the spirit of freedom had encompassed North, Central, and South America, they hoped it would do just as James Madison said -- spread abroad until it had become the heritage of "the whole human race."

## "Separatism" Replaced by "Internationalism"

"Separatism," and pursuing a "manifest destiny" to encourage the emancipation of "the whole human race," was the official policy of the United States for the first 125 years of its history.

Nevertheless, there were powerful influences congregating in the United States, particularly in financial circles, which wanted America in the thick of things, world-wide. Their opportunity came with the eruption of World War I. Congressional investigations by the Reece Committee revealed that long before the Lusitania sinking, these influences were agitating for U.S. involvement. (See report of Norman Dodd, *Freemen Digest*, June 1978, p. 5.)

Although the United States narrowly avoided becoming a member of the League of Nations after World War I, the stage was set for an accelerated involvement of the United States, both economically and politically, in foreign quarrels.

### Congressman Charles A. Lindbergh Counts American "Internationalism" a Serious Mistake

After World War I, Congressman Charles A. Lindbergh, Sr., father of the famous "Lone Eagle" who was the first to fly the Atlantic, asked the people of the United States to reconsider the policy Washington was pursuing in its foreign affairs. He was particularly concerned about how Americans were pushed into World War I. In 1923 he wrote:

"Take for example our entry into the World War [in 1917]. We did not think. We elected a president for a second term because he said he 'kept us out of war' in his first term. We proved by a large vote that we did not want to go to war, but no sooner was the president re-elected than the propaganda started to put us to war. Then we became hysterical, as people always have done in war, and we believed everything bad against our enemy and believed only good of our allies and ourselves. As a matter of fact all the leaders were bad and vicious. They lost their reason and the people followed....

"We cannot properly blame the people of any of the European nations, unless we blame ourselves. None of them were free from danger of the others.... We, however, were not in danger, statements by profiteers and militarists to the contrary notwithstanding.... The greatest good we could do the world at that time was to stay out, and that would have been infinitely better for ourselves, for we could have helped the world had we conserved our resources.

"There never was a nation that did a more un-statesmanlike thing than we did to enter the war. We came out without establishing a single principle for which we entered....

"The one compelling duty of America is to put its own house in shape, and to stand upon an economic system that will make its natural resources available to the intelligence, industry and use of the people. When we do that the way to world redemption from the folly of present chaos will stand out in our country so clearly, honestly and usefully that we shall be copied wherever peoples do their own thinking. (Charles A. Lindbergh, Sr., *The Economic Pinch*, 1923, reprint ed., Omni Publications, Hawthorne, California, 1976, pp. 233-235.)

### Visualizing America as a World Peacemaker

As World War II broke out in Europe during September 1939, there was widespread hope among Americans that the United States could somehow resist the temptation to become involved. Highly perceptive leaders who had served in Washington and knew the tragic consequences of "internationalism" as a basic foreign policy raised warning voices against participation in another world war. One of these was a former Under-Secretary of State and former ambassador to Mexico. As a prominent writer on Constitutional issues, he consistently reflected the views of the Founders. In 1939 he gave a speech urging American leaders to recognize the role of America as a great world peacemaker. Said he:

"America, multi-raced and multi-nationed, is by tradition, by geography, by citizenry, by natural sympathy, and by material interest, the great natural nation of the earth. God so designed it. Drawn from all races, creeds, and nations, our sympathies run to every oppressed people. Our feelings engaged on opposite sides of great differences, will in their natural course, if held in due and proper restraint, neutralize the one [with] the other. Directed in right channels, this great body of feeling for the one side or the other will ripen into sympathy and love for all misguided and misled fellowmen who suffer in any cause, and this sympathy and love will run out to all humanity in its woe....

"One of the great tragedies of the war [World War II] now starting is that every people now engaged in it have been led into it without their fully knowing just where they are bound. The people themselves are largely innocent of this slaughter.... As the great neutral of the earth, America may play a far greater part in this war.... It is our solemn duty to play a better part than we can do by participating in the butchery....

"... having in mind our position as the great world neutral, and remembering that the people of these warring nations have been led into this conflict largely unwittingly, and therefore are largely blameless, we should announce our unalterable opposition to any plan to starve these innocent peoples involved in this conflict -- the women, the children, the sick, the aged, and the infirm -- and declare that when actual and bonafide mass starvation shall come to any of them, no matter who they are, we shall do all that we properly may do to see that they are furnished with food....

"If we shall rebuild our lost moral power and influence by measures such as these which will demonstrate our love for humanity, our justice, our fair-mindedness ... we shall then be where ... we can offer mediation between the two belligerents.

"America, the great neutral, will thus become the peacemaker of the world, which is her manifest destiny if she lives the law of peace." (Quoted in the *Freemen Digest*, October 1978, pp. 2-3.)

### A New Role for America?

Since the former Under-Secretary of State, J. Reuben Clark, Jr., gave this speech, the United States has been involved in three major wars, including the holocaust of World War II. Looking back, one cannot help wondering how much happier, more peaceful, and more prosperous the world would be if the United States had been following a policy of "separatism" as the world's great peacemaker instead of "internationalism" as the world's great policemen.

# 26th

## Principle

**The core unit which determines the strength of any society is the family; therefore, the government should foster and protect its integrity.**

The family-centered culture which developed in America was not the austere pattern developed in England or the profligate pattern which characterized France. Alexis de Tocqueville compared the American family with that of Europe in the following words:

"There is certainly no country in the world where the tie of marriage is more respected than in America, or where conjugal happiness is more highly or worthily appreciated. In Europe almost all the disturbances of society arise from the irregularities of domestic life. To despise the natural bonds and legitimate pleasure of home is to contract a taste for excesses, a restlessness of heart, and fluctuating desires. Agitated by the tumultuous passions that frequently disturb his dwelling, the European is galled by the obedience which the legislative powers of the state exact. But when the American retires from the turmoil of public life to the bosom of his family, he finds in it the image of order and of peace. There his pleasures are simple and natural, his joys are innocent and calm; and as he finds that an orderly life is the surest path to happiness, he accustoms himself easily to moderate his opinions as well as his tastes. While the European endeavors to forget his domestic troubles by agitating society, the American derives from his own home that love of order which he afterwards carries with him into public affairs." (Alexis de Tocqueville, *Democracy in America*, 1:315.)

### Equality of Men and Women Under God's Law

The American Founders felt that the legal, moral, and social relationships between husband and wife were clearly established by Bible law under what Dr. H. Carlton Marlow has described as "differential" equality. (Carlton Marlow and Harrison M. Davis, *The American Search for Woman*, Clio Books, Santa Barbara, California, 1976, chapter 5.)

The husband and wife each have their specific rights appropriate to their role in life, and otherwise share all rights in common. The role of the man is "to protect and provide." The woman's role is to strengthen the family solidarity in the home and provide a wholesome environment for her husband and children. For the purpose of order, the man was given the decision-making responsibilities for the family; and therefore when he voted in political elections, he not only cast a ballot for himself, but also for his wife and children.

In theory, God's law made man first in governing his family, but as between himself and his wife he was merely first among equals. The Apostle Paul pointed out in his epistle to the Corinthians:

> "Neither is the man without the woman, neither the woman without the man, in the Lord." (*1 Corinthians* 11:11.)

### "Father" and "Mother" Treated Equally in Scripture

John Locke wrote his Second Essay Concerning Civil Government just as the colonies were becoming established, and his thinking was reflected in the family life-style of the American colonies more than in England itself. He stressed the equal responsibility of mother and father in rearing the children. He stated that the term *paternal authority,*

> "... seems so to place the power of parents over their children wholly in the father, as if the mother had no share in it; whereas if we consult reason or revelation, we shall find she has an equal title, which may give one reason to ask whether this might not be more properly called parental power? For whatever obligation Nature and the right of generation lays on children, it must certainly bind them equally to both the concurrent causes of it. And

accordingly we see the positive law of God everywhere joins them together without distinction, when it commands the obedience of children: 'Honor thy father and thy mother' (Exodus 20:12); 'Whosoever curseth his father or his mother' (Leviticus 20:9); 'Ye shall fear every man his mother and his father' (Leviticus 19:3); 'Children, obey your parents' (Ephesians 6:1), etc., is the style of the Old and New Testament." (John Locke, *Second Essay Concerning Civil Government*, p. 36, par. 52.)

### The Early New England Family

There is no doubt that the family life-style of early Americans contributed significantly to their success. Speaking of the early New England families, historian Wallace Notestein writes:

> "It was the duty of husbands to love their wives and to have due regard for them. It was even suggested they should make financial allowances for them, as some Puritan gentlemen did, and give them a certain control over the household. What is more significant, Puritan writers had a great deal to say about the family and its unity. From diaries and biographies one gains an impression that husbands and wives in their common effort to bring about the kingdom of God on earth lived happily with one another. A common purpose was the best of all ties." (Wallace Notestein, *The English People on the Eve of Colonization*, 1603-1630, Harper Brothers, New York, 1954, p. 168.)

### A Note on Benjamin Franklin

Not only was the unity of men and women emphasized, but also the complete interdependence of a man and a woman for their mutual happiness. It may seem strange to quote Benjamin Franklin on this subject, since certain historians have entertained the public for years with the alleged romantic profligacy of the famous Franklin. In point of fact, he admits in his autobiography that after running away from his home as a youth he fell in with certain rough companions and later had a son whom he named William. Nevertheless, he raised his son honorably, and William eventually became governor of New Jersey. With reference to Franklin's later life, a specialist on his papers and background at Yale University, Dr. Claude-Anne Lopez, says the stories about his "thirteen illegitimate children" and similar wild stories have proven to be myths. She says careful research is disclosing that Franklin was not the philanderer many writers have represented him to be. (See Alice J. Hail, "Benjamin Franklin: Philosopher of Dissent," *National Geographic*, July 1975, p. 118.)

### Benjamin Franklin's Comment on Marriage

From his own pen, we have Franklin at the age of 46 emphasizing the importance of marriage as he attempted to dissuade a young friend from taking a mistress. He wrote:

"Marriage is the proper remedy. It is the most natural state of man, and therefore the state in which you are most likely to find solid happiness. Your reasons against entering into it at present appear to me not well founded. The circumstantial advantages you have in view by postponing it are not only uncertain, but they are small in comparison with that of the thing itself, the being *married* and *settled* [emphasis by Franklin]. It is the man and woman united that make the complete human being. Separate, she wants his force of body and strength of reason; he, her softness, sensibility, and acute discernment. Together they are more likely to succeed in the world. A single man has not nearly the value he would have in that state of union. He is an incomplete animal. He resembles the odd half of a pair of scissors. If you get a prudent, healthy wife, your industry in your profession, with her good economy, will be a fortune sufficient." (Koch, *The American Enlightenment*, p. 70.)

### Responsibility of Parents to Children

The trilateral construction of the family, consisting of father, mother, and children, raises the basic question of the duty of the parents to the children and the respect which the children owe their parents. Locke stated that the authority of parents over children is based on an important principle of natural law:

"The power, then, that parents have over their children arises from that duty which is incumbent on them, to take care of their offspring during the imperfect state of childhood. To inform the mind, and govern the actions of their yet ignorant nonage, till reason shall take its place and ease them of that trouble, is what the children want, and the parents are bound to [provide]." (John Locke, *Second Essay Concerning Civil Government*, p. 37, par. 58.)

## What a Mature Adult Should Know

Locke then went on to point out that once a person has grown to adulthood and learned from experience and maturity the proper use of his reason, he should be capable of applying the revealed laws of God to his daily life:

"When he has acquired that state [of maturity], he is presumed to know how far that law is to be his guide, and how far he may make use of his freedom, and so comes to have it; till then, somebody else must guide him, who is presumed to know how far the law allows a liberty. If such a state of reason, such an age of discretion made him free, the same shall make his son free too. Is a man under the law of England? What made him free of that law -- that is, to have the liberty to dispose of his actions and possessions, according to his own will, within the permission of that law? A capacity of knowing that law, which is supposed, by that law, at the age of twenty one, and in some cases sooner. If this made the father free, it shall make the son free too. Till then, we see the law allows the son to have no will, but he is to be guided by the will of his father or guardian, who is to understand for him.... But after that [age of maturity is obtained] the father and son are equally free, as much as tutor and pupil after nonage, equally subjects of the same law together, without any dominion left in the father over the life, liberty, or estate of his son." (*Ibid.*, p. 37, par. 59.)

## Responsibility of Children to Parents

Locke said that the reciprocal responsibility of children to honor and obey their parents is equally specific:

"As He [God] hath laid on them [the parents] an obligation to nourish, preserve, and bring up their offspring, so He has laid on the children a perpetual obligation of honoring their parents, which, containing in it an inward esteem and reverence to be shown by all outward expressions, ties up the child from anything that may ever injure or affront, disturb or endanger the happiness or life of those from whom he received his [life], and engages him in all actions of defense, relief, assistance, and comfort of those by whose means he entered into being and has been made capable of any enjoyments of life. *From this obligation no state, no freedom, can absolve children."* (*Ibid.*, p. 39, par. 66; emphasis added.)

## The State Must Not Interfere with Legitimate Family Relations

The same permanence attaches to the responsibility which parents have for minor children. As Locke said:

> "The subjection of a minor places in the father a temporary government which terminates with the minority of the child.... The nourishment and education of their children [during their minority] is a charge so incumbent on parents for their children's good, *that nothing can absolve them from taking care of it."* (*Ibid.*, par. 67; emphasis added.)

It will be appreciated that the strength and stability of the family is of such vital importance to the culture that any action by the government to debilitate or cause dislocation in the normal trilateral structure of the family becomes, not merely a threat to the family involved, but a menace to the very foundations of society itself.

# 27th

## Principle

**The burden of debt is as destructive
to freedom as subjugation by conquest.**

"Think what you do when you run in debt; you give to
another the power over your liberty." -- Benjamin Franklin

Slavery or involuntary servitude is the result of either subjugation by
conquest or succumbing to the bondage of debt.

Debt, of course, is simply borrowing against the future. It exchanges
a present advantage for a future obligation. It will require not only the return of the original advance of funds, but a substantial compensation to
the creditor for the use of his money.

### How Debt Can Benumb the Human Spirit

The Founders knew that borrowing can be an honorable procedure
in a time of crisis, but they deplored it just the same. They looked upon
it as a temporary handicap which should be alleviated at the earliest possible moment. They had undergone sufficient experience with debt to see
its corrosive and debilitating effect, which tends to corrupt both individuals and nations.

In the case of the individual, excessive debt greatly curtails the freedom of the debtor. It benumbs his spirit, He often feels hesitant to seek a
new location or change a profession. He passes up financial opportunities
which a free man might risk. Heavy debt introduces an element of taint

into a man's search for happiness. There seems to be a perpetual burden every waking hour. There is a sense of being perpetually threatened as he rides the razor's edge of potential disaster.

There is also the sense of waste -- much like the man who has to make payments on a dead horse. It is money spent for pleasures or even needs that are long since past. It often means sleepless nights, recoiling under the burden of a grinding weight which is constantly increasing with every tick of the clock, and often at usurious rates.

## The Founders' Attitude toward Debt

The Founding Fathers belonged to an age when debt was recognized for the ugly spectre that it really is. They considered frugality a virtue, and even when an emergency compelled them to borrow, they believed in borrowing frugally and paying back promptly. Nearly everyone finds it to his advantage or absolute necessity to borrow on occasion. Debt becomes the only available means -- a necessary evil. Nevertheless, the Founders wanted the nature of debt to be recognized for what it is: evil, because it is a form of bondage.

As Thomas Jefferson wrote:

> "The maxim of buying nothing without the money in our pockets to pay for it would make our country one of the happiest on earth. Experience during the war proved this; and I think every man will remember that, under all the privations it obliged him to submit to during that period, he slept sounder and awoke happier than he can do now." (Ford, *Writings of Thomas Jefferson*, 4:414.)

## Debts from Splurge Spending

The Founders felt that the worst kind of debt is that which results from "splurge" borrowing -- going into debt to enjoy the temporary luxury of extravagantly living "beyond one's means." They knew the seductive snare which this possibility presents to the person who is watching other people do it. The English author William Makepeace Thackeray reflected those feelings when he wrote these words in Vanity Fair: "How well those live who are comfortably and thoroughly in debt: how they deny themselves nothing; how jolly and easy they are in their minds." (*Vanity Fair*, 2 vols. in 1, Thomas Y. Crowell Company, New York, 1893, 1:208.)

But, of course, all the reveling and apparitions of debt financed prosperity disappear like a morning mist when it comes time to pay. Extravagant living, waste, and hazardous borrowing against the future can reduce the best of us to bankruptcy, abject poverty, and even gnawing hunger from lack of the most basic necessities of life. Universal human experience verifies the bitter reality of the parable of the prodigal son, who "would fain have filled his belly with the husks that the swine did eat" (*Luke* 15:16).

The kind of frugality for which the Founders were famous was rooted in the conviction that debt should be abhorred like a plague. They perceived excessive indebtedness as a form of cultural disease.

## Benjamin Franklin on Splurge Spending

One of the Founders who made his fortune through frugality and financial discipline was Benjamin Franklin. He had this to say concerning splurge spending:

> "But what madness must it be to run in debt for these superfluities! We are offered, by the terms of this vendue, *six months' credit*; and that perhaps has induced some of us to attend it, because we cannot spare the ready money, and hope now to be fine without it. But, ah, think what you do when you run in debt; *you give to another power over your liberty*. If you cannot pay at the time, you will be ashamed to see your creditor; you will be in fear when you speak to him; you will make poor pitiful sneaking excuses, and by degrees come to lose your veracity, and sink into base downright lying; for, as *Poor Richard* says, the second vice is lying, the first is running in debt. And again, to the same purpose, lying rides upon debt's back. Whereas a freeborn Englishman ought not to be ashamed or afraid to see or speak to any man living. But poverty often deprives a man of all spirit and virtue. 'Tis hard for an empty bag to stand upright, as Poor Richard truly says." (Smyth, *Writings of Benjamin Franklin*, 3:416.)

## The Founders' Policy Concerning a National Debt

The pioneers of the American commonwealth had the wisdom born of experience to know that the debts of a nation are no different from the debts of an individual. The fact that the indebtedness is shared by the whole people makes it no less ominous. The Founders knew that dire circumstances, such as war or other emergency, could force a nation to borrow, so they authorized the federal government to do so in Article I of the Constitution. Nevertheless, they considered it a matter of supreme importance for the survival of a free people to get out of debt and enjoy complete solvency in order to prosper.

This is reflected in the declaration of Thomas Jefferson when he said:

> "I, however, place economy among the first and most important of republican virtues, and public debt as the greatest of the dangers to be feared." (Bergh, *Writings of Thomas Jefferson*, 15:47.)

## Should One Generation Impose Its Debts on the Next?

It has always been popular in some countries to justify the practice of passing on the debts incurred by one generation to the next for payment. This was justified, particularly in the case of war debts, by the rationalization that since war is fought to maintain the independence and integrity of the nation, future generations should bear the burden of the cost.

But this was not the view of the American Founding Fathers. They felt that the wars, economic problems, and debts of one generation should be paid for by the generation which incurred them. They wanted the rising generation to be genuinely free -- both politically and economically. It was their feeling that passing on their debts to the next generation would be forcing the children of the future to be born into a certain amount of bondage or involuntary servitude-something for which they had neither voted nor subscribed. It would be, in a very literal sense, "taxation without representation." Clearly, they said, it was a blatant violation of a fundamental republican principle.

## Jefferson Considered an Inherited Debt Immoral

Thomas Jefferson was particularly emphatic on this point. Said he:

> "That we are bound to defray [the war's] expenses within our own time, and unauthorized to burden posterity with them, I suppose to have been proved in my former letter.... We shall all consider ourselves morally bound to pay them ourselves; and consequently within the life [expectancy] of the majority....We must raise, then, ourselves the money for this war, either by taxes within the year or by loans; and if by loans, we must repay them ourselves, proscribing forever the English practice of perpetual funding." (*Ibid.*, 13:357-58.)

## The Founders Establish the Policy of Paying Debts Promptly

From the founding of the nation under the new Constitution, it became a policy of supreme importance to pay off the national debt. In his first term, President Washington wrote:

> "I entertain a strong hope that the state of the national finances is now sufficiently matured to enable you to enter upon a systematic and effectual arrangement for the regular redemption and discharge of the public debt, according to the right which has been reserved to the government. No measure can be more desirable, whether viewed with an eye to its intrinsic importance, or to the general sentiment and wish of the nation." (Fitzpatrick, *Writings of George Washington*, 32:211.)

The following year the President made it clear that this was no casual suggestion to Congress, but a matter of the highest priority:

> "No pecuniary consideration is more urgent than the regular redemption and discharge of the public debt; on none can delay be more injurious, or an economy of time more valuable." (*Ibid.*, 33:168.)

Just before leaving office, Washington made a final plea to the Congress to exert a greater effort to pay off the national debt, if only for the sake of the next generation. He said:

> "Posterity may have cause to regret if, from any motive, intervals of tranquility are left unimproved for accelerating this valuable end." (*Ibid.*, 35:319.)

## The History of the American National Debt

When we trace the history of the national debt, we find that the policy laid down by the Founders has been followed by every generation until the present one. One of the charts accompanying this chapter reflects the annual national debt from the days of George Washington to the present. By carefully tracing the pattern of these debts, we notice that after every war or financial emergency involving heavy indebtedness there was an immediate effort to pay it off as rapidly as possible. This policy was followed for the sake of the rising generation. The adult citizens of America wanted their children born in freedom, not bondage.

In our own day, however, a different attitude toward national fiscal policies has evolved. This is not only reflected in the skyrocketing thrust of an astonishing level of national indebtedness, but it has been accompanied by an equally profligate explosion in the cost of government operations, as reflected in the chart showing "Outlays of the Federal Government: 1789 to 2006."

## The Risk in Violating Fundamental Principles

America's contribution to mankind's 5,000-year leap was achieved by rather strict adherence to certain fundamental principles which were part of the Founders' phenomenal success formula. As we have already seen, some of these most important fundamentals are being neglected if not repudiated in our own day. A most important area of neglect is the advice of the Founders concerning national fiscal policies. As we examine the outlays of the federal government and the U.S. national debt throughout the history of the nation, we find a number of notable things.

First of all, as we have already observed, each generation of the past tried to pay off the national debt. In our own day, the importance of this policy has been de-emphasized. This development has occurred simultaneously with a policy of de-emphasizing the restraints and literal construction of the Constitution.

Beginning with the era of the Great Depression, all three branches of the federal government used the climate of emergency to overstep their Constitutional authority and aggressively undertake to perform tasks not authorized by the Founders. Extensive studies by Nobel Prize-winning economist Milton Friedman have demonstrated that every one of these adventures in non-Constitutional activities proved counter-productive, some of them tragically so.

Secondly, the people were induced to believe that these serious aberrations of Constitutional principles would provide a shortcut to economic prosperity, thereby lifting the people out of the depression. Unfortunately, it was successful only politically. It gave the people the illusion that by spending vast quantities of borrowed money they would prosper, when, as a matter of fact, the outcome was exactly the opposite, just as the Founders had predicted.

Dr. Milton Friedman points out that after the federal government had spent many billions of dollars and had seriously meddled with the Constitutional structure of the nation, the unemployment rate was higher in 1938 than it had been in 1932. Had not the crisis of World War II suddenly emerged, which required the spending of many additional billions of borrowed dollars and also resulted in absorbing the unemployed work force, the fiscal failure of the New Deal experiments would be better remembered by the American people.

# Outlays of the Federal Government: 1789 to 2006

| Year | Outlay | | Year | Outlay | | Year | Outlay |
|------|--------|---|------|--------|---|------|--------|
| | | | 1960 | 92,191,000,000 | | 1910 | 694,000,000 |
| | | | 1959 | 92,098,000,000 | | 1909 | 694,000,000 |
| | | | 1958 | 82,405,000,000 | | 1908 | 659,000,000 |
| | | | 1957 | 76,578,000,000 | | 1907 | 579,000,000 |
| 2006 | 2,473,298,000,000 | (est) | 1956 | 70,640,000,000 | | 1906 | 570,000,000 |
| | | | | | | | |
| 2005 | 2,399,843,000,000 | (est) | 1955 | 68,444,000,000 | | 1905 | 567,000,000 |
| 2004 | 2,318,834,000,000 | (est) | 1954 | 70,855,000,000 | | 1904 | 584,000,000 |
| 2003 | 2,157,637,000,000 | | 1953 | 76,101,000,000 | | 1903 | 517,000,000 |
| 2002 | 2,010,970,000,000 | | 1952 | 67,686,000,000 | | 1902 | 485,000,000 |
| 2001 | 1,863,770,000,000 | | 1951 | 45,514,000,000 | | 1901 | 525,000,000 |
| | | | | | | | |
| 2000 | 1,788,773,000,000 | | 1950 | 42,562,000,000 | | 1900 | 520,861,000 |
| 1999 | 1,701,891,000,000 | | 1949 | 38,835,000,000 | | 1895 | 356,195,000 |
| 1998 | 1,652,585,000,000 | | 1948 | 29,764,000,000 | | 1890 | 318,041,000 |
| 1997 | 1,601,250,000,000 | | 1947 | 34,496,000,000 | | 1885 | 260,227,000 |
| 1996 | 1,560,535,000,000 | | 1946 | 55,232,000,000 | | 1880 | 267,643,000 |
| | | | | | | | |
| 1995 | 1,515,802,000,000 | | 1945 | 92,712,000,000 | | 1875 | 274,623,000 |
| 1994 | 1,461,877,000,000 | | 1944 | 91,304,000,000 | | 1870 | 309,654,000 |
| 1993 | 1,409,489,000,000 | | 1943 | 78,555,000,000 | | 1865 | 1,297,555,000 |
| 1992 | 1,381,655,000,000 | | 1942 | 35,137,000,000 | | 1860 | 63,131,000 |
| 1991 | 1,324,369,000,000 | | 1941 | 13,653,000,000 | | 1855 | 59,743,000 |
| | | | | | | | |
| 1990 | 1,253,165,000,000 | | 1940 | 9,468,000,000 | | 1789-1849 | 1,090,000,000 |
| 1989 | 1,143,646,000,000 | | 1939 | 9,141,000,000 | | | |
| 1988 | 1,064,455,000,000 | | 1938 | 6,840,000,000 | | | |
| 1987 | 1,004,082,000,000 | | 1937 | 7,580,000,000 | | | |
| 1986 | 990,430,000,000 | | 1936 | 8,228,000,000 | | | |
| | | | | | | | |
| 1985 | 946,396,000,000 | | 1935 | 6,412,000,000 | | | |
| 1984 | 851,853,000,000 | | 1934 | 6,541,000,000 | | | |
| 1983 | 808,364,000,000 | | 1933 | 4,598,000,000 | | | |
| 1982 | 745,743,000,000 | | 1932 | 4,659,000,000 | | | |
| 1981 | 678,241,000,000 | | 1931 | 3,577,000,000 | | | |
| | | | | | | | |
| 1980 | 590,941,000,000 | | 1930 | 3,320,000,000 | | | |
| 1979 | 504,028,000,000 | | 1929 | 3,127,000,000 | | | |
| 1978 | 458,746,000,000 | | 1928 | 2,961,000,000 | | | |
| 1977 | 409,218,000,000 | | 1927 | 2,857,000,000 | | | |
| 1976 | 371,792,000,000 | | 1926 | 2,930,000,000 | | | |
| | | | | | | | |
| 1975 | 332,332,000,000 | | 1925 | 2,924,000,000 | | | |
| 1974 | 269,359,000,000 | | 1924 | 2,908,000,000 | | | |
| 1973 | 245,707,000,000 | | 1923 | 3,140,000,000 | | | |
| 1972 | 230,681,000,000 | | 1922 | 3,289,000,000 | | | |
| 1971 | 210,172,000,000 | | 1921 | 5,062,000,000 | | | |
| | | | | | | | |
| 1970 | 195,649,000,000 | | 1920 | 6,358,000,000 | | | |
| 1969 | 183,640,000,000 | | 1919 | 18,493,000,000 | | | |
| 1968 | 178,134,000,000 | | 1918 | 12,677,000,000 | | | |
| 1967 | 157,464,000,000 | | 1917 | 1,954,000,000 | | | |
| 1966 | 134,532,000,000 | | 1916 | 713,000,000 | | | |
| | | | | | | | |
| 1965 | 118,228,000,000 | | 1915 | 746,000,000 | | | |
| 1964 | 118,528,000,000 | | 1914 | 726,000,000 | | | |
| 1963 | 111,316,000,000 | | 1913 | 715,000,000 | | | |
| 1962 | 106,821,000,000 | | 1912 | 690,000,000 | | | |
| 1961 | 97,723,000,000 | | 1911 | 691,000,000 | | | |

(Source: www.gpoaccess.gov; The Statistical History of the United States [New York; Basic Books, Inc. 1976], p.1118; Statistical Abstract of the United States [Washington, D.C.; U.S. Bureau of the Census, 1978], p. 257.)

## US National Debt 1791 to 2006

| | | | |
|---|---|---|---|
| 2006................8,366,862,634,494 | | | |
| 2005................7,932,709,661,723 | 1985................1,945,941,616,459 | | 1885....................1,863,964,873 |
| 2004................7,379,052,696,330 | 1980..................930,210,000,000 * | | 1880....................2,120,415,.70 |
| 2003................6,783,231,062,743 | 1975..................576,649,000,000 * | | 1875....................2,232,284,531 |
| 2002................6,228,235,965,597 | 1970..................389,158,403,690 | | 1870....................2,480,672,427 |
| 2001................5,807,463,412,200 | 1965..................320,904,110,042 | | 1865....................2,680,647,869 |
| | | | |
| 2000................5,674,178,209,886 | 1960..................290,216,815,241 | | 1860......................64,842,287 |
| 1999................5,656,270,901,615 | 1955..................280,768,553,188 | | 1855......................35,586,956 |
| 1998................5,526,193,008,897 | 1950..................257,357,352,351 | | 1850......................63,452,773 |
| 1997................5,413,146,011,397 | 1945..................258,682,187,409 | | 1845......................15,925,303 |
| 1996................5,224,810,939,135 | 1940....................42,967,531,037 | | 1840........................3,573,343 |
| | | | |
| 1995................4,973,982,900,709 | 1935....................28,700,892,624 | | 1835...........................33,733 |
| 1994................4,692,749,910,013 | 1930....................16,185,309,831 | | 1830......................48,565,406 |
| 1993................4,411,488,883,139 | 1925....................20,516,193,887 | | 1825......................83,788,432 |
| 1992................4,064,620,655,521 | 1920....................25,952,456,406 | | 1820......................91,015,566 |
| 1991................3,665,303,351,697 | 1915......................3,058,136,873 | | 1815......................99,833,660 |
| | | | |
| 1990................3,233,313,451,777 | 1910......................2,652,665,838 | | 1810......................53,173,217 |
| 1989................2,857,430,960,187 | 1905......................2,274,615,063 | | 1805......................82,312,150 |
| 1988................2,602,337,712,041 | 1900......................2,136,961,091 | | 1800......................82,976,294 |
| 1987................2,350,276,890,953 | 1895......................1,676,120,983 | | 1795......................80,747,587 |
| 1986................2,125,302,616,658 | 1890......................1,552,140,204 | | 1791......................75,463,476 |

\* Rounded to Millions
(Source: Bureau of the Public Debt – United States Department of the
Treasury; www.publicdebt.treas.gov/opd/opd.htm)

## Splurge Spending Is Habit-Forming

It is highly significant that the political formula which Harry Hopkins recommended to keep a particular administration in power was "tax, tax – spend, spend -- elect, elect." Once the people have been encouraged by their political leaders to indulge in splurge spending, the result is like a snowball rolling downhill -- it increases in size and gains in speed. This is dramatically demonstrated in the charts. It will be noted that the national budget was less than a hundred billion dollars in 1960. Today we spend almost that much just for interest on the national debt. And that is more than the entire cost of World War I in real dollars!

## Today We Are Spending the Next Generations' Inheritance

The figures in these charts are astonishing, but not nearly as significant as the trend of thinking among the American people which the figures represent. For the first time in the entire history of the United States, a generation of Americans is squandering the next generations' inheritance. With the national debt as it stands today, there is no way in the foreseeable future whereby this generation could possibly liquidate such a mountain of accumulated debt.

The problem is aggravated by the fact that this generation has also committed itself to pay off additional liabilities in the future amounting to many trillions of dollars. Since 1972 an effort has been made to compute precisely how extensive these commitments really are, but it is feared that they may turn out to be even more than we have been previously told.

## The Problem of the "Fix"

Of course, the Founders would understand exactly what this generation is doing to itself. It is the very essence of human nature to pursue this disastrous course once the appetite has been created to demand it. As a result, American taxpayers now discover themselves playing a role almost identical to that of an addict on hard drugs. The addict denounces his "habit" and despises the "pusher" who got him into it, but when he is confronted with the crisis of needing a "fix" he will plead with tears of anguish for the narcotic remedy.

The "fix," of course, is not a remedy at all. The real remedy is "withdrawal." The addict must escape from the tortuous cycle of vicious repetition which is not solving his problem but compounding it. If withdrawal is painful, at least it is not prolonged. The problem is primarily a matter of will power -- the determination to change.

Every aspect of this reprehensible example applies to the mood of the American masses during recent years. Polemics against the government's profligate spending are vehement. The denunciation of high taxes is virtually universal. From banker to ditch-digger it is eloquently explained how this entire syndrome of big spending, high taxes, oppressive government regulations, and mountainous debt is stifling the economy, inhibiting the rate of production, and stagnating the wholesome development of the traditional American life-style. Yet, with all of that, any Congressman will verify that it has been, at least until recently, almost political suicide to try to change the trend. When it comes to cutting programs and reducing costs, balancing the budget, and eliminating deficit spending, it is amazing how few will make the necessary adjustment without the most violent outcries of protest when it affects them personally. But then, this would come as no surprise to the Founders. It is called "human nature." They would know that the only solution is to develop the will power to make the change. This is not easy, but it can be done.

### How Can the United States Return to the Founders' Formula?

In recent years, the number of Americans who have become reconciled to the inescapable necessity of returning to the Founders' formula has risen to millions. The very circumstances in which the American taxpayer finds himself are sufficient to awaken many to recognize the fiscal bottomless pit into which the nation is sinking. The vivid shock of that realization is precisely what is needed to arouse the majority of the people to the point where they are willing to go through fiscal withdrawal and kick the habit of splurge spending.

However, Congressmen, the President, and the taxpayers are all asking the same question: "Is there any way this can be accomplished without our going through the wringer of a deep depression?"

This writer believes that there is. By returning to the fundamental principles espoused by the Founding Fathers, we can reverse the trend and get America back to a formula of prosperity economics without a major crunch or depression.

# 28th
## Principle

**The United States has a manifest destiny to be
an example and a blessing to the entire human race.**

"I always consider the settlement of America with reverence and wonder, as the
opening of a grand scene and design in Providence for the illumination of the ignorant
and the emancipation of the slavish part of mankind all over the earth." -John Adams

All historians agree that a most singular and important feature of the
settlers of America was their overpowering sense of mission -- a conviction that they were taking part in the unfolding of a manifest destiny
of divine design which would shower its blessings on all mankind. As
historian John Fiske writes:

> "They believed that they were doing a wonderful thing. They
> felt themselves to be instruments in accomplishing a kind of
> 'manifest destiny.' Their exodus [from Europe] was that of a chosen people who were at length to lay the everlasting foundations
> of God's kingdom upon earth.... This steadfast faith in an unseen
> ruler and guide was to them a pillar of cloud by day and of fire
> by night. It was of great moral value. It gave them clearness of
> purpose and concentration of strength, and contributed towards
> making them, like the children of Israel, a people of indestructible vitality and aggressive energy." (Fiske, *The Beginnings of
> New England*, pp. 30, 45.)

This sense of manifest destiny has continued from that day to this and will be found expressed in nearly all of the inaugural addresses given by the presidents of the United States.

However, it is extremely important to distinguish between a sense of mission, and the spirit of perverted chauvinism associated with the idea of "racial superiority." The former is a call to exemplary leadership and service. The latter is the arrogant presumption of a self-appointed role to conquer and rule. The distinction between the two is readily perceived in the writings of the Founders. For example, John Adams wrote:

> "I always consider the settlement of America with reverence and wonder, as the opening of a grand scene and design in Providence for the illumination of the ignorant, and the emancipation of the slavish part of mankind all over the earth." (Quoted in Conrad Cherry, *God's New Israel*, Prentice-Hall, Englewood Cliffs, N.J., 1971, p. 65.)

Thomas Jefferson looked upon the development of freedom under the Constitution as "the world's best hope," and wrote to John Dickinson in 1801 that what had been accomplished in the United States "will be a standing monument and example for the aim and imitation of the people of other countries." (Bergh, *Writings of Thomas Jefferson*, 10:217.)

It was not uncommon for the Founders to stress the responsibility which had been placed upon them to perform a mighty task. As John Adams wrote from England while the Constitution was in preparation:

> "The people of America have now the best opportunity and the greatest trust in their hands that Providence ever committed to so small a number." (Koch, *The American Enlightenment*, p. 257.)

Alexander Hamilton emphasized the same point as the Constitution was presented to the people for their approval. He wrote:

> "It has been frequently remarked that it seems to have been reserved to the people of this country, by their conduct and example, to decide the important question, whether societies of men are really capable or not of establishing good government from reflection and choice, or whether they are forever destined to depend for their political constitutions on accident and force." (*The Federalist Papers*, No. 1, p. 33.)

### Failure Considered Treason Against the World

He went on to say that if the people of the United States failed in this mission, it would operate to "the general misfortune of mankind." (*Ibid.*, No. 1, p. 33.) John Adams later stated that if the people abandoned the freedom gained by the adoption of the Constitution, it would be "treason against the hopes of the world." (Koch, *The American Enlightenment*, p. 367.)

### John Jay Considers America to Be a Providential Blessing

After the task of structuring a constitutional government had been completed for the first free people in modern times, one of the Founders, John Jay, thought he saw in it a manifestation of divine approbation which was too obvious to be denied. He wrote:

"It has often given me pleasure to observe that independent America was not composed of detached and distant territories, but that one connected, fertile, wide-spreading country was the portion of our western sons of liberty. Providence has in a particular manner blessed it with a variety of soils and productions and watered it with innumerable streams for the delight and accommodation of its inhabitants. A succession of navigable waters forms a kind of chain round its borders, as if to bind it together; while the most noble rivers in the world, running at convenient distances, present them with highways for the easy communication of friendly aids and the mutual transportation and exchange of their various commodities."

John Jay continued:

"With equal pleasure I have often taken notice that Providence has been pleased to give this one connected country to one united people -- a people descended from the same ancestors, speaking the same language, professing the same religion, attached to the same principles of government, very similar in their manners and customs, and who, by their joint counsels, arms, and efforts, fighting side by side throughout a long and bloody war, have nobly established their general liberty and independence."

He then concluded as follows:

"This country and this people seem to have been made for each other, and it appears as if it was the design of Providence that an inheritance so proper and convenient for a band of brethren, united to each other by the strongest ties, should never be split into a number of unsocial, jealous, and alien sovereignties." (*The Federalist Papers*, No. 2, p. 38.)

Jay's estimate of the unique blessing of the land they had inherited proved correct. The Founders felt that ultimately their boundaries would extend to the western sea, as several of the original colonial charters had provided. When this had been accomplished, the vast Mississippi drainage basin, extending as it does from the Rockies in the west to the Appalachians in the east, turned out to be the most fertile and productive piece of real estate on this planet.

## Conclusion

The Founders knew they were sailing into uncharted waters, and they knew their ship of state was entirely different from anything else on the face of the earth. True, they had examined every kind of political operation known to man, and they had abstracted from history every lesson and precaution they could learn, but their own product was unique, bold, and filled with the promise of a better day. Probably no one summed it up better than James Madison when he wrote:

"Is it not the glory of the people of America that, whilst they have paid a decent regard to the opinions of former times and other nations, they have not suffered a blind veneration for antiquity, for custom, or for names, to overrule the suggestions of their own good sense, the knowledge of their own situation, and the lessons of their own experience?

"To this manly spirit posterity will be indebted for the possession, and the world for the example, of the numerous innovations displayed on the American theater in favor of private rights and public happiness.

"Had no important step been taken by the leaders of the Revolution for which a precedent could not be discovered, no government established of which an exact model did not present itself, the people of the United States might at this moment have been numbered among the melancholy victims of misguided councils, must at best have been laboring under the weight of some of those forms which have crushed the liberties of the rest of mankind."

Then he concluded:

"Happily for America, happily we trust for *the whole human race*, they pursued a new and more noble course. They accomplished a revolution which has no parallel in the annals of human society. They reared the fabrics of governments which have no model on the face of the globe. They formed the design of a great Confederacy, which it is incumbent on their successors, to improve and perpetuate." (*Ibid.*, No. 14, pp. 104-105; emphasis added.)

# Bibliography

Adams, John. *A Defense of the Constitutions of Government of the United States*. 3 vols., Philadelphia: Bud and Bartram, 1797.

*The Political Writings of John Adams*. Edited by George A. Peek, Jr. New York: Liberal Arts Press, 1954.

*The Works of John Adams*. Edited by Charles Francis Adams. 10 vols. Boston: Little, Brown and Company, 1850-56.

Adler, Mortimer J., et al., eds. *The Annals of America*. 18 vols. Chicago: Encyclopedia Britannica, Inc., 1968.

Bastiat, Frederic. *The Law*. Irvington-on-Hudson, New York: The Foundation for Economic Education, Inc., 1974.

Blackstone, William. *Commentaries on the Laws of England*. Edited by William Carey Jones. 2 vols. San Francisco: Bancroft-Whitney Company, 1916.

Carson, Clarence. *The American Tradition*. Irvington-on-Hudson, New York: The Foundation for Economic Education, Inc., 1970.

Chinard, Gilbert. *Thomas Jefferson: The Apostle of Americanism*. 2nd ed. rev. Ann Arbor: The University of Michigan Press, 1975.

Clark, J. Reuben, Jr. *Stand Fast by Our Constitution*. Salt Lake City: Deseret Book Company, 1973.

Ebenstein, William. *Great Political Thinkers*. New York: Holt, Rinehart and Winston, 1963.

Elliot, Jonathan, ed. *The Debates in the Several State Conventions on the Adoption of the Federal Constitution*. 5 vols. Philadelphia: J.B. Lippincott Company, 1901.

Fiske, John. *The Beginnings of New England*. The Historical Writings of John Fiske, vol. 6. Boston: Houghton, Mifflin and Company, 1902.

*Civil Government in the United States Considered with Some Reference to Its Origins*. Boston: Houghton, Mifflin and Company, 1890.

*The Critical Period of American History*, 1783-1789. The Historical Writings of John Fiske, vol. 12. Boston: Houghton, Mifflin and Company, 1916.

Franklin, Benjamin. *The Writings of Benjamin Franklin*. Edited by Albert Henry Smyth. 10 vols. New York: The Macmillan Company, 1905-7.

Hamilton, Alexander; Madison, James; and Jay, John. *The Federalist Papers*. New York: Mentor Books, 1961.

Hamilton, Alexander. *The Papers of Alexander Hamilton*. Edited by Harold C. Syrett et al. 19 vols. by 1973. New York: Columbia University Press, 1961.

Huszar, George B. de; Littlefield, Henry W.; and Littlefield, Arthur W.; eds. *Basic American Documents*. Ames, Iowa: Littlefield, Adams & Co., 1953.

Jefferson, Thomas. *The Papers of Thomas Jefferson*. Edited by Julian P. Boyd. 19 vols. by 1974. Princeton, New Jersey: Princeton University Press, 1950-.

*The Writings of Thomas Jefferson*. Edited by Albert Ellery Bergh. 20 vols. Washington: The Thomas Jefferson Memorial Association, 1907.

*The Writings of Thomas Jefferson*. Edited by Paul Leicester Ford. 10 vols. New York: G.P. Putnam's Sons, 1892-99.

Koch, Adrienne, ed. *The American Enlightenment*. New York: George Braziller, 1965.

Locke, John. *Concerning Human Understanding*. Great Books of the Western World, vol. 35. Chicago: Encyclopedia Britannica, Inc., 1952.

*Second Essay Concerning Civil Government*. Great Books of the Western World, vol. 35. Chicago: Encyclopedia Britannica, Inc., 1952.

Lovell, Colin Rhys. *English Constitutional and Legal History*. New York: Oxford University Press, 1962.

Madison, James. *The Complete Madison*. Edited by Saul K. Padover. New York: Harper & Brothers, 1953.

*Letters and Other Writings of James Madison*. Edited by William C. Rives and Philip R. Fendall. 4 vols. Philadelphia: J.B. Lippincott, 1865.

Montesquieu, Charles de Secondat, Baron de. *The Spirit of Laws*. Translated by Thomas Nugent. Revised by J. V. Prichard. Great Books of the Western World, vol. 38. Chicago: Encyclopedia Britannica, Inc., 1952.

Plato. *The Dialogues of Plato*. Translated by Benjamin Jowett. Great Books of the Western World, vol. 7. Chicago: Encyclopedia Britannica, Inc., 1952.

Sidney, Algernon. *Discourses on Government*. 3 vols. New York: Printed for Richard Lee by Deare and Andres, 1805.

Smith, Adam. *The Wealth of Nations*. "Heirloom Edition." 2 vols. New Rochelle, New York: Arlington House, n.d.

Story, Joseph. *Commentaries on the Constitution of the United States*. 3rd ed. 2 vols. Boston: Little, Brown and Company, 1858.

Tocqueville, Alexis de. *Democracy in America*. 2 vols. 1840. New York: Vintage Books, 1945.

Washington, George. *The Washington Papers*. Edited by Saul K. Padover. New York: Harper & Brothers, 1955.

*The Writings of George Washington*. Edited by John C. Fitzpatrick. 39 vols. Washington: United States Government Printing Office, 1931-44.

Wells, William V. *The Life and Public Services of Samuel Adams*. 3 vols. Boston: Little, Brown and Company, 1865.

Wood, Gordon S. *The Creation of the American Republic, 1776-1787*. Chapel Hill: The University of North Carolina Press, 1969.

# (Appendix A)

**The Mystery of the Anglo-Saxons**

*Excerpted from* The Making of America *by W. Cleon Skousen*
*(Washington, D.C., National Center for Constitutional Studies, 1986)*
*pp 54-62*

## The Mystery of the Anglo-Saxons

During the 1700s, one of the most fascinating and popular studies in England and America was unraveling the mystery of the Anglo-Saxons. Even today, English historian Sharon Turner, who wrote his three-volume classic in the days of the Founders, is still considered a leading authority on these amazing people who came from around the Black Sea in the first century B.C. and spread all across Northern Europe. In fact, they were the best organized, best governed people in their day. They not only conquered or intermarried with the royal families of every northern European country, but they set out in their open boats to chase the Irish out of Iceland, discover Greenland, and even establish temporary settlements in what is now Canada.

But the most important thing to Jefferson, Franklin, John Adams, and others who studied their culture was their institutes of constitutional government which were almost identical with those of ancient Israel.

The Anglo-Saxons first brought their culture to Britain around 450 A.D. when two brothers, Hengist and Horsa, were invited by the king of Kent to bring their relatives to southern Britain and fight off the king's enemies. The Anglo-Saxons were not only successful in this military venture, but they liked Britain so well they decided to stay. Before long they had virtually taken over the island of Britain and changed its name to England (Anglo-land or Engel-land).

## Jefferson Studied the Anglo-Saxons in Their Own Language

As we have already pointed out, Thomas Jefferson became remarkably proficient in five languages. One of them was the language of his ancestors, the Anglo-Saxons. He learned this language so he could study their laws in their original tongue. They not only had the major elements of People's Law, but they were organized and governed by principles similar to those of Moses. He made copies of the Anglo-Saxon laws and sent some of them to friends, along with his own translation.

His admiration for these laws is expressed in a letter to Edmund Pendleton [page 55] dated August 13, 1776, when he wrote:

> "Are we not better for what we have hitherto abolished of the feudal system: Has not every restitution of the ancient Saxon laws had happy effects? Is it not better now that we return at once into that happy system of our ancestors, the wisest and most perfect ever yet devised by the wit of man, as it stood before the eighth century?" [Julian P. Boyd, ed., *The Papers of Thomas Jefferson*, 20 vols. By 1982 (Princeton, J.J.: Princeton University Press, 1950-), 1:492]

### Some Interesting Aspects of the Anglo-Saxon Culture

Many have thought the Yinglings, or Anglo-Saxons, included a branch of the ancient Israelites because they came from the territory of the Black Sea (where the Ten Tribes disappeared), and because they preserved the same unique institutes of government as those which were given to the Israelites at Mount Sinai. But whether related or not, there is certainly irrefutable evidence of a cross-fertilization of laws and cultural values between these two peoples. [See Colin Rhys Lovell, *English Constitutional and Legal History* (New York: Oxford University Press, 1962)]

Here are some examples:

1. The Anglo-Saxons considered themselves a commonwealth of freemen.
2. They organized themselves into units identical to those of the Israelites.
   a. The head of 10 families was called a tithing-man.
   b. The head of 50 families became an obscure office but may have been a vil-man, or head of the village.
   c. The head of 100 families was called the hundred man.
   d. The head of 1,000 families was called the eolderman, later shortened to earl. The territory occupied by 1,000 families was called a shire, and the administrative assistant to the earl was called the "shire reef." We pronounce it sheriff.
3. All laws, as well as the election of leaders, had to be by the common consent of the people.

4. Authority granted to a chieftain in time of war was extremely limited and was taken away from him as soon as the emergency had passed.

5. Their system of justice was based on payment of damages to the victim rather than calling it a crime against the whole people.

When law books of both England and colonial America were crammed with bad procedures, unjust practices, and cruel punishments, the statutes of the Anglo-Saxons came to the Founders like a breath of fresh air. Here were "ancient principles" which could be employed to the advantage of the Founders as they developed their new success formula. To better appreciate the perspective, we will pause to examine the Anglo-Saxon precepts more closely.

### Summary of the Institutes of the Anglo-Saxons

Sharon Turner summarizes the substance of the Anglo-Saxon law as it existed up to the time of the Norman Conquest in 1066. As we have noted, Thomas Jefferson saw that the laws of the Anglo-Saxons were beginning to erode after the eighth century; nevertheless, a great many of the best features survived and were still in operation right up until the Norman Conquest.

Even though many years of war had compelled the Anglo-Saxons to confederate together under a king, he was still an elected monarch rather than a hereditary king and, initially, he was closely controlled by the Witen (the Anglo-Saxon parliament).

But as with kings in all ages, the centralization of power was beginning to concentrate extensive authority by 1066 A.D. He was not only the chief executive of the nation but played an essential role in the legislature. He received and expended all taxation and was even the center and source of authority for all jurisprudence. He was commander-in-chief of all the armies and when the Witen was summoned it was at his discretion. While it was in session, he presided over the proceedings.

The full name of the Anglo-Saxon parliament was the Witena-gemot which is usually referred to by the shorter name of Witen. The membership included representatives from each of the towns, regions, or clans as well as those who had been honored by the king for valiant military service. It also included the Thanes (major landowners) and Milites or knights.

The highest orders of nobility, which were granted for distinguished military service, were not designed for an aristocracy but were open to the lowest classes.

These titles included the title of Eolderman (Earl), Hold, Heretoch, Eorl, and Thegn or Thane. These titles were personal honors and were not passed on to the noblemen's successors.

Of course, land granted by the king for distinguished service was permanently retained by the recipient and could be transferred to his heirs. However, there was no feudal system of primogeniture which required that the nobleman's estate be assigned to an oldest son.

Any person holding land from the king was obligated to build castles and bridges and serve the king for a limited time in his military expeditions.

### The Freemen

The foundation of the Anglo-Saxon society was the freemen. They looked upon the king as their sovereign and defender but were subject to no other master except those whom they chose to serve.

The highest order of freemen was the Milites or knights. A freeman became a member of this order by the "investment of the military belt." He then became part of a privileged class that lived on the lands of the nobility but could not serve in the national army as a commanding officer unless appointed as such.

### Beginning of a Class of Bondsmen by 1066

During the latest states of Anglo-Saxon history, there had developed a substantial class of slaves, bondsmen, and others who were obligated to fulfill some degree of servility or compulsory employment. Nevertheless, the law protected them from abuse and provided certain regulations to promote their welfare and ultimate emancipation through good conduct.

### Property could not be taxed without the consent of the Witen.

All freemen were required to attach themselves to a tithing, which was a unit of administration originally consisting of ten families. Each member of a tithing had to put up a bond for his general good behavior and conduct himself according to certain regulations. (It's interesting that the very concept of a tithing, meaning one-tenth, comes from the Hebrews.)

### Reparation to the Victim

Originally a person found guilty of an offense was required to provide compensation only to the victim; however, the confederation under a permanent king resulted in additional fines going to the sovereign to cover the expense of "keeping the peace."

A value was placed on each individual according to his place in the social structure. This was called his "Were." An additional value was placed on each individual to protect his peace and security. This was called a "Mund." Offenders were fined proportionate to the amount of injury inflicted on a person's "life or limb" (his Were) or his peace and privacy (his Mund).

A high premium was placed on the personal liberty of each free subject so long as he was not violating any law. Heavy penalties were imposed on those who unlawfully imprisoned or restrained a freeman.

A person accused of a crime was permitted to defend himself by producing a certain number of his neighbors who were willing to swear that it was their complete conviction that he was innocent. This procedure was intended to impress on each person the necessity of maintaining a reputation of good character in his neighborhood so that in case of false accusation, his neighbors would come to his defense. Even today the use of "character witnesses" is a significant part of our judicial system.

### The Jury System

The Anglo-Saxons also employed trial by jury, but there is no record of the time when it was first inaugurated. It may have been instituted anciently or introduced by the Danish colonists who are known to have employed the jury system from remote antiquity.

Property rights were held to be sacred, and strict rules were employed concerning tenure and the transfer of titles.

Every man was required to honor the rights of others, just as he expected to have his own rights honored.

Judges were placed under obligation to carefully evaluate each offense and make the penalty commensurate with the seriousness of the crime.

All persons of means were emphatically enjoined to aid the poor, ameliorate the distress of widows and orphans, and treat strangers with kindness and fairness.

The Witen (or Parliament) was under obligation to make certain that the laws of the land conformed with the revealed laws of God. Any which did not were abolished and renounced as being unconstitutional and void. The Witen was also under obligation to see that every man, whether rich or poor, was fully protected in his common rights and treated with equal solicitude and care.

### Social Justice and the General Welfare

It was a fundamental precept that all laws must be for the "general welfare" of the people, collectively and individually. Frequently the Witen passed laws favorable to the emancipation of slaves, even though this was often done contrary to the wishes of those who held them in a state of involuntary servitude.

A fundamental requirement of the law was that all persons who had been offended should have the opportunity to petition for redress. In fact, there were heavy penalties enacted against shiremen or judges who refused or neglected to hear the petitions of the aggrieved.

The victim of an offense was not to avenge his injury personally until after legal justice had been sought.

The natural liberty of each individual was only to be restricted by those laws which were for the social good of the whole people.

To protect the life and liberty of all freemen, there was an established catalogue of penalties for the loss of each limb or any other act of maiming or injury to an individual.

There were laws to prohibit fighting and personal violence, as well as laws to punish robbery and rapine, which the "powerful and war-like" members of society sometimes imposed on weaker or unsuspecting victims.

There were heavy penalties for trespass, whether against a person's house or his private lands.

Every land owner was required to make hedges and fences to keep his cattle from injuring his neighbor.

The observance of Sunday as a day of rest "from all worldly labor" was strictly enforced.

The law provided that there is a "natural equality of man" which must not be violated by those in power.

To protect the various levels of nobility and civic responsibility among the people, the punishment for offenses increased with the rank of the person offended. It was presupposed that the higher the rank, the greater the offense against the welfare of the people whom he served.

### Channels of Justice

Each dimension and class of people had a procedure for the protection of their rights through designated channels, where redress could be sought. Each channel was kept distinct from interference by the others.

Not only was the property and life of the individual protected but his character was as well. Any slanderous words were subject to punishment.

The rights of women received special protection under the law. Upon the death of a father, the mother received the custody and care of the children. Women were protected by law from violence and abuse or forced marriages.

Parents were held responsible for any offense committed by their children against others.

Any person convicted of perjury was thereafter disqualified as a witness.

Every man was protected in his right to hunt in his own woods or fields. [Abstracted from Sharon Turner, *The History of the Anglo-Saxons*, 5th ed. (London: Longman, Rees, Orme, Brown, Green, and Longman, 1836), pp. 221-225.]

To the Founders, these principles seemed far advanced in both spirit and context compared with those which prevailed in any country of their day, including England.

As we indicated earlier, when Jefferson reflected on these ancient principles he could not help asking the leader in the Virginia House of Delegates, "Is it not better now that we return at once into that happy system of our ancestors, the wisest and most perfect ever yet devised by the wit of man?"

## Classical Studies of the Founders

It will be apparent from what we have seen thus far that, collectively speaking, the minds of the Founders were like a huge vacuum cleaner, sucking up knowledge of every sort from every available source.

When it came to politics, the minds of the leading Founders were as far ranging and profound as any collection of advanced scholars in the field of political studies today. Their correspondence, speeches, and commentaries disclose a penetrating understanding of both ancient and modern writers.

Often the Founders read the classics in their original language. They were familiar with Plato's Republic and his Laws; with Aristotle's Essays on Politics; with the political philosophy of the Greek historian, Polybius; with the great Roman defender of republican principles, Cicero; with the legal commentaries of Sir Edward Coke; with the essays and philosophy of Francis Bacon; with the essays of Richard Hooker; with the dark forebodings of Thomas Hobbes' Leviathan; with the more optimistic and challenging Essays on Civil Government, by John Locke; with the animated Spirit of the Laws, by Baron Charles de Montesquieu of France; with the three-volume work of Algernon Sidney, who was beheaded by Charles II in 1683; with the writings of David Hume; with the legal commentaries of Sir William Blackstone; and with the economic defense of a free market economy by Adam Smith called The Wealth of Nations.

The Founders knew their classics. They also knew their history — Biblical, Greek, Roman, European, and American. From all of these valuable sources they sorted out what they considered to be the best and most enduring for the prosperity and peace of a free people under a republican system of self-government.

# (Appendix B)

### The Secret to America's Strength
*By W. Cleon Skousen*
*An address to law school students, 1981*

### The Role of Religion in the
### Founding Fathers' Constitutional Formula

Americans of the Twentieth Century often fail to realize the supreme importance which the Founding Fathers originally attached to the role of religion in the structure of the unique civilization which they hoped would emerge as the first free people in modern times. Many Americans also fail to realize that the Founders felt the role of religion would be as important in our own day as it was in theirs.

In 1787, the very year the Constitution was written and approved by Congress, that same body of Congress passed the famous Northwest Ordinance. In it they outlawed slavery in the Northwest territory, they enunciated the basic rights of citizens in language similar to that which was later incorporated in the Bill of Rights, and they emphasized the essential need to teach religion and morality in the schools. Here is the way they said it:

> "Article 3: Religion, morality, and knowledge, being necessary to good government and the happiness of mankind, schools and the means of education shall forever be encouraged." (*Basic American Documents*, Littlefield, Adams & Co., Ames, Iowa, p. 66)

Notice that formal education was to include among its responsibilities the teaching of three important subjects:

1.   Religion, which might be defined as a "fundamental system of
     beliefs concerning man's origin and relationship to the cosmic
     universe as well as his relationship with his fellow men."
2.   Morality, which may be described as "a standard of behavior dis-
     tinguishing right from wrong."
3.   Knowledge, which is "an intellectual awareness and understand-
     ing of established facts relating to any field of human experience
     or inquiry, i.e., history, geography, science, etc."

We also notice that "religion and morality" were not required by the
Founders as merely an intellectual exercise, but they positively declared
their conviction that these were essential ingredients needed for "good
government and the happiness of mankind."

### Washington Describes the Founders' Position

The position set forth in the Northwest Ordinance was reemphasized
by President George Washington in his Farewell Address:

> "Of all the dispositions and habits which lead to political
> prosperity, religion and morality are indispensable supports....
> And let us with caution indulge the supposition that morality can
> be maintained without religion ... reason and experience both for-
> bid us to expect that national morality can prevail to the exclusion
> of religious principle.

> "It is substantially true that virtue or morality is a necessary
> spring of popular government." (*Basic American Documents*, pp.
> 108-109)

### The Teaching of Religion in Schools Restricted
### to Universal Fundamentals

Having established that "religion" is the foundation of morality and
both are essential to "good government and the happiness of mankind,"
the Founders then set about to exclude the creeds and biases or dissensions of individual denominations so as to make the teaching of religion
a unifying cultural adhesive rather than a divisive apparatus. Jefferson
wrote a bill for the "Establishing of Elementary Schools" in Virginia and
made this point clear by stating:

> "No religious reading, instruction or exercise, shall be pre-
> scribed or practiced inconsistent with the tenets of any religious

sect or denomination." (J. Randolph, editor, *Early History of the University of Virginia*, 1856, pp. 96-97)

Obviously, under such restrictions the only religious tenets to be taught in public schools would have to be those which were universally accepted by all faiths and completely fundamental in their premises.

## Franklin Describes the Five Fundamentals of "All Sound Religions"

Several of the Founders have left us with a description of their basic religious beliefs, and Benjamin Franklin summarized those which he felt were the "fundamental points in all sound religion." Here is the way he said it:

> "Here is my creed. I believe in one God, the Creator of the universe. That he governs it by his Providence. That he ought to be worshipped. That the most acceptable service we render to him is in doing good to his other children. That the soul of man is immortal, and will be treated with justice in another life respecting its conduct in this. These I take to be the fundamental points in all sound religion...." (Letter to Ezra Stiles, President of Yale University, Sparks, editor, *Works of Benjamin Franklin*, 1840, Vol. 10, pp. 423-424)

## The "Fundamental Points" to be Taught in the Schools

The five points of fundamental religious belief which are to be found in all of the principal religions of the world are those expressed or implied in Franklin's statement:

1.  Recognition and worship of a Creator who made all things.
2.  That the Creator has revealed a moral code of behavior for happy living which distinguishes right from wrong.
3.  That the Creator holds mankind responsible for the way they treat each other.
4.  That all mankind live beyond this life.
5.  That in the next life mankind are judged for their conduct in this one.

All five of these tenets run through practically all of the Founders' writings. These are the beliefs which the Founders sometimes referred to as the "religion of America," and they felt these fundamentals were so important in providing "good government and the happiness of mankind" that they wanted them taught in the public schools along with morality and knowledge.

### Statements of the Founders Concerning these Principles

Samuel Adams said these basic beliefs which constitute "the religion of America is the religion of all mankind." (W.V. Wells, *The Life and Public Services of Samuel Adams*, Vol. 3, p. 23) In other words, these fundamental beliefs belong to all world faiths and could therefore be taught without being offensive to any "sect or denomination" as indicated in the Virginia bill establishing elementary schools.

John Adams called these tenets the "general principles" on which the American civilization had been founded. (Letter to Jefferson cited in Burge, editor, *The Writings of Thomas Jefferson*, Vol. 13, p. 293)

Thomas Jefferson called these basic beliefs the principles "in which God has united us all." (*Ibid.*, Vol. 14, p. 198)

From these statements it is obvious how significantly the Founders looked upon the fundamental precepts of religion and morality as the cornerstones of a free government. This gives additional importance to the warning of Washington when he said: "Of all the dispositions and habits which lead to political prosperity, religion and morality are indispensable supports.... Who that is a sincere friend to it can look with indifference upon attempts to shake the foundation of the fabric?" (Littlefield, *Basic American Documents*, pp. 108-109)

Washington issued this solemn warning because in France, shortly before Washington wrote his Farewell Address (1796), the promoters of atheism and amorality had seized control and turned the French Revolution into a shocking blood-bath of wild excesses and violence. Washington never wanted anything like that to happen in the United States. Therefore he had said: "In vain would that man claim the tribute of patriotism, who should labor to subvert these great pillars of human happiness [religion and morality]." (*Ibid.*)

### Alexis de Tocqueville Discovers the Importance of Religion in America

When Alexis de Tocqueville visited the United States in 1831 he became so impressed with what he saw that he went home and wrote one of the most definitive studies on the American culture and Constitutional system that had been published up to that time. His book was called Democracy in America. Concerning religion in America, de Tocqueville said:

"On my arrival in the United States the religious aspect of the country was the first thing that struck my attention; and the longer I stayed there, the more I perceived the great political consequences resulting from this new state of things." (Alexis de Tocqueville, *Democracy in America*, Vol. 1, p. 319)

He described the situation as follows:

"Religion in America takes no direct part in the government of society, but it must be regarded as the first of their political institutions.... I do not know whether all Americans have a sincere faith in their religion — for who can search the human heart? — but I am certain that they hold it to be indispensable to the maintenance of republican institutions. This opinion is not peculiar to a class of citizens or to a party, but it belongs to the whole nation and to every rank of society." (*Ibid.*, p. 316)

## European Philosophers Turned Out To Be Wrong

In Europe it had been popular to teach that religion and liberty were inimical to each other. De Tocqueville saw the very opposite happening in America. He wrote:

"The philosophers of the eighteenth century explained in a very simple manner the gradual decay of religious faith. Religious zeal, said they, must necessarily fail the more generally liberty is established and knowledge diffused. Unfortunately the facts by no means accord with their theory. There are certain populations in Europe whose unbelief is only equaled by their ignorance and debasement; while in America, one of the freest and most enlightened nations in the world, the people fulfill with fervor all the outward duties of religion." (*Ibid.*, p. 319)

## A New Kind of Christianity Emerges in America

De Tocqueville points out that "in France I had almost always seen the spirit of religion and the spirit of freedom marching in opposite directions. But in America I found they were intimately united." (*Ibid.*) He then points out that the early American colonists "brought with them into the New World a form of Christianity which I cannot better describe than by styling it a democratic and republican religion. This contributed powerfully to the establishment of a republic and a democracy in public affairs; and from the beginning, politics and religion contracted an alliance which has never been dissolved." (*Ibid.*, p. 311)

However, he emphasized the fact that this religious under-girding of the political structure was a common denominator of moral teachings in different denominations and not the political pressure of some national church hierarchy. Said he:

> "The sects [different denominations] that exist in the United States are innumerable. They all differ in respect to the worship which is due to the Creator; but they agree in respect to the duties which are due from man to man. Each sect adores the Deity in its own peculiar manner, but all sects preach the same moral law in the name of God.... All the sects of the United States are comprised within the great unity of Christianity, and Christian morality is everywhere the same.... There is no country in the world where the Christian religion retains a greater influence over the souls of men than in America." (*Ibid.*, p. 314)

It was astonishing to de Tocqueville that liberty and religion could be combined in such a balanced structure of harmony and good order. He wrote:

> "... the revolutionists of America are obliged to profess an ostensible respect for Christian morality and equity, which does not permit them to violate wantonly the laws that oppose their designs.... Thus, while the law permits the Americans to do what they please, religion prevents them from conceiving and forbids them to commit, what is rash or unjust." (*Ibid.*, p. 316)

### De Tocqueville Describes the Role of Religion in the Schools

De Tocqueville found that the schools, especially in New England, incorporated the basic tenets of religion right along with history and political science in order to prepare the student for adult life. He wrote:

> "In New England every citizen receives the elementary notions of human knowledge; he is taught, moreover, the doctrines and the evidences of his religion, the history of his country, and the leading features of the Constitution. In the States of Connecticut and Massachusetts, it is extremely rare to find a man imperfectly acquainted with all these things, and a person wholly ignorant of them is a sort of phenomenon." (*Ibid.*, p. 327)

### De Tocqueville Describes the Role of the American Clergy

Alexis de Tocqueville saw a unique quality of cohesive strength emanating from the clergy of the various churches in America. After noting that all the clergy seemed anxious to maintain "separation of church and state," nevertheless, he observed that collectively they had a great influence on the morals and customs of public life. This indirectly reflected itself in the formulating of laws and ultimately in fixing the moral and political climate of the American commonwealth. As a result, he wrote:

> "This led me to examine more attentively than I had hitherto done the station which the American clergy occupy in political society. I learned with surprise that they filled no public appointments; I did not see one of them in the administration, and they are not even represented in the legislative assemblies." (*Ibid.*, p. 320)

How different this was from Europe where the clergy belonged to a national church, subsidized by the government. He wrote:

> "The unbelievers in Europe attack the Christians as their political opponents rather than as their religious adversaries; they hate the Christian religion as the opinion of a (political) party much more than as an error in belief; and they reject the clergy less because they are the representatives of the Deity than because they are the allies of government." (*Ibid.*, p. 325)

In America, he noted, the clergy remain politically separated from the government but nevertheless provide a moral stability among the people which permits the government to prosper. In other words, there is separation of church and state but not separation of church and religion.

### The Clergy Fuel the Flame of Freedom, Stress Morality and Alert the Citizenry to Dangerous Trends

The role of the churches to perpetuate the social and political culture of the United States provoked the following comment from de Tocqueville:

> "The Americans combine the notions of Christianity and of liberty so intimately in their minds that it is impossible to make them conceive the one without the other.... I have known societies formed by Americans to send out ministers of the Gospel into the new Western states, to found schools and churches there, lest religion should be allowed to die away in those remote settlements, and the rising states be less fitted to enjoy free institutions than the people from whom they came." (*Ibid.*, p. 317)

De Tocqueville discovered that while the clergy felt it would be demeaning to their profession to become involved in partisan politics, they nevertheless believed implicitly in their duty to keep religious principles and moral values flowing out to the people as the best safeguard for America's freedom and political security. In one of de Tocqueville's most frequently quoted passages, he stated:

> "I sought for the greatness and genius of America in her commodious harbors and her ample rivers, and it was not there; in her fertile fields and boundless prairies, and it was not there; in her rich mines and her vast world commerce, and it was not there. Not until I went to the churches of America and heard her pulpits aflame with righteousness did I understand the secret of her genius and power. America is great because she is good and if America ever ceases to be good, America will cease to be great."

### The Founders' Campaign for Equality of All Religions

One of the most remarkable attributes of the American Founders was undertaking to do something no other nation had ever successfully achieved —the task of providing legal equality for all religions, both Christian and non-Christian.

Jefferson and Madison were undoubtedly the foremost among the Founders in pushing through the first statutes in Virginia. Jefferson sought to dis-establish the official church of Virginia in 1776 but this effort was not completely successful until ten years later.

Meanwhile, in 1784, Patrick Henry was so enthusiastic about strengthening the whole spectrum of Christian churches that he introduced a bill "Establishing a Provision for Teachers of the Christian Religion." (This document is reproduced in the supplementary appendix of *Everson v. Board of Education*, 330 U.S. 1, 72.)

It was the intention of this bill to provide that each taxpayer would designate "to what society of Christians" his money should go. The funds collected by this means were to make "provision for a minister or teacher of the Gospel ... or the providing places of divine worship [for that denomination], and to none other use whatever...." (See the supplementary appendix of *Everson v. Board of Education*, 330 U.S. 1, 72, p. 94.)

Madison immediately reacted with his famous *Memorial and Remonstrance* in which he proclaimed with the greatest possible energy the principle that the State government should not prefer one religion over another. Equality of religions was the desired goal. He wrote:

"Who does not see that the same authority which can establish Christianity, in exclusion of all other religions, may establish with the same ease any particular sect of Christians, in exclusion of all other sects?... The bill violates that equality which ought to be the basis of every law." (*Letters and Other Writings of James Madison*, 1865, 1:163-164)

## Why the Founders Wanted the Federal Government Excluded From All Problems Relating to Religion and Churches

The Supreme Court has stated on numerous occasions that to most people freedom of religion is the most precious of all the inalienable rights next to life itself. When the United States was founded there were many Americans who were not enjoying freedom of religion to the fullest possible extent. At least seven of the states had officially established religions or denominations at the time the Constitution was adopted. These included: (Kruse, *The Historical Meaning and Judicial Construction of the Establishment of Religion Clause of the First Amendment*, 1962, Washburn, L. J., Vol. 2, pp. 65, 94-107.)

Connecticut (Congregational Church)
Delaware (Christian faith)
Maryland (Christian faith)
Massachusetts (Congregational Church)
New Hampshire (Protestant faith)
New Jersey (Protestant faith)
South Carolina (Protestant faith)

Under these circumstances the Founders felt it would have been catastrophic and might have precipitated civil strife if the federal government had tried to establish a national policy on religion or dis-establish the denominations which the States had adopted. Nevertheless, the Founders who were examining this problem were anxious to eventually see complete freedom of all faiths and an equality of all religions, both Christian and non-Christian. How could this be accomplished without stirring up civil strife?

### Justice Story Describes the Founders' Solution

In his famous Commentaries on the Constitution, Justice Story of the Supreme Court pointed out why the Founders as well as the States themselves felt the Federal Government should be absolutely excluded from any authority in the field of settling questions on religion. He states:

"In some of the states, Episcopalians constituted the predominant sect; in others, Presbyterians; in others, Congregationalists; in others, Quakers; and in others again, there was a close numerical rivalry among contending sects. It was impossible that there should not arise perpetual strife and perpetual jealousy on the subject of ecclesiastical ascendancy, if the national government were left free to create a religious establishment. The only security was in extirpating the power. But this alone would have been an imperfect security, if it had not been followed by a declaration of the right of the free exercise of religion, and a prohibition (as we have seen) of all religious tests. Thus the whole power over the subject of religion is left exclusive to the State Governments, to be acted upon according to their own sense of justice, and the State Constitutions...." (Article #1879 of the 1833 edition.)

This is why the First Amendment of the Constitution provides that "Congress shall make no law respecting an establishment of religion or prohibiting the free exercise thereof."

### Jefferson and Madison Emphasize the Intent of the Founders

It is clear from the writings of the Founders as well as the Commentaries of Justice Story that the First Amendment was designed to eliminate forever the interference of the Federal government in any religious matters within the various states. As Madison stated during the Virginia ratifying convention: "There is not a shadow of right in the general government to intermeddle with religion. Its least interference with it would be a most flagrant usurpation." (*The Elliot Debates*, Vol. 3, p. 330)

Jefferson took an identical position when he wrote the Kentucky-Virginia Resolutions of 1798: "... it is true as a general principle ... that no power over the freedom of religion, freedom of speech, or freedom of the press being delegated to the United States by the Constitution ... all lawful powers respecting the same did of right remain, and were reserved to the States, or to the people." (*The Kentucky-Virginia Resolutions and Mr. Madison's Report of 1799*, at 15-82)

### The Supreme Court as well as Congress Excluded from Jurisdiction Over Religion

In the Kentucky-Virginia Resolutions, Thomas Jefferson also made it clear that the Federal judicial system was likewise prohibited from intermeddling with religious matters within the States. He wrote:

"... special provision has been made by one of the amendments to the Constitution which expressly declares, the 'Congress shall make no law respecting an Establishment of religion, or prohibiting the free exercise thereof ... thereby guarding in the same sentence, and under the same words, the freedom of religion, of speech, and of the press, insomuch, that whatever violated either, throws down the sanctuary which covers the others, and that libels, falsehoods, and defamation, equally with hereby and false religions, are withheld from the cognizance of Federal tribunals." (*Ibid.*, p. 2-3 emphasis added)

### The Federal "Wall" Between Church and State

When Thomas Jefferson was serving in the Virginia legislature he introduced a bill to have a day of fasting and prayer, but when he became President, Jefferson said there was no authority in the Federal government to proclaim religious holidays. In a letter to the Danbury Baptist Association dated January 1, 1802, he explained his position and said the Constitution had created "a wall of separation between church and State." (Padover, *The Complete Works of Jefferson*, 1969, pp. 518-519)

In recent years the Supreme Court has undertaken to use this metaphor as an excuse for meddling in the religious issues arising within the various States. As we shall see later, it has not only presumed to take jurisdiction in these disputes, but has actually forced the States to take the same hands-off position toward religious matters even though this restriction originally applied only to the Federal government. This obvious distortion of the original intent of Jefferson (when he used the metaphor of a "wall" separating church and state) becomes entirely apparent when the statements and actions of Jefferson are examined in their historical context.

It will be recalled that Jefferson and Madison were anxious that the States intervene in religious matters until there was equality among all religions and that all churches or religions assigned preferential treatment should be disestablished from such preferment. They further joined with the other Founders in expressing an anxiety that all religions be encouraged in order to promote the moral fiber and religious tone of the people. This, of course, would be impossible if there were an impenetrable "wall" between church and state on the state level. Jefferson's "wall' was obviously intended only for the Federal government, and the Supreme Court application of this metaphor to the states has come under severe criticism. (Dallin Oaks, editor, *The Wall Between Church and State*, 1963, pp. 2-3)

## Religious Problems Must Be Solved Within The Various States

In Thomas Jefferson's second inaugural address, he virtually signaled the States to press forward in settling their religious issues since it was within their jurisdiction and not that of the Federal government:

> "In matters of religion, I have considered that its free exercise is placed by the Constitution independent of the powers of the general government. I have therefore undertaken, on no occasion, to prescribe the religious exercises suited to it; but have left them as the Constitution found them, under the direction and discipline of state or church authorities acknowledged by the several religious societies."

Jefferson, along with the other Founders, believed that it was within the power of the various States to eliminate those inequities which existed between the various faiths and then pursue a policy of encouraging religious institutions of all kinds because it was in the public interest to use their influence to provide the moral stability needed for "good government and the happiness of mankind." (*Northwest Ordinance*, Article 3)

Jefferson's Resolution for disestablishing the Church of England in Virginia was not to set up a wall between the State and the Church but simply, as he explained it, for the purpose of "taking away the privilege and preeminence of one religious sect over another, and thereby [establishing] ... equal rights among all." (J. Boyd, editor, *The Papers of Thomas Jefferson*, p. 531, note 1)

## Affirmative Programs to Encourage
## All Religions on the State Level

In view of the extremely inflexible and rigid position which the U.S. Supreme Court has taken in recent years concerning the raising up of a "wall" between State government and religion, it is remarkable how radically different the Founders looked upon such matters.

Take, for example, their approval of religious meetings in tax-supported public buildings. With the Founders there was no objection as to the propriety of using public buildings for religious purposes for that was to be encouraged. The only question was whether or not the facilities could be made available equally to all denominations desiring them. Notice how Jefferson reflects his deep satisfaction in the way the churches were using the local courthouse in Charlottesville, near Jefferson's home:

"In our village of Charlottesville, there is a good degree of religion, with a small spice only of fanaticism. We have four sects,
but without either church or meeting-house. The court-house is
the common temple, one Sunday in the month to each. Here,
Episcopalian and Presbyterian, Methodist and Baptist, meet together, join in hymning their Maker, listen with attention and devotion to each others' preachers, and all mix in society with
perfect harmony." (Ford, editor, *Works of Thomas Jefferson*, Vol.
12, pp. 270-271)

One cannot help asking the modern Supreme Court: "Where is the
wall of separation between church and state when the courthouse is approved for the common temple of all the religious sects of a village?"

Of course, Jefferson would be the first to require some other arrangement if all of the churches could not be accommodated equally, but so
long as they were operating equally and harmoniously together, it was
looked upon as a commendable situation. The fact that they were utilizing a tax-supported public building was not even made an issue.

### Jefferson Proposes Accommodations For
### Religious Instructions at a State School

Not only did the Congress of the Founders' day provide in the Northwest Ordinance that the basic tenets of religion and the fundamentals of
morality should be taught in the public schools, but Jefferson proposed
that the University of Virginia extend its facilities to the various denominations so that each student could worship and study in the church of his
choice. As Jefferson had written:

"Can the liberties of a nation be thought secure when we have
removed (by eliminating religious instruction) their only firm
basis — a conviction in the minds of the people that these liberties are of the gift of God? That they are not to be violated but
with his wrath?" (*Ibid.*, Vol. 4, p. 83)

To encourage religious studies by college students of different faiths,
Jefferson proposed the following:

1.  He suggested that the responsibility for teaching "the proofs of
    the being of a God, the creator, preserver, and supreme ruler of
    the universe, the author of all the relations of morality, and of the
    laws and obligations these infer, will be within the province of the
    professor of ethics." (Randolph, editor, Early History of the Uni-
    versity of Virginia, p. 441)

2.  The University faculty will also teach "the developments of these moral obligations, of those in which all sects agree, (together with) a knowledge of the languages, Hebrew, Greek, and Latin a basis will be formed common to all sects." (Ibid.)
3.  Encourage "the different religious sections to establish, each for itself, a professorship of their own tenets, on the confines (campus) of the university, so near ... that their students may attend the lectures there, and have the free use of our library, and every other accommodation we can give them; preserving, however, their independence of us and of each other." (Ibid., p. 475)
4.  Jefferson was also in favor of "enabling students of the University to attend religious exercises with the professor of their particular sect, either in the rooms of the buildings still to be erected (by each denomination on campus) ... or in the lecturing room of such professor." (Ibid.)
5.  Jefferson felt that students should be urged to participate in regular religious exercises but do so without conflicting with the established schedule of the University. Said he: "Should the religious sects of this State, or any of them, according to the invitation held out to them, establish within or adjacent to, the precincts of the University, schools for instruction in the religion of their sect, the students of the University will be free, and expected to attend religious worship at the establishment of their respective sects ... in time to meet their school in the University at its stated hour." (Padover, editor, The Complete Jefferson, p. 1110, emphasis added)

### Summary of Jefferson's Views

From these various documented sources it is apparent that Thomas Jefferson had a number of clearly defined views which he hoped would become the traditional American life-style with reference to religion and the Constitution. Perhaps these views might be summarized as follows:

1.  The First Amendment prohibits the Federal government from intermeddling in religious matters in any way. It is not to take any positive action which would tend to create or favor some "establishment of religion" nor is it to interfere or prohibit the free exercise of any religion.
2.  The individual state, however has the responsibility to see that laws and conditions are such that all religious denominations or sects receive equal treatment.
3.  There should be a regularly established policy of teaching the

fundamentals of religion and morality in the public schools.

4.  In addition, there should be an opportunity on the university level at least, for each denomination to be invited to build facilities on or adjacent to the campus where the students of that particular denomination could be expected to attend regular worship services and receive instructions in their particular faith.

5.  Professors might also hold special services or classes of religious instruction in the rooms assigned to them at the university in order to accommodate the needs of the students belonging to their particular faith.

6.  Students studying for the ministry at nearby seminaries should be allowed to have full access to the resources of the university library.

7.  However, in spite of all of these efforts to encourage religion indirectly, there must be no use of tax funds to subsidize any religion directly.

## Jefferson Sees Great Advantages in Following These Guidelines

By leaving it exclusively to the States to work out the equal encouragement of all religions, but at the same time give them no direct subsidy, Jefferson felt the goals of the Founders would be achieved. He felt their was a need to fill "the chasm" of religious ignorance which constituted a liability to society and at the same time leave "inviolate the constitutional freedom of religion, the most unalienable and sacred of all human rights." (Randolph, editor, *Early History of the University of Virginia*, p. 475)

Jefferson, like other leaders among the Founders, seemed anxious to not only encourage all religious faiths on a basis of equality but also to have them develop a spirit of toleration for each other. In referring to the university campus and its immediate environs where all faiths would be invited to provide facilities, Jefferson wrote:

> "... by bringing the sects together, and mixing them with the mass of other students, we shall soften their asperities, liberalize and neutralize their prejudices and make the general religion a religion of peace, reason and morality." (Ford, editor, *Works of Jefferson*, Vol. 12, p. 272)

## How the Courts Began Building a Wall
## Between Religion and the State

It is a well-known principle of substantive law that the Constitution and the law should be interpreted very strictly according to the original intent of those who created it. As Chief Justice Taney stated in the Dred Scott decision, "It (the Constitution) speaks not only in the same words, but with the same meaning and intent with which it spoke when it came from the hands of the framers...." (19 Howard 395)

In the case of Barron v. Baltimore (7 Peters 243; 8 L. Ed. 672-1833) Chief Justice Marshall affirmed that the Bill of Rights in the Constitution was a series of prohibitions against the Federal government to prevent it from encroaching on the States. With reference to religion, this meant that there was a Federal "wail" between the Federal government and any "establishment of religion "just as Jefferson had said.

However, in 1925, in the case of Gitlow v. New York (268 U.S. 652) the Supreme Court undertook to use certain provisions in the Federal Bill of Rights and apply them to the States. The court justified this action on the basis of the Fourteenth Amendment which provides that "No State shall make or enforce any law which shall abridge the privileges or immunities of citizens of the United States; nor shall any State deprive any person of life, liberty, or property, without due process of law; nor deny to any person within its jurisdiction the equal protection of the laws."

The opponents of traditional theistic religion and morality saw the Gitlow case as an opportunity to invoke the power of the Federal courts to build a wall between each of the States and any form of religious encouragement even though it was provided indirectly. In other words, they would review the Founders' original policy.

In 1940 the case of Cantwell v. Connecticut (310 U.S. 296) was the first ruling of the Supreme Court in which the "Gitlow doctrine" was applied to religious liberty and in 1947 Everson v. Board of Education (330 U.S. 1) was the first time the Supreme Court applied the "due process" clause of the Fourteenth Amendment to make the Federal wall of separation apply to religious matters among the individual States.

What this amounted to was the actual breaking down of the Federal wall set up by the First Amendment so that the Supreme Court actually usurped jurisdiction over religious matters in the States and began dictating what the States could or could not do with reference to religious questions. Without a doubt, there has been a severe wrenching of the Constitution from its original First Amendment moorings ever since this new trend began.

## In 1948 the Supreme Court Prohibited
## Teaching of Religion in Schools

It is interesting that in the debates over ratification Madison had stated the position of the Founders when he said: "There is not a shadow of right in the general government to intermeddle with religion. Its least interference with it would be a most flagrant usurpation." (Elliot Debates, Vol. 3, p. 330)

Nevertheless, in 1948 in McCollum v. Board of Education (333 U.S. 203), the Supreme Court interviewed in a religious question, used the Gitlow doctrine to tell a State Board of Education that it would not allow children, even with their parents' consent, to take religion classes in school. The students had been authorized by the Board of Education to sign up for these classes which were being taught by the representatives of their own particular faith and expected then to attend these classes as part of their regular studies just as Jefferson had recommended for the University of Virginia. The Court ignored the fact that there was equality of opportunity for any of the denominations to provide such classes and used the "wall" doctrine to outlaw use of tax-supported facilities for the teaching of religion by every denomination. There was a strong dissent by Justice Reed.

## In 1952 the Supreme Court Approved
## "Released Time" for Religious Education

It is of further interest that in 1952 the Supreme Court took its newly acquired jurisdiction over religious questions in State schools to announce in Zorach v. Clauson (343 U.S. 306) that it was very solicitous of religion and would approve classes in religion during the regular school day providing the classes were held separate from any tax-supported property. Justice Douglas wrote the opinion from the following frame of reference:

> "We are a religious people whose institutions presuppose a Supreme Being. We guarantee the freedom to worship as one chooses. We make room for a wide variety of beliefs and creeds as the spiritual needs of man deem necessary. We sponsor an attitude on the part of government that shows no partiality to any one group and that lets each flourish according to the seal of its adherents and the appeal of its dogma."

Justice Douglas even went further to state; "... we find no constitutional requirement which makes it necessary for government to be hostile to religion and to throw its weight against efforts to widen the effective scope of religious influence."

## The Cultural Vacuum Created by the
## Court: So-called "Neutrality"

However, in the 1947 case of Everson v. Board of Education (330 U.S. 1) the Supreme Court made it clear that neither the Federal government nor a State government could encourage religion in any way. Justice Black spoke for the Court and declared in his opinion, "Neither a State nor the Federal government ... can pass laws which aid one religion, aid all religions, or prefer one religion over another."

The Founders would have heartily endorsed Justice Black's "no-preference" doctrine, but they would have no doubt objected vigorously to the outlawing of indirect aid for and encouragement to "all religions." In the final analysis, it was "all religions" the Founders had said they were relying upon to undergird society with those moral teachings which are "necessary to good government and the happiness of mankind." (Northwest Ordinance previously cited)

No doubt they would have further objected to the Court's presumptive usurpation in taking jurisdiction over a religious question which had been specifically reserved by the First Amendment to the States themselves.

The Founders seemed fully aware that failure to encourage "all religions" in their important role of teaching fundamental morality would leave an empty void or cultural vacuum in their formula for a great new civilization of freedom and prosperity. It seems that all empirical evidence of history and human experience sustains their position. Then why did the Court take the position it did?

All of the cases from then until now suggest that the Court considered its position of "neutrality" more fair and more correct in administering true justice. What some legal scholars are beginning to point out however, is that the position of so-called neutrality has not achieved what the Court said it intended. It has indeed given "secularism" or the emphasis of non-spiritual and non-moral principles the clear advantage of a virtual monopoly in the arena of public education and the administering of public institutions.

## In 1962 the Supreme Court Outlawed
## Prescribed Prayers in School

In the case of Engel v. Vitale (370 U.S. 429) the issue was over the fact that the New York regents had prepared a nondenominational prayer for use in the public schools. The New York Court of Appeals upheld the prayer, but the Supreme Court once more intermeddled in a religious question of a State by ruling that a nondenominational prayer prescribed by the officials of the State was "establishing" a religion.

However, contrary to popular belief, the Court did not say that prayers were unlawful which were voluntary and prescribed or set by the State. Nevertheless, this case gave the advocates of secularism an excuse to push through ruling in many States that prayer would not be allowed in the schools.

## In 1963 the Supreme Court Outlawed the Lord's Prayer and Bible Reading in the Public Schools

In School District of Abington v. Schempp (374 U.S. 203) the Supreme Court ruled that opening exercises at the high school involving the recitation of the Lord's Prayer as well as reading Bible verses were unconstitutional. The Court rejected the proposition that the opening exercises had a secular purpose, namely, the "promotion of moral values, the contradiction to the materialistic trends of our times, the perpetuation of our institutions and the teachings of literature."

It was pointed out to the Court that "unless these religious exercises are permitted, a 'religion of secularism' is established in the schools," but the Court rejected this argument.

At this point it appears that for all intent and purpose the design of the Founding Fathers to have the public schools teach the fundamental principles of religion and morality was dead.

## Need for an Amendment

It is doubtful that the desires of the vast majority of American parents as well as the intent of the Founding Fathers to have these ideals taught in the schools will ever be restored without a Constitutional amendment further defining the right of the States to have exclusive jurisdiction over the determination of questions involving religious questions. At the same time it would undoubtedly be the further desire of the overwhelming majority of Americans that the States be required to give equality of encouragement to religion on a non-preference basis.

Since no State presently has an "establishment" or preferred religion and all the States require equal treatment of the churches, the remaining task is to adopt a Constitutional amendment somewhat along the following lines: "No branch or agency of the Federal government shall have any authority to influence or adjudicate any issue relating to questions of religion arising within the confines of any State.

Such an amendment would put the entire problem back where the Founders left it exclusively within the determination of each State.

### Daniel Webster Describes the Founders' Traditional Goal

In our own day of accelerating crimes of violence, narcotics addiction, billion-dollar pornography sales, hedonistic sexual aberrations, high divorce rates, and deteriorating family life, the American people might well recall the stirring words of Daniel Webster when he spoke to the New York Historical Society, February 22, 1852:

> "Unborn ages and visions of glory crowd upon my soul, the realization of all which, however, is in the hands and good pleasure of Almighty God; but, under his divine blessing, it will be dependent on the character and virtues of ourselves and of our posterity ... if we and they shall live always in the fear of God, and shall respect his commandments ... we may have the highest hopes of the future fortunes of our country.... It will have no decline and fall. It will go on prospering.... But if we and our posterity reject religious instruction and authority, violate the rules of eternal justice, trifle with the injunctions of morality, and recklessly destroy the political constitution which holds us together, no man can tell how sudden a catastrophe may overwhelm us, that shall bury all our glory in profound obscurity. Should that catastrophe happen, let it have no history! Let the horrible narrative never be written!"

Unfortunately, unless the present generation of American leadership returns to fundamental values, that history is being written right now.

# About the Author
## W. Cleon Skousen

**(1913-2006)**

W. Cleon Skousen was a world renowned teacher, lecturer and scholar for more than 60 years. Born in Raymond, Alberta, Canada on January 20, 1913, Dr. Skousen's growing up years were spent in Canada, Mexico, and California.

He attended college at the San Bernardino Junior College where he was elected Student Body President.

In 1934 he went to law school at George Washington University in Washington DC, where he earned his Juris Doctorate and was admitted to practice law in the District of Columbia. At this same time he was employed with the Federal Bureau of Investigation (FBI).

Dr. Skousen married Jewel Pitcher of San Bernardino, California, in August 1936. During their 69 years of marriage, they raised eight children and became the grandparents of 50 grandchildren and more than 90 great-grandchildren.

Dr. Skousen served the FBI for 16 years (1935-1951), and worked closely with J. Edgar Hoover including a hot-spot stint as the director of communications. As a prolific writer and speaker, he wrote his national best seller, "The Naked Communist" and later became the editor of the nation's leading police magazine, "Law And Order." In 1960 he began a speaking tour around the country addressing the important political issues facing America at that time. During this period, he averaged 300 speeches a year.

In 1972 Dr. Skousen organized a non-profit educational foundation named "The Freemen Institute." Later changed to "The National Center for Constitutional Studies" (NCCS), Dr. Skousen and his staff became the nation's leading organization in teaching students and legislators seminars on the Founding Fathers and the U.S. Constitution. His books "The Making of America" and "The 5,000 Year Leap" have been used nationwide to educate students on the original intent of the Founding Fathers.

His many books and recordings addressed diverse subjects ranging from the raising of boys, to the principles of good government, to prophetic history. Dr. Skousen accumulated a wealth of knowledge and optimism—information that he called the "diamond dust" of exciting history, natural law and eternal principles of hope. These principles he painstakingly distilled into the pages of over 40 books and pamphlets, to be shared in an exciting and inspirational manner. This is what made him so popular with audiences of millions around the world.

# INDEX

## A

Adams, John, helps produce original design for United States seal, 18-19; admired by American colonists for his virtue, 42; on relationship of religion and morality to survival of Constitution, 46-47; considers politics a "divine science," 50, 145; on motives of political leaders, 50; on his studies in governmental theory in preparation for political service, 50; his reflections on a life of public service, 50; on fundamental religious principles, 62; on true meaning of equality, 80; on essential nature of property rights, 96; on relationship of property rights to liberty, 127; an early advocate of separation-of-powers doctrine, 145-56; influence on state constitution of Massachusetts, 146-47; unappreciated for a century, 147; on capacity of Constitution to govern 300 million freemen, 147; on preservation of freedom by fixed laws, 174; on beginnings of public education in Massachusetts, 177; compares European and American literacy, 179; on manifest destiny of America, 194, 215-216

Adams, Samuel, on unconstitutionality of socialistic welfare state, 27, 90; on relationship of virtue to survival of free government in United States, 46-47, 207; on electing virtuous leaders, 47; sacrifices fortune to serve in politics, 50; on fundamental religious principles, 62-61 ; on man's responsibility to preserve his rights, 200-01

Alliances, Founders' warnings against, with foreign nations, 209, 189-193; see also Foreign Relations

America. See United States

Anarchy, as an extreme on Founders' political spectrum, 11-15; natural progression from, to tyranny, 19-20; United States brought too close to, under Articles of Confederation, 20; See also Political spectrum

Anglo-Saxons, Jefferson's admiration for institutes of freedom under, 13; basic characteristics of common law under, 14-15; common law under, compared with People's Law of ancient Israel, 15-18; represented in original design for United States seal, 18-19; law of reparation practiced by, 102; attitude toward divine law, 103; government of, based on consent of the people, 106; common law of, unwritten, 157; effects of Norman Conquest on, 157-70; local self-government among, 181-82.

Aristocracy, natural vs. artificial, 48-49; strengths and weaknesses of, 142-143

Aristotle, philosophical errors of, corrected by Cicero, 33-34; on superiority of government by law over government by men, 174

Articles of Confederation, United States brought too close to anarchy by weakness of, 20; weakened by requirement of unanimous consent for changes, 165

## B

Banking, establishment of national bank, 137; danger of allowing banks to issue currency, 137; problems created by fractional, 137-38; efforts of Jefferson, Jackson, and Lincoln to eliminate fractional, 138-39; Jefferson's criticisms of, 138-39. See also Money

Bastiat, Frederic, on protection of man's natural rights, 97-98

Beck, Glenn, Introduction to, The Five Thousand Year Leap, 1-7

Bible, Studied by Founders, 29; as basis of American political philosophy, 71; cultural influence of extensive reading of, 182; prohibited in today's public schools, 251

Bill of Rights (American), origin of, 21-22; added to Constitution to limit central government, 161-62

Bill of Rights (English), signed by William and Mary, 158

Black Panthers, 84

Blacks, experience of, as minority in United States, 83-85

Blackstone, Sir William, studied by Founders, 29; advocates natural law as only reliable basis for sound government, 33; on relationship of human laws to God's revealed law, 75-76; on supremacy of natural rights, 94; on man's three great natural rights, 96-97; on role of God's revealed law, 99-100; identifies natural law with Gods revealed law, 100-103; on supremacy of divine law, 104

## C

Carson, Clarence on true meaning of equality, 80

Chamberlain, John, on attitude of American intellectuals toward Adam Smith in 1920's, 134; on changes in governmental and economic theories in United States during Great Depression, 135; on rediscovery of Founders; and Adam Smith's ideas among American intellectuals, 136

Charles I (king of England), signs of English Petition of Rights, 158

Checks and balances, principle of, 149-156; relationship to separation of powers, 149-150; failure of, in recent years, 151-152; need for better understanding and enforcement of, 151; designed to protect will of the people, 151-153; examples of, under Constitution, 153-155

Chinese, success in overcoming disadvantages of minority in United States, 82

Churches. See Religion

Cicero, Marcus Tullius, studied by Founders, 29; a source of Founders' ideas about natural law, 33-43; brief sketch of his life, 35; identifies natural law with law of God, 36-37; comprehends two great commandments later taught by Jesus, 39-40; on God's Law of love as basis for justice, 40-41; warns against legislation in violation of natural law, 41-42; on virtue of statesmanship, 49

Clark, J. Reuben, Jr., on relationships of federal departments under Constitution, 49; warns against United States entrance into World War II, 256

Cleaver, Eldridge, story of, 84

Cleveland, Grover, on unconstitutionality of government welfare programs, 129

Coke, Sir Edward, studied by Founders, 29

Communism, as an extreme on today's political spectrum, 11; virtually identical with fascism, 11-12; unconstitutional in United States, 27

Communists, lessons from takeover in Hungary by, 88

Congress, function of, under Constitutional government, 23; has exclusive power to issue and control money supply, 136-137; imposition of excessive taxes by, 151; method of Senatorial elections changed by Seventeenth Amendment, 163; tendency to avoid responsibility to provide adequate national defense, 186; Washington's fifth annual address to, 186-187. See also Federal government

Connecticut, Fundamental Orders of, 158-159

Constitution (United States), not a "conglomerate of compromises," 21; ratification of three governmental branches under, 21-22; need for both problem-solving and conservation philosophies under, 24-29; those who would not uphold, have no right to public office, 25; responsibility of future Americans to preserve, 28; survival of, dependent on virtue in the people, 44; on exclusion of federal government from all religious matters, 61; built upon religious principles, 71; amendments to ensure equal rights, 85-86; does not authorize federal government to participate in public welfare programs, 91,129; ultimate authority of, resides in the people, 107; attacks on, 118; political leaders to be bound by "chains" of, 120; will never be obsolete, 122; distortion of "general welfare' clause, 128; gives Congress exclusive power to issue and control money supply, 137; requires gold or silver backing for currency, 137; partly based on Montesquieu's model constitution, 143; Franklin's attitude toward finished, 147; John Adams on capacity of, to govern 300 million freemen, 147; usurpation of power to be prevented by internal checks and balances, 153; evidence of divine influence on, 153; examples of checks and balances under, 153-54; provides for peaceful self-repair of government, 155-56; beginnings of, in Mayflower Compact in Fundamental Orders of Connecticut, 158; represents wisdom of many persons, 159; first ten amendments added to limit central government, 161-62; Ninth and Tenth Amendments quoted, 162; original balance between federal and state governments disturbed, 163; impact of Seventeenth Amendment on federal-state balance, 164-65; provisions in, for majority rule, 166-67; designed to prevent centralization of power, 169; 19th-century young children trained in, 181; authorizes government borrowing, 207; failure of unconstitutional practices by federal government, 210.

Constitutional Convention of 1787, 20-21; Madison attends, on borrowed money, 20, 52; Franklin's address on salaries for political offices, 52-55; Madison's acknowledgement of God's influences on, 77; debates on number of Presidents, 144; better document produced by, than could have been written by any individual, 159.

Constitutions, should be structured to protect against human frailties of rulers, 119; unalienable rights best preserved by written, 157-160; tradition or written, of American origin, 158.

Creator. See God

Currency. See Money

**D**

De Tocqueville, Alexis. See Tocqueville, Alexis de

Debt, immorality of passing public, to next generation, 27, 208; Jefferson's criticism of public, 138; destructive to freedom, 204-214; definition of, 204; individual, benumbs of the human spirit, 204-205; Founders' attitude toward, 205-208; history of United States national, 212; U.S. National, 1791-2006 (chart), 211-212; changing attitude of Americans toward public, 200, 212-213; compared to drug addiction, 214.

Declaration of Independence, meaning of "all men are created equal," 79-80; examples of unalienable rights not listed in, 94-95; other documents with similar language, 95; on people's right to alter or abolish a tyrannical government, 109-110.

Defense, strong military, necessary to preserve freedom, 183-187; Franklin's philosophy of, 184-185; duty of government to provide adequate military, 184; duty of people to pay for, 184-185; Washington's statements on national, 185-186.

Democracy, weaknesses of, 113-116, 142; contrasted with a republic, 114-117; modern confusion about meaning of, 115-119; United States erroneously identified as a, 117-119; relationship to socialism, 115-119; strengths of, 142.

Dickinson, John, chairs of committee which produced original version of Articles of Confederation, 20; uncertain whether Americans were virtuous enough for self-government, 42.

Duties, unalienable, accompany unalienable rights, 100-101; examples of public and private, 101-102.

## E

Ebenstein, William, on life of Cicero, 33-34; on forwardness of Cicero's ideas, 37.

Economics, experiments with communal, in early Jamestown, 3; beginnings of free-market, 3; progress resulting from free-market, in 1800s, 4-5; the poor benefit most under free-market, leads to prosperity, 131; formula for free-market, described by Adam Smith, 132; four laws of economic freedom, 132; proper role of government in, 133; movements away from free-market, in United States, 133; need for monetary reform in United States, 137; "boom and bust" pattern caused by fractional banking, 138. See also Banking; Debt; Money

Education, citizenry needs, to maintain government in balanced center of political spectrum, 28; importance of, in fostering virtue among youth,45; of virtuous citizens for service in political offices, 48-49; curriculum prescribed for public schools by Northwest Ordinance of 1787, 59-60; Jefferson's Bill for Establishing Elementary Schools in Virginia, 61; role of religion in early American schools, 64; preservation of freedom by, of electorate, 177-182; be-

ginnings of public, in Massachusetts, 177-178; importance of local school boards, 177; European and American literacy compared by John Adams, 179; Alexis de Tocqueville's observations on American, in 1831, 179; 19th-century young children trained in Constitution, 181; Bible reading prohibited in today's public schools, 182.

England, history of written guarantees of rights in, 157-158; undermining of local self-government in, 169.

Equality, meaning of, in free governments, 79-80; problems of minorities in attaining, 81-85; areas wherein, is impossible, 85; of men and women under God's law, 200.

Europe, Founders' warnings against United States involvement in affairs of, 192-193.

Executive, function of, under Constitutional government, 23; single, advocated by Montesquieu, 144; usurpation of power by the, 151.

## F

Family, duty of government to protect role of, 199-204; equality and roles of men and women under God's law, 200; unity of the, in early New England, 202; Franklin's observations on marriage, 202; parents' responsibility for children, 203; independence of adult children, 203; responsibility of children to parents, 203; location in normal structure of, a threat to foundations of society, 204.

Fascism, as an extreme in today's political spectrum, 11; virtually identical with communism, 11.

Federal government, separation of powers between states and, 22, 171; Founders' desire to exclude, from all religious matters, 241; not authorized by Constitution to participate in public welfare programs, 91, 128; usurpation of states' rights by, 151; original balance between states and, disturbed, 161-162; limited role of, under Constitution, 171-172; outlays of 1789-2006 (chart), 211; U.S. national debt, 1791-2006 (chart), 112; resistance to reductions in social programs of, 213. See also Congress; Executive; Government; Supreme Court; United States

Federal Reserve System, 137.

Federalist Party, monarchist fringe in, 25

Fiske, John, on the Fundamental Orders of Connecticut , 159; warns against administration of local affairs by federal government, 172; on importance of local school boards, 178; on sense of "manifest destiny" among early American settlers, 215-216.

Flood, Charles Bracelen, on Washington's acknowledgments of God's intervention during Revolutionary War, 76.

Foreign relations, Jefferson's famous rule for, of United States, 189; Founders' doctrine of "separatism" in, 189-194; Switzerland follows policy advocated by American Founders, 190; Jefferson anticipates Monroe Doctrine, 194; reconciliation of "separatism" replaced by "internationalism" in early twentieth century, 194; need for reconsideration of United States, 197. See also Alliances; Manifest Destiny; United States

Founding Fathers (American), assemble 28 great ideas into the success formula that helped change the world, 5; political spectrum used by, 11-12; efforts to establish and maintain a government in "balanced center" of political spectrum, 12, 18-28; study People's Law as practiced by Anglo-Saxons and ancient Israelites, 13; warnings against the welfare state, 27; origin of basic beliefs held in common by, 28-29; Cicero's ideas appreciated by, 34; desire to form a virtuous society, 40, 41-42, 44-45; on relationship of virtue to survival of free government under Constitution, 44-46, 187; writings of, as

source of formula for producing leaders of character and virtue, 56; basic beliefs of, 56-57; on fundamental religious principles, 60-62; desire for equality among all religious sects, 65-66, 69-70; want federal government excluded from all religious matters, 67-70; want state governments to encourage religion, 70-71; existence of God the fundamental premise of their political philosophy, 74-75; attitude toward God, 76-77; believe man's unalienable rights to come from God, 93; attitude toward people's right of self-government, 106; discredited by American intellectuals in first half of twentieth century, 135-136; need for return to economic ideas of, 136-137; Montesquieu's writings admired by, 143; their desires for a written constitution, 158; want American government formed by many persons, 159; attitude toward law, 175; education of, 178-179; policy of peace through strength, 187; views on United States foreign relations, 189-194; on manifest destiny of America, 193-195, 215-219; attitude toward debt, 206-207: United States can return to formula of, without economic depression, 214.

Franklin, Benjamin, helps produce original design for united States seal, 18-19; fears that American government will end in monarchy, 18-19, 54;on relationship of virtue to freedom, 41; on relationship of virtue to public well-being, 45; on salaries for political offices, 51-56; condemns politicians who seek office for selfish reasons, 52-53; praises for Washington for serving his country without salary, 54-55; describes his daily activities in summer of 1775, 55-56; on five fundamentals of all sound religion, 61-62; on government programs for the poor, 90-91; attitude toward finished Constitution, 147; limited formal education of,179; false stories about illegitimate children, 201-202; on marriage, 202; on debt, 207.

Freedom, worldwide spirit of, originates primarily in United States, 3; progress resulting from spirit of, in 1800s, 3-4; absence of, under Ruler's law, common law, 11-13; under Anglo-Saxton common law, 13-14; virtue required for survival of, 41-46, 187; cannot survive without religion, 59-71; dependent on maintenance of property rights, 123-129; four laws of economic, 132-133; local self-government as keystone to preserving, 169-172; preserved by fixed laws, 173-176; maintained by an educated electorate, 177-182; strong military defense necessary to preserve, 183-188; right to, a gift of God, 188; debt destructive to, 205-14.

Friedman, Milton, on failure of unconstitutional practices of American government, 210.

Frothingham, Richard, on undermining of local self-government in England, 169-170; on survival of instinct for self-government among emigration Englishmen, 170.

Fundamental Orders of Connecticut, 158-159.

proper role of, 87-91; what powers can be assigned to, 87-88; violates people's rights by redistributing wealth, 87-89; the people as a source of power in, 105-107, 151-52; people's right to alter or abolish a, 109-11; defined as force, 120; need for controls on, 120-21; primary purpose of, to protect property, 126-27; proper role of, in economics, 132-33; separation of powers in, 141-147; strengths and weaknesses of various forms of, 142; means for peaceful self-repair of, 155-156; importance of limiting and defining powers of, 161-64; majority rule in, 165-67; should be by law, not by men, 173-176; duty of, to provide adequate military defense, 184-84; duty of, to protect role of family, 199, 203-204. See also Checks and balances; Federal government; Political spectrum; Self-government; Separation of powers

Greece, unsuccessful attempts at democracy in, 113; conquered by rome, 141

Guizot, Francois, on survival of instinct for self-government among men, 170-71

# G

God, natural law identified with law of, 35, 101, 104; role of, in Founders' political philosophy, 73-77; reality and attributes of, 73-75; existence of, the Founders' fundamental premise, 74-75; revealed laws of, the foundation of a just society, 75; Founders' attitude toward, 76-77; source of man's unalienable rights, 93; role of divine law revealed by, 99-104; law of criminal justice revealed by, 102; supremacy of law revealed by, 104; property rights considered a gift of, under English common law, 123-24; right to freedom a gift of, 187-88; equality of men and women under law of, 200

Government, measurement of systems of, on Founders' political spectrum, 11-13;

# H

Hamilton, Alexander, on instability of national governments 18; on inevitability of inequality under free government, 85; on self-government, 107; on distrust of political leaders, 119-120; on need to limit power of government, 162; on need for balance between federal and state governments, 162-163; on majority rule in government, 166.

Happiness, object of human existence, 4; dependent on a return of fundamentals, 5; property rights essential to the pursuit of, 96.

Hengist and Horsa, represented in original design for United States seal, 18-19.

Henry, Patrick, introduces bill to provide for religious teachers, 66

Hooker, Thomas, writes Fundamental Orders of Connecticut, 15, 158-159; studied by Founders, 29.

Hoover, J. Edgar, attitude toward Japanese-Americans during World War II, 82.

Hopkins, Harry, political formula of "tax, spend, elect," 213.

Hungary, lessons from communist takeover in, 88.


# I

Intercollegiate Socialist Society, 113-114, 117, 134.

International relations. See Foreign relations

Israel (ancient), Angelo-Saxon common law compared with people's Law in, 14-17; represented in original design for United States seal, 18-19; law of reparation practiced by, 102; local self-government in, 169.


# J

Jackson, Andrew, efforts to establish sound monetary system, 138.

James I (king of England), Jamestown named after, 1-2.

Jamestown, Virginia, primitive conditions in early, 1; experiments with communal economics in, 1-2.

Japanese, success in overcoming disadvantages as minority in United States, 82.

Jay, John, uncertain whether Americans were virtuous enough for self-government, 42-45; on manifest destiny of America, 217.

Jefferson, Thomas, born in Virginia, 2; admiration for Anglo-Saxon heritage of People's Law, 13; helps produce original design for United States seal, 18-19; on need for both problem-solving and conservation philosophies under Constitution, 25; warns against extreme elements in political parties, 25-27; conversation with Washington about monarchists in national government, 25-27; on need to maintain balanced center of political spectrum, 28; warns against public welfare, 28; condemns deficit sending, 28, 206-207; on immorality of passing debt to next generation, 29, 208-209; on need for educated electorate, 29; on virtue, 45; on "natural aristocracy", 48; on educating citizens for service in political offices, 49; on teaching of religion in Virginia schools, 62; on fundamental religious principles, 68-69; attempts to disestablish state churches in Virginia, 66; on exclusion of federal government from all religious matters, 68-69; on separation of church and state, 69-71; on involvement of state governments in religious matters, 69-71; approves use of public buildings for religious worship, 70-71; on relationship of social duties to natural rights, 100; on people's right to alter or abolish a tyrannical government, 109; followers of, call United States a "democratic republic," 118; on binding political leaders by "the chains of the Constitution, " 119; on Adam Smith's The Wealth of Nations, 131; on danger of allowing banks to issue currency, 137; on fractional banking, 138; on public debt, 138; efforts to establish sound monetary system, 139; on currency problems created by banks, 139; on majority rule and minority rights, 162; on local self-government in New England townships, 169-170; on importance of local self-government, 170-171; on limited role of federal government under Constitution, 172; re-writes state laws of Virginia, 176; on manifest destiny of America, 193.

Jeremiah (Old Testament prophet), on liberty in ancient Israel, 16

Jesus, teachings of, studied by Founders, 29; teaches two great commandments identified by Cicero, 39.

Jethro (father-in-law of Moses), counsels Moses to establish People's Law in ancient Israel, 17.

John (king of England), forced to sign Magna Charta, 157

Judiciary, function of, under Constitutional government, 23-24; federal, restricted from jurisdiction in religious matters, 69; improper meddling of Supreme Court in religious matters, 69, 70-71; Montesquieu's views on need for independent, 143-144; usurpation of power by, 151. See also Supreme Court.

Justice, based on God's law of love, 38-39; provided only by legislation which conforms to natural law, 38-39; God's law of criminal, 102.

## K

Kentucky Resolutions of, 1798, on exclusion of federal government from all religious matter, 68; on binding political leaders by "the chains of the Constitution," 120.

Kings. See Monarchy

## L

Laidler, Harry W., co-director of Intercollegiate Socialist Society, 115.

Law, Definitions and basic characteristics of Ruler's, and People's, 11-14; human legislation should conform to natural, 38-39; God's revealed, the foundation of a just society, 35; role of God's revealed, 99-104; Sound principles of, all based on divine revelation, 99-100; divine, endows man with duties as well as rights, 100-101; God's of criminal justice, 102; attitude of Anglo-Saxons and ancient Israel toward divine, 103; supremacy of God's revealed, 104; government by, not by men, 173-176; preservation of freedom by established, 173-176; Founders' attitude toward, 175; should be understandable and sta-

ble, 175-176. See also Natural Law

League for Industrial Democracy, 115, 117.

League of Nations, 195.

Lee, Richard Henry, admired by American colonists for his virtue, 42.

"Left," confusion about meaning of, among today's political analysts, 11-12; Founders' warnings against drifting toward collectivists, 27-28.

Legislature. See Congress

Liberty. See Freedom

Life, all rights founded on protection of, 96-97.

Lincoln, Abraham, on desirability of private property and wealth, 126; efforts to establish sound monetary system 139.

Lindbergh, Charles A., Sr., on United States involvement in World War I, 195.

Livingston, Robert, uncertain whether Americans were virtuous enough for self-government, 42-44.

Locke, John, advocates separation of powers, 23; studied by founders, 29; on reality and attributes of God, 73-75; on inherent rights under natural law, 93-94; on supremacy of divine law, 104; on people's right of self-government, 105-106; on people's right to alter or abolish a tyrannical government, 110; on majority rule, 111, 165-166; on property rights as a gift of God, 123-124; on historical development of property rights, 123-125; on responsibility of government to protect property, 126; on difficulty of unanimous consent, 165; on preservation of freedom by fixed laws, 173-175; on equal responsibilities of fathers and mothers, 200; on parents' responsibility for children, 202-205; on independence of adult children, 203; on responsibility of children to parents, 203.

Lopez, Claude-Anne, 201.

Lovell, Colin Rhys, on Anglo-Saxons' attitude toward divine law, 103; on necessity of peoples consent in Anglo-Saxon government, 106; on nature of unwritten Anglo-Saxon law, 157.

# M

Madison, James, born in Virginia, 2; attends Constitutional Convention on borrowed money, 20, 52; role in preparing Bill of Rights, 22; on Constitutional powers delegated to federal and state governments, 22, 171; on responsibility of future Americans to preserve Constitution, 29; on spirit of liberty and patriotism at opening of American Revolution, 44; on relationship of virtue to survival of free government, 45; on need for controls on government, 47, 20-121; his "Memorial and Remonstrance" against religious assessments, 66; on exclusion of federal government from all religious matters, 68; acknowledges God's influence on Constitutional Convention, 76; on the people as ultimate authority in Constitutional government, 107; contrasts republics with democracies, 13-14, 116-117; on danger of gradual erosion of Constitutional rights, 120; on need to move quickly against encroachment on rights, 120-121; on responsibility of government to protect property, 127; on separation of powers, 149-50; pays tribute to Montesquieu, 150; on blending of governmental powers, 149-150; on the people as source of governmental power, 150-151; on dangers of frequent popular votes on constitutional issues, 151; on Constitutional checks and balances to prevent usurpation of power, 152; on origins of ancient governments, 159; on need for understandable and stable laws, 175-176; on manifest destiny of America, 194, 218-219.

Magna Charta, signed by King John, 157

Majority, governments should be established, altered, or abolished only by a, of the people, 110; necessity of rule by, 165-166.

Manifest Destiny, reconciliation of, with Founders' doctrine of "separatism," 194; Founders' views on, of United States, 194; sense of, among early American settlers, 215-216; distinguished from idea of racial superiority, 216.

Marriage. See Family

Marx, Karl, replaces Adam Smith in college economics courses in 1930's, 135.

Mason, George, born in Virginia, 2

Massachusetts, 1776 proclamation declaring right of self-government, 107; John Adams's experience in state constitutional convention, 146-147; separation-of-posers doctrine in constitution, 147; beginnings of public education in, 177-178.

Mayflower Compact, 158.

Minorities, problems of, in attaining equal rights, 81-85; United States a nation of, 81-82; Japanese and Chinese, 82; experience of black Americans, 83; Constitutional amendments to ensure equal rights to, 85; protection of equal rights of, 167-168.

Monarchy, Franklin fears that American government will end in, 18-19, 54; advocates of, in Federalist party, 25-26; Algernon Sidney beheaded for denying "divine right of kings," 105; strengths and weaknesses of, 142.

Money, Congress has exclusive power to issue and control gold or silver backing for currency, 135-136; need for currency backed by precious metals, 135-136; issuing of, turned over to private bankers, 136-138; efforts of Jefferson, Jackson, and Lincoln to establish sound monetary system, 139. See also Banking

Monroe Doctrine, Jefferson anticipates, 194; intent of, 194. See also Foreign relations

Montesquieu, Baron Charles de, advocates separation of powers, 23; studied by founders, 29; biographical sketch, 143; writes The Spirit of Laws, 143-144; views on separation of powers, 144; Madison's tribute to, 150; on wisdom of legislation by many persons, 159.

Morality, relationship of, to survival of free government, 44-45, 60, 62; relationship of, to survival of Constitution, 46; as part of school curriculum in Northwest Ordinance of 1787, 59-60; public and private, 100-101. See also Virtue

Morris, Robert, uncertain whether Americans were virtuous enough for self-government, 42-45.

Moses (Old Testament prophet), establishes Peoples Law in ancient Israel, 17.

### N

Natural Law, only reliable basis for sound government 37-40; identified with revealed law of God, 34-45; eternal and universal, 34-35; legislation should conform to, 38-39; man's inherent rights under, 93-94; based on divine revelation, 99-100; unalienable duties part of, 101. See also Law

New England, local self-government in townships of, 169-70; family relations in early, 201.

Norman Conquest, 157-158.

Northwest Ordinance of 1787, curriculum prescribed for public schools in, 59-60.

### O

Oaths, relationship of religious convictions to validity of public, 76-77.

Offices. See Political offices

### P

Page, John, on spirit of public virtue at openings of American Revolution, 44.

Paine, Thomas, assures Americans that they are virtuous enough for self-government, 42.

Parties. See Political parties

Paul (New Testament apostle), on equality of men and women under God's law, 201.

Peace, preparation for war necessary to preserve, 184-186. See also Defense

Pennsylvania, provision in state constitution on salaries for political offices, 56; provision in state constitution on natural rights, 97; state constitution revised to include separation of powers, 147; unsuccessful attempt to combat constitutional encroachments by a "Council of Censors, 152.

People's Law, definition of, 12; Founders' efforts to establish and maintain a system of, 12, 118-128; basic characteristics of, 13-15; contrasted with Ruler's Law, 15; under Anglo-Saxons and ancient Israel compared, 15-17. See also Government; Law

Petition of Rights (English) signed by Charles I, 158

Plato, philosophical errors of, corrected by Cicero, 33; on government by the few, 175

Political leaders those with virtuous motives regarded most highly by posterity, 50; Franklin's condemnation of those who seek political office for selfish reasons, 52-53; formula for producing, of character and virtue, 56; constitutions should be structured to protect against human frailties of, 119-122; to be bound by "the chains of the Constitution", 120.

Political offices, importance of electing virtuous persons to, 47-56; education of virtuous citizens for service in, a demonstration of virtue, 48-50; Franklin's address on salaries for, 51-52; provision in constitution of Pennsylvania on salaries for, 56-57.

Political parties, Jefferson's warnings against extreme elements in, 25-26.

Political spectrum, confusion created by modern, 11-12; the used by Founders, 11-13; Founders' effort to establish and maintain a government in "balanced center" of, 12-29; position of Articles of Confederation on Founders', 19-20; maintaining balanced center of, through separation of powers, 23-25; need for both problem-solving and conservation philosophies to maintain government in balanced center of, 25-29; educated electorate needed to maintain government in balanced center of, 29.

Politics, called a "divine science" by John Adams, 49-50, 145.

Polybius, advocates separation of powers, 23; studied by founders, 29; biographical sketch, 141-142; on strengths and weaknesses of various forms of government, 142; proposes a three-department government, 143.

Poor, benefit most under a free-market economy, 89; government programs for the, 90-91; federal government not authorized to participate in public welfare programs, 90-91; should be assisted through private charity, 127-129. See also Welfare

Power, Founders measure political systems in terms of, 11-12; abuse of, prevented by checks and balances, 149-159; the people as a source of governmental, 151-152; importance of limiting and defining a government's, 160-164; political, gravitates toward center, 169. See also Government; Separation of powers

Progress, results from spirit of freedom and free-market economics in 1800s, 3-4; in reverse, 4.

Property, right to, essential to pursuit of happiness, 96; right to, essential to security of life and liberty, 123-129; right to, considered a gift of God under English common law, 123-124; historical development of right to, 124-127; a

projection of life itself, 124; desirability of private, 123-124; primary purpose of government is to protect, 126-127; private, the foundation of all civilizations, 128.

Prosperity, protection of equal rights provides best atmosphere for, 89-90; under a free-market economy, 131-133. See also Wealth

# Q

Quincy, Josiah, admired by American colonists for his virtue, 42.

# R

Ramsay, David, on urgency of American independence for maintenance of public virtue, 44.

Reason, man endowed with gift of, for self government, 34, 36

Religion, free government cannot survive without, 44-46; as part of school curriculum in Northwest Ordinance o 1787, 59; Jefferson on teaching of, in Virginia schools, 60; Founders' views on fundamental principles of sound, 60-62; Alexis de Tocqueville on role of, in America, 62; Founders' desire for equality among all sects, 66-67, 69-70; Founders' desire to exclude federal government from all matters of, 67-70; officially established state denominations, "separation of church and state" meant to restrict only federal government, 70; Founders want to encourage, 70-71; principles of, undergird Constitutional government, 71; relationship of religious convictions to validity of public oaths, 76-77

Reparation, law of, a superior system of criminal justice, 62; law of, practiced by Anglo-Saxons and ancient Israel, 102; principle of, introduced into Utah criminal laws, 102.

Republic, United States a, 113-115; contrasted with democracy, 114-118; Polybius studies Roman, 102; Rome abandons principles of a, 102

"Right," confusion about meaning of, among today's political analysts, 11-12

Rights, lack of, under Ruler's Law, 11-13; meaning of equal, 79-81; problems of minorities in attaining equal, 81-85; Constitutional amendments to ensure equal, 84-85; governments should protect equal, not provide equal things, 87-91; people's violated by redistribution of wealth, 88-89: protection of equal, provides freedom to prosper, 88-90; man's unalienable, 93-97; natural vs. vested, 94-95; examples of unalienable, not listed in Declaration of Independence, 96-97; property essential to pursuit of happiness, 100-101; all, founded on protection of life, 105-107; unalienable, accompanied by unalienable duties, 100-101; right to govern vested in sovereign authority of whole people, 105-107; people's right to alter or abolish a tyrannical government, 109-111; danger of gradual erosion of Constitutional, 121; need to move quickly against encroachment on, 121-122; property, essential to the security of life and liberty, 123-129; unalienable, best preserved by a written constitution, 157-159; protection of equal, of minorities, 67; man's responsibility to preserve his, 186-187.

Rome, conquers Greece,141-142; Polybius studies republican form of government in, 142-143; abandons republican government, 143.

Roosevelt, Franklin, administration of, as watershed in changing role of American government, 135-136.

Rousseau, Jean Jacques, erroneous teachings about equality, 80.

Ruler's law, definition of, 11-13; basic characteristics of, 13-14; contrasted with People's Law, 14-15. See also Government; Law

Rush, Benjamin, 29, 145

# S

Schools. See Education

Self-government, man endowed with gift of reason for purposes of, 34-36; people's right of, 105-107; local, keystone to preserving freedom, 169-172; undermining of local in England, 170-171; survival of instinct for, among, emigrating Englishmen, 171; local, emphasized by Jefferson, 172.

Senate (United States). See Congress

Separation of powers, between federal and state governments, 22, 171-172; maintaining balanced center of political spectrum trough, 22-23; principle of, 141-147; proposed by Polybius, 142; Articulated by Montesquieu, 143-144; development of, in United States, 144-147; term prepared by checks and balances, 149-151; essential to liberty, 150.

Separatism. See Foreign relations

Sidney, Algernon, beheaded for denying "divine right of kings," 105; on people's right of self-government, 105-106.

Smith, Adam, writes The Wealth of Nations, 131-132; studied by Founders, 29; formula for free-market economics ideas of, in United States, 131-132; in disfavor among American intellectuals in 1920s, 134=135; replaced by Karl Marx in college economics courses in 1930s, 135; American intellectuals rediscovery of his economic ideas, 135-136.

Socialism, unconstitutional in United States, 27; governments not authorized to redistribute wealth, 87-92; definition of, 115; relationship to democracy, 115, 117-118; proven to be a failure formula, 118; books on failure of, 135.

States, separation of powers between federal government and, 22, 171-172; Founders want religious matters left exclusively to governments of, 67-70; officially established religious denominations in, 67-70; original balance between federal government and disturbed, 162-164.

Stiles, Ezra, Franklin's letter to, on religious beliefs, 61.

Story, Joseph, on exclusion of federal government from all religious matters, 67.

Supreme Court (United States), meddling in religious matters by, 69-71; distortion of "general welfare" clause by, 127-129. See also Federal government; Judiciary

Sutherland, George, on essential nature of property rights, 126.

Switzerland, follows foreign policy advocated by American Founders, 189.


**T**

Ten Commandments, 100-101.

Thackeray, William Makepeace, on comfortable life-style of debtors, 206.

Thomas, Norman, co-director of Intercollegiate Socialist Society, 115.

Tocqueville, Alexis de, on role of religion in America, 62-66; anecdote on relationship of religious convictions to validity of public oaths, 77; on American education in 1831, 179-80: compares European and American families, 199-200.

Tyranny, as an extreme on Founders' political spectrum, 12-13; natural progression from anarchy to, 18-19. See also Political spectrum


**U**

United States, worldwide spirit of freedom originates primarily in, 3; original design for official seal of, 18; brought too close to anarchy under Articles of Confederation, 19-21; importance of public virtue in minds of early Americans, 41-47; Revolution accelerated by reform movement during colonial period, 43-44; relationship of virtue to preservation of free government in, 46; Franklin fears that government of, will end in monarchy, 54; Alexis de Tocqueville on role of religion in, 62-65; a nation of minorities, 81-82, 167; a republic, 113-16; erroneously identified as a "democracy," 114-18; first nation to implement a free-market economy, 131; becomes richest industrial nation on earth, 132; movements away from free-market economics in, 132-34; changes in governmental and economic theories in, during Great Depression, 135-36; development of separation-of-powers doctrine in, 144-47; tradition of written constitution is of American origin, 158; John Adams compares literacy in Europe and, 178; Alexis de Tocqueville's observations on education in, in 1831, 179-80; use of English language in, 181; statements by Washington on national defense, 185-87; Founders' views on foreign relations of, 189-95; Founders' views on manifest destiny of, 194; foreign policy of "separatism" replaced by "internationalism" in early twentieth century, 216-219; involvement in World War I, 195; involvement in World War II, 196-97; as world peacemaker instead of world policeman, 197; Alexis de Tocqueville compares European families with those in, 199-200; Founders' views on national debt, 207-09; history of national debt, 209: changing attitude of Americans toward public debt, 209; outlays of federal government, 1789-2006 (chart), national debt, 211-212; failure of unconstitutional practices by federal government, 213; resistance to reductions in government social programs, 213-14; can return to Founders' formula without economic depression, 214; sense of "manifest destiny' among early settlers, 215-16. See also Federal government; Foreign relations

Utah, principle of reparation introduced

into criminal laws of, 102.

# V

Virginia, produces some of the early fore-most intellects in early America, 2; important role among the thirteen colonies, 3; Jefferson's Bill for Establishing Elementary Schools in, 60; Declaration of Rights similar to Declaration of Independence, 95-96; Declaration of Rights, on right of majority to alter or abolish a government, 111; state laws rewritten by Jefferson, 176. See also Jamestown

Virtue, in the people, required for survival of freedom under constitution, 41-46; importance of public, in minds of early Americans, 42-45; relationship of, to preservation of free government in United States, 46, 187; in the people secured by election of virtuous leaders, 47-57; demonstrated by service in political offices, 49; formula for producing leaders of character and, 56. See also Morality

Von Mises, Ludwig, on private property as the foundation of all civilizations, 128; economic ideas of, anticipated by Adam Smith, 136.

# W

War, preparation for, necessary to preserve peace, 184, 186. See also Defense

Washington, George, born in Virginia, 3; on prosperity and tranquility under new American government, 5; on natural progression from anarchy to tyranny, 19-20; attitude toward Articles of Confederation, 20-21; Jefferson's conversation with, about monarchists in national government, 25-26; on relationship of virtue to freedom, 46; admired by American colonists for his virtue, 42; on relationship of religion and morality to survival of free government, 44-45; declines salary as pres-

ident and Commander-in-Chief, 51; praised by Franklin for serving his country without salary, 54-55; acknowledges intervention of God in American affairs, 76; on relationship of religious convictions to validity of public oaths, 77; defines government as force, 130; on proper role of government in economics, 133; on use of gold or silver backing to prevent depreciation of currency, 137-138; on separation of powers and checks and balances, 155-156; limited formal education of, 179; on national defense, 185-186; on foreign relations of United States, 190-191; on urgency of eliminating national debt, 209-210.

Watergate scandal, 156.

Wealth, governments not authorized to redistribute, 87-91, 127-130; Abraham Lincoln on desirability of, 126.

Webster, Daniel, on use of English language in United States, 81; on cultural influence of extensive Bible reading, 182.

Welfare, Founders' warnings against public, 27; welfare state unconstitutional in United States, 89-90; Founders' ideas on government programs for the poor, 89-90; federal government not authorized to participate in public, 87-91, 127-130. See also, Poor

William and Mary (English monarchs), sign English Bill of Rights, 158.

Wilson, Woodrow, erroneous use of term "democracy" by, 117.

Wood, Gordon S., on importance of public virtue in minds of early Americans, 42; on reform movement during colonial period, 43; on urgency of American independence for maintenance of public virtue, 43.

World War I, United States involvement in, 195.

World War II, treatment of Japanese-Americans during, 82; United States involvement in, 196-197.

# The Constitution
# of the United States of America

## Preamble

We the People of the United States, in Order to form a more perfect Union, establish Justice, insure domestic Tranquility, provide for common defence, promote the general Welfare, and secure the Blessings of Liberty to ourselves and our Posterity, do ordain and establish this Constitution for the United States of America.

## Article I

**Section 1.** All legislative Powers herein granted shall be vested in a Congress of the United States, which shall consist of a Senate and House of Representatives.

**Section 2.** The House of Representatives shall be composed of Members chosen every second Year by the People of the several States, and the Electors in each State shall have the Qualifications requisite for Electors of the most numerous Branch of the State Legislature.

No Person shall be a Representative who shall not have attained to the Age of twenty five Years, and been seven Years a Citizen of the United States, and who shall not, when elected, be an Inhabitant of that State in which he shall be chosen.

Representatives and direct Taxes shall be apportioned among the several States which may be included within this Union, according to their respective Numbers, which shall be determined by adding to the whole Number of free Persons, including those bound to Service for a Term of Years, and excluding Indians not taxed, three fifths of all other Persons. The actual Enumeration shall be made within three Years after the first Meeting of the Congress of the United States, and within every subsequent Term of ten Years, in such Manner as they shall by Law direct. The Number of Representatives shall not exceed one for every thirty Thousand, but each State shall have at Least one Representative; and until such enumeration shall be made, the State of New Hampshire shall be entitled to chuse three, Massachusetts eight, Rhode-Island and Providence Plantations one, Connecticut five, New-York six, New Jersey four, Pennsylvania eight, Delaware one, Maryland six, Virginia ten, North Carolina five, South Carolina five, and Georgia three.

When vacancies happen in the Representation from any State, the Executive Authority thereof shall issue Writs of Election to fill such Vacancies.

The House of Representatives shall chuse their speaker and other Officers; and shall have the sole Power of Impeachment.

**Section 3.** The Senate of the United States shall be composed of two Senators from each State, chosen by the Legislature thereof for six Years; and each Senator shall have one Vote.

Immediately after they shall be assembled in Consequence of the first Election, they shall be divided as equally as may be into three Classes. The Seats of the Senators of the first Class shall be vacated at the Expiration of the second Year, of the second Class at the Expiration of the fourth Year, and of the third Class at the Expiration of the sixth Year, so that one third may be chosen every second Year; and if Vacancies happen by Resignation, or otherwise, during the Recess of the Legislature of any State, the Executive thereof may make temporary Appointments until the next Meeting of the Legislature, which shall then fill such Vacancies.

No Person shall be a Senator who shall not have attained to the Age of thirty Years, and been nine Years a Citizen of the United States, and who shall not, when elected, be an Inhabitant of that State for which he shall be chosen.

The Vice President of the United States shall be President of the Senate, but shall have no Vote, unless they be equally divided.

The Senate shall chuse their other Officers, and also a President pro tempore, in the Absence of the Vice President, or when he shall exercise the Office of President of the United States.

The Senate shall have the sole Power to try all Impeachments. When sitting for that Purpose, they shall be on Oath or Affirmation. When the President of the United States is tried, the Chief Justice shall preside: And no Person shall be convicted without the concurrence of two thirds of the Members present. Judgment in Cases of Impeachment shall not extend further than to removal from Office, and disqualification to hold and enjoy any Office of honor, Trust or Profit under the United States: but the Party convicted shall nevertheless be liable and subject to Indictment, Trial, Judgment and Punishment, according to law.

**Section 4.** The Times, Places and Manner of holding Elections for Senators and Representatives, shall be prescribed in each State by the Legislature thereof; but the Congress may at any time by Law make or alter such Regulations, except as to the Places of chusing Senators.

The Congress shall assemble at least once in every Year, and such Meeting shall be on the first Monday in December, unless they shall by Law appoint a different Day.

**Section 5.** Each House shall be the Judge of the Elections, Returns and Qualifications of its own Members, and a Majority of each shall constitute a Quorum to do business; but a smaller Number may adjourn from day to day, and may be authorized to compel the Attendance of absent Members, in such Manner, and under such Penalties as each House may provide.

Each House may determine the Rules of its Proceedings, punish its Members for disorderly Behaviour, and, with the Concurrence of two thirds, expel a Member.

Each House shall keep a journal of its Proceedings, and from time to time publish the same, excepting such Parts as may in their Judgment require Secrecy; and the Yeas and Nays of the Members of either House on any question shall, at the Desire of one fifth of those Present, be entered on the journal.

Neither House, during the Session of Congress, shall, without the Consent of the other, adjourn for more than three days, nor to any other place than that in which the two Houses shall be sitting.

**Section 6.** The Senators and Representatives shall receive a Compensation for their Services, to be ascertained by Law, and paid out of the Treasury of the United States. They shall in all Cases, except Treason, Felony and Breach of the Peace, be privileged from Arrest during their Attendance at the Session of their respective Houses, and in going to and returning from the same; and for any Speech or Debate in either House, they shall not be questioned in any other Place.

No Senator or Representative shall, during the Time for which he was elected, be appointed to any civil Office under the Authority of the United States, which shall have been created, or the Emoluments whereof shall have been encreased during such time; and no Person holding any Office under the United States, shall be a Member of either House during his Continuance in Office.

**Section 7.** All Bills for raising Revenue shall originate in the House of Representatives; but the Senate may propose or concur with Amendments as on other Bills.

Every Bill which shall have passed the House of Representatives and the Senate, shall, before it become a Law, be presented to the President of the United States; If he approve he shall sign it, but if not he shall return it, with his Objections to that House in which it shall have originated, who shall enter the Objections at large on their Journal, and proceed to reconsider it. If after such Reconsideration two thirds of that House shall agree to pass the Bill, it shall be sent, together with the Objections, to the other House, by which it shall likewise be reconsidered, and if approved by two thirds of that House, it shall become a Law. But in all such Cases the Votes of both Houses shall be determined by yeas and Nays, and the Names of the Persons voting for and against the Bill shall be entered on the Journal of each House respectively. If any Bill shall not be returned by the President within ten Days (Sundays excepted) after it shall have been presented to him, the Same shall be a Law, in like Manner as if he had signed it, unless the Congress by their Adjournment prevent its Return, in which Case it shall not be a Law.

Every Order, Resolution, or Vote to which the Concurrence of the Senate and House of Representatives may be necessary (except on a question of Adjournment) shall be presented to the President of the United States; and before the Same shall take Effect, shall be approved by him, or being disapproved by him, shall be repassed by two thirds of the Senate and House of Representatives, according to the Rules and Limitations prescribed in the Case of a Bill.

**Section 8.** The Congress shall have Power To lay and collect Taxes, Duties, Imposts and Excises, to pay the Debts and provide for the common Defence and general Welfare of the United States; but all Duties, Imposts and Excises shall be uniform throughout the United States;

To borrow Money on the credit of the United States;

To regulate Commerce with foreign Nations, and among the several States, and with the Indian Tribes;

To establish an uniform Rule of Naturalization, and uniform Laws on the subject of Bankruptcies throughout the United States;

To coin Money, regulate the Value thereof, and of foreign Coin, and fix the Standard of Weights and Measures;

To provide for the Punishment of counterfeiting the Securities and current Coin of the United States;

To establish Post Offices and post Roads;

To promote the Progress of Science and useful Arts, by securing for limited Times to Authors and Inventors the exclusive Right to their respective Writings and Discoveries;

To constitute Tribunals inferior to the supreme Court;

To define and punish Piracies and Felonies committed on the high Seas, and Offences against the Law of Nations;

To declare War, grant Letters of Marque and Reprisal, and make rules concerning Captures on Land and Water;

To raise and support Armies, but no Appropriation of Money to that Use shall be for a longer Term than two Years;

To provide and maintain a Navy;

To make Rules for the Government and Regulation of the land and naval Forces;

To provide for calling forth the Militia to execute the Laws of the Union, suppress Insurrections and repel Invasions;

To provide for organizing, arming, and disciplining, the Militia, and for governing such Part of them as may be employed in the Service of the United States, reserving to the States respectively, the Appointment of the Officers, and the Authority of training the Militia according to the discipline prescribed by Congress;

To exercise exclusive Legislation in all Cases whatsoever, over such District (not exceeding ten Miles square), as may, by Cession of particular States, and the Acceptance of Congress, become the Seat of the Government of the United States, and to exercise like Authority over all Places purchased by the Consent of the Legislature of the State in which the Same shall be for the Erection of Forts, Magazines, Arsenals, dock-Yards, and other needful Buildings;—And

To make all Laws which shall be necessary and proper for carying into Execution the foregoing Powers, and all other Powers vested by this Constitution in the Government of the United States, or in any Department or Officer thereof.

**Section 9.** The Migration or Importation of such Persons as any of the States now existing shall think proper to admit, shall not be prohibited by the Congress prior to the Year one thousand eight hundred and eight, but a Tax or duty may be imposed on such Importation, not exceeding ten dollars for each Person.

The Privilege of the Writ of Habeas Corpus shall not be suspended, unless when in Cases of Rebellion or Invasion the public Safety may require it.

No Bill of Attainder or ex post facto Law shall be passed.

No Capitation, or other direct, Tax shall be laid, unless in Proportion to the Census or Enumeration herein before directed to be taken.

No Tax or Duty shall be laid on Articles exported from any State.

No Preference shall be given by any Regulation of Commerce or Revenue to the Ports of one State over those of another; nor shall Vessels bound to, or from, one State, be obliged to enter, clear or pay Duties in another.

No money shall be drawn from the Treasury, but in Consequence of Appropriations made by Law; and a regular Statement and Account of the Receipts and Expenditures of all public Money shall be published from time to time.

No Title of Nobility shall be granted by the United States: And no Person holding any Office of Profit or Trust under them, shall, without the Consent of the Congress, accept of any present, Emolument, Office, or Title, of any kind whatever, from any King, Prince, or foreign State.

**Section 10.** No State shall enter into any Treaty, Alliance, or Confederation; grant Letters of Marque and Reprisal; coin Money; emit Bills of Credit; make any Thing but gold and silver Coin a Tender in Payment of Debts; pass any Bill of Attainder, ex post facto Law, or Law impairing the Obligation of Contracts, or grant any Title of Nobility.

No State shall, without the Consent of the Congress, lay any Imposts or Duties on Imports or Exports, except what may be absolutely necessary for executing it's inspection Laws: and the net Produce of all Duties and Imposts, laid by any State on Imports or Exports, shall be for the Use of the Treasury of the United States; and all such Laws shall be subject to the Revision and Controul of the Congress.

No State shall, without the Consent of Congress, lay any Duty of Tonnage, keep Troops, or Ships of War in time of Peace, enter into any Agreement or Compact with another State, or with a foreign Power, or engage in War, unless actually invaded, or in such imminent Danger as will not admit of delay.

### Article II

**Section 1.** The executive Power shall be vested in a President of the United States of America. He shall hold his Office during the Term of four Years, and, together with the Vice President, chosen for the same Term, be elected, as follows:

Each State shall appoint, in such Manner as the Legislature thereof may direct, a Number of Electors, equal to the whole Number of Senators and Representatives to which the State may be entitled in the Congress: but no Senator or Representative, or Person holding an Office of Trust or Profit under the United States, shall be appointed an Elector.

The Electors shall meet in their respective States, and vote by Ballot for two Persons, of whom one at least shall not be an Inhabitant of the same State with themselves. And they shall make a List of all the Persons voted for, and of the Number of Votes for each; which List they shall sign and certify, and transmit sealed to the Seat of the Government of the United States, directed to the President of the Senate. The President of the Senate shall, in the Presence of the Senate and House of Representatives, open all the Certificates, and the Votes shall then be counted. The Person having the greatest Number of Votes shall be the President, if such Number be a Majority of the whole Number of Electors appointed; and if there be more than one who have such Majority, and have an equal Number of Votes, then the House of Representatives shall immediately chuse by Ballot one of them for President: and if no Person have a Majority, then from the five highest on the List the said House shall in like Manner chuse the President. But in chusing the President, the Votes shall be taken by States, the Representation from each State having one Vote; A quorum for this Purpose shall consist of a Member or Members from two thirds of the States, and a Majority of all the States shall be necessary to a Choice. In every Case, after the Choice of the President, the Person having the greatest Number of Votes of the Electors shall be the Vice President. But if there should remain two or more who have equal Votes, the Senate shall chuse from them by Ballot the Vice President.

The Congress may determine the Time of chusing the Electors, and the Day on which they shall give their Votes; which Day shall be the same throughout the United States.

No Person except a natural born Citizen, or a Citizen of the United States, at the time of the Adoption of this Constitution, shall be eligible to the Office of President; neither shall any Person be eligible to that Office who shall not have attained to the Age of thirty five Years, and been fourteen Years a Resident within the United States.

In Case of the Removal of the President from Office, or of his Death, Resignation, or Inability to discharge the Powers and Duties of the said Office, the Same shall devolve on the Vice President, and the Congress may by Law provide for the Case of Removal, Death, Resignation or Inability, both of the President and Vice President, declaring what Officer shall then act as President, and such Officer shall act accordingly, until the Disability be removed, or a President shall be elected.

The President shall, at stated Times, receive for his Services, a Compensation, which shall neither be encreased nor diminished during the Period for which he shall have been elected, and he shall not receive within that Period any other Emolument from the United States, or any of them.

Before he enter on the Execution of his Office, he shall take the following Oath or Affirmation: "I do solemnly swear (or affirm) that I will faithfully execute the Office of President of the United States, and will to the best of my Ability, preserve, protect and defend the Constitution of the United States."

**Section 2.** The President shall be Commander in Chief of the Army and Navy of the United States, and of the Militia of the several States, when called into the actual Service of the United States; he may require the Opinion, in writing, of the principal Officer in each of the executive Departments, upon any Subject relating to the Duties of their respective Offices, and he shall have Power to grant Reprieves and Pardons for Offences against the United States, except in Cases of Impeachment.

He shall have Power, by and with the Advice and Consent of the Senate, to make Treaties, provided two thirds of the Senators present concur; and he shall nominate, and by and with the Advice and Consent of the Senate, shall appoint Ambassadors, other public Ministers and Consuls, Judges of the supreme Court, and all other Officers of the United States, whose Appointments are not herein otherwise provided for, and which shall be established by Law: but the Congress may by Law vest the Appointment of such inferior Officers, as they think proper, in the President alone, in the Courts of Law, or in the Heads of Departments.

The President shall have Power to fill up all Vacancies that may happen during the Recess of the Senate, by granting Commissions which shall expire at the End of their next Session.

**Section 3.** He shall from time to time give to the Congress Information of the State of the Union, and recommend to their Consideration such Measures as he shall judge necessary and expedient; he may, on extraordinary Occasions, convene both Houses, or either of them, and in Case of Disagreement between them, with Respect to the Time of Adjournment, he may adjourn them to such Time as he shall think proper; he shall receive Ambassadors and other public Ministers; he shall take Care that the Laws be faithfully executed, and shall Commission all the Officers of the United States.

**Section 4.** The President, Vice President and all civil Officers of the United States, shall be removed from Office on Impeachment for, and Conviction of, Treason, Bribery, or other High Crimes and Misdemeanors.

### Article III

**Section 1.** The judicial Power of the United States, shall be vested in one supreme Court, and in such inferior Courts as the Congress may from time to time ordain and establish. The Judges, both of the supreme and inferior Courts, shall hold their Offices during good Behaviour, and shall, at stated Times, receive for their Services, a Compensation, which shall not be diminished during their Continuance in Office.

**Section 2.** The judicial Power shall extend to all Cases, in Law and Equity, arising under this Constitution, the Laws of the United States, and Treaties made, or which shall be made, under their Authority;—to all Cases affecting Ambassadors, other public Ministers and Consuls;—to all Cases of admiralty and maritime jurisdiction;—to Controversies to which the United States shall be a Party;—to Controversies between two or more States;-between a State and Citizens of another State;—between Citizens of different States;—between Citizens of the same State claiming Lands under Grants of different States, and between a State, or the Citizens thereof, and foreign States, Citizens or Subjects.

In all Cases affecting Ambassadors, other public Ministers and Consuls, and those in which a State shall be Party, the supreme Court shall have original Jurisdiction. In all the other Cases before mentioned, the supreme Court shall have appellate Jurisdiction, both as to Law and Fact, with such Exceptions, and under such Regulations as the Congress shall make.

The Trial of all Crimes, except in Cases of Impeachment, shall be by Jury; and such Trial shall be held in the State where the said Crimes shall have been committed; but when not committed within any State, the Trial shall be at such Place or Places as the Congress may by Law have directed.

**Section 3.** Treason against the United States, shall consist only in levying War against them, or in adhering to their Enemies, giving them Aid and Comfort. No Person shall be convicted of Treason unless on the Testimony of two Witnesses to the same overt Act, or on Confession in open Court.

The Congress shall have Power to declare the Punishment of Treason, but no Attainder of Treason shall work Corruption of Blood, or Forfeiture except during the Life of the Person attainted.

## Article IV

**Section 1.** Full Faith and Credit shall be given in each State to the public Acts, Records, and judicial Proceedings of every other State. And the Congress may by general Laws prescribe the Manner in which such Acts, Records and Proceedings shall be proved, and the Effect thereof.

**Section 2.** The Citizens of each State shall be entitled to all Privileges and Immunities of Citizens in the several States.

A person charged in any State with Treason, Felony, or other Crime, who shall flee from justice, and be found in another State, shall on Demand of the executive Authority of the State from which he fled, be delivered up, to be removed to the State having Jurisdiction of the Crime.

No Person held to Service or Labour in one State, under the Laws thereof, escaping into another, shall in Consequence of any Law or Regulation therein, be discharged from such Service or Labour, but shall be delivered upon on Claim of the Party to whom such Service or Labour may be due.

**Section 3.** New States may be admitted by the Congress into this Union; but no new State shall be formed or erected within the Jurisdiction of any other State; nor any State be formed by the Junction of two or more States, or Parts of States, without the Consent of the Legislatures of the States concerned as well as of the Congress.

The Congress shall have Power to dispose of and make all needful Rules and Regulations respecting the Territory or other Property belonging to the United States; and nothing in this Constitution shall be so construed as to Prejudice any Claims of the United States, or of any particular State.

**Section 4.** The United States shall guarantee to every State in this Union a Republican Form of Government, and shall protect each of them against Invasion; and on Application of the Legislature, or of the Executive (when the Legislature cannot be convened) against domestic Violence.

## Article V

The Congress, whenever two thirds of both Houses shall deem it necessary, shall propose Amendments to this Constitution, or, on the Application of the Legislatures of two thirds of the several States, shall call a Convention for proposing Amendments, which, in either Case, shall be valid to all Intents and Purposes, as Part of this Constitution, when ratified by the Legislatures of three fourths of the several States, or by Conventions in three fourths thereof, as the one or the other Mode of Ratification may be proposed by the Congress; Provided that no Amendment which may be made prior to the Year One thousand eight hundred and eight shall in any Manner affect the first and fourth Clauses in the Ninth Section of the first Article; and that no State, without its Consent, shall be deprived of its equal Suffrage in the Senate.

## Article VI

All Debts contracted and Engagements entered into, before the Adoption of this Constitution, shall be as valid against the United States under this Constitution, as under the Confederation.

This Constitution, and the Laws of the United States which shall be made in Pursuance thereof; and all Treaties made, or which shall be made, under the Authority of the United States, shall be the supreme Law of the Land; and the Judges in every State shall be bound thereby, any Thing in the Constitution or Laws of any State to the Contrary notwithstanding.

The Senators and Representatives before mentioned, and the Members of the several State Legislatures, and all executive and judicial Officers, both of the United States and of the several States, shall be bound by Oath or Affirmation, to support this Constitution; but no religious Test shall ever be required as a Qualification to any Office or public Trust under the United States.

## Article VII

The Ratification of the Conventions of nine States, shall be sufficient for the Establishment of this Constitution between the States so ratifying the Same.

Done in Convention by the Unanimous Consent of the States present the Seventeenth Day of September in the Year of our Lord one thousand seven hundred and Eighty seven and of the Independence of the United States of America the Twelfth In witness whereof We have hereunto subscribed our Names:

Go. Washington — President and deputy from Virginia

Delaware: Geo. Read, Gunning Bedford, Jr., John Dickinson, Richard Bassett, Jaco. Broom

Maryland: James McHenry, Dan of St. Thos. Jenifer, Danl. Carroll

Virginia: John Blair, James Madison, Jr.

North Carolina: Wm. Blount, Richd. Dobbs Spaight, Hu Williamson

South Carolina: J. Rutledge, Charles Cotesworth Pinckney, Charles Pinckney, Pierce Butler

Georgia: William Few, Abr. Baldwin

New Hampshire: John Langdon, Nicholas Gilman

Massachusetts: Nathaniel Gorham, Rufus King

Connecticut: Wm. Saml. Johnson, Roger Sherman

New York: Alexander Hamilton

New Jersey: Wil. Livingston, David Brearley, Wm. Paterson, Jona. Dayton

Pennsylvania: B. Franklin, Thomas Mifflin, Robt. Morris, Geo. Clymer, Thos. FitzSimons, Jared Ingersoll, James Wilson, Gouv. Morris

## First Amendment

Congress shall make no law respecting an establishment of religion, or prohibiting the free exercise thereof; or abridging the freedom of speech, or of the press; or the right of the people peaceably to assemble, and to petition the Government for a redress of grievances.

## Second Amendment

A well regulated Militia, being necessary to the security of a free State, the right of the people to keep and bear Arms, shall not be infringed.

## Third Amendment

No Soldier shall, in time of peace be quartered in any house, without the consent of the Owner, nor in time of war, but in a manner to be prescribed by law.

## Fourth Amendment

The right of the People to be secure in their persons, houses, papers, and effects, against unreasonable searches and seizures, shall not be violated, and no Warrants shall issue, but upon probable cause, supported by Oath or affirmation, and particularity describing the place to be searched, and the persons or things to be seized.

## Fifth Amendment

No person shall be held to answer for a capital, or otherwise infamous crime, unless on a presentment or indictment of a Grand Jury, except in cases arising in the land or naval forces, or in the Militia, when in actual service in time of War or public danger; nor shall any person be subject for the same offence to be twice put in jeopardy of life or limb; nor shall be compelled in any criminal case to be a witness against himself, nor be deprived of life, liberty, or property, without due process of law; nor shall private property be taken for public use, without just compensation.

## Sixth Amendment

In all criminal prosecutions, the accused shall enjoy the right to a speedy and public trial, by an impartial jury of the State and district wherein the crime shall have been committed, which district shall have been previously ascertained by law, and to be informed of the nature and cause of the accusation; to be confronted with the witnesses against him; to have compulsory process for obtaining witnesses in his favor, and to have Assistance of Counsel for his defence.

## Seventh Amendment

In Suits at common law, where the value in controversy shall exceed twenty dollars, the right of trial by jury shall be preserved, and no fact tried by a jury, shall be otherwise reexamined in any Court of the United States, than according to the rules of the common law.

## Eighth Amendment

Excessive bail shall not be required, nor excessive fines imposed, nor cruel and unusual punishments inflicted.

## Ninth Amendment

The enumeration in the Constitution, of certain rights, shall not be construed to deny or disparage others retained by the people.

## Tenth Amendment

The powers not delegated to the United States by the Constitution, nor prohibited by it to the States, are reserved to the States respectively, or to the people.

## Eleventh Amendment

(Ratified in 1795.)

The Judicial power of the United States shall not be construed to extend to any suit in law or equity, commenced or prosecuted against one of the United States by Citizens of another State, or by Citizens or Subjects of any Foreign State.

## Twelfth Amendment

(Ratified in 1804.)

The Electors shall meet in their respective states and vote by ballot for President and Vice-President, one of whom, at least, shall not be an inhabitant of the same state with themselves; they shall name in their ballots the person voted for as President, and in distinct ballots the person voted for as Vice-President, and they shall make distinct lists of all persons voted for as President, and of all persons voted for as Vice-President, and of the number of votes for each, which lists they shall sign and certify, and transmit sealed to the seat of the government of the United States, directed to the President of the Senate;—The President of the Senate shall, in the presence of the Senate and House of Representatives, open all the certificates and the votes shall then be counted;—The person having the greatest number of votes for President, shall be the President, if such number be a majority of the whole number of Electors appointed; and if no person have such majority, then from the persons having the highest numbers not exceeding three on the list of those voted for as President, the House of Representatives shall choose immediately, by ballot, the President. But in choosing the President, the votes shall be taken by states, the representation from each state having one vote; a quorum for this purpose shall consist of a member or members from two-thirds of the states, and a majority of all the states shall be necessary to a choice. And if the House of Representatives shall not choose a President whenever the right of choice shall devolve upon then, before the fourth day of March next following, then the Vice-President shall act as President, as in the case of the death or other constitutional disability of the President.—The person having the greatest number of votes as Vice-President, shall be the Vice-President, if such number be a majority of the whole number of Electors appointed, and if no person have a majority, then from the two highest numbers on the list, the Senate shall choose the Vice-President; a quorum for the purpose shall consist of two-thirds of the whole number of Senators, and a majority of the whole number shall be necessary to a choice. But no person constitutionally ineligible to the office of President shall be eligible to that of Vice-President of the United States.

## Thirteenth Amendment

**Section 1.** Neither slavery nor involuntary servitude, except as a punishment for crime whereof the party shall have been duly convicted, shall exist within the United States, or any place subject to their jurisdiction.

**Section 2.** Congress shall have power to enforce this article by appropriate legislation.

# Fourteenth Amendment

(Ratified in 1868.)

**Section 1.** All persons born or naturalized in the United States, and subject to the jurisdiction thereof, are citizens of the United States and of the State wherein they reside. No State shall make or enforce any law which shall abridge the privileges or immunities of citizens of the United States; nor shall any State deprive any person of life, liberty, or property, without due process of law; nor deny to any person within its jurisdiction the equal protection of the laws.

**Section 2.** Representatives shall be apportioned among the several States according to their respective numbers, counting the whole number of persons in each State, excluding Indians not taxed. But when the right to vote at any election for the choice of electors for President and Vice President of the United States, Representatives in Congress, the Executive and Judicial officers of a State, or the members of the Legislature thereof, is denied to any of the male inhabitants of such State, being twenty-one years of age, and citizens of the United States, or in any way abridged, except for participation in rebellion, or other crime, the basis of representation therein shall be reduced in the proportion which the number of such male citizens shall bear to the whole number of male citizens twenty-one years of age in such State.

**Section 3.** No person shall be a Senator or Representative in Congress, or elector of President and Vice President, or hold any office, civil or military, under the United States, or under any State, who, having previously taken an oath, as a member of Congress, or as an officer of the United States, or as a member of any State legislature, or as an executive or judicial officer of any State, to support the Constitution of the United States, shall have engaged in insurrection or rebellion against the same, or given aid or comfort to the enemies thereof. But Congress may by a vote of two-thirds of each House, remove such disability.

**Section 4.** The validity of the public debt of the United States, authorized by law, including debts incurred for payment of pensions and bounties for services in suppressing insurrection or rebellion, shall not be questioned. But neither the United States nor any State shall assume or pay any debt or obligation incurred in aid of insurrection or rebellion against the United States, or any claim for the loss or emancipation of any slave; but all such debts, obligations and claims shall be held illegal and void.

**Section 5.** The Congress shall have power to enforce, by appropriate legislation, the provisions of this article.

# Fifteenth Amendment

(Ratified in 1870.)

**Section 1.** The right of citizens of the United States to vote shall not be denied or abridged by the United States or by any State on account of race, color, or previous condition of servitude.

**Section 2.** The Congress shall have power to enforce this article by appropriate legislation.

# Sixteenth Amendment

(Ratified in 1913.)

The Congress shall have power to lay and collect taxes on incomes, from whatever source derived, without apportionment among the several States, and without regard to any census or enumeration.

# Seventeenth Amendment

(Ratified in 1913.)

**Section 1.** The Senate of the United States shall be composed of two Senators from each State, elected by the people thereof for six years; and each Senator shall have one vote. The electors in each State shall have the qualifications requisite for electors of the most numerous branch of the State legislatures.

**Section 2.** When vacancies happen in the representation of any State in the Senate, the executive authority of such State shall issue writs of election to fill such vacancies: Provided, That the legislature of any State may empower the executive thereof to make temporary appointments until the people fill the vacancies by election as the legislature may direct.

**Section 3.** This amendment shall not be so construed as to affect the election or term of any Senator chosen before it becomes valid as part of the Constitution.

# Eighteenth Amendment

(Ratified in 1919.)

(Repealed in 1933 by Amendment XXI)

**Section 1.** After one year from the ratification of this article the manufacture, sale, or transportation of intoxicating liquors within, the importation thereof into, or the exportation thereof from the United States and all territory subject to the jurisdiction thereof for beverage purposes is hereby prohibited.

**Section 2.** The Congress and the several States shall have concurrent power to enforce this article by appropriate legislation.

**Section 3.** This article shall be inoperative unless it shall have been ratified as an amendment to the Constitution by the legislatures of the several States as provided in the Constitution, within seven years from the date of the submission hereof to the States by the Congress.

# Nineteenth Amendment

(Ratified in 1920.)

**Section 1.** The right of citizens of the United States to vote shall not be denied or abridged by the United States or by any State on account of sex.

**Section 2.** Congress shall have power to enforce this article by appropriate legislation.

# Twentieth Amendment

(Ratified in 1933.)

**Section 1.** The terms of the President and Vice President shall end at noon on the 20th day of January, and the terms of Senators and Representatives at noon on the 3d day of January, of the years in which such terms would have ended if this article had not been ratified; and the terms of their successors shall then begin.

**Section 2.** The Congress shall assemble at least once in every year, and such meeting shall begin at noon on the 3d day of January, unless they shall by law appoint a different day.

**Section 3.** If, at the time fixed for the beginning of the term of the President, the President elect shall have died, the Vice President elect shall become President. If a President shall not have been chosen before the time fixed for the beginning of his term, or if the President elect shall have failed to qualify, then the Vice President elect shall act as President until a President shall have qualified; and the Congress may by law provide for the case wherein neither a President elect nor a Vice President elect shall have qualified, declaring who shall then act as President, or the manner in which one who is to act shall be selected, and such person shall act accordingly until a President or Vice President shall have qualified.

**Section 4.** The Congress may by law provide for the case of the death of any of the persons from whom the House of Representatives may choose a President whenever the right of choice shall have devolved upon them, and for the case of the death of any of the persons from whom the Senate may choose a Vice President whenever the right of choice shall have devolved upon them.

**Section 5.** Sections 1 and 2 shall take effect on the 15th day of October following the ratification of this article.

**Section 6.** This article shall be inoperative unless it shall have been ratified as an amendment to the Constitution by the legislatures of three-fourths of the several States within seven years from the date of its submission.

## Twenty-first Amendment

(Ratified in 1933.)

**Section 1.** The eighteenth article of amendment to the Constitution of the United States is hereby repealed.

**Section 2.** The transportation or importation into any State, Territory, or possession of the United States for delivery or use therein of intoxicating liquors, in violation of the laws thereof, is hereby prohibited.

**Section 3.** This article shall be inoperative unless it shall have been ratified as an amendment to the Constitution by conventions in the several States, as provided in the Constitution, within seven years from the date of the submission hereof to the States by the Congress.

## Twenty-second Amendment

(Ratified in 1951.)

**Section 1.** No person shall be elected to the office of the President more than twice, and no person who has held the office of President, or acted as President, for more than two years of a term to which some other person was elected President shall be elected to the office of the President more than once. But this Article shall not apply to any person holding the office of President when this Article was proposed by the Congress, and shall not prevent any person who may be holding the office of President, or acting as President, during the term within which this Article becomes operative from holding the office of President or acting as President during the remainder of such term.

**Section 2.** This Article shall be inoperative unless it shall have been ratified as an amendment to the Constitution by the legislatures of three-fourths of the several States within seven years from the date of its submission to the States by the Congress.

## Twenty-third Amendment

(Ratified in 1961.)

**Section 1.** The District constituting the seat of Government of the United States shall appoint in such manner as the Congress may direct:

A number of electors of President and Vice President equal to the whole number of Senators and Representatives in Congress to which the District would be entitled if it were a State, but in no event more than the least populous State; they shall be in addition to those appointed by the States, but they shall be considered, for the purposes of the election of

President and Vice President, to be electors appointed by a State; and they shall meet in the District and perform such duties as provided by the twelfth article of amendment.

**Section 2.** The Congress shall have power to enforce this article by appropriate legislation.

## Twenty-fourth Amendment

(Ratified in 1964.)

**Section 1.** The right of citizens of the United States to vote in any primary or other election for President or Vice President, for electors for President or Vice President, or for Senator or Representative in Congress, shall not be denied or abridged by the United States or any State by reason of failure to pay any poll tax or other tax.

**Section 2.** The Congress shall have power to enforce this article by appropriate legislation.

## Twenty-fifth Amendment

(Ratified in 1967.)

**Section 1.** In case of the removal of the President from office or of his death or resignation, the Vice President shall become President.

**Section 2.** Whenever there is a vacancy in the office of the Vice President, the President shall nominate a Vice President who shall take office upon confirmation by a majority vote of both Houses of Congress.

**Section 3.** Whenever the President transmits to the President pro tempore of the Senate and the Speaker of the House of Representatives his written declaration that he is unable to discharge the powers and duties of his office, and until he transmits to them a written declaration to the contrary, such powers and duties shall be discharged by the Vice President as Acting President.

**Section 4.** Whenever the Vice president and a majority of either the principal officers of the executive departments or of such other body as Congress may by law provide, transmit to the President pro tempore of the Senate and the Speaker of the House of Representatives their written declaration that the President is unable to discharge the powers and duties of his office, the Vice President shall immediately assume the powers and duties of the office as Acting President.

Thereafter, when the President transmits to the President pro tempore of the Senate and the Speaker of the House of Representatives his written declaration that no inability exists, he shall resume the powers and duties of his office unless the Vice President and a majority of either the principal officers of the executive department or of such other body as Congress may by law provide, transmit within four days to the President pro tempore of the Senate and the Speaker of the House of Representatives their written declaration that the President is unable to discharge the powers and duties of his office. Thereupon Congress shall decide the issue, assembling within forty-eight hours for that purpose if not in session. If the Congress, within twenty-one days after receipt of the latter written declaration, or, if Congress is not in session, within twenty-one days after Congress is required to assemble, determines by two-thirds vote of both Houses that the President is unable to discharge the powers and duties of his office, the Vice President shall continue to discharge the same as Acting President; otherwise, the President shall resume the powers and duties of his office.

## Twenty-sixth Amendment

(Ratified in 1971.)

**Section 1.** The right of citizens of the United States, who are eighteen years of age or older, to vote shall not be denied or abridged by the United States or by any State on account of age.

**Section 2.** The Congress shall have power to enforce this article by appropriate legislation.

## Twenty-seventh Amendment

(Ratified in 1992.)

**Section 1.** No law varying the compensation for the services of the Senators and Representatives shall take effect, until an election of Representatives shall have intervened.

# The Declaration of Independence

In Congress, July 4, 1776
The Unanimous Declaration of The Thirteen United States of America

When in the Course of human events, it becomes necessary for one people to dissolve the political bands which have connected them with another, and to assume among the Powers of the earth, the separate and equal station to which the Laws of Nature and of Nature's God entitle them, a decent respect to the opinions of mankind requires that they should declare the causes which impel them to the separation. We hold these truths to be self-evident, that all men are created equal, that they are endowed by their Creator with certain unalienable Rights, that among these are Life, Liberty and the pursuit of Happiness. That to secure these rights, Governments are instituted among Men, deriving their just powers from the consent of the governed, That whenever any Form of Government becomes destructive of these ends, it is the Right of the People to alter or to abolish it, and to institute new Government, laying its foundation on such principles and organizing its powers in such form, as to them shall seem most likely to effect their Safety and Happiness. Prudence, indeed, will dictate that Governments long established should not be changed for light and transient causes; and accordingly all experience hath shown, that mankind are more disposed to suffer, while evils are sufferable, than to right themselves by abolishing the forms to which they are accustomed. But when a long train of abuses and usurpations, pursuing invariably the same Object evinces a design to reduce them under absolute Despotism, it is their right, it is their duty, to throw off such Government, and to provide new Guards for their future security.—Such has been the patient sufferance of these Colonies; and such is now the necessity which constrains them to alter their former Systems of Government. The history of the present King of Great Britain is a history of repeated injuries and usurpations, all having in direct object the establishment of an absolute Tyranny over these States. To prove this, let Facts be submitted to a candid world.

He has refused his Assent to Laws, the most wholesome and necessary for the public good.

He has forbidden his Governors to pass Laws of immediate and pressing importance, unless suspended in their operation till his Assent should be obtained; and when so suspended, he has utterly neglected to attend to them.

He has refused to pass other Laws for the accommodation of large districts of people, unless those people would relinquish the right of Representation in the Legislature, a right inestimable to them and formidable to tyrants only.

He has called together legislative bodies at places unusual, uncomfortable, and distant from the depository or their public Records, for the sole purpose of fatiguing them into compliance with his measures.

He has dissolved Representative Houses repeatedly, for opposing with manly firmness his invasions on the rights of the people.

He has refused for a long time, after such dissolutions, to cause others to be elected; whereby the Legislative powers, incapable of Annihilation, have returned to the People at large for their exercise; the State remaining in the mean time exposed to all the dangers of invasion from without, and convulsions within.

He has endeavoured to prevent the population of these States; for that purpose obstructing the Laws for Naturalization of Foreigners; refusing to pass others to encourage their migration hither, and raising the conditions of new Appropriations of Lands.

He has obstructed the Administration of Justice, by refusing his Assent to Laws for establishing Judiciary powers.

He has made Judges dependent on his Will alone, for the tenure of their offices, and the amount and payment of their salaries.

He has erected a multitude of New Offices, and sent hither swarms of Officers to harass our people, and eat out their substance.

He has kept among us, in times of peace, Standing Armies, without the Consent of our legislatures.

He has affected to render the Military independent of and superior to the Civil power.

He has combined with others to subject us to a jurisdiction foreign to our constitution, and unacknowledged by our laws; giving his Assent to their Acts of pretended Legislation:

For quartering large bodies of armed troops among us:

For protecting them, by a mock Trial, from Punishment for any Murders which they should commit on the Inhabitants of these States:

For cutting off our Trade with all parts of the world:

For imposing Taxes on us without our Consent:

For depriving us in many cases, of the benefits of Trial by Jury:

For transporting us beyond Seas to be tried for pretended offenses:

For abolishing the free System of English Laws in a neighboring Province, establishing therein an Arbitrary government, and enlarging its Boundaries so as to render it at once an example and fit instrument for introducing the same absolute rule into these Colonies:

For taking away our Charters, abolishing our most valuable Laws, and altering fundamentally the Forms of our Governments:

For suspending our own Legislatures, and declaring themselves invested with power to legislate for us in all cases whatsoever.

He has abdicated Government here, by declaring us out of his Protection and waging War against us.

He has plundered our seas, ravaged our Coasts, burnt our towns, and destroyed the lives of our people.

He is at this time transporting large Armies of foreign Mercenaries to compleat the works of death, desolation and tyranny, already begun with circumstances of Cruelty & perfidy scarcely paralleled in the most barbarous ages, and totally unworthy the Head of a civilized nation.

He has constrained our fellow Citizens taken Captive on the high Seas to bear Arms against their Country, to become the executioners of their friends and Brethren, or to fall themselves by their Hands.

He has excited domestic insurrections amongst us, and has endeavoured to bring on the inhabitants of our frontiers, the merciless Indian Savages, whose known rule of warfare, is an undistinguished destruction of all ages, sexes and conditions.

In every state of these Oppressions We have Petitioned for Redress in the most humble terms: Our repeated Petitions have been answered only by repeated injury. A Prince, whose character is thus marked by every act which may define a Tyrant, is unfit to be the ruler of a free people.

Nor have We been wanting in attentions to our Brittish brethren. We have warned them from time to time of attempts by their legislature to extend an unwarrantable jurisdiction over us. We have reminded them of the circumstances of our emigration and settlement here. We have appealed to their native justice and magnanimity, and we have conjured them by the ties of our common kindred to disavow these usurpations, which, would inevitably interrupt our connections and correspondence. They too have been deaf to the voice of justice and of consanguinity. We must, therefore, acquiesce in the necessity, which denounces our Separation, and hold them, as we hold the rest of mankind, Enemies in War, in Peace Friends.

We, Therefore, the Representatives of the United States of America, in General Congress, Assembled, appealing to the Supreme Judge of the world for the rectitude of our intentions, do, in the Name, and by Authority of the good People of these Colonies, solemnly publish and declare, That these United Colonies are, and of Right ought to be Free and Independent States; that they are Absolved from all Allegiance to the British Crown, and that all political connection between them and the State of Great Britain, is and ought to be totally disolved; and that as Free and Independent States, they have full Power to levy War, conclude Peace, contract Alliances, establish Commerce, and to do all other Acts and Things which Independent States may of right do.

And for the support of this Declaration, with a firm reliance on the protection of Divine Providence, we mutually pledge to each other our Lives, our Fortunes and our sacred Honor.

### Signers of the Declaration of Independence July 4, 1776

John Adams, Samuel Adams, Josiah Bartlett, Carter Braxton, Charles Carroll, Samuel Chase, Abraham Clark, George Clymer, William Ellery, William Floyd, Benjamin Franklin, Elbridge Gerry, Button Gwinnett, Lyman Hall, John Hancock, Benjamin Harrison, John Hart, Richard Henry Lee, Joseph Hewes, Thomas Heyward, Jr., William Hooper, Stephen Hopkins, Fras. Hopkinson, Samuel Huntington, Thomas Jefferson, Frans. Lewis, Francis Lightfoot Lee, Phil. Livington, Thomas Lynch, Jr., Thomas M'Kean, Arthur Middleton, Lewis Morris, Robert Morris, John Morton, Thomas Nelson, Jr., William Paca, John Penn, George Read, Caesar Rodney, George Ross, Benjamin Rush, Edward Rutledge, Roger Sherman, Jason Smith, Richard Stockton, Thomas Stone, George Taylor, Matthew Thornton, Robert Treat Paine, George Walton, William Whipple, William Williams, James Wilson, Johnothan Witherspoon, Oliver Wolcott, George Wythe.

# Common Sense

## by Thomas Paine

### Introduction

Perhaps the sentiments contained in the following pages, are not *yet* sufficiently fashionable to procure them general favour; a long habit of not thinking a thing *wrong*, gives it a superficial appearance of being *right*, and raises at first a formidable outcry in defense of custom. But the tumult soon subsides. Time makes more converts than reason.

As a long and violent abuse of power, is generally the Means of calling the right of it in question (and in Matters too which might never have been thought of, had not the Sufferers been aggravated into the inquiry) and as the King of England hath undertaken in his *own right*, to support the Parliament in what he calls *theirs*, and as the good people of this country are grievously oppressed by the combination, they have an undoubted privilege to inquire into the pretensions of both, and equally to reject the usurpation of either.

In the following sheets, the author hath studiously avoided every thing which is personal among ourselves. Compliments as well as censure to individuals make no part thereof. The wise, and the worthy, need not the triumph of a pamphlet; and those whose sentiments are injudicious, or unfriendly, will cease of themselves unless too much pains are bestowed upon their conversion.

The cause of America is in a great measure the cause of all mankind. Many circumstances hath, and will arise, which are not local, but universal, and through which the principles of all Lovers of Mankind are affected, and in the Event of which, their Affections are interested. The laying a Country desolate with Fire and Sword, declaring War against the natural rights of all Mankind, and extirpating the Defenders thereof from the Face of the Earth, is the Concern of every Man to whom Nature hath given the Power of feeling; of which Class, regardless of Party Censure, is the *Author*.

P.S. The Publication of this new Edition hath been delayed, with a View of taking notice (had it been necessary) of any Attempt to refute the Doctrine of Independance: As no Answer hath yet appeared, it is now presumed that none will, the Time needful for getting such a Performance ready for the Public being considerably past.

Who the Author of this Production is, is wholly unnecessary to the Public, as the Object for Attention is the *doctrine itself*, not the *man*. Yet it may not be unnecessary to say, That he is unconnected with any Party, and under no sort of Influence public or private, but the influence of reason and principle.

## Philadelphia, February 14, 1776

### Of the Origin and Design of Government in General. With Concise Remarks on the English Constitution

Some writers have so confounded society with government, as to leave little or no distinction between them; whereas they are not only different, but have different origins. Society is produced by our wants, and government by our wickedness; the former promotes our *positively* by uniting our affections, the latter *negatively* by restraining our vices. The one encourages intercourse, the other creates distinctions. The first a patron, the last a punisher.

Society in every state is a blessing, but government even in its best state is but a necessary evil; in its worst state an intolerable one; for when we suffer, or are exposed to the same miseries *by a government*, which we might expect in a country *without government*, our calamity is heightened by reflecting that we furnish the means by which we suffer. Government, like dress, is the badge of lost innocence; the palaces of kings are built on the ruins of the bowers of paradise. For were the impulses of conscience clear, uniform, and irresistibly obeyed, man would need no other lawgiver; but that not being the case, he finds it necessary to surrender up a part of his property to furnish means for the protection of the rest; and this he is induced to do by the same prudence which in every other case advises him out of two evils to choose the least. *Wherefore*, security being the true design and end of government, it unanswerably follows, that whatever *form* thereof appears most likely to ensure it to us, with the least expense and greatest benefit, is preferable to all others.

In order to gain a clear and just idea of the design and end of government, let us suppose a small number of persons settled in some sequestered part of the earth, unconnected with the rest, they will then represent the first peopling of any country, or of the world. In this state of natural liberty, society will be their first thought. A thousand motives will excite them thereto, the strength of one man is so unequal to his wants, and his mind so unfitted for perpetual solitude, that he is soon obliged to seek assistance and relief of another, who in his turn requires the same. Four or five united would be able to raise a tolerable dwelling in the midst of a wilderness, but *one* man might labour out of the common period of life without accomplishing any thing; when he had felled his timber he could not remove it, nor erect it after it was removed; hunger in the mean time would urge him from his work, and every different want call him a different way. Disease, nay even misfortune would be death, for though neither might be mortal, yet either would disable him from living, and reduce him to a state in which he might rather be said to perish than to die.

Thus necessity, like a gravitating power, would soon form our newly arrived emigrants into society, the reciprocal blessings of which, would supersede, and render the obligations of law and government unnecessary while they remained perfectly just to each other; but as nothing but heaven is impregnable to vice, it will unavoidably happen, that in proportion as they surmount the first difficulties of emigration, which bound them together in a common cause, they will begin to relax in their duty and attachment to each other; and this remissness will point out the necessity of establishing some form of government to supply the defect of moral virtue.

Some convenient tree will afford them a State-House, under the branches of which, the whole colony may assemble to deliberate on public matters. It is more than probable that their first laws will have the title only of *Regulations*, and be enforced by no other penalty than public disesteem. In this first parliament every man, by natural right, will have a seat.

But as the colony increases, the public concerns will increase likewise, and the distance at which the members may be separated, will render it too inconvenient for all of them to meet on every occasion as at first, when their number was small, their habitations near, and the public concerns few and trifling. This will point out the convenience of their consenting to leave the legislative part to be managed by a select number chosen from the whole body, who are supposed to have the same concerns at stake which those who appointed them, and who will act in the same manner as the whole body would act, were they present. If the colony continues increasing, it will become necessary to augment the number of the representatives, and that the interest of every part of the colony may be attended to, it will be found best to divide the whole into convenient parts, each part sending its proper number; and that the *elected* might never form to themselves an interest separate from the *electors*, prudence will point out the propriety of having elections often; because as the *elected* might by that means return and mix again with the general body of the *electors* in a few months, their fidelity to the public will be secured by the prudent reflection of not making a rod for themselves. And as this frequent interchange will establish a common interest with every part of the community, they will mutually and naturally support each other, and on this (not on the unmeaning name of king) depends the *strength of government, and the happiness of the governed.*

Here then is the origin and rise of government; namely, a mode rendered necessary by the inability of moral virtue to govern the world; here too is the design and end of government, viz. freedom and security. And however our eyes may be dazzled with show, or our ears deceived by sound; however prejudice may warp our wills, or interest darken our understanding, the simple voice of nature and of reason will say, it is right.

I draw my idea of the form of government from a principle in nature, which no art can overturn, viz. that the more simple any thing is, the less liable it is to be disordered; and the easier repaired when disordered; and with this maxim in view, I offer a few remarks on the so much boasted constitution of England. That it was noble for the dark and slavish times in which it was erected, is granted. When the world was overrun with tyranny the least remove therefrom was a glorious rescue. But that it is imperfect, subject to convulsions, and incapable of producing what it seems to promise, is easily demonstrated.

Absolute governments (tho' the disgrace of human nature) have this advantage with them, that they are simple; if the people suffer, they know the head from which their suffering springs, know likewise the remedy, and are not bewildered by a variety of causes and cures. But the constitution of England is so exceedingly complex, that the nation may suffer for years together without being able to discover in which part the fault lies; some will say in one and some in another, and every political physician will advise a different medicine.

I know it is difficult to get over local or long standing prejudices, yet if we will suffer ourselves to examine the component parts of the English constitution, we shall find them to be the base remains of two ancient tyrannies, compounded with some new republican materials.

*First*—The remains of monarchial tyranny in the person of the king.

*Secondly*—The remains of aristocratical tyranny in the persons of the peers.

*Thirdly*—The new republican materials in the persons of the commons, on whose virtue depends the freedom of England.

The two first, by being hereditary, are independent of the people; wherefore in a *constitutional sense* they contribute nothing towards the freedom of the state.

To say that the constitution of England is a *union* of three powers reciprocally *checking* each other, is farcical, either the words have no meaning, or they are flat contradictions.

To say that the commons is a check upon the king, presupposes two things:

*First*—That the king is not to be trusted without being looked after, or in other words, that a thirst for absolute power is the natural disease of monarchy.

*Secondly*—That the commons, by being appointed for that purpose, are either wiser or more worthy of confidence than the crown.

But as the same constitution which gives the commons a power to check the king by withholding the supplies, gives afterwards the king a power to check the commons, by empowering him to reject their other bills; it again supposes that the king is wiser than those whom it has already supposed to be wiser than him. A mere absurdity!

There is something exceedingly ridiculous in the composition of monarchy; it first excludes a man from the means of information, yet empowers him to act in cases where the highest judgment is required. The state of a king shuts him from the world, yet the business of a king requires him to know it thoroughly; wherefore the different parts, by unnaturally opposing and destroying each other, prove the whole character to be absurd and useless.

Some writers have explained the English constitution thus: The king, say they, is one, the people another; the peers are a house in behalf of the king, the commons in behalf of the people; but this hath all the distinctions of a house divided against itself; and though the expressions be pleasantly arranged, yet when examined, they appear idle and ambiguous; and it will always happen, that the nicest construction that words are capable of, when applied to the description of some thing which either cannot exist, or is too incomprehensible to be within the compass of description, will be words of sound only, and though they may amuse the ear, they cannot inform the mind, for this explanation includes a previous question, viz. *How came the king by a power which the people are afraid to trust, and always obliged to check*? Such a power could not be the gift of a wise people, neither can any power, *which needs checking*, be from God; yet the provision, which the constitution makes, supposes such a power to exist.

But the provision is unequal to the task; the means either cannot or will not accomplish the end, and the whole affair is a felo de se; for as the greater weight will always carry up the less, and as all the wheels of a machine are put in motion by one, it only remains to know which power in the constitution has the most weight, for that will govern; and though the others, or a part of them, may clog, or, as the phrase is, check the rapidity of its motion, yet so long as they cannot stop it, their endeavours will be ineffectual; the first moving power will at last have its way, and what it wants in speed, is supplied by time.

That the crown is this overbearing part in the English constitution, needs not be mentioned, and that it derives its whole consequence merely from being the giver of places and pensions, is self-evident, wherefore, though we have been wise enough to shut and lock a door against absolute monarchy, we at the same time have been foolish enough to put the crown in possession of the key.

The prejudice of Englishmen in favour of their own government by king, lords, and commons, arises as much or more from national pride than reason. Individuals are undoubtedly safer in England than in some other countries, but the *will* of the king is as much the *law* of the land in Britain as in France, with this difference, that instead of proceeding directly from his mouth, it is handed to the people under the more formidable shape of an act of parliament. For the fate of Charles the First hath only made kings more subtle—not more just.

Wherefore, laying aside all national pride and prejudice in favour of modes and forms, the plain truth is, that *it is wholly owing to the constitution of the people, and not to the constitution of the government*, that the crown is not as oppressive in England as in Turkey.

An inquiry into the *constitutional errors* in the English form of government is at this time highly necessary; for as we are never in a proper condition of doing justice to others, while we continue under the influence of some leading partiality, so neither are we capable of doing it to ourselves while we remain fettered by any obstinate prejudice. And as a man. who is attached to a prostitute, is unfitted to choose or judge a wife, so any prepossession in favour of a rotten constitution of government will disable us from discerning a good one.

## Of Monarchy and Hereditary Succession

Mankind being originally equals in the order of creation, the equality could only be destroyed by some subsequent circumstance; the distinctions of rich, and poor, may in a great measure be accounted for, and that without having recourse to the harsh, ill-sounding names of oppression and avarice. Oppression is often the *consequence*, but seldom or never the *means* of riches; and though avarice will preserve a man from being necessitously poor, it generally makes him too timorous to be wealthy.

But there is another and greater distinction, for which no truly natural or religious reason can be assigned, and that is, the distinction of men into KINGS and SUBJECTS. Male and female are the distinctions of nature, good and bad the distinctions of heaven; but how a race of men came into the world so exalted above the rest, and distinguished like some new species, is worth inquiring into, and whether they are the means of happiness or of misery to mankind.

In the early ages of the world, according to the scripture chronology, there were no kings; the consequence of which was, there were no wars; it is the pride of kings which throw mankind into confusion. Holland without a king hath enjoyed more peace for this last century than any of the monarchial governments in Europe. Antiquity favours the same remark; for the quiet and rural lives of the first patriarchs hath a happy something in them, which vanishes away when we come to the history of Jewish royalty.

Government by kings was first introduced into the world by the Heathens, from whom the children of Israel copied the custom. It was the most prosperous invention the Devil ever set on foot for the promotion of idolatry. The Heathens paid divine honours to their deceased kings, and the Christian world hath improved on the plan, by doing the same to their living ones. How impious is the title of *sacred majesty* applied to a worm, who in the midst of his splendor is crumbling into dust!

As the exalting one man so greatly above the rest cannot be justified on the equal rights of nature, so neither can it be defended on the authority of scripture; for the will of the Almighty, as declared by Gideon and the prophet Samuel, expressly disapproves of government by kings. All anti-monarchical parts of scripture have been very smoothly glossed over in monarchical governments, but they undoubtedly merit the attention of countries which have their governments yet to form. *Render unto Caesar the things which are Caesar's* is the scripture doctrine of courts, yet it is no support of monarchical government, for the Jews at that time were without a king, and in a state of vassalage to the Romans.

Near three thousand years passed away from the Mosaic account of the creation, till the Jews under a national delusion requested a king. Till then their form of government (except in extraordinary cases, where the Almighty interposed) was a kind of republic administered by a judge and the elders of the tribes. Kings they had none, and it was held sinful to acknowledge any being under that title but the Lord of Hosts. And when a man seriously reflects on the idolatrous homage which is paid to the persons of kings, he need not wonder that the Almighty, ever jealous of his honour, should disapprove of a form of government which so impiously invades the prerogative of heaven.

Monarchy is ranked in scripture as one of the sins of the Jews, for which a curse in reserve is denounced against them. The history of that transaction is worth attending to.

The children of Israel being oppressed by the Midianites, Gideon marched against them with a small army, and victory, through the divine interposition, decided in his favour. The Jews, elate with success, and attributing it to the generalship of Gideon, proposed making him a king, saying, *Rule thou over us, thou and thy son and thy son's son*. Here was temptation in its fullest extent; not a kingdom only, but an hereditary one, but Gideon in the piety of his soul replied, *I will not rule over you, neither shall my son rule over you,* THE LORD SHALL RULE OVER YOU. Words need not be more explicit; Gideon doth not decline the honour, but denieth their right to give it; neither doth he compliment them with invented declarations of his thanks, but in the positive style of a prophet charges them with disaffection to their proper Sovereign, the King of heaven.

About one hundred and thirty years after this, they fell again into the same error. The hankering which the Jews had for the idolatrous customs of the Heathens, is something exceedingly unaccountable; but so it was, that laying hold of the misconduct of Samuel's two sons, who were entrusted with some secular concerns, they came in an abrupt and clamorous manner to Samuel, saying, *Behold thou art old, and thy sons walk not in thy ways, now make us a king to judge us, like all other nations*. And here we cannot but observe that their motives were bad, viz. that they might be *like* unto other nations, i.e. the Heathens, whereas their true glory laid in being as much *unlike* them as possible. *But the thing displeased Samuel when they said, Give us a king to judge us; and Samuel prayed unto the Lord, and the Lord said unto Samuel, Hearken unto the voice of the people in all that they say unto thee, for they have not rejected thee, but they have rejected me,* THAT I SHOULD NOT REIGN OVER THEM. *According to all the works which they have since the day that I brought them up out of Egypt, even unto this day; wherewith they have forsaken me and served other Gods; so do they also unto thee. now therefore hearken unto their voice, howbeit, protest solemnly unto them and shew them the manner of the king that shall reign over them, i.e.* not of any particular king, but the general manner of the kings of the earth, whom Israel was so eagerly copying after. And notwithstanding the great distance of time and difference of manners, the character is still in fashion. *And Samuel told all the words of the Lord unto the people, that asked of him a king. And he said, This shall be the manner of the king that shall reign over you; he will take your sons and appoint them for himself, for his chariots, and to be his horseman, and some shall run before his chariots* (this description agrees with the present mode of impressing men) *and he will appoint him captains over thousands and captains over fifties, and will set them to ear his ground and reap his harvest, and to make his instruments of war, and instruments of his chariots; and he will take your daughters to be confectionaries, and to be cooks and to be bakers* (this describes the expense and luxury as well as the oppression of kings) *and he will take your fields and your olive yards, even the best of them, and give them to his servants; and he will take the tenth of your seed, and of your vineyards, and give them to his officers and to his servants* (by which we see that bribery, corruption, and favouritism are the standing vices of kings) *and he will take the tenth of your men servants, and your maid servants, and your goodliest young men and your asses, and put them to his work; and he will take the tenth of your sheep, and ye shall be his servants, and ye shall cry out in that day because of your king which ye shall have chosen,* AND THE LORD WILL NOT HEAR YOU IN THAT DAY. This accounts for the continuation of monarchy; neither do the characters of the few good kings which have lived since, either sanctify the title, or blot out the sinfulness of the origin; the high encomium given of David takes no notice of him *officially as a king,* but only as a *man* after God's own heart. *Nevertheless the people refused to obey the voice of Samuel, and they said, Nay, but we will have a king over us, that we may be like all the nations, and that our king may judge us, and go out before us, and fight our battles.* Samuel continued to reason with them, but to no purpose; he set before them their ingratitude, but all would not avail; and seeing them fully bent on their folly, he cried out, *I will call unto the Lord, and he shall send thunder and rain* (which then was a punishment, being in the time of wheat harvest) *that ye may perceive and see that your wickedness is great which ye have done in the sight of the Lord,* IN ASKING YOU A KING. *So Samuel called unto the Lord, and the Lord sent thunder and rain that day, and all the people greatly feared the Lord and Samuel. and all the people said unto Samuel, pray for thy servants unto the Lord thy God that we die not, for* WE HAVE

ADDED UNTO OUR SINS THIS EVIL, TO ASK A KING. These portions of scripture are direct and positive. They admit of no equivocal construction. That
the Almighty hath here entered his protest against monarchical government, is true, or the scripture is false. And a man hath good reason to believe that there is as much of kingcraft, as priestcraft, in withholding the
scripture from the public in Popish countries. For monarchy in every instance is the Popery of government.

To the evil of monarchy we have added that of hereditary succession;
and as the first is a degradation and lessening of ourselves, so the second,
claimed as a matter of right, is an insult and an imposition on posterity.
For all men being originally equals, no *one* by *birth* could have a right to
set up his own family in perpetual preference to all others for ever, and
though himself might deserve *some* decent degree of honours of his con-
temporaries, yet his descendants might be far too unworthy to inherit
them. One of the strongest *natural* proofs of the folly of hereditary right
in kings, is, that nature disapproves it, otherwise she would not so frequently turn it into ridicule by giving mankind an *ass for a lion.*

Secondly, as no man at first could possess any other public honours
than were bestowed upon him, so the givers of those honours could have
no power to give away the right of posterity. And though they might say,
"We chooses you for *our* head," they could not, without manifest injustice to their children, say, "that your children and your children's children
shall reign over *ours* for ever." Because such an unwise, unjust, unnatural compact might (perhaps) in the next succession put them under the
government of a rogue or a fool. Most wise men, in their private sentiments, have ever treated hereditary right with contempt; yet it is one of
those evils, which when once established is not easily removed; many
submit from fear, others from superstition, and the more powerful part
shares with the king the plunder of the rest.

This is supposing the present race of kings in the world to have had
an honourable origin; whereas it is more than probable, that could we take
off the dark covering of antiquities, and trace them to their first rise, that
we should find the first of them nothing better than the principal ruffian
of some restless gang, whose savage manners or preeminence in subtlety
obtained the title of chief among plunderers; and who by increasing in
power, and extending his depredations, overawed the quiet and defense-
less to purchase their safety by frequent contributions. Yet his electors
could have no idea of giving hereditary right to his descendants, because
such a perpetual exclusion of themselves was incompatible with the free
and unrestrained principles they professed to live by. Wherefore, hereditary succession in the early ages of monarchy could not take place as a

matter of claim, but as something casual or complemental; but as few or no records were extant in those days, and traditional history stuffed with fables, it was very easy, after the lapse of a few generations, to trump up some superstitious tale, conveniently timed, Mahomet like, to cram hereditary right down the throats of the vulgar. Perhaps the disorders which threatened, or seemed to threaten, on the decease of a leader and the choice of a new one (for elections among ruffians could not be very orderly) induced many at first to favour hereditary pretensions; by which means it happened, as it hath happened since, that what at first was submitted to as a convenience, was afterwards claimed as a right.

England, since the conquest, hath known some few good monarchs, but groaned beneath a much larger number of bad ones; yet no man in his senses can say that their claim under William the Conqueror is a very honourable one. A French bastard landing with an armed banditti, and establishing himself king of England against the consent of the natives, is in plain terms a very paltry rascally original. It certainly hath no divinity in it. However, it is needless to spend much time in exposing the folly of hereditary right; if there are any so weak as to believe it, let them promiscuously worship the ass and lion, and welcome. I shall neither copy their humility, nor disturb their devotion.

Yet I should be glad to ask how they suppose kings came at first? The question admits but of three answers, viz. either by lot, by election, or by usurpation. If the first king was taken by lot, it establishes a precedent for the next, which excludes hereditary succession. Saul was by lot, yet the succession was not hereditary, neither does it appear from that transaction there was any intention it ever should be. If the first king of any country was by election, that likewise establishes a precedent for the next; for to say, that the *right* of all future generations is taken away, by the act of the first electors, in their choice not only of a king, but of a family of kings for ever, hath no parallel in or out of scripture but the doctrine of original sin, which supposes the free will of all men lost in Adam; and from such comparison, and it will admit of no other, hereditary succession can derive no glory. For as in Adam all sinned, and as in the first electors all men obeyed; as in the one all mankind we re subjected to Satan, and in the other to Sovereignty; as our innocence was lost in the first, and our authority in the last; and as both disable us from reassuming some former state and privilege, it unanswerably follows that original sin and hereditary succession are parallels. Dishonourable rank! Inglorious connection! Yet the most subtle sophist cannot produce a juster simile.

As to usurpation, no man will be so hardy as to defend it; and that William the Conqueror was an usurper is a fact not to be contradicted.

The plain truth is, that the antiquity of English monarchy will not bear looking into.

But it is not so much the absurdity as the evil of hereditary succession which concerns mankind. Did it ensure a race of good and wise men it would have the seal of divine authority, but as it opens a door to the *foolish*, the *wicked*, and the *improper*, it hath in it the nature of oppression. Men who look upon themselves born to reign, and others to obey, soon grow insolent; selected from the rest of mankind their minds are early poisoned by importance; and the world they act in differs so materially from the world at large, that they have but little opportunity of knowing its true interests, and when they succeed to the government are frequently the most ignorant and unfit of any throughout the dominions.

Another evil which attends hereditary succession is, that the throne is subject to be possessed by a minor at any age; all which time the regency, acting under the cover a king, have every opportunity and inducement to betray their trust. The same national misfortune happens, when a king, worn out with age and infirmity , enters the last stage of human weakness. In both these cases the public becomes a prey to every miscreant, who can tamper successfully with the follies either of age or infancy.

The most plausible plea, which hath ever been offered in favour of hereditary succession, is, that it preserves a nation from civil wars; and were this true, it would be weighty; whereas, it is the most barefaced falsity ever imposed upon mankind. The whole history of England disowns the fact. Thirty kings and two minors have reigned in that distracted kingdom since the conquest, in which time there have been (including the Revolution) no less than eight civil wars and nineteen rebellions. Wherefore instead of making for peace, it makes against it, and destroys the very foundation it seems to stand on.

The contest for monarchy and succession, between the houses of York and Lancaster, laid England in a scene of blood for many years. Twelve pitched battles, besides skirmishes and sieges, were fought between Henry and Edward. Twice was Henry prisoner to Edward, who in his turn was prisoner to Henry. And so uncertain is the fate of war and the temper of a nation, when nothing but personal matters are the ground of a quarrel, that Henry was taken in triumph from a prison to a palace, and Edward obliged to fly from a palace to a foreign land; yet, as sudden transitions of temper are seldom lasting, Henry in his turn was driven from the throne, and Edward recalled to succeed him. The parliament always following the strongest side.

This contest began in the reign of Henry the Sixth, and was not entirely extinguished till Henry the Seventh, in whom the families were united. Including a period of 67 years, viz. from 1422 to 1489.

In short, monarchy and succession have laid (not this or that kingdom only) but the world in blood and ashes. Tis a form of government which the word of God bears testimony against, and blood will attend it.

If we inquire into the business of a king, we shall find that in some countries they have none; and after sauntering away their lives without pleasure to themselves or advantage to the nation, withdraw from the scene, and leave their successors to tread the same idle ground. In absolute monarchies the whole weight of business, civil and military, lies on the king; the children of Israel in their request for a king, urged this plea "that he may judge us, and go out before us and fight our battles." But in countries where he is neither a judge nor a general, as in England, a man would be puzzled to know what IS his business.

The nearer any government approaches to a republic the less business there is for a king. It is somewhat difficult to find a proper name for the government of England. Sir William Meredith calls it a republic; but in its present state it is unworthy of the name, because the corrupt influence of the crown, by having all the places in its disposal, hath so effectually swallowed up the power, and eaten out the virtue of the house of commons (the republican part in the constitution) that the government of England is nearly as monarchical as that of France or Spain. Men fall out with names without understanding them. For it is the republican and not the monarchical part of the constitution of England which Englishmen glory in, viz. the liberty of choosing an house of commons from out of their own body—and it is easy to see that when republican virtue fails, slavery ensues. Why is the constitution of England sickly, but because monarchy hath poisoned the republic, the crown hath engrossed the commons?

In England a king hath little more to do than to make war and give away places; which in plain terms, is to impoverish the nation and set it together by the ears. A pretty business indeed for a man to be allowed eight hundred thousand sterling a year for, and worshipped into the bargain! Of more worth is one honest man to society and in the sight of God, than all the crowned ruffians that ever lived.

## Thoughts on the Present State of American Affairs

In the following pages I offer nothing more than simple facts, plain arguments, and common sense; and have no other Preliminaries to settle with the reader, than that he will divest himself of prejudice and prepossession, and suffer his reason and his feelings to determine for themselves; that he will put ON, or rather that he will not put *off* the true character of a man, and generously enlarge his views beyond the present day.

Volumes have been written on the subject of the struggle between England and America. Men of all ranks have embarked in the controversy, from different motives, and with various designs; but all have been ineffectual, and the period of debate is closed. Arms, as the last resource, decide this contest; the appeal was the choice of the king, and the continent hath accepted the challenge.

It hath been reported of the late Mr. Pelham (who tho' an able minister was not without his faults) that on his being attacked in the house of commons, on the score, that his measures were only of a temporary kind, replied *"they will last my time."* Should a thought so fatal and unmanly possess the colonies in the present contest, the name of ancestors will be remembered by future generations with detestation.

The sun never shined on a cause of greater worth. 'Tis not the affair of a city, a county, a province, or a kingdom, but of a continent—of at least one eighth part of the habitable globe. 'Tis not the concern of a day, a year, or an age; posterity are virtually involved in the contest, and will be more or less affected, even to the end of time, by the proceedings now. Now is the seed-time of continental union, faith and honour. The least fracture now will be like a name engraved with the point of a pin on the tender rind of a young oak; the wound will enlarge with the tree, and posterity read it in full grown characters.

By referring the matter from argument to arms, a new aera for politics is struck; a new method of thinking hath arisen. All plans, proposals, &c. prior to the nineteenth of April, *i.e.* to the commencement of hostilities, are like the almanacs of the last year; which, though proper then are superseded and useless now. Whatever was advanced by the advocates on either side of the question then, terminated in one and the same point. viz. a union with Great-Britain: the only difference between the parties was the method of effecting it; the one proposing force, the other friendship; but it hath so far happened that the first hath failed, and the second hath withdrawn her influence.

As much hath been said of the advantages of reconciliation which, like an agreeable dream, hath passed away and left us as we were, it is but right, that we should examine the contrary side of the argument, and inquire into some of the many material injuries which these colonies sustain, and always will sustain, by being connected with, and dependent on Great Britain: To examine that connection and dependence, on the principles of nature and common sense, to see what we have to trust to, if separated, and what we are to expect, if dependant.

I have heard it asserted by some, that as America hath flourished under her former connection with Great Britain that the same connection is necessary towards her future happiness, and will always have the same effect. Nothing can be more fallacious than this kind of argument. We may as well assert that because a child has thrived upon milk that it is never to have meat, or that the first twenty years of our lives is to become a precedent for the next twenty. But even this is admitting more than is true, for I answer roundly, that America would have flourished as much, and probably much more, had no European power had any thing to do with her. The commerce, by which she hath enriched herself, are the necessaries of life, and will always have a market while eating is the custom of Europe.

But she has protected us, say some. That she has engrossed us is true, and defended the continent at our expense as well as her own is admitted, and she would have defended Turkey from the same motive, viz. the sake of trade and dominion.

Alas, we have been long led away by ancient prejudices, and made large sacrifices to superstition. We have boasted the protection of Great Britain, without considering, that her motive was *interest* not *attachment*; that she did not protect us from *our enemies* on *our account*, but from *her enemies* on *her own account*, from those who had no quarrel with us on any *other account*, and who will always be our enemies on the *same account*. Let Britain wave her pretensions to the continent, or the continent throw off the dependence, and we should be at peace with France and Spain were they at war with Britain. The miseries of Hanover last war ought to warn us against connections.

It has lately been asserted in parliament, that the colonies have no relation to each other but through the parent country, *i.e.* that Pennsylvania and the Jerseys, and so on for the rest, are sister colonies by the way of England; this is certainly a very round-about way of proving relationship, but it is the nearest and only true way of proving enemyship, if I may so call it. France and Spain never were. nor perhaps ever will be our enemies as *Americans*, but as our being the *subjects of Great Britain*.

But Britain is the parent country, say some. Then the more shame upon her conduct. Even brutes do not devour their young, nor savages make war upon their families; wherefore the assertion, if true, turns to her reproach; but it happens not to be true, or only partly so and the phrase *parent* or *mother country* hath been jesuitically adopted by the king and his parasites, with a low papistical design of gaining an unfair bias on the credulous weakness of our minds. Europe, and not England, is the parent country of America. This new world hath been the asylum for the persecuted lovers of civil and religious liberty from *every part* of Europe. Hither have they fled, not from the tender embraces of the mother, but from the cruelty of the monster; and it is so far true of England, that the same tyranny which drove the first emigrants from home, pursues their descendants still.

In this extensive quarter of the globe, we forget the narrow limits of three hundred and sixty miles (the extent of England) and carry our friendship on a larger scale; we claim brotherhood with every European Christian, and triumph in the generosity of the sentiment.

It is pleasant to observe by what regular gradations we surmount the force of local prejudice, as we enlarge our acquaintance with the world. A man born in any town in England divided into parishes, will naturally associate most with his fellow-parishioners (because their interests in many cases will be common) and distinguish him by the name of *neighbour*; if he meet him but a few miles from home, he drops the narrow idea of a street, and salutes him by the name of *townsman*; if he travel out of the county, and meet him in any other, he forgets the minor divisions of street and town, and calls him *countryman*, i.e. *countryman*; but if in their foreign excursions they should associate in France or any other part of *Europe*, their local remembrance would be enlarged into that of *Englishmen*. And by a just parity of reasoning, all Europeans meeting in America, or any other quarter of the globe, are *countrymen*; for England, Holland, Germany, or Sweden, when compared with the whole, stand in the same places on the larger scale, which the divisions of street, town, and county do on the smaller ones; distinctions too limited for continental minds. Not one third of the inhabitants, even of this province, are of English descent. Wherefore I reprobate the phrase of parent or mother country applied to England only, as being false, selfish, narrow and ungenerous.

But admitting, that we were all of English descent, what does it amount to? Nothing. Britain, being now an open enemy, extinguishes every other name and title: And to say that reconciliation is our duty, is truly farcical. The first king of England, of the present line (William the Conqueror) was a Frenchman, and half the Peers of England are descendants from the same country; therefore, by the same method of reasoning, England ought to be governed by France.

Much hath been said of the united strength of Britain and the colonies, that in conjunction they might bid defiance to the world. But this is mere presumption; the fate of war is uncertain, neither do the expressions mean any thing; for this continent would never suffer itself to be drained of inhabitants, to support the British arms in either Asia, Africa, or Europe.

Besides what have we to do with setting the world at defiance? Our plan is commerce, and that, well attended to, will secure us the peace and friendship of all Europe; because, it is the interest of all Europe to have America a *free port*. Her trade will always be a protection, and her barrenness of gold and silver secure her from invaders.

I challenge the warmest advocate for reconciliation, to shew, a single advantage that this continent can reap, by being connected with Great Britain. I repeat the challenge, not a single advantage is derived. Our corn will fetch its price in any market in Europe, and our imported goods must be paid for, buy them where we will.

But the injuries and disadvantages we sustain by that connection, are without number; and our duty to mankind at large, as well as to ourselves, instruct us to renounce the alliance: Because, any submission to, or dependence on Great Britain, tends directly to involve this continent in European wars and quarrels; and sets us at variance with nations, who would otherwise seek our friendship, and against whom, we have neither anger nor complaint. As Europe is our market for trade, we ought to form no partial connection with any part of it. It is the true interest of America to steer clear of European contentions, which she never can do, while by her dependence on Britain, she is made the make-weight in the scale of British politics.

Europe is too thickly planted with kingdoms to be long at peace, and whenever a war breaks out between England and any foreign power, the trade of America goes to ruin, *because of her connection with Britain*. The next war may not turn out like the last, and should it not, the advocates for reconciliation now, will be wishing for separation then, because, neutrality in that case, would be a safer convoy than a man of war. Every thing that is right or natural pleads for separation. The blood of the slain, the weeping voice of nature cries, 'TIS TIME TO PART. Even the distance at which the Almighty hath placed England and America, is a strong and natural proof, that the authority of the one, over the other, was never the design of Heaven. The time likewise at which the continent was discovered, adds weight to the argument, and the manner in which it was peopled increases the force of it. The reformation was preceded by the discovery of America, as if the Almighty graciously meant to open a sanctuary to the Persecuted in future years, when home should afford neither friendship nor safety.

The authority of Great Britain over this continent, is a form of government, which sooner or later must have an end: And a serious mind can draw no true pleasure by looking forward under the painful and positive conviction, that what he calls "the present constitution" is merely temporary. As parents, we can have no joy, knowing that *this government* is not sufficiently lasting to ensure any thing which we may bequeath to posterity: And by a plain method of argument, as we are running the next generation into debt, we ought to do the work of it, otherwise we use them meanly and pitifully. In order to discover the line of our duty rightly, we should take our children in our hand, and fix our station a few years farther into life; that eminence will present a prospect, which a few present fears and prejudices conceal from our sight.

Though I would carefully avoid giving unnecessary offense, yet I am inclined to believe, that all those who espouse the doctrine of reconciliation, may be included within the following descriptions. Interested men, who are not to be trusted; weak men, who *cannot* see; prejudiced men, who *will not* see; and a certain set of moderate men, who think better of the European world than it deserves; and this last class, by an ill-judged deliberation, will be the cause of more calamities to this continent, than all the other three.

It is the good fortune of many to live distant from the scene of sorrow; the evil is not sufficient brought to *their* doors to make *them* feel the precariousness with which all American property is possessed. But let our imaginations transport us far a few moments to Boston, that seat of wretchedness will teach us wisdom, and instruct us for ever to renounce a power in whom we can have no trust. The inhabitants of that unfortunate city, who but a few months ago were in ease and affluence, have now, no other alternative than to stay and starve, or turn and beg. Endangered by the fire of their friends if they continue within the city, and plundered by the soldiery if they leave it. In their present condition they are prisoners without the hope of redemption, and in a general attack for their relief, they would be exposed to the fury of both armies.

Men of passive tempers look somewhat lightly over the offenses of Britain, and, still hoping for the best, are apt to call out, *"Come, Come, we shall be friends again, for all this."* But examine the passions and feelings of mankind, Bring the doctrine of reconciliation to the touchstone of nature, and then tell me, whether you can hereafter love, honor, and faithfully serve the power that hath carried fire and sword into your land? If yon cannot do all these, then are you only deceiving yourselves, and by your delay bringing ruin upon posterity. Your future connection with Britain, whom you can neither love nor honor will be forced and unnatural, and being formed only on the plan of present convenience, will in a little time fall into a relapse more wretched than the first. But if you say, you can still pass the violations over, then I ask, Hath your house been burnt? Hath your property been destroyed before your face! Are your wife and children destitute of a bed to lie on, or bread to live on? Have you lost a parent or a child by their hands, and yourself the ruined and wretched survivor! If you have not, then are you not a judge of those who have. But if you have, and still can shake hands with the murderers, then are you unworthy the name of husband, father, friend, or lover, and whatever may be your rank or title in life, you have the heart of a coward, and the spirit of a sycophant.

This is not inflaming or exaggerating matters, but trying them by those feelings and affections which nature justifies, and without which, we should be incapable of discharging the social duties of life, or enjoying the felicities of it. I mean not to exhibit horror for the purpose of provoking revenge, but to awaken us from fatal and unmanly slumbers, that we may pursue determinately some fixed object. It is not in the power of Britain or of Europe to conquer America, if she do not conquer herself by *delay* and *timidity*. The present winter is worth an age if rightly employed, but if lost or neglected, the whole continent will partake of the misfortune; and there is no punishment which that man will not deserve, be he who, or what, or where he will, that may be the means of sacrificing a season so precious and useful.

It is repugnant to reason, to the universal order of things, to all examples from former ages, to suppose, that this continent can longer remain subject to any external power. The most sanguine in Britain does not think so. The utmost stretch of human wisdom cannot, at this time, compass a plan short of separation, which can promise the continent even a year's security. Reconciliation is *now* a fallacious dream. Nature hath deserted the connection, and Art cannot supply her place. For, as Milton wisely expresses, "never can true reconcilement grow, where wounds of deadly hate have pierced so deep."

Every quiet method for peace hath been ineffectual. Our prayers have been rejected with disdain; and only tended to convince us, that nothing Batters vanity, or confirms obstinacy in Kings more than repeated petitioning—and nothing hath contributed more than that very measure to make the Kings of Europe absolute: Witness Denmark and Sweden. Wherefore, since nothing but blows will do, for God's sake, let us come to a final separation, and not leave the next generation to be cutting throats, under the violated unmeaning names of parent and child.

To say, they will never attempt it again is idle and visionary, we thought so at the repeal of the stamp-act, yet a year or two undeceived us;

as well may we suppose that nations, which have been once defeated, will never renew the quarrel.

As to government matters, it is not in the power of Britain to do this continent justice: The business of it will soon be too weighty, and intricate, to be managed with any tolerable degree of convenience, by a power so distant from us, and so very ignorant of us; for if they cannot conquer us, they cannot govern us. To be always running three or four thousand miles with a tale or a petition, waiting four or five months for an answer, which when obtained requires five or six more to explain it in, will in a few years be looked upon as folly and childishness—There was a time when it was proper, and there is a proper time for it to cease.

Small islands not capable of protecting themselves, are the proper objects for kingdoms to take under their care; but there is something very absurd, in supposing a continent to be perpetually governed by an island. In no instance hath nature made the satellite larger than its primary planet, and as England and America, with respect to each other, reverses the common order of nature, it is evident they belong to different systems; England to Europe, America to itself.

I am not induced by motives of pride, party, or resentment to espouse the doctrine of separation and independance; I am clearly, positively, and conscientiously persuaded that it is the true interest of this continent to be so; that every thing short of *that* is mere patchwork, that it can afford no lasting felicity,—that it is leaving the sword to our children, and shrinking back at a time, when, a little more, a little farther, would have rendered this continent the glory of the earth.

As Britain hath not manifested the least inclination towards a compromise, we may be assured that no terms can be obtained worthy the acceptance of the continent, or any ways equal to the expense of blood and treasure we have been already put to.

The object, contended for, ought always to bear some just proportion to the expense. The removal of North, or the whole detestable junto, is a matter unworthy the millions we have expended. A temporary stoppage of trade, was an inconvenience, which would have sufficiently balanced the repeal of all the acts complained of, had such repeals been obtained; hut if the whole continent must take up arms, if every man must be a soldier, it is scarcely worth our while to fight against a contemptible ministry only. Dearly, dearly, do we pay for the repeal of the acts, if that is all we fight for; for in a just estimation, it is as great a folly to pay a Bunker-hill price for law, as for land. As I have always considered the independancy of this continent, as an event, which sooner or later must arrive, so from the late rapid progress of the continent to maturity, the event could not be far off. Wherefore, on the breaking out of hostilities, it was not worth while to have disputed a matter, which time would have finally redressed, unless we meant to be in earnest; otherwise, it is like wasting an estate on a suit at law, to regulate the trespasses of a tenant, whose lease is just expiring. No man was a warmer wisher for reconciliation than myself, before the fatal nineteenth of April 1775, but the moment the event of that day was made known, I rejected the hardened, sullen tempered Pharaoh of England for ever; and disdain the wretch, that with the pretended title of FATHER OF HIS PEOPLE can unfeelingly hear of their slaughter, and composedly sleep with their blood upon his soul.

But admitting that matters were now made up, what would be the event? I answer, the ruin of the continent. And that for several reasons.

*First.* The powers of governing still remaining in the hands of the king, he will have a negative over the whole legislation of this continent. And as he hath shewn himself such an inveterate enemy to liberty. and discovered such a thirst for arbitrary power; is he, or is he not, a proper man to say to these colonies, *"You shall make no laws but what I please."* And is there any inhabitant in America so ignorant as not to know, that according to what is called the *present constitution*, that this continent can make no laws but what the king gives leave to; and is there any man so unwise, as not to see, that (considering what has happened) he will suffer no law to be made here, but such as suit HIS purpose. We may be as effectually enslaved by the want of laws in America, as by submitting to laws made for us in England. After matters are made up (as it is called) can there be any doubt, but the whole power of the crown will be exerted, to keep this continent as low and humble as possible? Instead of going forward we shall go backward, or be perpetually quarrelling or ridiculously petitioning.—We are already greater than the king wishes us to be, and will he not hereafter endeavour to make us less? To bring the matter to one point. Is the power who is jealous of our prosperity, a proper power to govern us? Whoever says *No* to this question, is an *independant*, for independancy means no more, than, whether we shall make our own laws, or whether the king, the greatest enemy this continent hath, or can have, shall tell us *"there shall be no laws but such as I like."*

But the king you will say has a negative in England; the people there can make no laws without his consent. In point of right and good order, there is something very ridiculous, that a youth of twenty-one (which hath often happened) shall say to several millions of people, older and wiser than himself, I forbid this or that act of yours to be law. But in this place I decline this sort of reply, though I will never cease to expose the absurdity of it, and only answer, that England being the King's residence, and America not so, makes quite another case. The king's negative *here* is ten times more dangerous and fatal than it can be in England, for *there* he will scarcely refuse his consent to a bill for putting England into as strong a state of defense as possible, and in America he would never suffer such a bill to be passed.

America is only a secondary object in the system of British politics, England consults the good of *this* country, no farther than it answers her *own* purpose. Wherefore, her own interest leads her to suppress the growth of *ours* in every case which doth not promote her advantage, or in the least interferes with it. A pretty state we should soon be in under such a secondhand government, considering what has happened! Men do not change from enemies to friends by the alteration of a name: And in order to shew that reconciliation now is a dangerous doctrine, I affirm, *that it would be policy in the king at this time, to repeal the acts for the sake of reinstating himself in the government of the provinces;* in order, that HE MAY ACCOMPLISH BY CRAFT AND SUBTLETY, IN THE LONG RUN, WHAT HE CANNOT DO BY FORCE AND VIOLENCE IN THE SHORT ONE. Reconciliation and ruin are nearly related.

*Secondly.* That as even the best terms, which we can expect to obtain, can amount to no more than a temporary expedient, or a kind of government by guardianship, which can last no longer than till the colonies come of age, so the general face and state of things, in the interim, will be unsettled and unpromising. Emigrants of property will not choose to come to a country whose form of government hangs but by a thread, and who is every day tottering on the brink of commotion and disturbance; and numbers of the present inhabitants would lay hold of the interval, to dispense of their effects, and quit the continent.

But the most powerful of all arguments, is, that nothing but independence, i.e. a continental form of government, can keep the peace of the continent and preserve it inviolate from civil wars. I dread the event of a reconciliation with Britain now, as it is more than probable, that it will be followed by a revolt somewhere or other, the consequences of which may be far more fatal than all the malice of Britain.

Thousands are already ruined by British barbarity; (thousands more will probably suffer the same fate) Those men have other feelings than us who have nothing suffered. All they *now* possess is liberty, what they before enjoyed is sacrificed to its service, and having nothing more to lose, they disdain submission. Besides, the general temper of the colonies, towards a British government, will be like that of a youth, who is nearly out of his time; they will care very little about her. And a government which cannot preserve the peace, is no government at all, and in that case we pay our money for nothing; and pray what is it that Britain can do, whose power will he wholly on paper. should a civil tumult break out the very day after reconciliation! I have heard some men say, many of whom I believe spoke without thinking, that they dreaded an independence, fearing that it would produce civil wars. It is but seldom that our first thoughts are truly correct, and that is the case here; for there are ten times more to dread from a patched up connection than from independence. I make the sufferers case my own, and I protest, that were I driven from house and home, my property destroyed, and my circumstances ruined, that as man, sensible of injuries, I could never relish the doctrine of reconciliation, or consider myself bound thereby.

The colonies have manifested such a spirit of good order and obedience to continental government, as is sufficient to make every reasonable person easy and happy on that head. No man can assign the least pretence for his fears, on any other grounds, than such as are truly childish and ridiculous, viz. that one colony will be striving for superiority over another.

Where there are no distinctions there can be no superiority, perfect equality affords no temptation. The republics of Europe are all (and we may say always) in peace. Holland and Switzerland are without wars, foreign or domestic: Monarchical governments, it is true, are never long at rest; the crown itself is a temptation to enterprising ruffians at *home*; and that degree of pride and insolence ever attendant on regal authority, swells into a rupture with foreign powers, in instances, where a republican government, by being formed on more natural principles, would negotiate the mistake.

If there is any true cause of fear respecting independence, it is because no plan is yet laid down. Men do not see their way out—Wherefore, as an opening into that business, I offer the following hints; at the same time modestly affirming, that I have no other opinion of them myself, than that they may be the means of giving rise to something better. Could the straggling thoughts of individuals be collected, they would frequently form materials for wise and able men to improve into useful matter.

LET the assemblies be annual, with a President only. The representation more equal. Their business wholly domestic, and subject to the authority of a Continental Congress.

Let each colony be divided into six, eight, or ten, convenient districts, each district to send a proper number of delegates to Congress, so that each colony send at least thirty. The whole number in Congress will be at least 390. Each Congress to sit and to choose a president by the following method. When the delegates are met, let a colony be taken from the whole thirteen colonies by lot, after which, let the whole Congress choose (by ballot) a president from out of the delegates of *that* province. In the next Congress, let a colony be taken by lot from twelve only, omitting that colony from which the president was taken in the former Congress, and so proceeding on till the whole thirteen shall have had their proper rotation. And in order that nothing may pass into a law but what is satisfactorily just not less than three fifths of the Congress to be called a majority—He that will promote discord, under a government so equally formed as this, would have joined Lucifer in his revolt.

But as there is a peculiar delicacy, from whom, or in what manner, this business must first arise, and as it seems most agreeable and consistent, that it should come from some intermediate body between the governed and the governors, that is, between the Congress and the people. Let a CONTINENTAL CONFERENCE be held, in the following manner, and for the following purpose.

A committee of twenty-six members of Congress, viz. two for each colony. Two Members from each House of Assembly, or Provincial Convention; and five representatives of the people at large, to be chosen in the capital city or town of each province, for and in behalf of the whole province, by as many qualified voters as shall think proper to attend from all parts of the province for that purpose; or, if more convenient, the representatives may be chosen in two or three of the most populous parts thereof. In this conference, thus assembled, will be united, the two grand principles of business *knowledge* and *power*. The members of Congress, Assemblies, or Conventions, by having had experience in national concerns, will be able and useful counsellors, and the whole, being empowered by the people, will have a truly legal authority.

The conferring members being met, let their business be to frame a CONTINENTAL CHARTER, Or Charter of the United Colonies; (answering to what is called the Magna Carta of England) fixing the number and manner of choosing members of Congress, members of Assembly, with their date of sitting, and drawing the line of business and jurisdiction between them: (Always remembering, that our strength is continental, not provincial:) Securing freedom and property to all men, and above all things, the free exercise of religion, according to the dictates of conscience; with such other matter as is necessary for a charter to contain. Immediately after which, the said Conference to dissolve, and the bodies which shall be chosen comformable to the said charter, to be the legislators and governors of this continent for the time being: Whose peace and happiness may God preserve, Amen.

Should any body of men be hereafter delegated for this or some similar purpose, I offer them the following extracts or that wise observer on governments *Dragonetti[1]*. "The science" says he "of the politician consists in fixing the true point of happiness and freedom. Those men would deserve the gratitude of ages, who should discover a mode of government that contained the greatest sum of individual happiness, with the least national expense.

But where, says some, is the King of America? I'll tell you. Friend, he reigns above, and doth not make havoc of mankind like the Royal Brute of Britain. Yet that we may not appear to be defective even in earthly honors, let a day be solemnly set apart for proclaiming the charter; let it be brought forth placed on the divine law, the word of God; let a crown be placed thereon, by which the world may know, that so far we approve of monarchy, that in America THE LAW IS KING. For as in absolute governments the King is law, so in free countries the law *ought* to be King; and there ought to be no other. But lest any ill use should afterwards arise, let the crown at the conclusion of the ceremony, be demolished, and scattered among the people whose right it is.

A government of our own is our natural right: And when a man seriously reacts on the precariousness of human affairs, he will become convinced, that it is infinitely wiser and safer, to form a constitution of our own in a cool deliberate manner, while we have it in our power, than to trust such an interesting event to time and chance. If we omit it now, some[2] Massanello may hereafter arise, who laying hold of popular disquietudes, may collect together the desperate and the discontented, and by assuming to themselves the powers of government, may sweep away the liberties of the continent like a deluge. Should the government of America return again into the hands of Britain, the tottering situation of things will be a temptation for some desperate adventurer to try his fortune; and in such a case, that relief can Britain give? Ere she could hear the news, the fatal business might be done; and ourselves suffering like the wretched Britons under the oppression of the Conqueror. Ye that oppose independence now, ye know not what ye do; ye are opening a door to eternal tyranny, by keeping vacant the seat of government. There are thousands, and tens of thousands, who would think it glorious to expel from the continent that barbarous and hellish power, which hath stirred up the Indians and Negroes to destroy us; the cruelty hath a double guilt, it is dealing brutally by us, and treacherously by them.

To talk of friendship with those in whom our reason forbids us to have faith, and our affections wounded through a thousand pores instruct us to detest, is madness and folly. Every day wears out the little remains of kindred between us and them, and can there be any reason to hope, that as the relationship expires, the affection will increase, or that we shall agree better, when we have ten times more and greater concerns to quarrel over than ever?

Ye that tell us of harmony and reconciliation, can ye restore to us the time that is past? Can ye give to prostitution its former innocence? Neither can ye reconcile Britain and America. The last cord now is broken, the people of England are presenting addresses against us. There are injuries which nature cannot forgive; she would cease to be nature if she did. As well can the lover forgive the ravisher of his mistress, as the continent forgive the murders of Britain. The Almighty hath implanted in us these unextinguishable feelings for good and wise purposes. They are the guardians of his image in our hearts. They distinguish us from the herd of common animals. The social compact would dissolve, and justice be extirpated the earth, or have only a casual existence were we callous to the touches of affection. The robber, and the murderer, would often escape unpunished, did not the injuries which our tempers sustain, provoke us into justice.

O ye that love mankind! Ye that dare oppose, not only the tyranny, but the tyrant, stand forth! Every spot of the old world is overrun with oppression. Freedom hath been hunted round the globe. Asia, and Africa, have long expelled her—Europe regards her like a stranger, and England hath given her warning to depart. O! receive the fugitive, and prepare in time an asylum for mankind.

## Of the Present Ability of America, with Some Miscellaneous Reflections

I have never met with a man, either in England or America, who hath not confessed his opinion that a separation between the countries, would take place one time or other: And there is no instance, in which we have shewn less judgement, than in endeavouring to describe, what we call the ripeness or fitness of the Continent for independence.

As all men allow the measure, and vary only in their opinion of the time, let us, in order to remove mistakes, take a general survey of things, and endeavour, if possible, to find out the *very* time. But we need not go far, the inquiry ceases at once, for, the *time hath found us*. The general concurrence, the glorious union of all things prove the fact.

It is not in numbers, but in unity, that our great strength lies; yet our present numbers are sufficient to repel the force of all the world. The Continent hath, at this time, the largest body of armed and disciplined men of any power under Heaven; and is just arrived at that pitch of strength, in which no single colony is able to support itself, and the whole, when united, can accomplish the matter, and either more, or, less than this, might be fatal in its effects. Our land force is already sufficient, and as to naval affairs, we cannot be insensible, that Britain would never suffer an American man of war to be built, while the continent remained in her hands. Wherefore, we should be no forwarder an hundred years hence in that branch, than we are now; but the truth is, we should be less so, because the timber of the country is every day diminishing, and that, which will remain at last, will be far off and difficult to procure.

Were the continent crowded with inhabitants, her sufferings under the present circumstances would be intolerable. The more seaport towns we had, the more should we have both to defend and to lose. Our present numbers are so happily proportioned to our wants, that no man need be idle. The diminution of trade affords an army, and the necessities of an army create a new trade.

Debts we have none; and whatever we may contract on this account will serve as a glorious memento of our virtue. Can we but leave posterity with a settled form of government, an independent constitution of its own, the purchase at any price will be cheap. But to expend millions for the sake of getting a few vile acts repealed, and routing the present ministry only, is unworthy the charge, and is using posterity with the utmost cruelty; because it is leaving them the great work to do, and a debt upon their backs, from which they derive no advantage. Such a thought is unworthy of a man of honor, and is the true characteristic of a narrow heart and a peddling politician.

The debt we may contract doth not deserve our regard, if the work be but accomplished. No nation ought to be without a debt. A national debt is a national bond; and when it bears no interest, is in no case a grievance. Britain is oppressed with a debt of upwards of one hundred and forty millions sterling, for which she pays upwards of four millions interest. And as a compensation for her debt, she has a large navy; America is without a debt, and without a navy; yet for the twentieth part of the English national debt, could have a navy as large again. The navy of England is not worth, at this time, more than three millions and an half sterling.

The first and second editions of this pamphlet were published without the following calculations, which are now given as a proof that the above estimation of the navy is just one.[3]

The charge of building a ship of each rate, and furnishing her with masts, yards, sails and rigging, together with a proportion of eight months boatswain's and carpenter's seastores, as calculated by Mr. Burchett, Secretary to the navy.[4]

```
For a ship of a 100 guns ...............35,553
                    90.....................29,886
                    80.....................23,638
                    70.....................17,795
                    60.....................14,197
                    50.....................10,606
                    40......................7,558
                    30......................5,846
                    20......................3,710
```

And from hence it is easy to sum up the value, or cost rather, of the whole British navy, which in the year 1757, when it was at its greatest glory consisted of the following ships and guns:

| Ships | Guns | Cost of one | Cost of all |
|-------|------|-------------|-------------|
| 6 | 100 | 35,553 | 213,318 |
| 12 | 90 | 29,886 | 358,632 |
| 12 | 80 | 23,638 | 283,656 |
| 43 | 70 | 17,785 | 764,755 |
| 35 | 60 | 14,197 | 496,895 |
| 40 | 50 | 10,606 | 424,240 |
| 45 | 40 | 7,558 | 340,110 |
| 58 | 20 | 3,710 | 215,180 |
| 85 Sloops, bombs, and fireships, one with another, | | 2,000 | 170,000 |

Cost   3,266,786

Remains for guns,   233,214

3,500,000

No country on the globe is so happily situated, or so internally capable of raising a fleet as America. Tar, timber, iron, and cordage are her natural produce. We need go abroad for nothing. Whereas the Dutch, who make large profits by hiring out their ships of war to the Spaniards and Portuguese, are obliged to import most of their materials they use. We ought to view the building a fleet as an article of commerce, it being the natural manufactory of this country. It is the best money we can lay out. A navy when finished is worth more than it cost. And is that nice point in national policy, in which commerce and protection are united. Let us build; if we want them not, we can sell; and by that means replace our paper currency with ready gold and silver.

In point of manning a fleet, people in general run into great errors; it is not necessary that one fourth part should he sailors. The *Terrible* privateer, Captain Death, stood the hottest engagement of any ship last war, yet had not twenty sailors on board, though her complement of men was upwards of two hundred. A few able and social sailors will soon instruct a sufficient number of active landmen in the common work of a ship. Wherefore, we never can be more capable to begin on maritime matters than now, while our timber is standing, our fisheries blocked up, and our sailors and shipwrights out of employ. Men of war of seventy and eighty guns were built forty years ago in New-England, and why not the same now? Ship-building is America's greatest pride, and in which she will in time excel the whole world. The great empires of the east are mostly inland, and consequently excluded from the possibility of rivalling her. Africa is in a state of barbarism; and no power in Europe hath either such an extent of coast, or such an internal supply of materials. Where nature hath given the one, she has withheld the other; to America only hath she been liberal of both. The vast empire of Russia is almost shut out from the sea: wherefore, her boundless forests, her tar, iron, and cordage are only articles of commerce.

In point of safety, ought we to be without a fleet? We are not the little people now, which we were sixty years ago; at that time we might have trusted our property in the streets, or fields rather; and slept securely without locks or bolts to our doors or windows. The case now is altered, and our methods of defense ought to improve with our increase of property. A common pirate, twelve months ago, might have come up the Delaware, and laid the city of Philadelphia under instant contribution, for what sum he pleased; and the same might have happened to other places. Nay, any daring fellow, in a brig of fourteen or sixteen guns might have robbed the whole continent, and carried off half a million of money. These are circumstances which demand our attention, and point out the necessity of naval protection.

Some, perhaps, will say, that after we have made it up Britain, she will protect us. Can we be so unwise as to mean, that she shall keep a navy in our harbours for that purpose? Common sense will tell us, that the power which hath endeavoured to subdue us, is of all others the most improper to defend us. Conquest may be effected under the pretence of friendship; and ourselves after a long and brave resistance, be at last cheated into slavery. And if her ships are not to be admitted into our harbours, I would ask, how is she to protect us? A navy three or four thousand miles off can be of little use, and on sudden emergencies, none at all. Wherefore, if we must hereafter protect ourselves, why not do it for ourselves?

The English list of ships of war, is long and formidable, but not a tenth part of them are at any one time fit for service, numbers of them not in being; yet their names are pompously continued in the list, f only a plank be left of the ship: and not a fifth part of such as are fit for service, can be spared on any one station at one time. The East and West Indies, Mediterranean, Africa, and other parts over which Britain extends her claim, make large demands upon her navy. From a mixture of prejudice and inattention, we have contracted a false notion respecting the navy of England, and have talked as if we should have the whole of it to encounter at once, and for that reason, supposed, that we must have one as large; which not being instantly practicable, have been made use of by a set of disguised Tories to discourage our beginning thereon. Nothing can be farther from truth than this; for if America had only a twentieth part of the naval force of Britain, she would be by far an overmatch for her; because, as we neither have, nor claim any foreign dominion, our whole force would be employed on our own coast, where we should, in the long run, have two to one the advantage of those who had three or four thousand miles to sail over, before they could attack us, and the same distance to return in order to refit and recruit. And although Britain, by her fleet, hath a check over our trade to Europe, we have as large a one over her trade to the West Indies, which, by laying in the neighbourhood of the continent, is entirely at its mercy.

Some method might be fallen on to keep up a naval force in time of peace, if we should not judge it necessary to support a constant navy. If premiums were to be given to merchants, to build and employ in their service ships mounted with twenty, thirty, forty or fifty guns, (the premiums to be in proportion to the loss of bulk to the merchants) fifty or sixty of those ships, with a few guardships on constant duty, would keep up a sufficient navy, and that without burdening ourselves with the evil so loudly complained of in England, of suffering their fleet, in time of peace to lie rotting in the docks. To unite the sinews of commerce and defense is sound policy; for when our strength and our riches play into each other's hand, we need fear no external enemy.

In almost every article of defense we abound. Hemp flourishes even to rankness, so that we need not want cordage. Our iron is superior to that of other countries. Our small arms equal to any in the world. Cannon we

can cast at pleasure. Saltpetre and gunpowder we are every day producing. Our knowledge is hourly improving. Resolution is our inherent character, and courage hath never yet forsaken us. Wherefore, what is it that
we want? Why is it that we hesitate? From Britain we can expect nothing
but ruin. If she is once admitted to the government of America again, this
Continent will not be worth living in. Jealousies will be always arising;
insurrections will be constantly happening; and who will go forth to quell
them? Who will venture his life to reduce his own countrymen to a foreign obedience? The difference between Pennsylvania and Connecticut,
respecting some unlocated lands, shews the insignificance of a British
government, and fully proves, that nothing but Continental authority can
regulate Continental matters.

Another reason why the present time is preferable to all others, is,
that the fewer our numbers are, the more land there is yet unoccupied,
which instead of being lavished by the king on his worthless dependants,
may be hereafter applied, not only to the discharge of the present debt, but
to the constant support of government. No nation under heaven hath such
an advantage as this.

The infant state of the Colonies, as it is called, so far from being
against, is an argument in favour of independance. We are sufficiently
numerous, and were we more so, we might be less united. It is a matter
worthy of observation, that the mare a country is peopled, the smaller
their armies are. In military numbers, the ancients far exceeded the
modems: and the reason is evident. for trade being the consequence of
population, men become too much absorbed thereby to attend to anything
else. Commerce diminishes the spirit, both of patriotism and military defence. And history sufficiently informs us, that the bravest achievements
were always accomplished in the non-age of a nation. With the increase
of commerce, England hath lost its spirit. The city of London, notwithstanding its numbers, submits to continued insults with the patience of a
coward. The more men have to lose, the less willing are they to venture.
The rich are in general slaves to fear, and submit to courtly power with the
trembling duplicity of a Spaniel.

Youth is the seed time of good habits, as well in nations as in individuals. It might be difficult, if not impossible, to form the Continent into
one government half a century hence. The vast variety of interests, occasioned by an increase of trade and population, would create confusion.
Colony would be against colony. Each being able might scorn each other's
assistance: and while the proud and foolish gloried in their little distinctions, the wise would lament, that the union had not been formed before.
Wherefore, the *present time* is the *true time* for establishing it. The inti-

macy which is contracted in infancy, and the friendship which is formed in misfortune, are, of all others, the most lasting and unalterable. Our present union is marked with both these characters: we are young and we have been distressed; but our concord hath withstood our troubles, and fixes a memorable are for posterity to glory in.

The present time, likewise, is that peculiar time, which never happens to a nation but once, viz. the time of forming itself into a government. Most nations have let slip the opportunity, and by that means have been compelled to receive laws from their conquerors, instead of making laws for themselves. First, they had a king, and then a form of government; whereas, the articles or charter of government, should be formed first, and men delegated to execute them afterward but from the errors of other nations, let us learn wisdom, and lay hold of the present opportunity—*To begin government at the right end.*

When William the Conqueror subdued England, he gave them law at the point of the sword; and until we consent, that the seat of government, in America, be legally and authoritatively occupied, we shall be in danger of having it filled by some fortunate ruffian, who may treat us in the same manner, and then, where will be our freedom? where our property?

As to religion, I hold it to be the indispensable duty of all government, to protect all conscientious professors thereof, and I know of no other business which government hath to do therewith, Let a man throw aside that narrowness of soul, that selfishness of principle, which the niggards of all professions are willing to part with, and he will be at delivered of his fears on that head. Suspicion is the companion of mean souls, and the bane of all good society. For myself, I fully and conscientiously believe, that it is the will of the Almighty, that there should be diversity of religious opinions among us: It affords a larger field for our Christian kindness. Were we all of one way of thinking, our religious dispositions would want matter for probation; and on this liberal principle, I look on the various denominations among us, to be like children of the same family, differing only, in what is called, their Christian names.

In page three-hundred-fourteen, I threw out a few thoughts on the propriety of a Continental Charter, (for I only presume to offer hints, not plans) and in this place, I take the liberty of rementioning the subject, by observing, that a charter is to be understood as a bond of solemn obligation, which the whole enters into, to support the right of every separate part, whether of religion, personal freedom, or property. A firm bargain and a right reckoning make long friends.

In a former page I likewise mentioned the necessity of a large and equal representation; and there is no political matter which more deserves our attention. A small number of electors, or a small number of representatives, are equally dangerous. But if the number of the representatives be not only small, but unequal, the danger is increased. As an instance of this, I mention the following; when the Associators petition was before the House of Assembly of Pennsylvania; twenty-eight members only were present, all the Bucks county members, being eight, voted against it, and had seven of the Chester members done the same, this whole province had been governed by two counties only, and this danger it is always exposed to. The unwarrantable stretch likewise, which that house made in their last sitting, to gain an undue authority over the delegates of that province, ought to warn the people at large, how they trust power out of their own hands. A set of instructions for the Delegates were put together, which in point of sense and business would have dishonoured a schoolboy, and after being approved by a *few*, a *very few* without doors, were carried into the House, and there passed *in behalf of the whole colony;* whereas, did the whole colony know, with what ill-will that House hath entered on some necessary public measures, they would not hesitate a moment to think them unworthy of such a trust.

Immediate necessity makes many things convenient, which if continued would grow into oppressions. Expedience and right are different things. When the calamities of America required a consultation, there was no method so ready, or at that time so proper, as to appoint persons from the several Houses of Assembly for that purpose; and the wisdom with which they have proceeded hath preserved this continent from ruin. But as it is more than probable that we shall never be without a CONGRESS, every well wisher to good order, must own, that the mode for choosing members of that body, deserves consideration. And I put it as a question to those, who make a study of mankind, whether *representation and election* is not too great a power for one and the same body of men to possess? When we are planning for posterity, we ought to remember, that virtue is not hereditary.

It is from our enemies that we often gain excellent maxims, and are frequently surprised into reason by their mistakes, Mr. Cornwall (one of the Lords of the Treasury) treated the petition of the New-York Assembly with contempt, because *that* House, he said, consisted but of twenty-six members, which trifling number, he argued, could not with decency be put for the whole. We thank him for his involuntary honesty.[5]

TO CONCLUDE, however strange it may appear to some, or however unwilling they may be to think so, matters not, but many strong and striking reasons may be given, to shew, that nothing can settle our affairs so expeditiously as an open and determined declaration for independence. Some of which are,

*First.*— It is the custom of nations, when any two are at war, for some other powers, not engaged in the quarrel, to step in as mediators, and bring about the preliminaries of a peace: hut while America calls herself the Subject of Great Britain, no power, however well disposed she may be, can offer her mediation. Wherefore, in our present state we may quarrel on for ever.

*Secondly.*— It is unreasonable to suppose, that France or Spain will give us any kind of assistance, if we mean only, to make use of that assistance for the purpose of repairing the breach, and strengthening the connection between Britain and America; because, those powers would be sufferers by the consequences.

*Thirdly.*— While we profess ourselves the subjects of Britain, we must, in the eye of foreign nations. be considered as rebels. The precedent is somewhat dangerous to *their peace*, for men to be in arms under the name of subjects; we, on the spot, can solve the paradox: but to unite resistance and subjection, requires an idea much too refined for common understanding.

*Fourthly.*— Were a manifesto to be published, and despatched to foreign courts, setting forth the miseries we have endured, and the peaceable methods we have ineffectually used for redress; declaring, at the same time, that not being able, any longer, to live happily or safely under the cruel disposition of the British court, we had been driven to the necessity of breaking off all connections with her; at the same time, assuring all such courts of our peaceable disposition towards them, and of our desire of entering into trade with them: Such a memorial would produce more good effects to this Continent, than if a ship were freighted with petitions to Britain.

Under our present denomination of British subjects, we can neither be received nor heard abroad: The custom of all courts is against us, and will be so, until, by an independance, we take rank with other nations.

These proceedings may at first appear strange and difficult; but, like all other steps which we have already passed over, will in a little time become familiar and agreeable; and, until an independance is declared, the Continent will feel itself like a man who continues putting off some unpleasant business from day to day, yet knows it must be done, hates to set about it, wishes it over, and is continually haunted with the thoughts of its necessity.

# Appendix

Since the publication of the first edition of this pamphlet, or rather, on the same day on which it came out, the King's Speech made its appearance in this city. Had the spirit of prophecy directed the birth of this production, it could not have brought it forth, at a more seasonable juncture, or a more necessary time. The bloody mindedness of the one, shew the necessity of pursuing the doctrine of the other. Men read by way of revenge. And the Speech, instead of terrifying, prepared a way for the manly principles of Independance.

Ceremony, and even, silence, from whatever motive they may arise, have a hurtful tendency, when they give the least degree of countenance to base and wicked performances; wherefore, if this maxim be admitted, it naturally follows, that the King's Speech, as being a piece of finished villany, deserved, and still deserves, a general execration both by the Congress and the people. Yet, as the domestic tranquillity of a nation, depends greatly, on the *chastity* of what may properly be called NATIONAL MANNERS, it is often better, to pass some things over in silent disdain, than to make use of such new methods of dislike, as might introduce the least innovation, on that guardian of our peace and safety. And, perhaps, it is chiefly owing to this prudent delicacy, that the King's Speech, hath not, before now, suffered a public execution. The Speech if it may be called one, is nothing better than a wilful audacious libel against the truth, the common good, and the existence of mankind; and is a formal and pompous method of offering up human sacrifices to the pride of tyrants. But this general massacre of mankind. is one of the privileges, and the certain consequence of Kings; for as nature knows them *not*, they know *not her*, and although they are beings of our *own* creating, they know not *us*, and are become the gods of their creators. The Speech hath one good quality, which is, that it is not calculated to deceive, neither can we, even if we would, be deceived by it. Brutality and tyranny appear on the face of it. It leaves us at no loss: And every line convinces, even in the moment of reading, that He, who hunts the woods for prey, the naked and untutored Indian, is less a Savage than the King of Britain.

Sir John Dalrymple, the putative father of a whining jesuitical piece, fallaciously called, "*The address of the people of* ENGLAND *to the inhabitants of* AMERICA ," hath, perhaps, from a vain supposition, that the people here were to be frightened at the pomp and description of a king, given, (though very unwisely on his part) the real character of the present one: "But" says this writer, "if you are inclined to pay compliments to an administration, which we do not complain of," (meaning the Marquis of Rockingham's at the repeal of the Stamp Act) "it is very unfair in you to withhold them from that prince *by whose* NOD ALONE *they were permitted to do any thing*." This is toryism with a witness! Here is idolatry even without a mask: And he who can calmly hear, and digest such doctrine, hath forfeited his claim to rationality an apostate from the order of manhood; and ought to be considered as one, who hath not only given up the proper dignity of man, but sunk himself beneath the rank of animals, and contemptibly crawl through the world like a worm.

However, it matters very little now, what the king of England either says or does; he hath wickedly broken through every moral and human obligation, trampled nature and conscience beneath his feet; and by a steady and constitutional spirit of insolence and cruelty, procured for himself an universal hatred. It is *now* the interest of America to provide for herself. She hath already a large and young family, whom it is more her duty to take care of, than to be granting away her property, to support a power who is become a reproach to the names of men and Christians— YE, whose office it is to watch over the morals of a nation, of whatsoever sect or denomination ye are of, as well as ye, who, are more immediately the guardians of the public liberty, if ye wish to preserve your native country uncontaminated by European corruption, ye must in secret wish a separation—But leaving the moral part to private reflection, I shall chiefly confine my farther remarks to the following heads.

First. That it is the interest of America to be separated from Britain.

Secondly. Which is the easiest and most practicable plan, RECONCILIATION OR INDEPENDANCE? With some occasional remarks.

In support of the first, I could, if I judged it proper, produce the opinion of some of the ablest and most experienced men on this continent; and whose sentiments, on that head, are not yet publicly known. It is in reality a self-evident position: For no nation in a state of foreign dependance, limited in its commerce, and cramped and fettered in its legislative powers, can ever arrive at any material eminence. America doth not yet know what opulence is; and although the progress which she hath made stands unparalleled in the history of other nations, it is but childhood, compared with what she would be capable of arriving at, had she, as she ought to have, the legislative powers in her own hands. England is, at this time, proudly coveting what would do her no good, were she to accomplish it; and the Continent hesitating on a matter, which will be her final ruin if neglected. It is the commerce and not the conquest of America, by which England is to he benefited, and that would in a great measure continue, were the countries as independant of each other as France and Spain; because in many articles, neither can go to a better market. But it is the independance of this country on Britain or any other, which is now the main and only object worthy of contention, and which, like all other truths discovered by necessity, will appear clearer and stronger every day.

First. Because it will come to that one time or other.

Secondly. Because, the longer it is delayed the harder it will be to accomplish.

I have frequently amused myself both in public and private companies, with silently remarking, the specious errors of those who speak without reflecting. And among the many which I have heard, the following seems the most general, viz. that had this rupture happened forty or fifty years hence, instead of *now*, the Continent would have been more able to have shaken off the dependance. To which I reply, that our military ability, *at this time*, arises from the experience gained in the last war, and which in forty or fifty years time, would have been totally extinct. The Continent, would not, by that time, have had a General, or even a military officer left; and we, or those who may succeed us, would have been as ignorant of martial matters as the ancient Indians: And this single position, closely attended to, will unanswerably prove, that the present time is preferable to all others. The argument turns thus—at the conclusion of the last war, we had experience, but wanted numbers; and forty or fifty years hence, we should have numbers, without experience; wherefore, the proper point of time, must be some particular point between the two extremes, in which a sufficiency of the former remains, and a proper increase of the latter is obtained: And that point of time is the present time.

The reader will pardon this digression, as it does not properly come under the head I first set out with, and to which I again return by the following position, viz.

Should affairs he patched up with Britain, and she to remain the governing and sovereign power of America, (which, as matters are now circumstanced, is giving up the point entirely) we shall deprive ourselves of the very means of sinking the debt we have, or may contract. The value of the back lands which some of the provinces are clandestinely deprived of, by the unjust extension of the limits of Canada, valued only at five pounds sterling per hundred acres, amount to upwards of twenty-five millions, Pennsylvania currency; and the quit-rents at one penny sterling per acre, to two millions yearly.

It is by the sale of those lands that the debt may be sunk, without burthen to any, and the quit-rent reserved thereon, will always lessen, and in time, will wholly support the yearly expence of government. It matters not how long the debt is in paying, so that the lands when sold be applied to the discharge of it, and for the execution of which, the Congress for the time being, will be the continental trustees. . .

I proceed now to the second head, viz. Which is the easiest and most practicable plan, RECONCILIATION or INDEPENDANCE; With some occasional remarks.

He who takes nature for his guide is not easily beaten out of his argument, and on that ground, I answer *generally—That* INDEPENDANCE *being a* SINGLE SIMPLE LINE, *contained within ourselves; and reconciliation, a matter exceedingly perplexed and complicated, and in which, a treacherous capricious court is to interfere, gives the answer without a doubt.*

The present state of America is truly alarming to every man who is capable of reflexion. Without law, without government, without any other mode of power than what is founded on, and granted by courtesy. Held together by an unexampled concurrence of sentiment, which, is nevertheless subject to change, and which, every secret enemy is endeavouring to dissolve. Our present condition, is, Legislation without law; wisdom without a plan; a constitution without a name; and, what is strangely astonishing, perfect Independance contending for dependance. The instance is without a precedent; the case never existed before; and who can tell what may be the event? The property of no man is secure in the present unbraced system of things. The mind of the multitude is left at random, and seeing no fixed object before them, they pursue such as fancy or opinion starts. Nothing is criminal; there is no such thing as treason; wherefore, every one thinks himself at liberty to act as he pleases. The Tories dared not have assembled offensively, had they known that their lives, by that act, were forfeited to the laws of the state. A line of distinction should be drawn, between, English soldiers taken in battle, and inhabitants of America taken in arms. The first are prisoners, but the latter traitors. The one forfeits his liberty, the other his head.

Notwithstanding our wisdom, there is a visible feebleness in some of our proceedings which gives encouragement to dissensions. The Continental Belt is too loosely buckled. And if something is not done in time, it will be too late to do any thing, and we shall fall into a state, in which, neither *reconciliation* nor *independance* will be practicable. The king and his worthless adherents are got at their old game of dividing the Continent, and there are not wanting among us, Printers, who will be busy in spreading specious falsehoods. The artful and hypocritical letter which appeared a few months ago in two of the New York papers, and likewise in two others, is an evidence that there are men who want either judgment or honesty.

It is easy getting into holes and corners and talking of reconciliation: But do such men seriously consider, how difficult the task is, and how dangerous it may prove, should the Continent divide thereon. Do they take within their view, all the various orders of men whose situation and circumstances, as well as their own, are to be considered therein. Do they put themselves in the place of the sufferer whose *all* is *already* gone, and of the soldier, who hath quitted *all* for the defence of his country. If their ill judged moderation be suited to their own private situations *only*, regardless of others, the event will convince them, that "they are reckoning without their Host."

Put us, says some, on the footing we were on in sixty-three: To which I answer, the request is not now in the power of Britain to comply with, neither will she propose it; but if it were, and even should be granted, I ask, as a reasonable question, By what means is such a corrupt and faithless court to be kept to its engagements? Another parliament, nay, even the present, may hereafter repeal the obligation, on the pretense, of its being violently obtained, or unwisely granted; and in that case, Where is our redress?—No going to law with nations; cannon are the barristers of Crowns; and the sword, not of justice, but of war, decides the suit. To be on the footing of sixty-three, it is not sufficient, that the laws only be put on the same state, but, that our circumstances, likewise, be put on the same state; Our burnt and destroyed towns repaired or built up, our private losses made good, our public debts (contracted for defence) discharged; otherwise, we shall be millions worse than we were at that enviable period. Such a request, had it been complied with a year ago, would have won the heart and soul of the Continent—but now it is too late, "The Rubicon is passed."

Besides, the taking up arms, merely to enforce the repeal of a pecuniary law, seems as unwarrantable by the divine law, and as repugnant to human feelings, as the taking up arms to enforce obedience thereto. The object, on either side, doth not justify the means; for the lives of men are too valuable to be cast away on such trifles. It is the violence which is done and threatened to our persons; the destruction of our property by an armed force; the invasion of our country by fire and sword, which conscientiously qualifies the use of arms: And the instant, in which such a mode of defence became necessary, all subjection to Britain ought to have ceased; and the independancy of America, should have been considered, as dating its a era from, and published by, *the first musket that was fired against her*. This line is a line of consistency; neither drawn by caprice, nor extended by ambition; but produced by a chain of events, of which the colonies were not the authors.

I shall conclude these remarks with the following timely and well intended hints. We ought to reflect, that there are three different ways by which an independancy may hereafter be effected; and that *one* of those *three*, will one day or other, be the fate of America, viz. By the legal voice of the people in Congress; by a military power; or by a mob—It may not always happen that *our* soldiers are citizens, and the multitude a body of reasonable men; virtue, as I have already remarked, is not hereditary, neither is it perpetual. Should an independancy be brought about by the first of those means, we have every opportunity and every encouragement before us, to form the noblest purest constitution on the face of the earth. We have it in our power to begin the world over again. A situation, similar to the present, hath not happened since the days of Noah until now. The birthday of a new world is at hand, and a race of men, perhaps as numerous as all Europe contains, are to receive their portion of freedom from the event of a few months. The Reflexion is awful—and in this point of view, How trifling, how ridiculous, do the little, paltry cavillings, of a few weak or interested men appear, when weighed against the business of a world.

Should we neglect the present favourable and inviting period, and an Independance be hereafter effected by any other means, we must charge the consequence to ourselves, or to those rather, whose narrow and prejudiced souls, are habitually opposing the measure, without either inquiring or reflecting. There are reasons to be given in support of Independance, which men should rather privately think of, than be publicly told of. We ought not now to be debating whether we shall be independant or not, but, anxious to accomplish it on a firm, secure, and honorable basis, and uneasy rather that it is not yet began upon. Every day convinces us of its necessity. Even the Tories (if such beings yet remain among us) should, of all men, be the most solicitous to promote it; for, as the appointment of committees at first, protected them from popular rage, so, a wise and well established form of government, will be the only certain means of continuing it securely to them. *Wherefore*, if they have not virtue enough to be *Whigs*, they ought to have prudence enough to wish for Independance.

In short, Independance is the only *Bond* that can tye and keep us together. We shall then see our object, and our ears will be legally shut against the schemes of an intriguing, as well, as a cruel enemy. We shall then too, be on a proper footing, to treat with Britain; for there is reason to conclude, that the pride of that court, will be less hurt by treating with the American states for terms of peace, than with those, whom she denominates, "rebellious subjects," for terms of accommodation. It is our delaying it that encourages her to hope for conquest, and our backwardness tends only to prolong the war. As we have, without any good effect therefrom, withheld our trade to obtain a redress of our grievances, let us *now* try the alternative, by *independantly* redressing them ourselves, and then offering to open the trade. The mercantile and reasonable part in England, will be still with us; because, peace *with* trade, is preferable to war *without* it. And if this offer be not accepted, other courts may be applied to.

On these grounds I rest the matter. And as no offer hath yet been made to refute the doctrine contained in the former editions of this pamphlet, it is a negative proof, that either the doctrine cannot be refuted, or, that the party in favour of it are too numerous to be opposed. WHEREFORE, instead of gazing at each other with suspicious or doubtful curiosity; let each of us, hold out to his neighbour the hearty hand of friendship, and unite in drawing a line, which, like an act of oblivion shall bury in forgetfulness every former dissension. Let the names of Whig and Tory be extinct; and let none other be heard among us, than those of a *good citizen, an open and resolute friend, and a virtuous supporter of the* RIGHTS *of* MANKIND *and of the* FREE AND INDEPENDANT STATES OF AMERICA.

*To the Representatives of the Religious Society of the People called Quakers, or to so many of them as were concerned in publishing the late piece, entitled* "THE ANCIENT TESTIMONY and PRINCIPLES of the People called QUAKERS renewed, with Respect to the KING and GOVERNMENT, and touching the COMMOTIONS now prevailing in these and other parts of AMERICA addressed to the PEOPLE IN GENERAL."

The Writer of this, is one of those few, who never dishonours religion either by ridiculing, or cavilling at any denomination whatsoever. To God, and not to man, are all men accountable on the score of religion. Wherefore, this epistle is not so properly addressed to you as a religious, but as a political body, dabbling in matters, which the professed Quietude of your Principles instruct you not to meddle with.

As you have, without a proper authority for so doing, put yourselves in the place of the whole body of the Quakers, so, the writer of this, in order to be on an equal rank with yourselves, is under the necessity, of putting himself in the place of all those, who, approve the very writings and principles, against which, your testimony is directed: And he hath chosen this singular situation, in order, that you might discover in him that presumption of character which you cannot see in yourselves. For neither he nor you can have any claim or title to *Political Representation*.

When men have departed from the right way, it is no wonder that they stumble and fall. And it is evident from the manner in which ye have managed your testimony, that politics, (as a religious body of men) is not your proper Walk; for however well adapted it might appear to you, it is, nevertheless, a jumble of good and bad put unwisely together, and the conclusion drawn therefrom, both unnatural and unjust.

The two first pages, (and the whole doth not make four) we give you credit for, and expect the same civility from you, because the love and desire of peace is not confined to Quakerism, it is the *natural*, as well the religious wish of all denominations of men. And on this ground, as men labouring to establish an Independant Constitution of our own, do we exceed all others in our hope, end, and aim. *Our plan is peace for ever.* We are tired of contention with Britain, and can see no real end to it but in a final separation. We act consistently, because for the sake of introducing an endless and uninterrupted peace, do we bear the evils and burthens of the present day. We are endeavoring, and will steadily continue to endeavour, to separate and dissolve a connexion which hath already filled our land with blood; and which, while the name of it remains, will he the fatal cause of future mischiefs to both countries.

We fight neither for revenge nor conquest; neither from pride nor passion; we are not insulting the world with our fleets and armies, nor ravaging the globe for plunder. Beneath the shade of our own vines are we attacked; in our own houses, and on our own lands, is the violence committed against us. We view our enemies in the character of Highwaymen and Housebreakers, and having no defence for ourselves in the civil law, are obliged to punish them by the military one, and apply the sword, in the very case, where you have before now, applied the halter—Perhaps we feel for the ruined and insulted sufferers in all and every part of the continent, with a degree of tenderness which hath not yet made its way into some of your bosoms. But be ye sure that ye mistake not the cause and ground of your Testimony. Call not coldness of soul, religion; nor put the *Bigot* in the place of the *Christian*.

O ye partial ministers of your own acknowledged principles. If the bearing arms be sinful, the first going to war must be more so, by all the difference between wilful attack, and unavoidable defence. Wherefore, if ye really preach from conscience, and mean not to make a political hobbyhorse of your religion convince the world thereof, by proclaiming your doctrine to our enemies, *for they likewise bear* ARMS . Give us proof of your sincerity by publishing it at St. James's, to the commanders in chief at Boston, to the Admirals and Captains who are piratically ravaging our coasts, and to all the murdering miscreants who are acting in authority under HIM whom ye profess to serve. Had ye the honest soul of Barclay[6] ye would preach repentance to *your* king; Ye would tell the Royal Wretch his sins, and warn him of eternal ruin. Ye would not spend your partial invectives against the injured and the insulted only, but, like faithful ministers, would cry aloud and *spare none*. Say not that ye are persecuted, neither endeavour to make us the authors of that reproach, which, ye are bringing upon yourselves; for we testify unto all men, that we do not complain against you because ye are *Quakers*, but because ye pretend to *be* and are NOT Quakers.

Alas! it seems by the particular tendency of some part of your testimony, and other parts of your conduct, as if, all sin was reduced to, and comprehended in, *the act of bearing arms*, and that by the *people only*. Ye appear to us, to have mistaken party for conscience; because, the general tenor of your actions wants uniformity—And it is exceedingly difficult to us to give credit to many of your pretended scruples; because, we see them made by the same men, who, in the very instant that they are exclaiming against the mammon of this world, are nevertheless, hunting after it with a step as steady as Time, and an appetite as keen as Death.

The quotation which ye have made from Proverbs, in the third page of your testimony, that, "when a man's ways please the Lord, he maketh even his enemies to be at peace with him"; is very unwisely chosen on your part; because, it amounts to a proof, that the king's ways (whom ye are desirous of supporting) do *not* please the Lord, otherwise, his reign would be in peace.

I now proceed to the latter part of your testimony, and that, for which all the foregoing seems only an introduction viz.

"It hath ever been our judgment and principle, since we were called to profess the light of Christ Jesus, manifested in our consciences unto this day, that the setting up and putting down kings and governments, is God's peculiar prerogative; for causes best known to himself: And that it is not our business to have any hand or contrivance therein; nor to be busy bodies above our station, much less to plot and contrive the ruin, or overturn of any of them, but to pray for the king, and safety of our nation. and good of all men—That we may live a peaceable and quiet life, in all godliness and honesty; *under the government which God is pleased to set over us*"—If these are *really* your principles why do ye not abide by them? Why do ye not leave that, which ye call God's Work, to be managed by himself? These very principles instruct you to wait with patience and humility, for the event of all public measures, and to *receive that event* as the divine will towards you. *Wherefore*, what occasion is there for your *political testimony* if you fully believe what it contains? And the very publishing it proves, that either, ye do not believe what ye profess, or have not virtue enough to practise what ye believe.

The principles of Quakerism have a direct tendency to make a man the quiet and inoffensive subject of any, and every government *which is set over him*. And if the setting up and putting down of kings and governments is God's peculiar prerogative, he most certainly will not be robbed thereof by us: wherefore, the principle itself leads you to approve of every thing, which ever happened, or may happen to kings as being his work. OLIVER CROMWELL thanks you. CHARLES, then, died not by the hands of man; and should the present Proud Imitator of him, come to the same untimely end, the writers and publishers of the Testimony, are bound, by the doctrine it contains, to applaud the fact. Kings are not taken away by miracles, neither are changes in governments brought about by any other means than such as are common and human; and such as we are now using. Even the dispersion of the Jews, though foretold by our Saviour, was effected by arms. Wherefore, as ye refuse to be the means on one side, ye ought not to be meddlers on the other; but to wait the issue in silence; and unless ye can produce divine authority, to prove, that the Almighty who hath created and placed this new world, at the greatest distance it could possibly stand, east and west, from every part of the old, doth, nevertheless, disapprove of its being independent of the corrupt and abandoned court of Britain, unless I say, ye can shew this, how can ye on the ground of your principles, justify the exciting and stirring up the people "firmly to unite in the *abhorrence* of all such *writings*, and *measures*, as evidence a desire and design to break off the *happy* connexion we have hitherto enjoyed, with the kingdom of Great-Britain, and our just and necessary subordination to the king, and those who are lawfully placed in authority under him." What a slap of the face is here! the men, who in the very paragraph before, have quietly and passively resigned up the ordering, altering, and disposal of kings and governments, into the hands of God, are now, recalling their principles, and putting in for a share of the business. Is it possible, that the conclusion, which is here justly quoted, can any ways follow from the doctrine laid down? The inconsistency is too glaring not to be seen; the absurdity too great not to be laughed at; and such as could only have been made by those, whose understandings were darkened by the narrow and crabby spirit of a despairing political party; for ye are not to be considered as the whole body of the Quakers but only as a factional and fractional part thereof.

Here ends the examination of your testimony; (which I call upon no man to abhor, as ye have done, but only to read and judge of fairly;) to which I subjoin the following remark; "That the setting up and putting down of kings," most certainly mean, the making him a king, who is yet not so, and the making him no king who is already one. And pray what hath this to do in the present case? We neither mean to *set up* nor to *put down*, neither to *make* nor to *unmake*, but to have nothing to *do* with them. Wherefore, your testimony in whatever light it is viewed serves only to dishonor your judgement, and for many other reasons had better have been let alone than published.

*First*, Because it tends to the decrease and reproach of all religion whatever, and is of the utmost danger to society to make it a party in political disputes.

*Secondly*, Because it exhibits a body of men, numbers of whom disavow the publishing political testimonies, as being concerned therein and approvers thereof.

*Thirdly*, because it hath a tendency to undo that continental harmony and friendship which yourselves by your late liberal and charitable donations hath lent a hand to establish; and the preservation of which, is of the utmost consequence to us all.

And here without anger or resentment I bid you farewell. Sincerely wishing, that as men and christians, ye may always fully and uninterruptedly enjoy every civil and religious right; and be, in your turn, the means of securing it to others; but that the example which ye have unwisely set, of mingling religion with politics, *may be disavowed and reprobated by every inhabitant of* AMERICA .

FINIS.

# Notes

1. Dragonetti on virtue and rewards

2. Thomas Anello otherwise Massanello a fisherman of Naples, who after spiriting up his countrymen in the public marketplace, against the oppressions of the Spaniards, to whom the place was then subject prompted them to revolt, and in the space of a day became king.

3. See Entic's naval history, intro. page 56.

4. pounds Sterling

5. Those who would fully understand of what great consequence a large and equal representation is to a state, should read Burgh's political disquisitions.

6. "Thou hast tasted of prosperity and adversity; thou knowest what it is to be banished thy native country, to be over-ruled as well as to rule, and set upon the throne; and being oppressed thou hast reason to know how hateful the oppressor is both to God and man: If after all these warnings and advertisements, thou dost not turn unto the Lord with all thy heart, but forget him who remembered thee in thy distress, and give up thyself to fallow lust and vanity, surely great will be thy condemnation.—Against which snare, as well as the temptation of those who may or do feed thee, and prompt thee to evil, the most excellent and prevalent remedy will be, to apply thyself to that light of Christ which shineth in thy conscience, and which neither can, nor will flatter thee, nor suffer thee to be at ease in thy sins."—Barclay's address to Charles II.

# 101 Constitutional Questions To Ask Candidates

Produced by W. Cleon Skousen
in 1980 for training purposes

Because so many millions of Americans finally realize that something is seriously wrong with the way the government is handling our affairs, people are continually asking: "Do you think there is still time to turn it around?"

When you ask, "Still time before what?" they usually reply: "Before total disaster overtakes." For those who wonder about such things the answer is this: "Yes, there is still time, but not much."

The next question is: "What can we do to get America turned around and regain our national sanity?" The answer is: "Elect a President and a majority in Congress who still believe in the Constitution and will fight to return America to her original moorings."

### Identifying Constitutional Candidates

"But how can you tell when a candidate for political office is really a Constitutionalist?" If the candidate is already in office he will have a voting record which will clearly show whether or not he is a Constitutionalist. Several organizations monitor the Congress and publish the results. However, if the candidate is a newcomer to politics you will have to test his knowledge of Constitutional principles by asking a few questions.

### What Kind of Questions Should Be Asked?

1. Under the Constitution, who has the sovereign authority to govern?

   The founders said it is in the people "by God's own allowance". No branch or agency of the government should be allowed to operate in violation of the expressed will of the people. Their collective will is set forth in the Constitution and the laws passed by the people's representatives.

2. In what way are "all men created equal?"

   All humanity are equal in three ways: 1. Equal before God, 2. Equal before the law, 3. Equal in their rights. In all other respects people are different.

3.  What is an inalienable right?

    An inalienable right is one which comes as an "endowment from the
    Creator" and cannot be violated without coming under the judgment
    of God.

4.  Which inalienable rights were listed in the Declaration of
    Independence?

    The Declaration of Independence lists the right to life, liberty and
    the pursuit of happiness.

5.  What did the founders mean by the "pursuit of happiness?"

    This is a collective phrase designed to cover all of the other inalien-
    able rights.

6.  Give an example of an inalienable right which is essential to the
    pursuit of happiness.

    The Founders believed, for example, that human happiness requires
    that each of us enjoy the right to acquire, develop and dispose of
    property. They believed that without the protection of property rights,
    all other rights are placed in serious jeopardy.

7.  What are some of the other inalienable rights?

    The inalienable rights of mankind include such things as the right of
    self government; the right of human beings to beget their own kind;
    the right of parents to rear their children free from outside interfer-
    ence (unless there is criminal abuse or neglect); the right to freedom
    of belief; the right to freedom of speech; the right to assemble; the
    right to petition; the right to change residence; the right to change
    jobs, etc.

8.  What is the purpose of government?

    The Founders said the basic reason for creating a government is to
    protect the inalienable rights of the people. The government is to pro-
    vide "liberty under law," which means that no law should be passed
    unless it is specifically designed to protect the freedom, liberty, and
    well-being of the people.

### The American Structure of Government

9.  What is a democracy?

    A democracy is a government wherein decisions are made by the
    masses of the people rather than by elected representatives.

## 10. What is a republic?

A republic is a system in which the laws are passed and decisions made by the elected representatives of the people.

## 11. Why did Jefferson call the American system a democratic-republic?

Because the system allows the masses of qualified voters to participate in the election of their officials (democracy) and then the people's elected representatives enact the laws and administer the affairs of the people under majority rule but with the equal protection of individual rights (a republic.)

## 12. Is it a mistake, therefore, to call the United States a democracy?

Yes. The only part of the American system which is borrowed from "democracy" is the popular election of government officials. Except for this, the Founders strongly emphasized the republican aspects of the American system. A republic places the responsibility for sound government and decision-making on the people's elected representatives rather than allowing the fluctuating and superficial emotions of the people to override law and order or the rights of minorities. The classical example of government functioning on republican principles and prevailing over "pure democracy" would be the case of a sheriff protecting a prisoner against a lynch mob.

### The Task of Controlling Power

## 13. Why is separation of power safer than concentration of power?

Government is "force" which Washington compared to "fire" and said government is a "dangerous servant" and a "fearful master." Power should be dispersed among the people where they can keep it under control.

## 14. How should the powers of government be separated?

First of all the Founders wanted political power separated vertically.

They considered the principal power base of society to be the family. However, there are a few things which a community of families can provide better than a single family (police, fire, water, utilities, etc.). Power to perform these functions is therefore delegated to the community. Then there are a few things which groups of communities can do better than the single community. These tasks are assigned to the higher level of the county. There are also a few things that a group of counties can do better than a single county and these are assigned to the State level. The Founders also discovered that there were certain matters dealing with foreign affairs, problems of war and peace, imports, etc. which need to be handled in behalf of all the states. These responsibilities are therefore assigned to the Federal Government. It should be noted that the Founders' pyramid of power provided that the greatest number of responsibilities should rest with the family. Only a few responsibilities were assigned to the levels of government above the family and the Federal Government was to have the least of all.

15. What remedies did the Founders provide if government officials violated the channel of power assigned to them?

Administrative pressures from other departments are provided and if his offenses are serious he can be impeached for treason, bribery, high crimes or misdemeanors.

16. Why did the Founders want the powers of government to flow from the bottom up rather than the top down?

Jefferson stated that a political unit governs best which governs least. In other words, the services which the people need from government are relatively simple and when circumstances are normal the people like to conduct their affairs with as little interference from the government as possible. Consequently, in the Founders' original plan for a happy and prosperous society, the functions of government were designed to be relatively simple and remarkably cheap.

17. Then why do we have such a complicated and expensive government today?

The professional politicians learned that in a war, depression, or a serious crisis, the people will endure higher taxes and a far greater concentration of authority on the higher levels of government. Certain politicians therefore set out to exploit every emergency as an excuse for the acquiring of more power. During most of the twentieth century ambitious politicians trumpeted the message that the government can solve practically all problems better than the people. Today, as a result, Americans are being literally "programmed" to death. And taxes have skyrocketed.

### Separating Power Horizontally

18. How did the Founders separate power horizontally?

There are three functions of government at each level of society. One function is to make the law, another is to administer the law and a third is to interpret the law. These are all on the same horizontal level and are referred to as the legislative, executive, and judicial functions of government. The Founders wanted these three functions to be separated into equal, independent departments. At the same time, they wanted to coordinate these functions so that one department could not function without the other two. Each department was therefore assigned to serve as a check on the others. The idea of the Founders was to have these functions of government "coordinated but never consolidated." This was one of the most ingenious devices contributed by the Founders.

19. What happens if the separation of powers breaks down either vertically or horizontally?

The Founders warned that if the vertical separation of power should ever break down so that all power began to be concentrated in Washington, there would be a severely arrogant abuse of the people by government officials. They also said that if the legislative executive and judicial departments failed to act as a check on each other, there would be tyranny and the people would lose their freedom. For more than one full generation this is what has been happening.

## Americans Experiment with Another System

20. Is the consolidation of government functions the trend today?

Yes. Consolidation of power is gravitating toward Washington at a pace which would have greatly alarmed the Founders.

21. What has caused this?

Beginning around 1900 certain wealthy influential groups lost confidence in the original American system and began propagandizing the people into believing that a "redistribution of the wealth" by the government would greatly improve the American life style. This theory of economics with its concentration of political power at the center of government is usually referred to as socialism. Samuel Adams vigorously warned against these principles. He said socialism violates equal protection of rights and completely destroys the concept of limited government. In fact, he said the Founders had done everything possible to make these collectivist policies "unconstitutional."

22. What has been the result?

These policies launched the United States on a wild and dizzy trajectory which has resulted in run-away inflation; a huge burden of national debt; taxes which are devouring nearly half of the peoples' earning power; a serious invasion of individual rights; and a virtual collapse of states rights.

23. Has socialism or "collectivism" worked anywhere in the world?

Unfortunately, it has not. In fact, the militant forms of socialism such as Communism, Nazism, and Fascism have caused more wars and shed the blood of more human beings than any system of government in the history of the world. Even the so-called "peaceful" forms of socialism such as Democratic Socialism and Fabian Socialism, have proven counter-productive and have continuously crept along the razor's edge of perpetual bankruptcy. Americans have sent over hundreds of billions of dollars in foreign aid trying to help the socialist nations survive. Now we are bordering on bankruptcy ourselves.

24. How did the Founders structure the American system so that socialism would be unconstitutional?

They did it by setting up a "limited" form of government with carefully enumerated powers. Jefferson called these limitations on government the "chains" of the Constitution.

## American Leaders Began to Abandon the Founders Success Formula

25. Does this mean Theodore Roosevelt was In error when he said the President could do anything except that which the Constitution forbids?

Yes, he was turning the Constitution upside down. The President and all other officials of the government are only allowed to do that which is expressly authorized. The Founders referred to any exercise of power outside of these Constitutional chains as "usurpation."

26. Was President Woodrow Wilson also in error when he said the United States should become involved in the political and economic affairs of the world?

Yes. The Founders had continually warned against foreign, entangling alliances. The Founders believed the United States should try to be friendly with all nations, but beholden to none. They knew that political interdependence leads to the development of power blocs, and power blocs ultimately lead to war.

27. Was Franklin D. Roosevelt in error when he structured the New Deal?

Yes. The New Deal was structured on collectivist principles designed by such men as Harry Hopkins who saw socialism as a tremendous vehicle to acquire power over the people and their resources. His famous formula was "tax, tax — spend, spend — elect, elect!"

28. Was Lyndon Johnson in error when he said, "We will take from the haves and give to the have nots!"

The Founders would certainly have called it an error. There is absolutely no Constitutional authority for the government to engage in any such invasion of private property rights. Throughout history it has always been popular for governments to pretend they are going to "soak the rich," but such programs have always ended up with government officials using this newly acquired power to violate the inalienable rights of both rich and poor. It is a political trick to build bigger government with bigger debts and bigger taxes.

29. Was President Nixon in error when he continually tried to involve the United States in a "New World Order"?

Yes. It is extremely dangerous for Americans to enter into foreign engagements where decisions for Americans are made by non-Americans. The Founders believed that we should coordinate but never consolidate our free and independent society with foreign nations.

30. Was President Carter in error when he began meddling in domestic affairs of foreign nations?

Yes. The Monroe Doctrine specifically promised that the United States would never undertake to meddle in the domestic affairs of other countries. Any President or Secretary of State who has followed a policy of "interventionism," has operated outside of his Constitutional authority.

## Presidential Violations of the Constitution

31. What about executive orders which are treated as laws after being published in the federal register?

In the eyes of the Founders these would be considered unconstitutional. The President can issue executive orders to the administrative branches of government under his supervision but he has no authority whatever to make "laws" for the people since the Constitution assigns that authority exclusively to the Congress. An act of Congress could stop this whole illegal procedure.

32. What about executive agreements between the President and heads of foreign governments?

This procedure is also unconstitutional. The Founders provided that all agreements with foreign nations must have the advice and consent of the Senate. Since American Presidents began holding summit conferences with the heads of foreign governments, they have been entering into secret engagements which very often never see the light of day let alone receive the advice and consent of the Senate. Each year there are many more executive agreements signed by the President than there are treaties ratified by the Senate.

## Judicial Violations of the Constitution

33. What about new laws laid down by the Supreme Court?

This is called "judicial legislation." This occurs when the Supreme Court creates a new law by pretending to interpret an old one. In the Federalist Papers the Founders specifically warned against this type of arrogance by the Supreme Court.

34. How is the Supreme Court supposed to interpret the Constitution?

The Founders made it very clear that the Supreme Court would be violating its assignment if it substituted its own opinions for that of the Founders. Until recently it has always been an established principle that the Constitution must be interpreted the way the Founders intended it and not according to the whims or caprice of modern justices.

35. Is there any way to curb the Supreme Court from exercising its power in an unconstitutional manner?

Yes. A Judicial Reform Amendment would allow any Supreme Court decision to be overturned by two-thirds of the House and two-thirds of the Senate. A decision could also be overturned by concurring resolutions from three-fourths of the State Legislatures. Had this procedure been available the States would have' undoubtedly outlawed forced busing of school children at least twenty years ago.

## Unconstitutional Edicts of Regulatory Agencies

36. Is it Constitutional for an agency of the Federal Government to write rules and regulations which are enforced in the courts as "laws?"

No. This is a recent development in governmental procedures. It is called "administrative law." The Founders provided no power in any agency of government to make laws except the Congress.

## Blurring the Founders' Division of Labor Between the States and the Federal Government

37. How did the Founders intend to divide the problem-solving powers between the States and the Federal Government?

James Madison spelled it out in the Federalist Papers, No. 45. He wrote: "The powers delegated by the proposed Constitution to the Federal Government are few and defined.... The powers reserved to the several states will extend to all the objects which, in the ordinary course of affairs, concern the lives, liberties, and the properties of the people, and the internal order, improvement and prosperity of the State."

38. How did the Founders know whether to assign a problem to the State or Federal Governments?

If a problem involved foreign relations (war, peace, treaties, etc.) or matters which could not be handled by any one of the states (regulating interstate commerce, crimes on the high seas, navigable waters, naturalization, etc.) it went to the Federal Government. All other powers were retained by the States.

39. How many areas of power were ultimately assigned to the Federal Government?

The Constitution gives the Federal Government twenty powers. These are set forth in Article I, Section 8.

40. What if the Federal Government thinks it needs more power?

The government cannot legally exercise any powers except those which are specifically granted to it by the Constitution. The only way Washington can get any additional legitimate power is by an amendment.

41. Where does it say that the Federal Government is specifically restricted from exercising any power not granted to it by the States?

### The Tenth Amendment

42. Then how did the government get so much power?

The dominating arrogance of the Federal Government today came about primarily through three channels: 1. outright usurpation of power, 2. an edict by the Supreme Court in the Butler Case in 1936 reversing the original meaning in the Welfare Clause, and 3. distorting the Commerce Clause as the means of shattering the restrictive chains of the Constitution and expanding Federal jurisdiction into hundreds of areas never intended by the Founders..

### Subverting Two Important Constitutional Clauses

43. What was the Butler Case?

In this decision, Justice Roberts included in his opinion a dictum that the Congress would no longer be restricted in its taxing and spending powers so long as it was in the "general welfare" of the nation.

This immediately opened the U.S. Treasury to looting for all kinds of give-away programs which politicians began using to buy votes.

44. In what way has the Commerce Clause been distorted to give the Federal Government unconstitutional powers?

This clause was simply designed to give the Federal Government sufficient power to insure the "free flow" of commerce so that the States would not interfere with inter-state shipments as they had done in the past. Since 1936 the original intent of the Founders has been expanded to include Federal control over practically everything which affects inter-state commerce either directly or indirectly. This usurpation of authority by Congress (which has been upheld by the Supreme Court), has shattered some of the most important restrictions on Federal intervention in the business and commercial life of the nation.

## Some Practical Questions

45. Doesn't the more complex nature of modern society require a far more extensive control of the economy by the Federal Government?

No. The more complex society becomes the more it needs the automatic problem-solving devices of a free-market economy operating with the least possible interference from government. As Adam Smith pointed out, government interference only adds to the complexity of the system and results in a serious deterioration of individual freedom.

46. What is a modern example of the Founders' original success formula solving some of the highly complex problems of a modern society?

No nation could have had a much more complex situation than West Germany right after World War II. Every major city in Germany was bomb-gutted and the people were surviving in basements and make-shift hovels. Chancellor Konrad Adenauer of West Germany took over in 1949 and immediately initiated the basic economic principles advocated by the Founding Fathers. By using freedom instead of heavy-handed government regulations, West Germany achieved the highest standard of living in Western Europe within eight years. The West Germans were not only fully employed but importing foreign labor besides. Clothing, food and housing were abundant and cheap. West Germany became so prosperous she was the envy of socialized Sweden. It will be recalled that Sweden wasn't even in the war and had boasted of the superiority of her socialist controls. However, in Sweden a young married couple has to wait ten years to get a one-room apartment because of the government monopoly over housing. It was obvious West Germany had chosen a better way.

## Questions About Money and the Budget

47. What happened to the Federal budget after the "Butler" case?

In 1936 (the year of the Butler case) the Federal budget was around six billion dollars. By 1980 the looting of the American taxpayer had pushed the Federal budget to more than six hundred billion dollars!

48. Is it Constitutional for the government to spend more money that it takes in?

Yes. The Constitution allows the government to borrow in emergencies. Unfortunately, during the last 50 years Congress has continually found excuses to borrow whether there was an emergency or not. The only way to stop this is to replace the big spenders in Congress with Constitutionalists who recognize that we are presently on a disaster course.

## The National Debt

49. How much is the national debt today?

The U.S. National Debt is nearly a trillion dollars (extremely higher today!) requiring interest payments which cost more each year than the entire cost of World War I. Future liabilities to which the government is already committed will require taxation of an additional six to seven trillion.

50. How does the U.S. debt compare with the debts of other nations?

The United States now owes more than all of the rest of the nations of the world combined.

51. Why would the Founders have considered this gigantic indebtedness immoral?

The Founders said that no generation should go so deeply in debt that it becomes guilty of squandering the next generation's inheritance. They said such extravagance is immoral. All past generations tried to pay off all the debts accrued during their time. Ours is the first generation which has deliberately squandered the inheritance of its children.

## What About Welfare?

52. But hasn't much of our money been spent for welfare and other Important social programs?

> This was the main excuse for sky-rocketing taxation and deficit spending. Tragically, however, the money has been squandered primarily to build a vast bureaucracy. It is amazing how many of the government's multibillion dollar social programs have provided only a pittance to trickle down to the poor, the sick and the elderly.

53. But didn't the government have to try to do something to help those in need?

> The Founders specifically warned against this type of political deception where the compassion of the people is exploited to build big government and raise taxes. They said that all types of charity and welfare should be handled on the local level where abuses could be quickly detected and corrected.

54. But what if the states do not provide needed services?

> The existence of a need on a State level does not create a power on the Federal level. When a State fails to fulfill its obligation the pressure should be exerted on the State, not the Federal government.
>
> Jefferson said there is no way to preserve freedom if all political power gravitates to Washington.

## The National Debt and Foreign Aid

55. In view of America's tremendous national debt, why do we continue giving foreign aid to over a 125 countries?

> This whole procedure violates the Constitution and common sense. What started out as part of the defense program in the interest of the United States has turned into an international Santa Claus give-away program. similar to the extravagant give-away programs at home. Tens of billions given away each year automatically add to the national debt.

## Social Security

56. Is Social Security an insurance plan or a welfare plan?

> The Supreme Court has held that it is a welfare plan. This means that it can be terminated at anytime. It also means the government can distribute its proceeds arbitrarily. The contributor to social security payments acquires no rights and receives only what the government

condescends to distribute to him as "payments" if he qualifies under the government's arbitrary poverty level.

57. Is there a better way?

Yes. It is called an annuity program. If the money contributed by an employee (and his employer) between 25 and 65 were invested in American industries under an annuity plan, the fund could be built to a quarter of a million dollars by the time he retires. An annuity fund of this kind would permit an employee to retire at $1,200 to $1,500 per month. Furthermore, the money is his. He does not have to be poor to get it. If he dies it goes to his widow and children. He earned it. He owns it. [these figures would be higher now]

58. Is the Federal Income Tax Constitutional?

Yes. The Sixteenth Amendment was adopted according to the requirements of the constitution.

59. Is this the type of tax which the Founding Fathers would have employed?

No. They provided that direct taxes be apportioned to the States according to population, not according to the incomes of the people.

60. Has income tax been administered uniformly?

No. A graduated income tax violates the equal protection of rights. It violates the principle of uniformity required by the Constitution and makes the property of accumulated wealth less sacred than those who have less.

61. Is it possible to administer the Income Tax fairly?

No. This could only be done by setting up a universal monitoring system similar to a "police state." This would violate all of the basic rights guaranteed in the Fourth Amendment.

62. Would it ever be possible to repeal the Federal Income Tax?

Yes. By phasing out governmental activities which are clearly outside the Constitution, the cost of government would be greatly reduced and the income tax could be safely eliminated.

63. Would the repeal of the Sixteenth Amendment interfere with defense and other legitimate Federal responsibilities?

No. Corporate taxes and other sources of Federal revenue would more than adequately provide for the legitimate expenses of the Federal Government if its unconstitutional expenses were phased out. Who knows, there might even be a surplus!

64. What about the thousands of Federal-aid programs covering nearly every aspect of American life?

> Federal grants are unconstitutional unless directly related to some power specifically delegated to the Federal Government. A strict interpretation of the Constitution would probably wipe out at least 95% of the Federal-aid programs presently plaguing the nation.

## Federal Regulatory Agencies

65. What about EPA?

> The Environmental Protection Act involves problems which the Founders delegated exclusively to the States where local supervision could prevent abuses and deal with over-regulation more readily. Today, federal control over air, water, and land environment is strangling the economy and suppressing the development of energy and natural resources.

66. What about OSHA?

> Occupational safety and health are important responsibilities but they should never have been delegated to the Federal level. The Founders knew that government is too big, and the legal machinery too expensive for most citizens to handle. They therefore endure the disruptive and oppressive edicts of this agency because it has been too big for the average citizen to fight.

67. What about the Federal Communications Commission?

> This agency was designed to "police" the traffic on the air waves but the FCC has used its licensing power to control the editorial content of programs. This is in direct violation of the First Amendment.

68. What about the Pure Food and Drug Administration?

> There is no authority for this agency under the Constitution. If it is in the national interest to have such an agency it should have been authorized by an amendment. There is already a wide-spread criticism of the arbitrary manner in which this agency has exercised its broad spectrum of power.

69. What about Consumer Protection?

> Here again we have an exercise of power unauthorized by the Constitution. Do we really want that much power allocated to the Federal level where the agency is so big and powerful that not even the largest corporations are able to cope with its abuses?

## What About the Government Setting Up Business Operations?

70. Is there any authority in the Constitution for the government to set up tax-exempt corporations or business operations to compete with tax-paying citizens?

> The answer is no, unless the corporation or business is directly connected with an area of Federal responsibility enumerated in the Constitution. For example, an independent government corporation to provide mail service would be constitutional. However, a corporation set up to compete in the production of electricity, the manufacturing of clothes, or the operating of a chain of public restaurants, would not.

71. How many corporations and businesses does the government operate at the present time which are unauthorized by the constitution?

> Around 700 corporations and 11,000 businesses. [much higher now]

72. Are all of these tax-exempt?

> Yes. They are not only tax-exempt but most of them are being subsidized out of tax funds because they are not being operated efficiently.

## What Caused the "Sagebrush Rebellion?"

73. Shouldn't all of the states have been admitted to the Union on an equal basis?

> Yes. This was set forth by Congress in the Northwest Ordinance of 1787.

74. Which states were strong-armed into accepting statehood without being admitted on an equal footing?

> All of the Western States and Alaska.

75. In what way were they forced to accept statehood unequally?

> Large regions of these states were retained by the Federal Government for purposes not authorized by the Constitution in Article I, Section 8, Clause 17.

76. About how much of the land did the Federal Government usually withhold from these states?

> The government retained around 50% of the land in most Western States, but 79% of Nevada and 96% of Alaska.

77. Are any of these states attempting to get this land back?

> Yes. The press has labeled this effort the "Sagebrush Rebellion," but it is not a rebellion. These states are simply following the legal and Constitutional procedures necessary to have this land turned back to them.

## What About Locking Up State Territory As Wilderness Areas?

78. Does the Constitution authorize the President and the Secretary of the Interior to lock up large blocks of land within a state as a "wilderness reserve?"

> No. This violates the express provisions of the Constitution but was upheld by the Supreme Court on extremely tenuous grounds.

79. Does the Constitution authorize the Federal Government to have a national forest within the confines of a state?

> No. This is not included in the list of territories which the Federal Government is allowed to occupy with the consent of the State. (See Article I, Section 8, Clause 17) The Supreme Court had to distort the Constitution to justify it. Historically, the States have had fewer forest fires and have maintained the State forests on a higher level than the national forests.

80. Does the Constitution authorize the Federal Government to have national parks within the confines of a State?

> No. For the same reasons as those cited above, the Supreme Court should have disallowed them. It has been observed that as a rule State Parks are better maintained and provide better facilities than those operated by the Federal Government.

## What About Federal Control of Energy Resources?

81. Does the Constitution authorize the government to control, regulate, or inhibit the production of energy resources within a state?

> No.

## Problems with Government Monopolies

82. What about the widely expanded activities of the Interstate Commerce Commission?

> The Founders never intended the "regulation of commerce" to include cartel monopolies, fixing prices, fixing routes, and regulating industries into bankruptcy. The recent deregulation of airlines dra-

matically demonstrated the advantage of free-market competition over a system of unconstitutional governmental regulations.

83. Does the Constitution authorize the Federal Government to set prices?

Not in time of peace.

84. Does the Constitution authorize the Federal Government to set wages?

Not in time of peace.

### The National Labor Relations Board

85. Does the Constitution authorize the Federal Government to enter into labor-management disputes in the private sector?

No. This area of Federal usurpation occurred during the "New Deal" days by completely distorting the original intent of the Commerce Clause.

### The Department of HEW

86. Is there any Constitutional foundation for the extravagant and wasteful expenditures of the Department of Health, Education and Welfare?

No. Each of the agencies under HEW has developed since the Butler Case. The dictum in this case authorized the general welfare clause to be interpreted in a manner which extended government intrusion into areas specifically excluded from Federal jurisdiction by the Founders.

87. About how much of the Federal budget Is spent each year on these unconstitutional activities?

Around 201 billion dollars in 1980 which is approximately 1/3 of the Federal budget.

88. Would it require an amendment to the Constitution to eliminate the Department of HEW?

No. An act of Congress could dismantle this extremely costly department which has probably been more wasteful and nonproductive in its assigned area of activity than any other branch of the government.

## The Equal Rights Amendment

89. Why are so many millions of American women now opposing the passage of the Equal Rights Amendment?

In the beginning nearly everyone assumed that this amendment was designed to provide equal rights for women. This supposed objective was widely approved. It was only after 30 states had ratified this amendment that it was realized that the simple wording of this amendment would actually destroy a broad spectrum of rights which American women already have.

90. What are some of the rights of American women which ERA would destroy?

At present American women enjoy both the common law right as well as the statutory right to be supported, along with their children, by their husbands. ERA would not only destroy this right but also eliminate many rights relating to employment, maternity leave, insurance and survival rights which are presently provided by law.

91. Would passage of the Equal Rights Amendment give women any more rights than they now have?

No. All of the rights which the advocates of ERA claim they are getting for women through the passage of this amendment are already provided by law.

92. Would the passage of ERA further damage the original separation of powers instituted by the Founders?

Yes. For example, it would transfer a large percentage of cases involving family and other domestic problems from the State courts to the Federal judiciary which is already smothered with legal problems.

## Abortions

93. Is Federal funding of abortion a violation of the Constitution?

Yes. The specific and limited authority granted to the Federal Government does not include any funding for abortions.

## The Gold and Silver Standard

94. Was the United States taken off the gold and silver standard in violation of the Constitution?

Yes. The gold standard is written into the Constitution (Article I, Section 10, Clause 1) and was removed by several acts of Congress without an amendment to the Constitution between 1934 and 1964. From the Founding Fathers standpoint this whole procedure was illegal.

## The Federal Department of Education

95. Is it Constitutional for Federal funds to be used in the financing of local schools?

No. The Founding Fathers warned against the funding of schools by the Congress. In fact, education in the U.S. has seriously deteriorated since Federal funding began. James Madison equated the Federal funding of schools as extremely dangerous and said it was almost as bad as funding and controlling the churches of the nation.

96. Should the members of State and educational associations be required by law to pay dues to the National Educational Association?

No. The NEA is a private lobby with an annual budget of nearly $60 million dollars. It succeeded in getting the States to pass a law requiring the educators in State associations to pay dues to the NEA.

These laws should be repealed. Teachers find themselves compelled to pay dues to this private organization which often advocates policies that are inimical to the best interests of American education.

## Taxes on Dividends

97. Should stockholders be required to pay income taxes on their dividends when the corporation has already been subject to a corporate tax?

No. The stockholders are the owners of the company. They have already paid around 48% tax on the company's earnings. The residue should be distributed among the stockholders as funds on which the required tax has already been paid.

## Control of Firearms

98. Should the Federal Government pass laws providing for the control of guns?

No. The Founders left gun control under the exclusive jurisdiction of the State. They felt it was extremely dangerous to allow the Federal Government to "infringe" on the right to bear arms even in the slightest degree.

## The Modem Method of Electing Senators

99. Should the Seventeenth Amendment be repealed?

> The Founders would undoubtedly say yes. They set up a House of Representatives to represent the people and set up a Senate to represent the individual States. Senators were originally appointed by State legislatures and were the watchdogs of States rights. The Seventeenth Amendment took away the authority of the State Legislatures to appoint Senators. and therefore required Senatorial candidates to appeal to the people in a popular election. This resulted in the Senators frequently ignoring States rights in an effort to get more money for their States just as Congressmen do. States' rights have been seriously deteriorating since the Seventeenth Amendment was adopted in 1913. It destroyed an important element of balance which the founders built into the Constitution.

## The BLM

100. Should the Bureau of Land Management be abolished?

> Yes. This bureau has been rapidly phasing out the traditional grazing rights of ranchers and setting up impossible regulations on land which should have been turned over to the States when they were admitted into the Union.

## Government Expenses

101. Can you find out how the government spends its money?

> Yes. A complete breakdown of government spending is published each year by the Government Printing Office. This is required by the Constitution.

## Conclusion

Now, as nearly as we can ascertain from the writings of the Founding Fathers, this is about the way they would have answered each of these 101 questions. We have also tried to reflect the line of reasoning which their writings portray when similar questions were raised in their own day.

It is believed their point of view deserves careful consideration in view of the rather calamitous consequences which modern Americans have encountered as a result of following a different line of thinking. The socialist or collectivist formula has not worked for Americans; nor any one else for that matter.

It is believed this generation of Americans could earn the eternal gratitude of their descendants if they would immediately undertake to restore the Constitution in the tradition of the Founding Fathers.

# Credits

**Cover Design**
Evan Frederickson

**Page Layout**
Carlos Packard

**Editors**
James Michael Pratt, Glenn Kimber,
Paul Skousen, Brent Skousen, Harold Skousen

**Image Credits**
Page 33, Cicero - Flickr.com/antmoose
Page 73, Galaxy - Flickr.com/xamad
Page 113, American Flag - Flickr.com/repres
Page 119, Thomas Jefferson - Flickr.com/Tony the Misfit
Page 123, Farm House - Flickr.com/ken ratcliff
Page 165, Statue of Liberty - Flickr.com/wwarby
Page 199, Family - Flickr.com/rolands.lakis
Page 205, Benjamin Franklin - Flickr.com/ jaycross

# American Documents Publishing & PowerThink
## Proudly Present

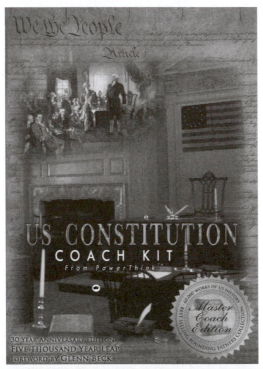